SCARS OF WAR

A captain in 148 Commando Forward Observation Battery, Hugh McManners served with the Special Boat Squadron during the Falklands War. *Falklands Commando,* his account of his experiences, was acclaimed by *The Times Literary Supplement* as 'an immensely detailed but wholly real picture of what soldiering is like', and by the *Daily Telegraph* as 'exciting, well told, and frequently hair-raising'.

Hugh McManners joined the British Army in 1972 and was commissioned into the Royal Artillery. In 1975 the army sponsored him to read Geography at Oxford University. Subsequently he spent thirteen years with 3 Commando Brigade. Before leaving the army in 1989, he joined a mountaineering expedition in China, about which he wrote in *Crowning the Dragon: Adventures in the Chinese Karakoram.*

He is now a television documentary producer, freelance writer and editor of *Command* magazine.

'A noble and courageous approach to an aspect of war concealed too often and too easily . . . Hugh McManners has made a valuable and important breach into the citadel of a subject which has been guarded in silence for too long'

ROBERT FOX, Daily Telegraph

'A stirring and disturbing book'   *The Times*

D0889621

HUGH McMANNERS

The Scars of War

HarperCollins*Publishers*

HarperCollins*Publishers*
77–85 Fulham Palace Road,
Hammersmith, London W6 8JB

This paperback edition 1994
5 7 9 8 6 4

First published in Great Britain by
HarperCollins*Publishers* 1993

ISBN 0 586 21129 2

Set in Sabon by
Rowland Phototypesetting Ltd
Bury St Edmunds, Suffolk

Printed in Great Britain by
HarperCollinsManufacturing Glasgow

For my Deborah,
with love.

CONTENTS

LIST OF ILLUSTRATIONS

PREFACE

The individuals who appear throughout this book are telling stories that many others in the Falklands and other wars could equally have told. After their experience of combat, some left the armed forces, while others continued in their military careers and were still serving when I interviewed them. I have not attempted in editing their accounts to select only the highlights of what they had to say, but have included most of the memories and impressions that they feel are significant.

This is important, because through having in some respects been deliberately non-selective about the men I interviewed and the material I then included in this book, I have been able to create what I hope is an accurate impression of what the modern battlefield is really like. (Mostly it is boring, uncomfortable and very worrying.) There is however one common denominator shared by all my interviewees; they are thinking men, deeply affected by what they went through, with the intelligence, perception and humility to dig back into their broom cupboard of painful memories. Nearly nine years on, having deliberately repressed all but a few happier memories of the war, it takes courage to speak honestly about what really happened.

These interviews were difficult, particularly at the start of each one. As a combat veteran myself, however, I was able to ask the right questions, and avoid the stupid ones that would cause the shutters to come down abruptly. (I was also able to identify and challenge when, on a very few occasions, I was spun a yarn, or when something unpleasant was glossed over.) Each interview was a journey to a foreign land and another time, a harsh, hostile place with strange, absolute rules, where people behaved very differently. Some of the memories bubbled up like marsh gas, with a smell that made you realize the nature of the swamp. At the end, however, there was a feeling of relief and remarks like 'You are the first person I've ever said any of this to'; 'Not even my wife knows what I've just told you'; and 'I feel a lot better, like having got something off my chest at last'. I am deeply grateful to each of my interviewees for having been so frank.

Catharsis was also one of my motives in writing this book. Equally, writing in the shadow of the Gulf War (the 'mother of all battles', in which chemical and biological weapons seemed likely to be used) I wanted to put on record a few things about modern wars and their effect on the people who fight them, the reality that most civilians never consider. Apart from the very small number of military personnel who have personally experienced combat, nobody has the faintest idea of what it is actually like – and why should they? This almost total ignorance gives rise to many unfortunate attitudes during and after wars, epitomized by newspaper headlines like 'Gotcha!' (after the sinking of the Argentine battle cruiser *General Belgrano*) or 'Up Yours Galtieri'; or, at the other extreme, by the Synod of the Church of England agonizing over the morality of the Gulf War at the same time as British soldiers were sweating it out in their anti-chemical suits. The attitudes and debates at home are often so far removed from the reality of the battlefield as to make soldiers feel isolated and even bitter.

Media coverage of the Gulf War (and the same will probably apply to all future wars) made most of us back at home angry at its incredible waste – of life, technology and money, not to mention the wasted hours, stretching into days and weeks, of being glued to radio and television sets. By its unseemly end, people were fed up with the war, many cynical about its aims and result. Although the USA, enjoying victory after decades of military disappointment, welcomed her soldiers home with a defiant, ticker-tape celebration, in Britain, troops and electorate alike were uneasy about the triumph, unwilling to revel in its dubious glory.

For those of us born into the second half of this century, conscription and general war affecting whole nations is impossible to imagine. The generations that did not fight the World Wars do not understand what war is really like – and the generation that did is loath to talk about it. This is entirely understandable – and proper. Life should not be about fighting, violence and death, but about living.

It is however important to get war into the right perspective. War is far from being an entirely miserable experience; rather it is a peculiar mixture of pain, horror, and heady excitement, creating an emotional cocktail that some combatants actually relish. Mercenaries have been a constant factor in military history, as they are today even in the confusion of the present Yugoslav civil war. Modern mercenaries risk life and limb as much because they enjoy it as for the money. We can assume that their historical forebears were similarly motivated.

Fighting can provide a diversion from the misery of a campaign that actually buoys people up and keeps them going. I 'enjoyed' the Falklands War; being part of a brotherhood of dedicated, like-minded people I knew very well, and the excitement of doing the job I'd trained to do, in a unique atmosphere of almost cavalier professionalism.

Indeed, many combatants consider 'the war' to have been the most rewarding time of their lives, a time when human relations were at their most honourable, when life had a clear purpose. Without personal experience of war, it seems very strange that something so essentially terrible could be remembered in such a way. It is perhaps an indication of the extent to which war affects combatants that they should return to normal society with such feelings.

After a war, however, combatants do not just turn smartly to the right and march off into the sunset, starting their normal life from where it was interrupted. There is a price to be paid for the basic freedoms that we enjoy and the things that governments do in our name (whether or not we agree with them). Because we have professional armed forces to do the dirty work on our behalf, we remain blissfully unaware of that price, while our servicemen pay it. This book is about the emotional overdraft that combat veterans run up in war, which afterwards many never manage to pay off.

INTRODUCTION

War is by far the most traumatic 'life event' that any human can experience, a damaging combination of danger, uncertainty and horror. Civilian experiences, no matter how terrible, are simply not in the same league. Steven Hughes, today an orthopaedic surgeon, as an army captain was 2nd Battalion the Parachute Regiment's doctor throughout the battles for Goose Green and Wireless Ridge during the Falklands War:

I can't think of a civilian experience of similar magnitude – not even the Clapham train disaster, King's Cross fire or whatever. It's like willingly taking part in the disaster – all of you going to King's Cross, including setting fire to the place yourselves . . . It also lasted for a sustained period of time.

Psychologists have identified a scale of normal human occurrences, such as divorce, bereavement, changing job, moving house and so on, which seriously affect all of us at various times in our lives. These 'life events' can occur simultaneously; for example divorcing, moving house and changing job often go together. It is accepted that the upward spiral of stress created by experiencing two or more 'life events' at the same time can have marked and injurious effects on the health of the unfortunate individuals going through the emotional mill.

On the battlefield, in addition to the ordinary stress of being separated from their families and doing a 'new job' somewhere strange, professional soldiers suffer frequent bereavements and an increasing sense of danger and personal vulnerability – in addition to the horrors they see and the terrible things they find themselves doing. They are bolstered to an extent by their training and by unit esprit de corps, but being human they suffer nevertheless. Many experience serious psychological problems on the battlefield, and many more develop long-term problems when they return to peacetime life.

This book takes a hard look at the realities of modern warfare, not from a historical or military point of view, but from an emotional perspective, through the eyes of the individuals who do the fighting. Although it concentrates on the Falklands War (because I fought in it), it draws from other modern wars in order to establish the common truths of what really happens when men use modern weapons against each other. I realize that for veterans of the two World Wars, the shortness of modern wars is something that differentiates their experiences from those of today's combatants. For various reasons, modern wars fought with modern weapon systems are likely to be short and furious – requiring peacetime troops to be constantly ready for imminent combat, with a significant psychological shock factor when they are used in battle. There can be no sensible comparison of relative difficulty, unpleasantness or potential psychological effect between the World Wars, in which time was both help and hindrance, and those of today.

It is equally impossible to rank the unpleasantness of even earlier wars with those of today. Dramatic improvements in hygiene, rations, medical services and personal equipment which make the lot of the modern soldier easier have been more than equalled by increases in weapon lethality. This book however is not about the battles of history, but about what faces servicemen and women today, on modern battlefields. The horrors of medieval warfare, or the bloodbaths of the First World War are relevant to this book only in so far as they help us to understand what happens today. I would certainly never presume to lessen the memory or the achievements of those who fought in those battles in any way.

Writing as a former professional soldier, I begin by looking at life in a peacetime army, describing the lifestyle, aspirations and motivations that men take with them to war. We then follow the 'blooding' process, in which a soldier's career steps up several gears and peacetime professionals become combat-hardened troops.

The threats and strictures of military law in modern volunteer armies play different roles in peacetime and in war. These roles, which very much affect men's behaviour in battle, can only be understood if military law is examined in its historical context. Within modern professional armies, although the full punitive force of military law still lurks in the shadows, it is no longer the prime motivator that forces men to fight. On today's technical and increasingly individual battlefield (the comradeship of 18th-century infantry square formations has gone), self-motivation created through training is far more effective. Military law underpins this self-motivation, however, and has a more subtle and complex role to play, thus earning a chapter of its own.

Unlike virtually any other profession, members of the armed forces prepare for something they hope never to have to do. Without the experience of real operations, practising and training can easily become the perceived purpose of peacetime armed forces who, when they are required to fight, have problems sloughing off misapprehensions and bad practices. However the selection and training of special forces creates an expectation and commitment in each man of the likelihood of having to fight (Chapter 4), which makes the process of going into battle for the first time (Chapter 5: 'First Blood'), much easier.

Special forces refer to combat as 'doing business' – their job, the way they earn their pay. 'Doing business' varies greatly for the different armed services in psychological attitude, physical conditions, personal stress and actual danger. The common denominator is death, hence the uncertainty with which each person fights his war. Combat at sea, on land and in the air have therefore a chapter each.

Commanders also have a chapter, from those at the very top to the platoon commanders and their sergeants at the bottom who actually fight the war. Confusion in war is total, command exercised by determined men feeling their way often blindly through the smoke. The only certain products of their efforts are death and terrible injury, which combatants have to be able to cope with, both physically in order to save lives, and mentally in order to be able to continue fighting. 'Coping with Carnage' therefore has a chapter of its own.

And when the war is over, the 'Aftermath' is often as difficult to handle as the fighting, the time when men become aware of what they have done, and when enormous efforts must be made to re-establish the rules of law and civilization. In the moment of survival, men wonder why they are living, and why their friends died (Chapter 12: 'The Quick and the Dead'), wondering who protected them, or at the god that allowed such carnage to occur. The aftermath is also the time when those products of war – the dead – must be disposed of, some into unmarked pits, others with the care and emotion of grieving friends.

The final chapter takes us beyond victory parades and retrospective television documentaries ('Was it all worthwhile?'), to see what happens when combatants return to normal life. Unfortunately, they do not simply march off into the sunset, putting the horrors of the war behind them. The long-term emotional effect of combat becomes 'Another Kind of War' (Chapter 13). Perhaps the reason for old soldiers never dying (merely fading away) is that after the war, like so many of their comrades, emotionally they were dead already.

The individual is often forgotten when studies are made of battles, or when regimental histories are compiled. The lives of great commanders are researched avidly, but because so many individuals were involved in achieving the victories that these great men planned, it is impossible to see it through their many and different eyes. For the individual, war is a very parochial, localized experience, almost impossible to relate to a battle or campaign as a whole. Nevertheless, it is the individual who wins wars. Chinagraph arrows drawn by generals on large-scale maps have never yet hurt anybody. The actual killing must be done by a vast variety of people, each with different hopes, fears and aspirations. The individual is the most important and most interesting part of the military machine – purely because, despite enormous pressures to conform and become a mere component in the apparatus, in battle most military people remain human and act according to their individual strengths and weaknesses. Furthermore, their individuality is often the vital spark that creates victory from the potential defeat that every battle starts out as being.

Individual memories of combat are often at odds with history books, autobiographies and official regimental diaries. For many reasons, whether humane or for all manner of expediency, the unpalatable is often altered or omitted from published accounts. For those without experience of it, combat can appear (in comparison to what actually happened) sanitized and gentlemanly, or excitingly heroic in the 'John Wayne' tradition. Individuals also edit their own memories, because remembering the truth is often too painful for them to bear. Breaking through what to outsiders can seem a conspiracy of silence, is only really possible for someone who has been in combat too – who can understand and ask the right questions. I achieved breakthroughs in many of my interviews and was quite surprised at some of the things I learned.

For combat veterans the war does not end as the peace treaty is signed. For many the scars do not emerge for months, years or even decades after the last shot was fired. The war lives on in their imaginations, a vivid, terrifying nightmare of guilt, bereavement and black impending doom souring their lives thereafter. Although these long-term effects are only now being identified and accepted by the medical profession, thousands of veterans from past wars have suffered them (and still suffer) in silence – often without realizing the nature of their pain.

The power and range of modern weapons, and the ability of technology to eliminate darkness so that fighting can take place around the clock, makes modern war very much more stressful than it has been hitherto. The numbers of men suffering long-term psychological injury are thus likely to increase dramatically. Indeed, some experts feel that war and modern weapons are now so destructive that their human operators will no longer be able to cope with the strain of the modern battlefield environment – as seen in the complete disintegration of the Iraqi Army under the Allies' air and artillery bombardment in February 1991. To fight future wars, men will have to train specifically to withstand psychological as well as physical hardship, and might even need to resort to the official use of stress and fatigue reducing drugs more sophisticated than the benzedrine 'uppers' and alcohol of past wars.

Unfortunately, many peacetime military men prefer not to think realistically enough about this dimension of combat. They see 'cracking up' as a sign of personal weakness – particularly if it comes as the result of combat. The military 'stiff upper lip' must not be seen to quiver, either during the fighting or afterwards. This intolerance of perceived weakness is a tribal belief, which many individual military men privately deplore. It is in fact the intolerance and not the cracking up that is the real problem – an intolerance born of ignorance and perhaps even fear. Without an honest acceptance of the harsh realities of the modern battlefield by the military in general (and their leaders in particular), their troops may indeed crack under the strain and, like the poor Iraqi Army, be unable to fire a shot.

This military problem aside, from the perspective of the individual, the long-term effects of the stress of battle are more important than the problems facing military authorities in fighting wars. There is nothing new about these long-term effects. After the Second World War the members of an entire generation were personally affected by their experiences. Afterwards, they put the war behind them and concentrated on winning the peace – no mean task. They were all in it together, which may partly explain the reluctance with which they as individuals admit to having been adversely affected by it.

Unlike the Second World War generation, today's professional servicemen (and women) are a minority in the population of their countries. In the years and decades following wars, one might therefore think that their long-term, post-combat psychological problems should thus be more easily identifiable. However this has proved not to be the case. The minority status of combat veterans, among a peacetime population that seems unwilling to remember wars fought in the past in their name, has made isolation an even greater problem. In the future, combat veterans are likely to feel even more isolated from the rest of their generation, unable to talk with civilians, about either their war experiences or the psychological after-effects.

For humans, both on the battlefield and afterwards in civilian life, isolation can be an enemy more damaging than weapons.

This book is about modern war fought by professional, career soldiers, a new and very different sort of war from that fought by conscripted amateurs in the past. Expertise apart, technology and politics have also changed the way battles are fought: short and very sharp rather than drawn-out campaigns.

In the British Army, the 2nd Battalion of the Parachute Regiment is the only unit since the Korean War to have fought two consecutive, full-scale modern battles in the same campaign – the Falklands. Their experience is unique, and so in extracts from my interviews with war veterans I have drawn upon their experience (and that of their sister battalion 3 Para) as much as possible.

In November 1990, I was invited back to the British Army Staff College at Camberley in Surrey, for a two-day study period on 'The Realities of War', covering topics like the effect of firepower on morale, becoming a prisoner of war and the stress of higher command. When I was a student there in 1984, the same lectures, given by many of the same people, had been called 'The Stress Study'. I wondered if the change of name had any significance.

My role second time round was as a veteran of the Falklands. Apart from enjoying splendid lunches and a regimental dinner, I listened to the lectures then, with a distinguished cadre of Second World War veterans, joined one of the student 'syndicates' for group discussion – in which they were supposed to gain insight from my (and my more experienced elders') experience. In the second lecture, about the Falklands, one of the speakers had explained the reason for the name change; 'The Stress Study' seemed to concentrate on the psychological problems of combat, and not on the positive things that military leaders must do to motivate soldiers to fight. Psychiatrists had become involved, and were thought by the military men to be turning combat stress into an acceptable reason for failure of nerve on the battlefield. In changing the name to 'The Realities of War', the military were bringing the subject back into familiar territory, back under their control, reasserting time-honoured and hard-learned values of discipline and leadership, which psychiatrists in their researches seemed to be only rediscovering. In any case, military people know that common sense is better than psychological self-indulgence.

From the military point of view, it all boils down to a question of discipline. When faced with problems, individuals have the choice of reacting positively, or of being overwhelmed by events and crumbling under the strain. Discipline can help the individual by programming him into positive reaction – resolving the dilemma by removing the element of choice. This absence of choice is seen by military people as being 'well disciplined'.

It is well known that stress can be either a healthy stimulant or, if not handled correctly, a killer. The positive military reaction to the whole question of battle stress, illustrated by this simple changing of the name of the Camberley study period, is to face up to the harsh realities of war rather than become neurotic about the effects of the stress that they cause.

The attitudes of servicemen to battle stress and the psychological effect of battle on combatants are understandably very sensitive. Everybody knows that war is bloody awful, but if you are a professional soldier, sailor or airman, there's no point in dwelling on it. All military forces practise some kind of 'machismo' or 'stiff upper lip', which keeps them going in adversity, but can make them seem blind and insensitive. From the point of view of professional institutions like the Staff College, both staff and students know that wars have to be planned and fought. Ignoring unpleasant facts would be stupid, but becoming obsessed with the dreadful conditions of future battlefields is not the true function of military men.

Before the Falklands War, the Royal Navy in particular was oriented towards a peacetime existence: official trips to exotic ports, bands, flags, cocktail parties and bunting. In the Falklands, some naval personnel, finding themselves involved in a full-blown modern war, were taken by surprise. Service psychiatrists, particularly those of the Royal Navy, attempted to draw attention to the various post-Falklands problems of many veterans. These problems equate with those suffered by Vietnam veterans, and are grouped together under the label of Post Traumatic Stress Disorder (PTSD). However, few members of such a rational group of people as the armed services have much time for psychiatrists, especially 'shrinks in uniform' who point accusing fingers at the way fighting men fight their wars.

In the sometimes narrow-minded politics of service life, minority points of view (and opposition to them) are often overstated in order to be heard, or are used as platforms for individual reputations. Views become polarized, then common sense evaporates. This process may unfortunately have confused the very important debate within the armed forces over combat stress and its long-term effects. In their publicizing of PTSD, military psychiatrists have a very important contribution to make towards the training of men for war, and their psychological care afterwards. However, I realized during this 1990 Staff College study period that the psychiatrists had (temporarily) lost their case. At that time, within the Services, PTSD had become a rather tedious subject, regarded with varying degrees of scorn or indifference, even as an indication of weakness of character. One lecturer, a doctor serving with the Royal Navy, referred to it as 'Compensationitis'.

Most of the other combat veterans present at the study period had served in the Second World War. In syndicate discussions, several made very disparaging comments about combat stress, recounted ordering gibbering men to 'pull themselves together', and drawing their pistols as further encouragement. Their clear-cut response to battle stress problems was greeted with relieved laughter, the experts seeming to have contradicted the psychiatrists' depressing predictions. But these Second World War veterans were less than keen to talk about battle stress, and seemed happier telling war stories than answering the students' questions. I came away with the strong feeling that we had been given sanitized versions of a very different reality.

Perhaps because the Second World War affected everyone in that generation, they rarely talked openly about it. There are some Second World War autobiographies in which the unvarnished reality comes through, but many more are in the *Boy's Own Paper* style, in which everybody seems to behave stereotypically. Forty years of telling abridged versions of war stories to children could have had something to do with it; we were always asking our father to 'tell us a story from the war', and only once did he let slip something unpleasant.

There is no doubt that many who served in the Second World War were deeply affected by what they had seen and experienced. In the first three months of the Blitz, 12,696 Londoners were killed. When the worst was supposed to be over, in November alone, 4,558 were killed in Britain and thousands more injured. Civilians (let alone military personnel) saw grotesque horrors equal to those of the Falklands or the Gulf, yet they appear to have learned to cope. After the war, 'winning the peace' was more important than dwelling on the past, and frank talk about the war was confined to Old Comrades reunions, many of which (participants' health permitting) flourish today. At the end of his excellent book *18 Platoon* (1987), Sydney Jary declares that he did not suffer 'nervously or emotionally' as a result of his battle experiences. He won an MC as a platoon commander in the Somerset Light Infantry, fighting from the Normandy landings in June 1944 until the end of the war in Bremen. It is clear from the final pages of his book, however, that normal life was pallid and unsatisfactory to him afterwards, and that as a sensitive man and first-class soldier, he had been very deeply affected. It could be that the enormous stress of the Second World War, a desperate struggle for freedom against a very tangible evil, affected an entire generation. Everyone lived in the fast lane of life; falling in love, marrying and parting within days, losing their children to unknown foster parents and their homes to the Luftwaffe.

We who did not live through those years think of the dead of that war as mere names on memorials, as the forgotten people who never completed their journey. We never knew them. We can only know the *survivors* of that war, and we base most of our impressions of it upon what they remember. In so doing, maybe we are forgetting the nature of their journey, and the significance of all those who died along the way? Many people lost all their friends in the war, and in their hearts wish that they too had died with them. War and youth were synonymous, and with the peace came a realization that the one had taken the other for ever. Perhaps an entire generation was burnt out by the emotional experiences of the Second World War, never to regain fully its zest and youthfulness? Such a suggestion would not be disputed in the Soviet Union where, despite the tribulations that followed the war against Hitler, war memories are sombre and hatreds well preserved.

But one must not generalize about the collective effects of individual trauma on nations: the Japanese reaction to defeat and the atomic destruction of two major cities made them the second most economically powerful nation in the world. Germany has succeeded in an equally miraculous way.

There is however no doubt of the suffering of the war generation in Germany. Today they suffer doubly the shame of their children: for what happened, and also for joining and so tacitly supporting the moral degeneracy that allowed the worst of the Nazi excesses to take place. Some of that older generation have become stridently defensive, but most refuse to talk about it.

Humans are very tough and resourceful, solving most of their emotional and psychological problems without professional help. The most common self-therapies for PTSD are hard work to keep the memories at bay, and drugs (usually alcohol) to induce sleep at night. Today, psychiatrists are discovering that the suppressed emotions of the war generation are giving way to a very delayed PTSD, forty years on. The young men who survived the Second World War are now in their late sixties and recently retired. Their wives may have died, and for the first time since the war they find themselves with time to spare. Many Second World War veterans are seeking medical help with PTSD problems now, as their memories catch up with them.

The psychological problems created by war are hardly an indication of weakness or defective character. On the contrary, all these stress-related symptoms are a normal, sane response to its horrors. Wars, however, are not all horror; on the battlefield many find humour, comradeship, self-sacrifice, human dignity and even love, a richness of life that can make peacetime seem selfish, mean and rather squalid. War affects people in different ways: some become clinically mad, others live perfectly happy, normal lives. It is true to say, however, that everyone is to some extent affected. Only a psychopath could claim otherwise. Most war veterans are made stronger by their experiences, seeing life through new and more grateful eyes. Some slip in and out of various forms of depression – like everybody else.

However, unlike most people, war vets are very tough people who know how to endure pain.

ACKNOWLEDGEMENTS

Before specifying the particular people who went out of their way to help me produce this book, I'd like to thank all those who were kind enough to allow me to interview them. Whether their names or words appear or not, each interview helped me confirm either my own ideas or the words of others.

Particular thanks to Dr Richard Fargher, Oxford don and wartime artillery officer, who proofread the book. His pages of notes, comments and suggestions were both comprehensive and invaluable. Any mistakes that might have survived his exacting eye are therefore mine alone.

I am also very grateful to my father, Dr the Rev John McManners FBA, historian and wartime infantry officer, for literary advice throughout the writing of this book, but more importantly (with Richard Fargher) for reluctantly recalling (considerable) personal Second World War combat experience in order to help me. In so doing they remembered things they'd manged to forget – for which I apologize.

Brigadier Tony Dixon and the staff of the excellent and highly effective Ex-Servicemen's Mental Welfare Society (of which he is General Secretary) helped me to understand the extent to which war affects people, but also to realize that servicemen and women suffer from 'ordinary' mental problems too – a form of double jeopardy.

Various Ministry of Defence people have also helped: in the Surgeon General's Department, members of the Royal Army Medical Corps, the Army and Navy Historical Branches, Staff College Camberley's library, and in the Directorate of Public Relations (Army).

For this paperback edition, I'm particularly grateful to the following people, whose comments on the hardback enabled me to update, correct and improve the text: Major General Julian Thompson was particularly helpful with his classic Staff College Camberley 'red ink correction'; Lieutenant Colonel David Bonest of the Parachute Regiment (who was Signals Officer for 2 Para throughout the Falklands War), for his thorough and most helpful comments; and Brigadier Rickett, late the Welsh Guards.

My editor Richard Johnson has been supportive, understanding and considerate, both in terms of excellent and judicious editorial advice, but also with respect to deadlines – for which I am most grateful. His staff have been equally impressive: sub-editor Betty Palmer applied a deeply sensitive and perceptive expertise to the manuscript despite finding some of it particularly harrowing; editor Robert Lacey performed miracles of pagination in allowing me to add text well beyond the last possible moment; and Katherine Everett for her help with the illustrations. And finally my literary agent Barbara Levy.

Hugh McManners
May 1993

1

FIGHTING THE PEACE

The distinguished psychologist Norman F. Dixon quotes a scathing description of the militarist, whose characteristics he ascribes to all soldiers:

'The militarist is a relatively prejudiced and authoritarian person. He is emotionally dependent, socially conformist and religiously orthodox. His interest in the welfare of others is relatively low. He is extremely distrustful of the new and strange.' Such people are also 'uncreative, unimaginative, narrow-minded, security-seeking, prestige-orientated, parochial, ultra-masculine, anti-intellectual, extraversive [extrovert], and severely socialized as children'. They are lacking in aesthetic appreciation, complexity of thinking, independence, self-expression and altruism, and relatively high in anxiety. Finally, military professionals are lower in self-esteem than any other occupational group.[1]

If all soldiers fitted the description, then an army would at least consist of like-minded people, but every person is different. Some people are as he describes but may not show it. Some are partly militarist with other characteristics, and others are not militarist at all. There is however an 'official' military attitude or outlook, a sort of common denominator that everybody in a military organization understands – and will ultimately defer to.

When young men enquire about joining the armed forces, the recruiters do not include quotations like that in the pamphlets they hand out. Instead they emphasize certain aspects of military life (prestige, masculinity, 'extrovert-ism' and security) and make virtues of other aspects (conformism, discipline, authoritarianism and anti-intellectualism). Recruits either accept the recruiters' picture, which is strongly confirmed throughout basic training, or they find military life intolerable and leave.

Military selection and training sets great store on moulding individuals into membership of the military team – on fitting in.

Conformism is possibly the most important personal characteristic, particularly for officers. Armies tend to get rid of misfits and only tolerate odd-ball characters if (paradoxically) they happen to fit in, because they have something to offer like sporting prowess, an amusing and acceptable eccentricity, or they can be adopted as mascots. The stress of peacetime life in the armed forces is in many ways related to this constant pressure to conform. Peace is so different from war that, to survive the peace, armies have to change (often radically) in character. Some excellent soldiers become frustrated in peacetime and misbehave; the hierarchy will not tolerate their antics, even though it accepts their worth in war.

When a peacetime army goes to war, its attitudes, prejudices and habits often have to be rapidly and radically changed if the unit is to become combat effective. Some units, like the Israeli Defence Force and British paratroopers and marines, are already oriented towards combat. Others, like the British Army of the Rhine in the autumn of 1990, were more oriented towards military routines established by forty years of peace. British combat units in Germany, particularly the armour, were often as much as two-thirds below their proper fighting strength, with inadequately maintained vehicles. In getting to combat strength, the rest of the British Army was plundered of men, spare parts and vehicles – effectively put out of action in order to send two brigades into the field. Geographically (and psychologically), British Gulf troops underwent a severe transformation, from a damp German autumn to the heat of the Saudi desert. Luckily there was plenty of time, and once units were acclimatized a gruelling programme of tough exercises knocked everybody into shape.

Each individual who goes to war is under tremendous pressure anyway. In the enormous emotional upheaval of leaving family and friends, each combatant takes a whole catalogue of personal problems on to the battlefield. It is accepted by psychiatrists that men with the additional burden of personal problems are more likely to become psychological battle casualties. When individuals return from war, peacetime attitudes are reimposed with depressing swiftness, seeming to wipe out everything that has been learned in combat. The individual, however, may not be able to re-adjust as quickly as the mechanisms of the military system, and so finds himself an outsider in the army for which he has just been fighting. If he is parted from those with whom he fought, he will begin to feel seriously isolated, and the pressures of peacetime army life will bear heavily upon him.

One of the critical personnel problems suffered by very large armies is a loss of personal identity caused by the sheer scale of the organization. It is vitally important, regardless of the size of the army, for each soldier to feel that his individual effort counts towards the whole. Keeping people together for as long as possible is important, too; enabling individuals to perceive the vast, monolithic organization of the army proper as being split into small, family-type units with which they can identify. Soldiers generally prefer this kind of stability. The Israeli Defence Force do exactly this, keeping the same groups of soldiers together in the same units during and after training. Individual soldiers thus identify strongly with their units, and the leaders get to know their men really well. In the intimacy that develops in such close-knit groups, each man knows his role and worth. Some British regiments derive tremendous strength from the continuity of their personnel. There are still examples of whole families serving in the same regiment; father as the RSM with sons as private soldiers and NCOs in the rifle companies. Several generations of officers from the same families might be commissioned into the same regiment – and even command it.

However, some armies, notably the US Army, rotate individuals between units on short (two-year) postings. An average US Army platoon is therefore rarely the same from one week to the next, with individuals being drafted in and others moving out at the end of their postings. In the British Army, the Royal Engineers operate a similar system for both officers and soldiers (to give everyone a wide range of engineering experience), whereas in the Royal Artillery and the service corps, only the officers rotate between units.

In really large armies, individuals often feel lost within the system, being moved like driftwood on an enormous beach. Most military people are forced into adopting peculiar attitudes towards friendship, based on the knowledge that most of the people they meet will soon be posted away, never to be seen again. Although people become adept at picking up friendships again (often many years later) the relationships they make tend to be only transitory, and easily discarded. Children who grow up in the military environment ('army brats') move around with their parents, and so must adopt the same attitude to their own friends. If sent to boarding school, although they gain a degree of stability, they will see little of their parents. However, military fathers are not often at home anyway, spending around seven months each year away (in my personal experience). In eighteen years, a father could easily be absent for a total of eight years, his child attending nine different schools and the family moving twelve times.[2]

In the turbulence of peacetime military life, it is hardly surprising therefore that individuals ignore the need to plan ahead, perhaps behaving irresponsibly in failing to prepare for their own futures. Being mucked about by the army is part of the job; as British soldiers say, 'If you can't take a joke, you shouldn't have joined.' Planning anything outside the army can easily come to grief, so most don't bother.

In some armies, notably in China, and the permanent cadre of the former Soviet Red Army, soldiers and their families are treated very much better than the rest of the population. The US Army, despite its highly disruptive posting system, goes to great lengths to make moving easier, and keep wives and families happy. Such American measures as 'spouse satisfaction' are treated as jokes by British Army personnel staff officers – who by contrast with the professional attitude of their US Army counterparts, can seem uncaring amateurs. Whereas the US Army pays all movement costs, British Army personnel must endure an inefficient and desperately bureaucratized movement system, and end up paying from their own pockets every time they are posted somewhere new (this system is under review).

The environment from which individuals proceed into combat determines the level of personal stress that they are suffering from to start with. The level of this pre-combat stress determines to a great extent how an individual will cope with the greatly increased stress of combat. This psychological concept translates directly into a well-known military maxim: that high morale is essential for troops going into battle. Family and personal welfare contribute towards morale, as does the standard of administration practised in each unit. The domestic, social and administrative peculiarities of peacetime armies, and the stress that peacetime military life places upon individuals and their families is critical to understanding how individuals are affected, in both the short and long term, by the savageries of war.

Military life always has preparation for war as its background, even though individuals join for reasons other than any desire to go to war. They want to travel, to improve themselves by gaining useful qualifications, and because they 'always wanted to'. One British Army psychiatrist told me that he had never taken a history from a patient who said he'd joined in order to defend his country. (Rather than indicating that few join 'for Queen and country', this surprising statement suggests that individuals who fail to think through the full implications of joining the army are prone to develop psychological problems. They might also be reticent about admitting patriotic motives.)

On joining the army, many young people find themselves away

from home and family for the first time, suffering the homesickness that boarding-school pupils get out of their systems very early in their lives. In addition, during those difficult first few months, the nature of their new career is made apparent to them in a demonstration of military weapons that can be watched either with glee or with the sober realization of their killing power. Firepower demonstrations and other events in training that bring home the reality of what weapons are designed ultimately to do, force individuals to think through the real implications of being in the armed forces. The possibility of having to use real, killing weapons against real people – and having similar weapons firing back – must be accepted by every service person early on in their career.

If we were to compare a military career with one in medicine, a significant difference would be that all doctors are certain to encounter death in their work. Medical students must face death very early in their training, to the extent of spending the first term hunched over corpses in the dissecting room. In the process of learning anatomy, they also learn to shut off the grim reality of what they are doing with macabre jokes and the beginnings of a detached, professional manner. Soldiers in western peacetime armies, by contrast, may never have shots fired at them in anger, or encounter death. For them, accepting the darker side of their military career is not therefore always necessary. At the start of hostilities in the Falklands, particularly when the Argentine air force began to sink British ships, a significant number of individuals found that being personally involved in a real war was a shock to them, something they had not expected. After years of carefree military duty (one man in particular had done 22 years in the navy) they were having to face up to all the implications of being members of the armed forces, under the awesome pressure of real enemy fire.

Conversely, peacetime soldiering is stressful in ways that can make real combat seem a release – and almost a relief. The psychology of this is related to the army's ultimate role. If the aim of peacetime training is clearly understood by everybody to be the realistic preparation for war, individuals can think themselves into the jobs they will have to do, come to terms with the risks and practise with a strong sense of purpose. In those circumstances, life is simple, satisfying and clearly directed. If, however, individuals disbelieve that they will ever have to do their jobs in combat, their motivations and perception change. The army becomes a peacetime career for them, with well-defined hurdles to be overcome and promotion as the reward. Life in a 'career' army becomes very complicated. Personal

motivation can be split two ways: between the logical requirements of the job, and the irrational demands of superiors who
must be obeyed and satisfied if the individual is to be promoted.
All successful career soldiers must master this essentially political
system.

Peacetime forces resemble any large organization, with petty politics and high levels of bureaucratic and social stress. Two additional
factors increase the stress beyond that found in civilian life: military
rank and commitment. Military rank and authority are absolute so,
unlike in a civilian office, there is little effective recourse available to
a disgruntled subordinate. Commitment is long term, which forcibly
prevents a subordinate from walking out on a superior. But more
importantly, good soldiers suffer in silence because they are proud
of their units and care about what they are doing.

In peacetime, life in the armed forces is a peculiar mixture of
military preparedness in the shadow of war, and boredom. This
has long been recognized; in the past, when less time was spent on
equipment maintenance and large-scale exercises, the officer class in
particular was able to revel in sports and games, riding, shooting,
pig-sticking and so on. The use of alcohol is an institutionalized ritual
for all ranks in the British Army, to the extent that in some units,
not drinking is considered a sign of weakness. (The US armed forces,
by contrast, are particularly strict about *not* drinking during working
hours.) Many units do not have a real job to do in peacetime, so they
invent activities: inspections, complicated administration, tests and
training exercises.

Armed forces need good people to make them work. Without the
right men and women in the right jobs, and the best leaders out in
front, neither technology, training nor sheer force of numbers can
win wars. The pyramid shape of any military organization contains
large numbers of low-level leaders who at the same time are also
being led by those above them in the structure. The type and quality
of military leadership is therefore the single most significant deter-
minant of what one might call the psychological tone of the organization – the attitudes, lifestyles and social structure within which
everybody lives and works. In all armies, good leaders must also be
good followers. In western armies, there is no clear dividing line
between leaders and followers; even the men at the very base of
the pyramid structure are considered potential leaders and trained
accordingly. Professional, career troops expect promotion at regular
intervals, so very soon after leaving basic training each person
becomes a leader. Leadership is dynamic and shapes every aspect of

life in the armed forces, for better and for worse. The psychology (and tradition) behind the concepts of leadership practised in various armies is fundamental to the way their soldiers are motivated, and to the way they fight. It also determines how the individual reacts to the traumatic experience of combat. Psychological tone is possibly even more important in armies than in navies or air forces because of the numbers of people involved. An army has many more people in its ranks; as individuals they are the weapons with which the war is fought. Navies and air forces use their people to crew ships and aircraft, to operate the technology and service the machinery that does the fighting for them. Individual soldiers must actually be able to kill the enemy. Their discipline, obedience, group cohesion, team spirit, training, all of which create high morale, are determined by leadership, in peacetime as well as in war.

The only product of a peacetime army, navy or air force, apart from the intangible deterring of potential aggressors and the providing of aid to civilian authorities in times of national disaster, is the capacity to select and nurture the right military leaders who will keep the forces up to combat standard in peace, and win battles if war is necessary. One inescapable paradox is that the men who rise to the top in peace are not always the best war leaders. Peacetime armed forces are caught in the dilemma of knowing that many of their leaders may not be cut out for war, but needing to have careful, bureaucratic individuals keeping the military machine ready to fight. Of course there were many excellent peacetime leaders in World War Two: Auchinleck, Wavell, Slim, Dempsey, Horrocks and so on. But the immediate demands of peacetime override those of some future, theoretical war – which everyone hopes in their hearts is never going to happen. Volatile men of outstanding combat ability, like Patton or Montgomery (whose feud with each other would never have been tolerated by a peacetime commander-in-chief), rarely get the chance to prove their worth in peace, being too unpopular with superiors to gain promotion.[3]

Ordinary soldiers also suffer from this same paradox. 'Fighters' can seem over-keen on practising their military skills to be tolerated in peacetime units. Elite cadres like the British SAS attract men frustrated by the peacetime attitudes of their parent units. These men are often identified by their officers as being particularly good at their jobs and likely to perform well in combat. Nevertheless, in peacetime, other qualities are required to earn promotion (usually tact and diplomacy). These individuals get passed over in favour of other more personable men.

Before he had experienced battle, Second World War infantry platoon commander Sydney Jary would have listed masculine qualities like aggression, physical stamina, a competitive nature and hunting instinct as the necessary qualities of a good soldier. After fighting from 1944 until the end of the war, from Normandy into Germany, his ideas had changed radically.

. . . sufferance, without which one could not survive. Secondly a quiet mind which enables the soldier to live in harmony with his fellows through all sorts of difficulty and dreadful conditions . . . there is simply no room for the assertive or acrimonious. Thirdly . . . a sense of the ridiculous, which helps the soldier surmount the unacceptable. Add to these physical fitness and professional competence and you have a soldier for all seasons.[4]

Given the choice between sportsmen and poets for a dangerous mission, Jary declares he 'would unhesitatingly recruit from the latter', men who in peacetime would probably not even have joined the army, let alone been considered for promotion.

The armed forces of many countries are an interesting reflection of the social structure of the rest of their societies. Each is organized according to the nature of the society which it serves and defends. Some armed forces epitomize the ideology of the governing class and its attempts to shape the social order: the erstwhile Soviet Union and China clearly so; and, more subtly, the English class system and the American pseudo-egalitarian myth.

Through its regimental system, the British Army perpetuates an obsolescent dream of English upper-middle-class life. Technology and the need for intelligent, well-trained men in all ranks has largely eliminated this from the Royal Navy and the RAF. By contrast, the US Army's classless officer corps selects its members from the same backgrounds as the men, but then has the problem of making them different enough from the other ranks to stand out as officers. The Israeli Defence Force avoids all these problems by selecting officers from the best NCOs. Ironically, soldierly skill is not nearly so important for a British Army officer. In the conformist environment of a British officers' mess his social standing can be more important, not only with brother officers, but particularly with the other ranks. In Highland regiments, for example, many of the men prefer their officers to speak with upper-class English accents. In regiments like the Guards, the men like their officers to be 'toffs', partly because in the past they have often been absurdly brave and colourful – but more importantly, perhaps, because they are predictable.

The influence of class in the British Army is far stronger than in most other parts of British society, which keep mostly within their own class boundaries. Each regiment is a microcosm in which people of every social class work unusually closely together. Military rank is more important among the other ranks than between officers. For officers, status is much more a question of education and social class than of military rank. The noble lord who is only a captain, does not feel inferior to the majors. Because the smartest regiments take officers only from the upper classes, the regimental cap badge becomes an indication of the individual's class – except in the unlikely event of a particular upper-class individual 'slumming it' in a lower-class regiment. In a staff headquarters, although officers from different regiments and corps work together, the horizontal social hierarchy (based firmly upon class and not rank) continues strongly, and can create pretension and occasional strife. Inside smart regiments, officers from the Ordnance, Engineers, Artillery and REME may be attached, any one of whom may drop his aitches. On peacetime exercises, social superiority and inferiority can adversely affect the integration of these vital specialists into the organization. How words are pronounced can be as important as their meaning.

As an institution the British Army lives in the past – and not simply because of its traditions. Its isolation from the rest of society offers a purely social reason for its being so class-oriented. This isolation is particularly apparent in the British Army of the Rhine and the time lag is significant, something in the order of a decade and more. Within the institution of the army, individuals behave, dress and think according to their own inclinations, but conform to the official, time-lagged, upper-class norm when required. A small number of officers and NCOs blot out their private persona, being and living exactly in the army's image. As such officers achieve promotion, this will stand them in good stead. An even smaller number are so pukka as to try to live as an officer might have done in India between the wars. They are regarded by most as eccentrics, but this does not harm their promotion prospects – rather the opposite.

English public schools epitomize the English class system, and are very important to the British Army. Lt Colonel Tim Spicer (Scots Guards, educated at Sherborne):

Public schools drum into their pupils the need to set a good example, and provide the means to becoming a good, overall sort of chap. The public-school boy tends to be naturally better at the sort of leadership required by the British Army because he has been practising it throughout his school life. Although other sorts of school might also provide individuals who happen to be good leaders, they do not give them the same tremendous advantage – and head start.

Of course not all public-school boys do well in the army; some fail on entry, and others survive without really pulling their weight. The public-school boys who get to the top of the army usually have the added advantage of brain power, which adds up to being the best sort of officer leader.

By coming straight into the army, a public-school boy moves from one institution to another, compounding the narrowness of his outlook. (This happens in other professions too, the law in particular.) Narrow-mindedness is inevitable, which in the army (where the upper and lower classes of British society work together with unparalleled intimacy) could become an increasingly serious disadvantage. Lt Colonel Spicer:

Eton College gives possibly the broadest approach to life and a better understanding of the outside world. Etonians do well in the Army, and in combat. Colonel 'H' Jones [CO 2 Para in the Falklands] went to Eton ... Public school gives an advantage in the army because of a general inhibition [held by army officers] about those who went to other schools – that they might eat their peas with a knife or something.

However good the qualities they promote, public schools cast a divisive shadow over life in the officer corps of the modern British Army. Public-school manners and self-confidence are easily recognizable standards of behaviour that the army believes are synonymous with being an officer. Thus officers who did not go to public school (the majority) can feel at a disadvantage, socially inferior, even to the extent of not being 'proper' officers.

Inside the British Army, the effect of institutionalized snobbery is insidious and widespread, although few would admit that it even exists. To a varying extent it inhibits individuals from doing and saying what they actually think. Peacetime army life can be highly stressful for those who continually have to keep up socially. Because such people can never entirely relax and be themselves, their lives become unnecessarily uncomfortable – regimented in every sense.

All armies have elite units which attract the best officers and soldiers, and are accepted as having the highest military standards. The British Army, however, is unique in that it has two sorts of elite unit: military elites like the SAS and the Parachute Regiment; and socially elite units like the Life Guards, Foot Guards and Cavalry. This concept of socially elite units is essentially European, the product of military history and tradition (today's social elites being yesterday's military elites). The idea of a privileged officer caste monopolizing units like the Household Cavalry would be intolerable to the Israeli Defence Force, although Israel's best soldiers do come from the best educated and most prosperous strata of Israeli society. The IDF exists only to ensure the survival of the State of Israel and is therefore geared solely to war. The elitism of IDF units is related to public opinion, based upon well-informed public knowledge of units' performance in combat operations. The units deemed most significant in the defence of Israel have the best reputations. While there is no doubt of the quality of the British Army's military elite units, in recent years its socially elite units have been nothing like so consistent. It could be argued that the Household Cavalry and Foot Guards demonstrate high standards by doing two jobs – public duties and normal military training. However, public duties such as mounting guard at St James's Palace and Buckingham Palace, turning out to receive foreign dignitaries and rehearsing parades – all in London – are a daily grind. They simply do not allow time for more than rudimentary military training, achieving standards about equal to those of a Territorial Army unit, according to one Irish Guards officer.

The difference in military capability between socially elite regiments and military elite units in one respect may not be as unequal as it seems. Winning modern battles on the playing fields of Eton might sound ridiculous, but it is undeniably true that the British upper classes have always produced good soldiers, from top generals to unconventional fighters like David Stirling (who started the SAS) and Lord Lovat. Nobody can deny that the socially elite Scots Guards were successful in achieving an apparently impossible five-week transformation from public duties in London to being combat-effective in the Falklands. It must also be said that their success was due to the realistic leadership of their professional and perceptive commanding officer, and not to their Guards antecedents. Socially elite regiments believe that somehow their social status will translate itself into an equal level of military expertise. This attitude is a form of self-delusion and is drawn from a deep well of collective over-confidence, which under an unrealistic commanding officer can become dangerous. (Believing your own PR has also brought down many high-flying business organizations and individuals.) Socially elite units believing themselves to be inherently good, tend to attempt to 'cuff' or 'wing it' without proper preparation, with the result that unrealistically difficult exercises are imposed on undertrained troops who make a mess of them. The individual soldiers in these regiments are expected to be elite, too, to avoid making mistakes regardless of the standard of their training. According to an army psychiatrist, the pressure this places on some men can lead to serious psychotic reactions.

Military elite units approach training with a very different attitude, with an intimate knowledge of their soldiers' limitations. (The 'invincible' SAS rehearse everything they do ad nauseam, as would a professional theatre company.) The standard and difficulty of training is steadily built up until the required level is reached. A British Army psychiatrist:

The special units have got the psychology of it right; keeping people within their capabilities, then training them well beyond the standard of that required in war. They have tight-knit groups, which stay together, and train for jobs exhaustively, in manageable parts. Some people can do certain things well, and are not so good at other things. Nobody can do everything well. The army is not good at being honest about this. These social elites need to be brought down to earth, from the fantasy of fancy ceremonial. Regimental tradition is all right, but all the donkey work has to be done by the soldiers – who enjoy the military side of their jobs, but not the ceremonial. What are these socially elite units actually better at? They have this irrational feeling of superiority, but what is it actually based on?

In any army it is healthy for units to believe they are the best. Social elitism in the British Army, however, is far deeper than that, being based solely upon the class of the officers. The socially elite units in the British Army identify completely with their own perceived social status. Their officers socialize with each other rather than with officers of lesser regiments, and their soldiers feel themselves to be the best because their officers are the best – from the top public schools and top-drawer families. The subject of military efficiency does not arise where pedigree and quality are beyond question.

The list of socially elite regiments is headed by the Household Cavalry, then the Foot Guards and some Cavalry regiments. The Royal Green Jackets (infantry) slide into this batting order near the top. Some regiments are considered less elite than others; the cavalry talked disparagingly of the 'vulgar fractions' (regiments like the former 15/19th King's Hussars or the 9/12th Lancers), and the infantry of 'fish and chip' regiments. The importance of an established pecking order among British regiments has long been recognized. The strict precedence of British Army regiments is actually laid down in Queen's Regulations, the more senior regiments positioned 'to the right of the line'. Today the official precedence of Queen's Regulations is hopelessly out of date. When 'right of the line' is quoted, the Royal Artillery on parade with its guns takes the premier position – which everyone would agree does not demonstrate its current social superiority. Despite the strict ordering of QRs, psychological elitism remains competitive and based upon the perceptions of the regiments themselves.

Initiation ceremonies are very basic human events, carried out by all societies. Unofficial military initiations are additional to that provided officially by basic training, and can be seen as a sign that the members of the regimental 'club' do not respect the selectivity of basic training. Their aim is to degrade the initiand, cutting him down to size before allowing him 'club' membership. There have been tragedies, and countless other narrow and very frightening escapes. In one case, a boy was tied into a chair then thrown from a second floor window. He was so badly affected by this, he started drinking and was eventually medically boarded and left the army, because he constantly associated green uniforms with this terrifying experience.

Initiation ceremonies are particularly common among the soldiers of socially elite regiments. The Household Cavalry, for example, dunk new men into various unpleasant horsy by-products. Hair is often cropped and boot polish smeared on parts of the anatomy. Military elite units have no need for this kind of ritual as each man has already been initiated in the severe selection process through which each man must go, by which he earns the respect of his peers. Initiation ceremonies have received so much bad press that they have become serious offences. Unfortunately, the adjutants of many battalions simply deny that they take place.

The Guards, Household Cavalry and some other regiments, despite their regular denials, also practise an informal but active colour bar. For their soldiers, regimental tradition has acquired a Masonic quality that has nothing to do with military efficiency, in which the members of the regiment take it upon themselves to decide who will be admitted. As an Irish Guards officer said to me: 'The Micks would never tolerate a black man in *their* regiment.'

The position of ordinary soldiers in socially elite regiments is very different from the egalitarian mutual respect of the military elites. In upper-class regiments soldiers are often little more than servants to the officers and senior NCOs. Private soldiers have to polish the boots and ceremonial uniforms of officers, which is certainly not what most of them joined the army for. In other regiments, such impositions would be regarded as degrading.

Although the vital logistic services like ordnance, transport, electrical and mechanical engineers should be highly regarded by military men, the sad fact is that they are often looked down upon – as 'tradesmen'. Most armies have this attitude towards their logisticians. The 'teeth arms' who do the fighting feel superior to the service corps, who try to take comfort from doing an essential job, but nevertheless feel inferior. The service corps become the last resort of the less able or less well-regarded officer cadets. In Zugbach's sociological study of Sandhurst in the mid-seventies only one logistic service officer admitted to having wanted to be commissioned into his corps.[5] All the others would have preferred to go to a teeth arm.

The status of non-combat arm officers in the Israeli Defence Force is even worse. They are actively discriminated against, rarely being promoted before the minimum time limit and always slower than combat officers. Non-combat officers with specialist qualifications (doctors, attorneys, engineers) receive only one month's basic training and three months' officer training (very similar to that given to British Army 'vicars and tarts' courses for padres, lawyers et al). Although these specialists join the IDF directly as officers, they are not given the same respect, nor regarded as 'proper' officers.

A British Army psychiatrist believes that service corps personnel maintain personal self-respect by concentrating on their technical expertise: 'The service corps see themselves as superior technicians and the infantry and armour as cannon fodder. Without fuel and transport, the tanks and infantry are useless.' Their defence is fragile, particularly as they often work on attachment to smarter regiments:

The socially elite units have fewer people commissioned through the ranks. When the service corps mix with these regiments, very experienced ex-rankers come up against very inexperienced, upper-class officers who feel and behave in an unreasonably superior manner, causing great tension. Defence mechanisms are elaborate and very divisive, and the ex-ranker has no acceptable or secure basis on which he can answer back.

A service corps officer, promoted from the ranks, attached to a smart regiment, does not feel a full member of the team – because of the social difference. In war, he is likely to feel very isolated. Also, because he is a military expert, with over twenty years' experience, he will be much more experienced than the officers of the regiment to which he is attached.

Delegation is a vital management skill in the armed forces, as in any organization. There is a fine line between letting subordinates take decisions and offloading onerous responsibilities. The 'dumping' of responsibilities downwards is very common in peacetime armies. The expertise of logistics and service corps officers makes them prime targets, and they usually end up doing all the work, particularly if they are older, more experienced men, former warrant officers commissioned from the ranks: 'Inevitably, a lot of real and serious problems will be dumped on the ex-ranker – problems deemed too mundane for the "proper" regimental officers to be bothered with. In fact the regimental officers rarely have the experience to solve the stores, transport, maintenance and repair problems that ex-rankers handle.' In war, this practice is potentially disastrous as these few individuals end up shouldering an enormous personal burden of worry. Having 'dumped' responsibility and perhaps interest, their superiors are unlikely to understand the problems these people face. Pulled between the demands of superiors and the double burden of their jobs and their responsibilities, they may be more likely to become psychological casualties than their 'teeth arm' comrades.

The army is supposed to be one big happy family, a stable structure, carefully layered, with everyone knowing his or her place within the system. In fact below the surface things are not quite so happy and the similarities to a family become even more apparent. In psychological terms, family dynamics can be applied to the services as a whole, to the army as a whole, and to each of the regiments and units. Like all biological families, there are times when the military family is happy, and other times when it is distinctly miserable.

The regiment is the most traditional and well-known of the army's family units. Artillery batteries are closer, tighter and smaller, and much more independent than their infantry or armoured equivalents (companies and squadrons). The regimental family has its CO as the father figure, its adopted and foster children who don't quite fit in (for example the REME Light Aid Detachment commander and his troop), its cousins who are tolerated (the artillery battery commander and his forward observation officers) – and also its enemies. It is common (and traditional) for young men from broken homes to join the army in order to belong to a family. The British Army's image (and peculiar tribalism) has always been that of a close-knit family, although in the last two decades recruiters have made efforts to compare it favourably with industry – as a 'caring employer' or industrial skills trainer.

When the family of the army is happy and working, the system works very well. In war its purpose is quite clear and, because military units are tailor-made for war, everything falls into place: the family's whole raison d'être is to fight. In peacetime, however, when war is considered to be unlikely, the aims of the military family can become confused, and relations within it strained and uncertain. The family identity becomes all-important, and must be defended. Soldiers from different regiments fight each other off duty, young officers raid the messes of their rivals, regimental headquarters try to deflect on to rival regiments unreasonable demands for manpower from brigade and divisional headquarters . Preparation for war is taken less seriously than 'doing well' on exercises. Competing against rival regiments, 'for the honour of the regiment', or impressing the commander can become the aims of peacetime training.

Competition can be a substitute for war and bind units together, but can also become an expression of the ability of individual COs as they jockey for position in the promotion race. Difficulties may be glossed over and short-cuts taken, to the extent that people come to believe that what they are doing is realistic preparation for war. At the bottom of the rank structure, the soldiers are well aware when things are not being done properly, and learn to play the same game. Training becomes routine and predictable. The important thing is never to be caught out making a mistake. Unfortunately, war is far from being predictable; mistakes are made all the time. The secret of survival in war is to be able to recover from mistakes in time, the key scenario that much peacetime training never addresses.

The unreality of peacetime training also makes it difficult to keep teams together and practise effectively. So many compromises are made to achieve peacetime ends, that soldiers can become confused about their real roles. As a result, the military family loses cohesion, which adversely affects its battle efficiency.

Most military promotion systems are based upon the judgement of officers as to the suitability of their subordinates. In the British Army, platoon commanders evaluate their soldiers and junior NCOs; company commanders, commanding officers, brigade commanders and so on evaluate the officers under their command. The promotion of the right men at the right time, and the selection of the best candidates for responsible posts, is the single most important administrative task in any army. Good men passed over for promotion too often eventually become unhappy, and inadequate men promoted to positions of responsibility become liabilities. Therefore it is logical (and essential) for armed forces to devote considerable effort to running promotion systems that train and promote the right people to the right jobs at the right time.

Up to 1941, British regiments selected officers primarily by means of interviews that ruled out people from the wrong backgrounds – regardless of their ability. By 1942, expansion and casualties had seriously depleted the officer corps and more were required. The interview system, in which public schools, fathers' regiments, private incomes and so on were used to determine the social status of candidates, was not producing enough men of the right quality. Up to half the officer candidates were failing their training courses, with high levels of psychological breakdown. At the same time, many suitable candidates, in every way perfect, some proven in combat but lacking the right education and social background, remained in the ranks, reluctant to push for a commission, believing that the selection system was prejudiced against them.

The Adjutant General of the time, General Sir Ronald Adam, decided that psychological tests were required to override the highly subjective character judgement by which officers were then selected. These tests were to be a yardstick independent of the social standing of candidates. The 'Bion Leaderless Group Test' was devised. Groups of strangers were set a complicated task, then watched closely to see how each contributed. Some took charge, others followed; some worked wholeheartedly towards the group aim and others did nothing. A formal selection course was developed, which in time became the model for officer selection tests in the armies of several other countries. These new psychological tests were very carefully evaluated by the British Army, and were discovered to equate accurately to the subsequent performance of candidates on officer training courses. In the first six months of the implementation of the new tests, when it became known throughout the army that class-determining questions about schooling and private income were no longer part of officer selection, 25 per cent more applicants for commissions came forward.

The army's suspicion of psychologists parallels that of the general public. Giving the vital job of officer selection to 'shrinks' was doubly perplexing and worrying for senior officers as it seemed to cast doubt on one of their most vital skills. Army officers have always been used to judging and evaluating men; it is considered a stock in trade, like a gentleman's ability to ascertain the soundness of a horse, or the steadiness of a gun dog. So using psychologists to select the raw material for the British Army's officer caste was seen by some as an insult, and by others as an unfortunate necessity of war – to be dispensed with as soon as possible afterwards. The military establishment resisted the new tests, but high-powered champions of the new system (Field Marshal Auchinleck for one) held sway until 1948 when the psychologists were voted off the selection boards.

The army then slipped back into its old ways, which even today still play a part in the way some individual regiments select new officers. The army's formal officer aptitude selection (the Regular Commissions Board) is regarded by the smarter regiments as merely one of various inconvenient hoops through which the individuals they have chosen must jump. The Guards and Household Cavalry, in particular, choose only from the 'gentry', giving weight to family pedigree and existing family ties with the regiment. Today, psychologists do not play an active part in officer or soldier selection, although psychological tests are widely used and military staff may have some psychological training. During officer selection for the SAS, an anonymous psychologist is reputed to sleuth around the officers' mess eavesdropping on the conversations of candidates, but his views would certainly not be afforded anything like the same emphasis as those of the selection course instructors.

The Regular Commissions Board takes three days and is partly physical, looking for the *potential* to become an officer. The individual assault course is a particularly interesting test of fitness, agility and strength, cleverly coupled with judgement and quick thinking. There are also group discussions, written papers, interviews and psychological tests, all carefully observed by Board selection officers. The RCB looks for a type of leadership described by sociologists as 'leader-centred'. It believes in what it calls 'natural leadership' (a stereotype clearly understood by Board staff), selecting those who are able to alternate easily between leading and following, as all military leaders, regardless of seniority, must take orders from someone else. The RCB tends to reject democratically inclined leaders as 'not hard enough' or 'indecisive'. 'Positive' candidates are preferred, the sort who might push others aside in their keenness to lead. According to von Zugbach, autocratic and authoritarian personalities are favoured. Precocious types tend to fare badly, being judged immature, perhaps being invited to try again in a year or so.

According to another categorization of leadership, into Types A and B, RCB selects Type A leaders – the noisy, extrovert, authoritarian ones – while discounting Type B leaders, who are quiet, thoughtful and inward-looking, leading quietly and without fuss. Several studies show that in the stress of combat, Type A leaders tend to become subdued to the point where their leadership is ineffective, whereas Type B leaders continue quietly as they had always done, in the process drawing their men even closer to them, increasing the effectiveness of their leadership. The combat experience of many individuals to whom I have spoken corroborates this. RCB selectors like robust, outward-looking people, who engage in tough, manly activities. In sociological terms, they exercise 'anti-intraception', disliking introspection and tender-mindedness in candidates (as manifested in writing poetry or playing musical instruments, for example).

Independent psychological testing of successful RCB candidates has revealed stronger Super Egos and weaker Egos than in a control group of civilians. (The Freudian 'Super Ego' can be loosely translated into military terminology as 'sense of duty'.) The same testing revealed weaker Ids in the military group (less primitive drive and creativity). Translated into English, RCB chooses individuals likely to be dominated by their sense of duty, but less able to satisfy their instinctual drives (libido), a personality that could to some extent became unbalanced or frustrated. These psychological tests also noted 'much higher levels of authoritarian aggression' in successful candidates; 'a tendency to condemn, reject and punish people who violate conventional values'.[6]

This rejection of 'people who violate conventional values' is an important aspect of RCB selection. In a complicated social system like the army, individuals must fit in without difficulty. To an extent candidates need to understand and accept the social conventions of the army before they join – hence the preponderance of individuals with parents or close family already in the army. The RCB will not take risks with unconventional candidates, regardless of how admirable they might be in other ways. The stakes are simply too high. In enforcing the army's conventional values, RCB selectors practise stereotyping, identifying categories into which individuals can be accurately placed. All army officers learn to judge and categorize men, developing their skills on serving soldiers. However, in entering the army, completing basic training and joining a particular regiment, soldiers are already very thoroughly categorized. RCB stereotyping is therefore to an extent flawed through military stereotypes being used to judge civilians – a very different animal. Candidates who do not fit the RCB's stereotype image are rejected, often for showing 'argumentativeness' or a 'lack of clarity of thought'. Intellectuals are regarded with hostility and suspicion, deemed 'too clever to see the plain facts'. Deviance from middle-class norms is considered 'weakness of character' or 'immaturity'. Zugbach commented: 'RCB punishes by giving low grades to those who deviate from their consensus of conventionality, and high grades to those who conform.'[7] It must be said that RCB's experience is enormous, and it makes relatively few mistakes.

Because of the enormous social differences between its regiments, the RCB is the British Army's standard yardstick, the common denominator from which all its leaders are selected. The Board is expected to identify future officers from wildly differing backgrounds. The aristocracy, intending to enter the Household Cavalry, the Guards or a cavalry regiment, compete with the sons of working men (who would not be welcome in those and other similar regiments). In fact, working-class candidates try hard and do well at RCB, possibly because they have nothing to lose. Zugbach believes, however, that subsequent success in the army requires individuals to reject their working-class origins, a burning of bridges that happens in other professions but is particularly important where there is a very rigid correlation between rank and apparent social class. The vast majority of RCB candidates are middle-class, from military backgrounds. Moving sideways, from one institution into a very similar military version, public-school boys find themselves on familiar ground. The process of socialization into the army is very much easier for them, and they find their feet to out-perform others much earlier. The Royal Military Academy – Sandhurst – is highly competitive, and places in the best regiments have to be won against stiff opposition. A head start is a great advantage, and in any case, the smarter regiments prefer public-school boys.

Although it would be absurd to equate young people from Israeli kibbutzim and moshavim with British public-school boys, communal living does create a sense of social duty that is peculiarly suited to military life. Kibbutzniks and moshavim members do particularly well in Israeli Defence Force aptitude tests – known as 'kaba'. The lower kaba scores tend to come from under-privileged families, often immigrants from Islamic states (Sephardim). Israel's population is small by comparison with the potentially hostile nations that surround it. In defending the nation, the Israeli Defence Force must make the best military use of the population, carefully selecting conscripts for exactly the right jobs. The sophisticated selection procedure was developed for this purpose, to grade recruits initially, then be updated throughout an individual's career, to be used for his or her selection as an NCO and officer, and for subsequent appointments and promotions.

Unlike the British Army's Sum Selection Grading tests (SSG – used to measure British recruits' potential on entry to the army), kaba is used throughout soldiers' careers and is particularly useful for charting their progress in comparison with that of their peers. The word 'kaba' is an acronym for a Hebrew phrase meaning 'quality category'. Kaba calculates a 'quality group score' for each individual by measuring intelligence, formal education, and command of the Hebrew language. (Many conscripts are recent immigrants and may not have learned Hebrew. Each IDF soldier must at least be able to read a written order, fill in a form and understand the spoken word.) The final and most important kaba index, which is determined by interview, measures the individual's personal motivation to serve, particularly in a combat unit. Known as 'Tsadach', this measure is not applied to women.

The kaba indices work by identifying three categories of recruit: low quality (with scores of 41 to 46), moderate (47–50) and high quality (51–56). The very best become pilots, naval officers, high-grade technicians and special unit personnel. Most graded 'high' will go on to become NCOs or officers. (All officers score between 51 and 56, with the NCOs spread from around 47 upwards.) Those graded 'moderate' go to logistic units, and the lowest category to auxiliary units for non-combat jobs. Both the 'high' and 'moderate' categories are earmarked for combat units, where failure (in action) can least be tolerated. The tests are first taken in the year before conscription, allowing IDF planners to calculate how many potential officers, paratroopers, pilots etc. it can expect from each new intake of conscripts. In addition to getting the right people into the right jobs, kaba is therefore a vital planning tool to allow the optimal utilization of Israel's very limited human resources. Furthermore, after much experience and investigation, the IDF have found that kaba scores relate very closely to the subsequent performance of individuals in battle, which makes it possible for IDF planners to go one stage further and evaluate accurately the battle potential of their units and staff them with the right people.

Israeli experience over many years has proved that conscripts from prosperous, well-educated, 'comfortable' families obtain by far the best kaba scores, and go on to do correspondingly well in combat. Thus in Israeli society, conscripts from the upper classes make the most useful and most highly motivated soldiers – a deduction that Wellington would certainly have agreed with.

In the British Army, the advantage of a good education (at a public school) increases as an officer rises through the officer ranks. In the seventies, virtually every general of three stars and higher in the British Army was a former public-school boy,[8] with around a quarter of them having been to Eton. It would be impossible to determine the extent to which the ability nurtured by public schools and the accompanying style and manners contribute respectively to these statistics; but the predominance of former public-school boys at the top of the army certainly ensures the domination of the initial selection process and later army life by public-school men and their values.

The whole process of military training and promotion is full of paradoxes. Leadership is very difficult to measure and test. Superiors tend to judge subordinates using themselves as the standard, giving the most credit to those whose leadership (and personal style) most exactly resembles their own. In turn, ambitious subordinates learn to act like their superiors. Leaders tend therefore to be chosen according to their ability to follow, rather than their ability to do things in their own way. A free spirit is unlikely to do well – at least in peacetime. Those who accept and obey are more rapidly promoted to high rank than those who raise objections. The ability to think can therefore be a serious handicap, as breadth of thought is not required of young officers. In the lower echelons of the army particularly, those who think and evaluate the world for themselves can be at a distinct disadvantage to those who merely accept. Thinkers waste time and mental energy when action is required. Military men generally are intolerant of ambiguity and of those who question. And yet after decades of obedience and confining thought to very narrow bands of concern, when an officer reaches the upper echelons of the army, thinking suddenly becomes a required part of the job.

Another dimension of military conformism is that in order for anybody at any rank to be successful in the army, the correct image is vital, tailored to the particular requirements (or idiosyncrasies) of one's immediate superior. As an individual advances up the promotion ladder, his deference to authority must grow, until it extends well beyond that necessary in combat, dominating his behaviour (and possibly that of his wife) even at social events during off-duty hours. The psychologist Norman F. Dixon believes that the end result of all this complicated moulding and self-constriction is to make military men over-cautious. When playing the promotion game in a peacetime army, it is important not to rock the boat. It can be dangerous to use your own knowledge to influence superiors who, because nobody speaks frankly to them, are likely to be out of touch with events. Ministries of Defence all over the world shelter plenty of examples of this phenomenon.

The overriding need to conform has a psychiatric dimension too. Conforming is so important in military life that quite minor behavioural aberrations can become problems: sleepwalking for example. An acceptable response to such things is to refer the non-conformists to military psychiatrists. A soldier who, after his girl-friend had jilted him, stole a tank and until capture drove around wrecking an army camp, would be regarded by military men as mad. However, without certain symptoms, for example voices which told him to do it, he could only be diagnosed as suffering from an 'acute situational disturbance'. He would certainly not be considered psychiatrically ill. Despite military discipline, bad behaviour does not equate to psychiatric disorder, in the same way that chest pain alone does not indicate a heart attack, or headache a brain tumour. In the army, the idea that a regiment could produce a soldier capable of such criminal misuse of military hardware is unthinkable. Military selection and training cannot be thought capable of producing joy-riders; what might a man with a 175mm howitzer or Rapier anti-aircraft missile system be capable of doing?

The official, almost knee-jerk reaction of superior headquarters when incidents of this sort occur is to examine the general standard of discipline in the regiment concerned, with the implication that the incident was *allowed* to happen. A traditional view is that private soldiers are not supposed to be responsible for anything themselves (as an artillery CO once told me). Following this logic, the joy-rider's spree of destruction must therefore be the result of either poor leadership or sudden madness. For the sake of the career of the man's commanding officer, it is more convenient that army psychiatrists declare the soldier mentally ill (an aberrant individual, nothing to do with the regiment), which also lets the regiment off the hook.

Military discipline puts tremendous pressure on individuals to conform, and this is particularly stressful as the purpose of military discipline is to make people do things they don't actually want to do. When a private soldier is promoted, he moves from being one of the disciplined, to become a leader and discipliner. He is suddenly expected to take charge of his former fellows and friends, with only a single 'tape' on his arm as authority. This first promotion is an added burden, for with only one tape, he remains firmly among the ranks of the disciplined, but with additional responsibilities. On the promotion ladder, this first step is easily the most difficult, and many experienced soldiers have been demoted at this stage (usually for misbehaviour while celebrating).

The promotion of an individual upsets the established balance of a group, particularly when privates are promoted. Those who were not promoted (but perhaps felt they should have been) are often not prepared to examine their own deficiencies, and can become very bitter about the army, their careers and about life in general. They may become critical of authority, and adopt an injured, surly attitude that hampers or prevents their due promotion, fuelling their feelings of injustice.

The stress created by promotions is felt very much more among other ranks than among officers, although when officers reach certain critical career points (being 'pink-listed' for promotion to Lt Colonel for example), disappointments can be felt very keenly. Individuals who have devoted their lives to getting on in the army can find being passed over for promotion (and seeing their contemporaries listed) very hard to bear. Such people usually have few interests outside the army or army life. Not being promoted can seem like being rejected; I knew personally one major who committed suicide after not appearing on the promotion list. Such desperate disappointment is unbalanced, particularly as in such people it is based on an exaggeration of their own military worth. Throughout their careers they have usually been ultra-conformist, giving their all in order to be promoted. Having subordinated everything in their lives to the army (wife, family, private interests and so on), not being promoted makes the self-sacrifice (and so life) seem suddenly worthless. Among other ranks, the effect of promotion (and lack of it) is more directly felt in their day-to-day lives. A corporal is given a room of his own and becomes a member of the corporals' club, and a sergeant joins the inner circle of the sergeants' mess. Promotion affects directly who your friends are and how everybody reacts towards you. In the officers' mess, by contrast, rank is less important.

Although the British Army does all it can to keep its NCO corps strong (they are the ones who actually fight and win battles), increasingly its best are being siphoned off, promoted to cover officer shortages, peacetime career considerations overriding the need for mature, strong NCOs in war. Sergeants are being promoted younger, partly as an effect of increasing commissioning from the ranks, but also because today's top NCOs are not as prepared as their forebears to wait for promotion. The traditional father-like, older platoon sergeant, who takes his young officer firmly in hand, is more likely today to be commanding the platoon himself, due to a shortage of officers. Young officers are very much affected by this. Fresh from Sandhurst, they find themselves teamed up with a sergeant who may be even younger, and who therefore is less likely to get a grip on them and teach them the reality of their responsibilities. The combination of a young sergeant and a freshly commissioned 'rupert' (a common nickname for young second lieutenants) creates extra work for others, particularly the company sergeant major, as inevitably inexperience leads to administrative problems.

Rivalries among NCOs, particularly sergeants, are very much greater than among officers – as young officers invariably discover on social visits to the sergeants' mess. This rivalry extends from winning military competitions and general military accomplishment, to social attributes – in which drinking can play an important part. Young officers invited into the sergeants' mess are required to match drink for drink with the sergeants, usually being judged sympathetically by their willingness and application rather than by the end result.

All young officers arriving at their first regiment are keen to establish credibility for themselves with their soldiers. The first vital step is to gain some sort of status and relationship with their platoon sergeant – and the competition involved in this process can be fierce. Not all officers succeed. Those who fail have no choice but to put the experience behind them, and possibly invent another leadership personality for themselves to use when they take up another job with a new group of soldiers. Officers can choose how to play their relations with NCOs and soldiers. They can be equally successful, by either being completely pukka and unattainable, or by being themselves and meeting NCOs and soldiers at their own level. The latter approach is more difficult, which may be the reason why some officers from comparatively ordinary backgrounds adopt the role of the 'proper' army officer.

Israeli society is aggressively egalitarian, with little room for an aristocracy or the concept of gentle breeding. IDF officers are not required to be gentlemen, nor to have any sort of social, academic or even educational superiority over their subordinates. The officers themselves place little value on such things, although there is a growing realization that the sophistication of military technology makes some kind of science degree a prerequisite for officers[9] – an unavoidable concession to non-military qualification. Theirs is a very demanding occupation. Conscripts selected for officer training must sign on for at least one extra year of service, and in peacetime officers work particularly long and unsociable hours. They are three to four times more likely than other ranks to become casualties in combat, the inevitable product of high profile, 'follow-me' leadership, and they retire earlier than their western counterparts, some (particularly during the war years) exhausted by years of long hours on duty and stress. In return for this significant burden of responsibility, Israeli society accords a very high status to IDF officers, which is a significant motivating factor in becoming one.

Performance in combat is the prime criterion by which the IDF judges its leaders. Apart from those doctors, engineers and other specialists who join at senior level, all officers have served in the ranks and must then have served, and excelled, as NCOs. There is only one route for promotion, from NCO to officer, with nothing like the parallel career structure offered by most other armies, with NCOs and officers in two separate castes. As a result, IDF NCOs are notably young and inexperienced. There is no equivalent to the mature, experienced, cautious (and possibly paternal) senior NCO character that exists in most other armies. The IDF officer must therefore be responsible for much of his senior NCOs' work, as well as his own – a burden that British officers rarely have to shoulder.

Israeli Defence Force officers are the survivors of rigorous testing and hard work. After basic training and five months with their units (patrolling, training and on operations) they are graded – by kaba score and their unit commander's evaluation of performance – and must be in the top 50 per cent of their intake. Most are then selected for three- to four-month NCO leadership courses – considered the toughest in the IDF. Much of the time on these courses is spent on exercise, deprived of sleep, proper food and shelter. They learn leadership and technical military skills, being evaluated as they perform a wide variety of different military jobs.

The training is personal, and very intense. For example, on the NCO tank commanders course, students form tank crews which stay with the same instructors for the duration of the course. The instructors take time to get to know each crew member, determining how to bring out the best in him. The instructors have been carefully selected from the previous batch of conscripts and so are the same age as their pupils. To the students, they are known as 'Gananimm' (kindergarten teachers).

After these NCO command courses, and a further 6–10 months as team leaders back with their units, all NCOs are considered for their potential as officers. Those with the highest kaba scores (51 to 56) undergo a series of peer ratings, commanders' recommendations and psychological evaluations. Sociability, social intelligence, emotional stability, leadership, devotion to duty, decisiveness and perseverance under stress are measured.[10] Because the IDF officer candidate already has two years of military experience, his training concentrates on human leadership and tactical problems rather than (as at Sandhurst) teaching military skills as well. Tuition comes in the form of practical exercises rather than formal teaching. Student teams discuss problems, plan, then take turns to actually lead the exercise operation that is the result.

Most armies tend to teach conservative tactics, so that their students learn the basics thoroughly while ensuring that from the beginning officers make realistic plans. There is no point in creating a plan so daring or different that soldiers refuse to carry it out. The IDF philosophy is very different. Its style of leadership is very clearly defined, characterized by adventurous officers leading from the front, using initiative, improvisation and flexibility rather than going by the book. Officers and NCOs are always the best soldiers in their units, a principle developed from the pre-Independence days of the Palmach and Haganah (the guerrilla groups which provide the IDF's only military traditions). By leading through personal example (the 'follow-me' style), Israeli officers believe they can 'pull' their men with them into more daring tactical solutions than otherwise might be possible or prudent. Creative thinking and improvisation is particularly encouraged, stimulated by the instructors who introduce unexpected problems to the field training exercises. In their tactical solutions to problems, IDF officer trainees do not have to conform to text-book tactics, or to what is referred to in the British Army as the 'DS solution' – that is, the procedures laid down by the Directing Staff, who are always right.

The US Army's officer training academy at West Point, like Soviet Army equivalents, offers an academic as well as a military training. West Point is very different from the British equivalent at Sandhurst in both training and attitude, and, interestingly, is the older of the two. Whereas the Sandhurst motto 'Serve to Lead' is commonly corrupted into 'Skive to Survive', West Pointers are subject to the notorious 'Honor Code', in which a cadet promises that he will not 'lie, cheat or steal, nor tolerate anyone else who does so'. The Honor Code's purpose is to give each cadet the opportunity to live a perfect life for the few years he is under training, like a knight of Arthurian legend. In reality, it seems to have upset some as well as ennobled others. Honour has not, for example, deterred notorious examination scandals at West Point – in which incidents of organized cheating have led to savage witch-hunts.

West Point creates a strange elite within the ranks of the US Army officer corps. Its graduates are in a minority compared with the numbers of officers from lesser officer training establishments. Generals like MacArthur were great 'Corpsmen', believing that the Corps of West Point cadets (and its graduates) were the cream, vital to the future of the US Army. They might seem to an outsider to be an equivalent to the officers of the British Army's socially elite regiments. West Pointers do not however have the same social exclusivity as British officers are supposed (or assumed) to have. They come from a very wide range of different backgrounds, some being sponsored by Congressmen and a number by Congressional Medal of Honor winners (the US equivalent of the Victoria Cross). West Point's elitism is created by the academy itself, and spreads beyond the US Army into business and social circles. The academy homogenizes all the various social and cultural backgrounds of each cadet until they pass out as fully fledged 'West Pointers', of the same stamp, which they will carry for the rest of their lives, inside and outside the US Army. The personal prestige is considerable.

The army is not as integrated into American society, nor as generally socially accepted as in Britain – or certainly in Israel. Since the US Cavalry was sent out to subdue the Sioux and Apache, the army has tended to be based in some of the more remote areas of the USA. (Its Staff College at Fort Leavenworth, in the depths of Kansas, is deliberately located well away from the distractions and fun of city life.) US military 'Forts' are independent, self-contained townships, complete with supermarkets, bowling alleys, churches, petrol stations and so on. As a result, servicemen have no need to become involved with the communities or areas in which they live. They move on posting from one Fort to the next, overseas and at home, like Indian fighters moving through hostile territory. One effect of this isolation is to make joining the US Army a serious psychological burning of bridges, each soldier becoming 'Army' oriented more than in many other armies. This strong identification is also a form of psychological inflexibility, which in combat can make the personality brittle and less able to cope.

Vietnam had a severe and damaging effect on the US public's opinion of its armed forces – particularly the army. And more particularly, West Pointers became identified with the keen, career-oriented sort of officer who got his men killed unnecessarily. The shining armour of the West Point 'Corps of Cadets' was battered and stained by Vietnam, and remained so during the seventies and eighties.

Commanding officers, particularly of British battalions, have enormous personal power. They are responsible for everything that happens in their unit, with a great deal of choice in how they exercise their power. In both the Chinese People's Liberation Army, and until recently in the Soviet Army (and communist armies in general), for political reasons command is shared between the commander and his political commissar. Commander and commissar have equal powers but clearly defined areas of responsibility: the commander for training and operational military matters, the commissar for the welfare and morale of the men.

Western commanders regard this sort of duality as one of the worst manifestations of Communism, but in the PLA it appears to work well. The commissar frees the commander from everything but military matters: organizing entertainment for the troops, sorting out personal problems, running political meetings and smoothing relations with the civilian population. Jobs of this nature are regarded by most commanders as necessary but irksome, and many western military leaders would actually welcome someone else doing them. Sharing command in this way is however alien to most military people. The military ethos is based upon decisions being made by one person, who then issues orders that subordinates must obey. Having to debate decisions with another person is a complication fraught with difficulty. In the communist system, disagreements between commander and commissar are supposed to be referred to the unit's Party committee – a further complication. In battle particularly, an unresolved disagreement could be disastrous for the unit as commander and commissar have equal power and status.

Western COs are subjected to the pressures of coping with the problems of the families as well as training and commanding their soldiers. In war the job would in many ways be simpler, a matter of keeping the men fighting. In starting out as a CO, every lieutenant colonel has several fundamental decisions to make, that will affect the rest of his career. To achieve promotion he has toed the line, getting 'Excellent' grades in his confidential reports and a string of recommendations for command. Does he continue to build his career, safeguarding his own future by making the decisions that he knows (or guesses) his superior would want, or does he do what is best for his battalion? (There will be occasions when these two responsibilities are at odds.) He is father to the unit, but how does he choose to deal with the problems? He can remain aloof, only getting involved when there is a problem, or make himself available and known as a caring person, and so pre-empt problems.

Peacetime COs have very different aims and motives from wartime COs. In peace they command for a fixed period of time. Ambitious men therefore ride their regiments hard for two and a half years, ensuring that everything looks good, so that they do well personally and receive good confidential reports. Some may not be interested in knowing what is really wrong inside their battalions, just so long as their superiors are happy with what they see. Such personal ambition is usually accompanied by the ruthless will to ensure that no mistakes are made that could be blamed on them while they are in command. For peacetime brigade commanders (sweating on getting a clean sheet from their brigades), trouble-free units are clearly preferable; their COs must be reliable and therefore predictable. Some peacetime COs find it much easier to be sociable to superiors while keeping a distance from subordinates. They may even deliberately make their soldiers frightened of them, using their personal power and rank as a weapon of subjugation. One CO told me he did this as part of preparing the men for combat. 'If they are frightened of me, what chance have they against the Russians?'

By contrast, in the Israeli Defence Force popularity is considered a particularly important leadership quality. Popularity is formally measured as a 'peer rating', which includes frank appraisals from all members of the unit. Most pilots (for example) emerge at the end of their training and selection as men who have proved themselves very popular with everyone – almost celebrities. By setting such stock on peer rating, the IDF ensure that their soldiers are led by officers they respect rather than by those appointed from above. The IDF officer caste is thus not artificially elevated, nor are its leaders and followers distanced from each other in the way the British Army believes necessary.

In war, it is essential that everybody in a unit trusts the commanding officer. For this trust to develop, the CO must have some kind of sensible and genuine relationship with his officers, NCOs and soldiers. In terms of personal qualities, the basic essential is integrity of character; if a CO is really a shy, aloof person, it cuts no ice for him to pretend he is something different. He must also be honest with his soldiers – 'straight'. The best war COs are genuinely concerned and approachable, but also ruthless enough in battle to force their men to do things they don't want to do. In good units, the ruthlessness works both ways; Private Nick Taylor of 2 Para in the Falklands comments on his CO:

'H' Jones wasn't really discussed afterwards. He'd been doing the right thing, the thing we expected of him – doing his job. He knew most people's surnames, and knew most of us pretty well. He talked to us at our level, whereas some of them don't even bother their arses. During the battle, when he was killed, I just thought, 'Tough'.

Some men have a need to be liked, others are shy. Both these characteristics can create pressure, and cannot be eradicated by military training. The best training can achieve is to force the individual to adopt some kind of defence mechanism behind which he can hide what in the army (and in some other careers) are considered personal weaknesses. Problems arise through the behavioural artificiality of the defence mechanisms, which can appear to subordinates as irrational behaviour.

Beyond the rank of lieutenant colonel, isolation from ordinary soldiers and the real military world becomes an increasing problem. Successful commanders in peacetime armies are able to organize things both at unit level dealing with soldiers, and in staff HQ dealing with paperwork. To be promoted to high rank in peacetime, senior officers must be able to run a neat, efficient office – a far cry from fighting battles. The prime quality for officers working in head-quarters is good organization, which in the army is judged by produc-ing accurate work on time, and being good with fine detail – the vital 'nitty gritty' of plans. This starts from the very beginning, at Sandhurst where officer cadets are constantly urged to 'pay attention to detail'. Appearances are important too, taken as signs of under-lying efficiency: neat handwriting, a tidy desk – some of the indi-cators psychologist Norman Dixon says point towards obsessional personalities. It is however entirely reasonable for good organizers, in whatever walk of life, to have clear 'In' and 'Out' trays, to think ahead and to be reliable and predictable. But in the civilian world, the sort of 'good organization' some senior officers insist on might be regarded as unreasonable and obsessional. Nevertheless, military headquarters are different; doing things exactly to the letter is very important, particularly in war when men's lives depend on getting it right under pressure.

Norman Dixon's theory of increasing obsessional behaviour in military officers as they are promoted, although a generalization, does however help illustrate what life can be like within military organizations. He argues that obsessional personalities do well in peacetime; they ensure that things are done exactly correctly, follow orders to the letter, and are very dedicated.

Unfortunately, obsessional people contain within them the seeds of their own destruction. The higher up the military tree an officer progresses, the more his job increases in complexity. The pressure builds up, too, particularly for the obsessional who cannot do every-thing himself, but is forced to delegate to others. According to Dixon, he therefore visits his obsessions on subordinates, who are told to do things in exactly the way he would do them himself. Their work never reaches his standards, so the obsessed senior officer spends more time on the backs of his subordinates checking their work than he does working himself, becoming unpopular in the process. Eventually, in his crusade to be better organized (and promoted), the obsessional reaches the point where he cannot cope, ultimately becoming depressed and falling ill. It is a no win situation. In peace-time, Dixon says, senior officers get to the top through being obses-sional, and when obsession gets the better of them, are left stranded beyond their true capabilities. With no other personal abilities to fall back on, such individuals can only struggle, each reaching what Dixon calls 'their own level of incompetence'.

Although Dr Dixon exaggerates, there is something of the obses-sional in most successful staff officers. In all armies, selection for promotion is through the personal recommendations of superiors. Because obsessionals insist that work be done in exactly the same manner that they themselves would do it, they choose fellow obses-sionals, or at least people with similar characteristics to their own, for promotion. Once an officer reaches the rank of brigadier, the generals who decide which brigadiers will become major generals will probably know him well. Promotion to lieutenant general and higher is even more based upon personal knowledge. The top men choose people like themselves as their successors; reliable, neat, logi-cal men, who pay attention to detail ...

At the end of a military career, letting go can be difficult. For some, retiring from the army can be very depressing. A former RSM finds himself a nobody in the outside world, suddenly devoid of rank and power, and without any sort of status. Military discipline does not work in Civvy Street; shouting at subordinates is more likely to start a fight than to get the job done. The more military minded an individual has become (or 'khaki-brained'), the harder it is for him to leave the army. As a result, significant numbers of retiring officers prefer to stay under the military umbrella after retirement age, in underpaid, often mundane, Retired Officer posts.

The peacetime army is a strange, stressful environment, a highly structured society in miniature. When this pressurized society goes off to war, much of its social tension and tribalism becomes irrelevant. In war the only important factor is professional competence. Putting aside the habits of peace at the right time may not be easy.

Isolation is the most damaging psychological enemy of the battle-field, stripping men of courage and the will to continue. In peace, the overriding importance of conforming and the social divisions of the British Army, particularly within its officer caste, can create unpleasant situations for particular individuals. In war these divisions could make people feel terribly alone, and so create serious problems. Because social division is not considered a problem by most people in the British Army, individuals become used to coping with it. Most would not be prepared to admit even to being aware of it. In war, when the psychological pressures increase and comradeship becomes essential for survival, those of the same social level would feel confident enough to confide in their equals, dispelling their own fears by talking about them. The outsiders however have nobody to whom they can turn and could therefore become psychiatric casualties. The British Army's regimental system is a wonderful source of comradeship and motivation for its card-carrying members, but can slam the door in the face of those who for one reason or another are outsiders.

An Army psychiatrist, pondering the motives of ambitious officers, comments (in a rather wild generalization) on what he feels is a basic part of Army psychology:

The Army is all about power and privilege. Shouting is encouraged, starting from the parade square, extending into all aspects of army life. There's also the staff cars, commanders' houses, house staff, perks et cetera . . . It can't be because of the money.

The personal power of military commanders is far greater than that enjoyed by civilian employers. This power must however be used for purely military purposes, and should not be translated across into ordinary life. Status goes with rank and appointment, commanding officers in particular being given a whole package of privileges that emphasize the singularity of their position. Military commanders become adept at exercising personal power, using their official authority to manipulate others into getting the job done. Many feel a sense of anti-climax on leaving the forces, not only leaving the military family, but losing a whole raft of status, position and authority.

2

IN THE SHADOW OF WAR

Throughout the world, different armies make different assumptions about whether they are likely to have to use their skills in combat, and the nature of that combat. For example, expecting to have to fight against guerrillas is very different from preparing for conventional warfare. Some South American armies (notably that of Argentina before the Falklands War) have become used to fighting guerrillas and revolutionaries – and now drug barons. Such armies become militarized police, unable and even unwilling to fight effectively in a conventional war. Conversely, an army might have no expectation of fighting anybody in any circumstances, happily going through the motions of preparing and training secure in the knowledge that it would only be committed to war in time of dire and therefore unlikely emergency. Until recent years, NATO forces in Europe, facing a Soviet Armageddon, had much this sort of attitude, preparing for something that everybody hoped was too terrible ever to actually happen. Training realistically in such an environment becomes very difficult, and individual motives complex.

Military elite units, however, gain much of their strength and effectiveness from training realistically in the shadow of war. Their soldiers believe that they will have to fight, and many genuinely hope that they will be able to put their hard-won skills to the test in real combat. Small-scale conflicts provide good training for keen soldiers – as long as casualties are light. The 'war' in Northern Ireland has given British Army junior NCOs invaluable practice in commanding their teams under stress, keeping alive the psychological expectation of fighting in the midst of prolonged peace.

Members of military elite units see themselves as living constantly in the shadow of war, their lives dedicated to the pursuit of military excellence. My own unit was bombarded with telephone calls from former members begging to be allowed to return for the Falklands, and in 1990 I met senior majors in the Parachute Regiment who felt (in every sense) marooned in staff jobs and were bitterly disappointed at not being sent to the Gulf. As in Israel, British military elite units enjoy considerable public support, and react positively to the consequent high levels of public expectation when they go into action. The British media in particular are skilled at building this expectation to fever pitch when any hint of war seems likely.

Fighter aircrew (fast jet pilots and navigators) are among the cream of the elite personnel of all armed forces. The best regarded units in the Israeli Defence Force are those that take only volunteers, with air force pilots enjoying the highest status of all. Their slogan 'Hatovimm Latyees', literally translated, means 'the best to pilots', which the IDF personnel selection process ensures is literally true. Paratroopers are the elite of IDF ground forces, followed by other combat units that have distinguished themselves in past wars, for example the 'Golan' infantry brigade. The IDF has always lived in the shadow of imminent war, and so the reputations of its elite units are fresh and beyond dispute. The motivation for their best units to maintain high standards is also very strong – for reasons of self-preservation as well as martial pride.

Public perception is generally fickle, but nevertheless affects the self-perception of military people, confirming very strongly their own opinions of themselves. An embarrassingly exaggerated newspaper story about the prowess of the local infantry regiment is likely to be particularly popular with individual members of the 'embarrassed' regiment. Fifty years ago, after the Battle of Britain, Spitfire pilots were the heroes of the day. The beleaguered Israeli public today similarly lionize their jet pilots and paratroopers. However, after over forty years of peace, until the Gulf War the British public did not include RAF pilots in the same heroic mould that they invented for the paras or commandos after the Falklands.

The public image of the Royal Air Force was developed to a great extent after the Second World War, through works like Paul Brickhill's *Reach for the Sky* (about Douglas Bader), the film based on the Dam Busters' exploits and the desperate romance that came to be associated with the Battle of Britain. But although they took part in countless support operations all over the world after 1945, until the Gulf War the RAF had had no recent opportunity to try out their skills in combat. Even now, actual combat experience in the RAF is very restricted. A sizeable portion of the RAF was not involved at all in the Gulf air war, and due to the lack of Iraqi air force retaliation, only a few aircrew (and no ground crew) actually experienced combat. Most flew well above the air defences, bombing from high altitude. Only the Tornado crews flying low level against Iraqi runways had to run the gauntlet of flak – and paid a high price for it.* Most of them flew only a few such missions.

Nevertheless, the RAF's lack of combat experience is not quite the problem it would be for army or perhaps navy units, because life as aircrew in a peacetime air force is notably dangerous. Aircraft crash; friends and colleagues are killed. The tight-knit life of an operational fast jet squadron therefore has all the traditions and character of a wartime unit, with enough real danger and tragedy to keep everyone thinking realistically. In peacetime, fast jet aircrew take risks in training simply in order to push their skills to the standard required of them in combat. These risks are carefully calculated, but accidents are almost an accepted part of peacetime military aviation.

The risks, danger and perception of air force personnel are very different from those of soldiers. Training and tradition prepare individuals for the sort of combat that each service expects to fight. Fighter aircrew are used to short, sharp bursts of aggressive activity, returning to comfortable airfields to rest between missions. Ground crew are trained to cope with their airfield being attacked, and to working wearing NBC (nuclear, biological and chemical) protection equipment. The prolonged, endless misery of the soldier, living in muddy trenches, marching mindlessly from one concentration area to the next, without sleep or warm food is unimaginable to naval or air force personnel – as incomprehensible as the horror of an air crash or a below-decks fire to a soldier.

The really fundamental difference in perception between armies, navies and air forces comes from the essential nature of the combat that each must fight. Naval and air force personnel fight their wars impersonally, using technical expertise and sophisticated weapons. Most of their personnel, moreover, do not control actual weapon systems, or fly combat aircraft, but work to support the few who do, and their equipment. Soldiers, however, regardless of whether they are missile operators, truck drivers or storemen, are all trained as basic infantrymen, and so expect to have to fight personally against the enemy. In the very last resort, when a soldier has run out of ammunition, he may have to bayonet another human being. Sailors

---

* Exactly *how* RAF aircraft were downed in the Gulf War, and how they were flying, has important technological and security implications. This is a very sensitive area. (See Appendix 1, p. 407.)

and airmen are not individually conditioned to this idea of personal physical combat.

Training prepares individuals for what they may face in action, and is tailored to the particular job that each must do. However, in war, individuals from different units and even services find themselves side by side, facing the same situations. Soldiers stuck below decks in naval ships during air raids will feel helpless and terrified, while their naval counterparts calmly shoot down the incoming aircraft. Soldiers riding in combat aircraft, even on peacetime training sorties, may be airsick and terrified. Training is a conditioning and educating process which takes place over the years of an individual's service. Each one, through his particular experience, finds his own way of coping with the stress of combat, and the circumstances in which he is likely to be exposed to it. If an individual finds himself in a battle situation for which he has not been trained, his lack of knowledge will make him much more frightened than others who have been properly trained. Of course, if everyone is new to the situation, then everyone will be equally frightened – and there is some comfort in that. The RAF Parachute Training School (at RAF Brize Norton in Oxfordshire) has as its motto 'Knowledge Dispels Fear', a concise description of the method used there to train sane men to overcome the very strong and sensible instinct not to jump from perfectly serviceable aircraft.

In the same way that training prepares individuals for the particular circumstances of their sort of combat, it also conditions individuals to some of the implications of the jobs they do, to the effect of their actions on other human beings – the enemy. Infantrymen know that the last phase of an attack, as they fight through the enemy trench positions, is likely to be a cruel and bloody business. To an extent, having thought it through in training, they are as prepared as anyone can be for the reality of hand-to-hand combat. Similarly, an artilleryman understands the capabilities of the ammunition he orders his guns to fire on targets: Variable Time fuses bursting overhead like enormous shotgun blasts to kill troops in the open, Fuse Delay to explode just below the surface to collapse trenches, and White Phosphorus to create dense clouds of white smoke and burn deeply into any person it splashes. An artillery forward observer is to an extent prepared through his training for the horrors his fire will create on the enemy position his formation is attacking.

Tough though the infantry might be, when they assault the enemy position, they may not be prepared for the sight of this carnage. Individuals are seriously affected by what they see in combat, and without having undergone realistic training as preparation their reaction would certainly be worse. For soldiers, being shelled is perhaps the single most psychologically damaging situation. The fear of imminent death or mutilation, and the sense of complete helplessness, cause more battlefield psychiatric casualties than anything else.

In 1980, Squadron Leader Dennis Marshall-Hasdell (then a Flight Lieutenant), after several tours as a fast jet navigator flying Phantoms, volunteered to join 3 Commando Brigade as their Forward Air Controller (directing air attacks on ground targets). He regarded this new job as an adventure – an alternative to taking up a routine flying post as a navigation trainer. Well over six feet tall, of athletic build with dark hair, moustache and an irrepressible sense of humour, he thoroughly enjoyed being a commando, and was very popular indeed with everyone he came in contact with in the Commando Brigade. However, because of his RAF background, his training and mental conditioning were very different from that of the commando soldiers with whom he found himself working. Despite his enormously positive attitude, the disparity between his training and the training and experience of his new comrades was to give him serious problems during and after the Falklands campaign.

Dennis Marshall-Hasdell joined the RAF in July 1972 following in the footsteps of both his father and grandfather. It seemed 'an almost natural thing to do'. He had originally wanted to be a doctor, but his A-level grades were not good enough. At Bedford Recruiting Office, a squadron leader navigator persuaded Dennis to sign up as a first choice, fast-jet navigator. At that time the RAF was keen to recruit directly from schools rather than colleges or universities, and were short of navigators. Influenced by the recruiter, and flattered at having such personal interest taken in him, he fell into line with the requirements of the system – his first act of conformity.

Even at that early stage, I was being told what to do. The recruiter's style was to flatter by appearing to be interested, and I went along with his pitch. I was ambitious. I wanted to be Chief of the Air Staff – to do as well as I possibly could. All fast-jet aircrew are the same. I wanted some fun, too, and no other fun job paid so well. There's nothing quite like using up Her Majesty's fuel by flying low-level to drop Her Majesty's practice bombs! I expected a hard slog too. And the training, apart from a few downs, was enjoyable.

After public school, Dennis found no surprises at RAF Henlow, in Bedfordshire, and a social environment similar to home. A gregarious person, he had always been at the front in school – captain of cricket, a leader and never a follower, always pulling others along. The initial four weeks of 'Bull' were 'amusing', and even from those early days, when mixing with fellow cadets he felt the elitism of being graded 'aircrew'. Within an air force very few people actually fly, most working to keep aircraft serviceable, handling the vast range of spares, keeping airfields working and the paperwork flowing. This vast administrative 'tail' regards aircrew as the elite, their respect increasing with aircraft speed. Real men fly fast jets.

For Dennis Marshall-Hasdell, RAF flying training, at Church Fenton and Finningley in Yorkshire, was hard work and totally absorbing:

I had no spare capacity to think over the moral or ethical side – what I was doing or why I was here ... why do I want to be in co-charge of a war machine? ... beyond accepting that's what I would have to do if required. There were Moral Leadership lectures and Padres' Chats – but I don't remember any of them. The padres' reasoning can't have seemed very relevant or I'd have remembered some of it.

Eighteen-year-olds can't seriously consider the reality of modern exploding bombs – it looks fun. It's a sort of acceptance created by circumstances; you're not forced into it, but it grows all the same. All your awareness is channelled in particular directions. There are too many new ideas and values to absorb, so perhaps you remain unaware of the more crucial questions.

After all the interviews and selection board quizzings, young officer cadets have already learned the correct answers to difficult questions about whether or not they would be prepared to go to war: 'When asked, "Would you do it?" you answer that you would. I was one hundred per cent committed to becoming a navigator – to passing the next stage of training. Nothing could have put me off.'

Flying is a specific skill that has to be learned. Objectives are set then achieved, against the constant threat of failure. Fresh objectives allow no time for reflection. Acceptance becomes a vital part of learning; flying has to be learned and there is no time for questioning what is taught. Acceptance rapidly becomes a habit of necessity.

For me flying training was quite straightforward, with no set-backs. Until 1982, I was intolerant of other people's ineptitude – an attitude that could be associated with arrogance. I'd always wanted to be better than others. If I failed in this, I regarded it as a set-back. The flying instructors were good at detecting when I failed to match up to my self-created standards – attempting through this to get at what they probably saw as my arrogance. Often others didn't match up to my own particular standards, and with the naivety of youth, if I didn't achieve these standards, I took it out on others.

In my reports, I'm referred to as 'arrogant' and 'flippant'. I was a very open person, cheeky, with enormous ambition, drive and energy, which the instructors channelled, but never managed to control.

Twelve of us survived the course, and were very close indeed. At the end of the fourteen months, only five actually graduated. It was team work – mutual support in order to survive. I always sought the help of the others when I had problems, rather than keeping them to myself.

I'd always enjoyed being in a team – but in order to organize and run it myself. I've found that after a limited time of doing what someone else has planned, I wanted to start doing it in my own way. I therefore needed to go into Phantoms or Buccaneers – aircraft with only two seats – rather than Vulcans, Shackletons, Hercules, that have a large crew.

Progress from flying training to an operational squadron in the Royal Air Force is a gradual process. Navigating at low level starts with Jet Provosts, then moves to the Operational Conversion Unit at Coningsby, Lincolnshire, where the trainee navigators are crewed-up with pilots – in Dennis's case with a very good, experienced Canadian Air Force pilot on an exchange posting to the RAF. Dennis became the junior member of a very good team, the progression up the ladder being part of the fun. There were no real responsibilities: 'Coningsby had the standard fighter aircrew atmosphere. You just had to do your best.'

Operational Conversion lasted seven months, followed by a lead-in of six months with 29 Squadron before becoming fully operational. This six months lead-in is compulsory for all aircrew entering the squadron, from the OC downwards:

My only worries were my own ability to cope with the job. In fact, apart from the odd nerves before some important test, I had no hangups at all. The danger aspect of the job was something I accepted. Our reactions to dangerous situations were thoroughly and completely conditioned by drills learned in the simulator until they were second nature. In fast-jets, seconds are vital, so reactions to danger have got to become instinctive.

Air emergencies were practised so much that the correct response became conditioned reflexes, drummed relentlessly into the students. The lessons had to be accepted and fully understood: 'Because they might save your life'.

Most of what you learn in flying training is essential, very objective stuff – nothing you can really question. You can't experiment too much in an aircraft – it's been done already. The training aims to produce a human who becomes an element of the machine, who will make the machine work really well. The quality of the human crew makes the difference between the flying machine being just okay, or absolutely superb.

Training was a risky business; the squadron lost two aircraft, with the deaths of four crew members. 'There were lots of the usual emergencies – with a high degree of danger if you didn't get it right. Everyone faced the same potential threats; for instance, my Canadian pilot had to eject on one occasion.'

Air force aircrew believe that it is only a question of time before anyone is involved in some kind of an accident. Strangely, the first friend Dennis lost was not killed flying, but decapitated by a steel hawser whilst riding his moped home in the dark. This friend had already suffered two bad car accidents and was considered jinxed.

The first air accident Dennis was involved with took place in Malta. The squadron had just landed and were watching as a Vulcan bomber under-shot on landing, knocking the port undercarriage up into the wing. The impact broke a fuel line, releasing fuel and setting the engines on fire. Unable to slow down without explosion, the pilot took off again and circled the airfield, trying to get his crew safely out of the aircraft's side doors. The doors however had jammed in the heat of the fire. Eventually, after five minutes of burning, the pilot and co-pilot ejected and the aircraft crashed, killing the remaining five men.

His second experience of an air accident occurred several years later. He was flying with another Phantom, making a low-level radar-controlled attack on Harrier targets. His aircraft was the first to attack, then ten seconds later, the second Phantom turned in to make its attack. Looking back they saw a cloud of smoke, so they called the other Phantom on the radio. Receiving no reply, they flew over the site – a North German village. The second aircraft had crashed:

It was a horrible thing to have to do. We circled overhead to report the incident, then stayed for another fifteen or twenty minutes to co-ordinate the rescue. There were no signs of life, just smoke and debris everywhere and a big hole with some burning – but no real fire. The worst thing was when we got back to base. The Board of Inquiry was immediate and we had to fly back up to the crash site in a helicopter to make statements and help gather the evidence. It was crucial to find out what had happened quickly.

The devastation in the village was amazing but only one small girl was hurt – with a broken arm. The aircraft was in little pieces, except for the engines which were one solid lump. Five tons of engine at 500 mph had gone clean through a house and just missed the occupants. There were chalk marks in the road, of the footprints of an old lady who'd stood stock still as the crash happened around her. She was taken immediately to hospital with shock. All around her footprints were bits of plane . . . everywhere.

An engine lay twenty feet away. And just behind her, the pilot, after he'd ejected.

I can understand the old lady's shock. The kinetic energy involved in the crash, at 500 mph plus the ejection, was enormous. The effect on the pilot, who must have been killed instantaneously, was to extrude him out of the safety straps of his seat. The seat was still sitting on the road the right way up, facing forwards. Its shoulder, lap and crutch straps were still done up, but the pilot lay a few feet from it. Although his arms and legs had been severed by the straps, his body was still completely intact. The poor old soul must have emerged from the shock of the impact, smoke, dust and debris, to see this terrible fresh 'thing' on the road beside her . . .

The other pilot had completely vanished in the smoking crater. His aircrew watch was found, intact and still functioning, buried ten feet into the impacted earth. A memorial service was held at the village three weeks later. The squadron were welcomed by the villagers, and a plaque was laid.

The plane had missed buildings and people, and it looked like they'd done their best [the crew] to steer away, so the villagers were grateful.

I could never work out just how much genuine concern [for where the plane will crash] there could be in such circumstances – as opposed to controlled panic. The navigator has his own ejector and so can bang-out if he wants to. I wondered why it doesn't happen more often, why navigators don't just bail out of the aircraft? I would guess that with the tremendous trust that builds up between a navigator and pilot, if in an emergency the pilot says he's got it [control of the aircraft], the nav believes him and tends to stay on board.

The standard practice on most squadrons after a crash or accident, particularly if someone has been killed, is to close down, go to the bar and drink – on the dead man's mess bill [which in Second World War tradition, the squadron subsequently pays]. The next day, everyone goes flying. An unexplained crash is much worse – and can lead to all aircraft of that type being grounded until a cause is determined, hence the need for immediate Boards of Inquiry.

I regarded these particular deaths as a bit of a personal milestone of my life in the air force, but they were also normal events, a part of the process [of becoming operational]. The law of averages means you sometimes lose aircraft – this is an accepted fact in the air force, rather than being a conscious thought. Causes of crashes are always very complex, each one different, and pilot error will be only one of many variables. An identified pilot error reaffirms everyone's desire to do things correctly. For a time after the accident I was more cautious, the deaths drumming home all the lessons I'd been taught in training.

Surviving death can also be strangely comforting, giving renewed confidence to the survivors: 'The crash reaffirmed my belief that had it been me, I would have survived – by banging-out [ejecting].'

Aircrew find it easier to come to terms with crashes that have obvious causes: mechanical failure, weather or damage. In such crashes, the participants exercise a very fine line of judgement between crashing, ejecting and carrying on. The early days of jet fighter flying were filled with uncertainty. Men were killed almost by chance, unable to influence events. The F104 Starfighter became known universally as the 'Widowmaker', its wing shape making it dangerously unstable under certain conditions. At times, aircraft were crashing almost weekly.

In order to be able to fly safely, individuals must accept the danger of what they are doing. But once in the air, there is no time for uncertainty:

Although I accepted the danger, I've never been consciously aware of it in the air, so I've never been affected by it. Things can just happen, like what are called 'uncommanded aileron roll problems', in which the plane inexplicably rolls and you hope to get it back okay. You are aware of the risk of such things happening, but carry on.

Excellence in fast-jet flying isn't possible without danger. Working hard at the extreme limits of safety is more risky, but somehow one's physical and mental ability rises to cope. It's quite hard to overload in these situations – quick thinking, rapid decisions, with the willingness to take it to the limits, and accept the danger of crashing. There's a particular pass through the hills in Germany that only the best pilots will take at low level. To do it, you have to skim up into the cloud base, which sits at around a thousand feet, losing vision until you make it to the other side. It's like flying into a letter box. You really have to go for it.

Aircrew relationships are all about trust, and with trust, risk perception gets less. I've never flown with anyone I didn't trust, but they have varied from exceptional down to average. There are few fast-jet pilots in the RAF who might be classed as below average.

In some ways, apart from the improvements of modern technology, the sheer expense of modern aircraft has made them safer to fly. Each Tornado costs around £25m, and is therefore too expensive to crash. The solution, for peacetime training, has been to narrow the flying parameters so that larger safety margins can minimize the chances of losses.

In January 1980, as a flight lieutenant, Dennis Marshall-Hasdell was posted to the School of Navigation at Finningley as an instructor. At 26 with two full flying tours under his belt, he was too young to be promoted to squadron leader so this posting was a sensible career

move. However, enjoying his responsibilities and with high expectations of life, all Dennis actually wanted to do was fly Phantoms at
low level.

Then his boss showed him a DCI (Defence Council Instruction)
asking for fit, fast-jet crew volunteers to serve with Commando
Forces as Forward Air Controllers (FACs). Sitting in a smoky crew
room at RAF Wildenrath in Northern Germany, this seemed an interesting and challenging way of getting out of the Finningley job.
Dennis was chain-smoking King Edward cigars at the time, and the
physical realities of commando service were completely unknown to
him. However, having decided to go for it, he stopped smoking and
tried to get fit – without any idea of what this new job might entail.
Perhaps strangely, he made no effort to find out. It seemed the ideal
move; in keeping with his wild, punchy character.

The first step was the FAC course at RAF Brawdy in south-west
Wales, where, meeting army people, he found out more. A Royal
Artillery officer who had just failed the commando course was understandably full of doom and despondency, telling him to break-in at
least two pairs of boots as he'd wear out the ones he already had,
and to soften-up his brand-new 58 pattern webbing equipment in
water for at least three days 'lest it cut your waist and shoulders to
ribbons'. This latter advice Dennis ignored; his RAF issue webbing
looked too nice and new for that. For someone used to sitting in a
jet cockpit, the FAC course (talking to pilots from the ground) was
very easy.

Visiting Stonehouse Barracks in Plymouth – the headquarters of 3
Commando Brigade – Dennis was made to feel welcome. He realized
that the commando course would not be pleasant and so, his resolve
fortified, he returned home to Aberporth in West Wales to get properly fit. Four weeks of running up hills wearing heavy boots, and
work as a builder's labourer to toughen his hands and upper body
made him fit enough for the pre-commando course 'beat-up' at Stonehouse Barracks. Although he was unworried by the beat-up, he realized he knew nothing about soldiering and had not the least idea of
how to live in the field. RAF recruit exercises at Henlow had been
like Girl Guides' camp by contrast. By the time Dennis went to the
Commando Training Centre at Lympstone in Devon, he had evolved
a policy of survival through use of good humour. Universally referred
to as 'Biggles', he had half his moustache shaved off for him – so he
left it like that for several days before completing the job himself. He
liked commando people and was determined to become one of them:
'I really wanted a green beret.'

Marshall-Hasdell succeeded in becoming a member of two quite different military elites, fast-jet aircrew and the commandos, a remarkable achievement. He had very little personal experience of soldiering, which he had to learn very quickly. His life experience was with the air force and, having been conditioned for years as a jet fighter man, going to war on his feet was a serious test of his strength of character – which he was to pass with flying colours. As we shall see, however, like a newly arrived visitor to a hot country who stays out in the sun too long, he was burned.

Getting into any elite unit is a long, hard process, which both trains and tests the candidates, while allowing the instructors to pick out the most promising among them. Commando and parachute selection courses are very different – although to the outsider the constant running and marching with heavy loads might seem equally painful.

The aim of the commando course is to produce a man who regards being cold, wet and tired as normal and therefore irrelevant. He has been mucked about for five weeks by experts and it no longer bothers him – he just carries on doing his job. He has also been taught specific commando skills: to help him get from the sea on to the shore, to work completely by night if required and to carry on functioning for that little bit longer than other troops. The tests range from the 'thirty miler' on Dartmoor, the assault course and Tarzan ropes course, the seven miles of water-filled tunnels and running of the Endurance Course, the Nine Mile Speed March and the Load Carry. All the tests are preceded by long, uncomfortable and gruelling exercises.

The paratrooper has to be able to turn on his maximum effort for the length of time it takes for his forward parachute drop zone to be resupplied and his unit to be relieved – around thirty-six hours. Before he even arrives on the battlefield he is likely to be exhausted – from the long and probably turbulent flight, the heavy parachute equipment he has been wearing in the aircraft and the frantic period of preparation over the two days or so before the airborne assault. He jumps into battle tired out – and with a peculiar sense of relief that at last the agony of waiting is over.

The P Company tests are designed to produce maximum effort from each individual. In his introductory talk, the course officer summarizes the primary requirements for airborne soldiers as 'Go, Guts and Gumption', first formulated by Brigadier Hill, Commander of 3 Airborne Brigade for the jump into Normandy followed by the Rhine crossing in 1944:

'Go' is the spirit to get up off your backside and do something; the spirit that dominates life rather than vice versa. By volunteering for this course, you have shown a good spirit, as you have volunteered to push yourselves to the limit and beyond, something most people never volunteer to do. So well done. You will need the same get up and go to attack all the events on P Company.

Guts. This course will push you hard and it will hurt. You will require guts to persevere, to smash through the pain barrier on a bi-daily basis. It will take courage and commitment to drive on. But take comfort from the fact that all your colleagues are suffering just as much as you are.

Gumption – the mental approach required for success – and therefore the most important of the three. You must stay switched on at all times, particularly when tired. Twenty-five per cent of you will fail through injuries collected on this course. Be aware that injuries happen primarily to the unfit; when tiredness sets in, the body slows and the mind switches off. That is when you make mistakes, roll an ankle, break a leg. You must stay switched on to respond to commands at all times.

After each event you must immediately sort yourself out, to get yourself to the next start line with the right kit in the right condition and in the right frame of mind – this is standard battle procedure.

There is no physical stereotype of the airborne soldier, but there is a common mental attitude. This is the attitude that is prepared to push the body beyond the limits that are considered normal, a refusal to accept the standard limits and a willingness to drive on into the unknown. This course will push you to the limit of your fitness, and then the testing will begin; you will be driven by your mental resolve rather than your physical fitness. That is when we on P Company assess your suitability for airborne soldiering . . .

My P Company staff are on your side, and everything they do is designed to help you push yourselves further than you want to go. You may find their brand of man management somewhat out of step with contemporary standards, but as we are asking you to perform extraordinary feats, so we need to provide extraordinary motivation. You will never forget your P Company instructors; they will help you achieve great things if you work with them.

A sense of humour is vital. Let the course get on top of you and this three weeks will be a nightmare – for you and for us. However, approach it with a sense of humour and you will find the course rewarding and maybe even enjoyable![1]

The tests themselves, the Stretcher Race, Assault Course, Milling (a one-minute fight requiring total aggression; although gloves are worn, boxing skills are forbidden), Battle Marches, Speed Marches, and Load Carries, cannot easily be compared with those of the Commando Course because most take place straight from camp without the gruelling field exercises that precede the commando tests. Although there are strict minimum times for the completion of these tests, the instructors set more stock by observing the reactions of individuals, and ensuring that everybody reaches his own personal limits of endurance. They are interested in seeing a man's conduct when he reaches his limits, rather than his athletic prowess. Also on P Company the tests themselves are very severe, more severe than those of the commando course, and there is very little extra aggravation from the instructors – provided the men on the course are always smart, punctual and enthusiastic.

On both courses, potential commando or parachute padres receive particular attention. They are respectfully urged to perform ecclesiastical tricks – walking on water is the usual one, although transforming water into wine is often requested. All members of the airborne brigade are required to pass P Company, including doctors. Being non-military, like the padres they are watched very carefully. On one P Company speed march, a suffering doctor was noticed to be coughing, right hand thrust down the front of his trousers. His reply to the instructor's indelicate inquiry was that he was sure that something was seriously wrong with him, but he was having problems deciding what exactly it was.

The Special Air Service selection course is said by some to be comparable to P Company in purely physical terms – the important difference being that, unlike parachute or commando selection, SAS selection is a totally individual effort. There is no deliberate fostering of team spirit and group effort, each man being free to pull out at any time with only his own determination to drive him on. The aim is to select men who in war can be relied upon to continue with a mission even when all the other members of their unit are dead, wounded or captured.

The initial three weeks of the SAS course are preparatory training (polishing up map reading skills and fitness), but are very tiring. The fourth week, Test Week, is an exhausting, lonely series of individual marches against the clock, carrying a minimum weight of 25 kilos plus a rifle. The extreme changeability of weather conditions and the usual driving rain of the Brecon Beacons in Wales are an additional serious (and often dangerous) factor. Those on the winter course must cope with snow drifts, starting and ending the marches in darkness. The summer courses have the disadvantage of possible very hot weather, plus the same sudden impenetrable mists, cold, rain and sleet of winter. The Beacons themselves are wet, exposed and

dangerous, huge glaciated hills populated only by sheep – an unforgiving environment.

Throughout Test Week, early each morning SAS candidates leave
the base at Hereford in the backs of four-ton trucks. They start each
march alone, knowing only the next RV (rendezvous) for which they
must head. The weight of their bergan rucksacks is checked sporadi-
cally – any found to be less than the required 25 kilos incurs (for a
first offence) a heavy extra weight penalty. Each march must be
completed within a set time, which is determined by weather conditions. The candidates do not know the time limit, nor the route or
the number of RVs to which they will be sent.

Each day the marches lengthen: the 'Fan Dance' is an early pipe-
opener (a brisk hack up and over the 3000-foot Pen y Fan, then back
again); 'Point to Point', 'Pipe Line' . . . all permutations of routes
that involve climbing and descending the highest mountains in the
area. Staff at the RVs check each candidate's condition before giving
the grid reference of his next RV. Those who are going too slowly
will be warned, and if a candidate seems unlikely to complete the
march in time (or looks too tired to continue safely) staff will pull
him off the course, to be sent back to his parent unit. Navigation
skills and will-power are tested under pressure during Test Week. By
the last day, candidates are very short of sleep. At the end of each
day, the course returns to barracks in Hereford late at night, then
parades in the early hours for the next day's march. They are foot-
sore, often injured and exhausted before even they start the final,
longest march. Some will already be under pressure, having completed previous marches in slightly more than the minimum times.
(They are permitted to continue provided the lost time is clawed
back.) As one simple map-reading error can easily cost an hour of
hard slog, the pressure of the ticking clock is great.

The final march is the longest – around 35 miles, according to
how accurately you navigate. It is a feat of endurance, usually completed in under 18 hours. Taking terrain into account, an average
speed of four miles per hour as the crow flies must be maintained
(up mountain slopes, around corries and across ridgelines) in order
to pass. This involves running down hills and on the level, which,
with the weight of the bergan, makes injury very likely. Those who
do pass Selection have usually pushed themselves through it nursing
some sort of injury.

In addition to Selection, officers must undergo a week in which
their judgement and ability to plan under pressure is intensively
tested. Four weeks of jungle training and a period of specialized

weapon handling precede the last hurdle – Combat Survival. For the individual, after all the determination, pain and action of the previous months, learning to eat berries and squirrels while wandering the countryside dressed like a tramp seems an anti-climax. The final week, however, more than makes up for this. The surviving candidates are given ragged Second World War uniforms, then set loose in remote countryside to be hunted by police and soldiers with dogs and helicopters as they make their way between RVs with 'agents' using a rough sketch map. If captured, they suffer twenty-four hours of exposure to the elements and extreme discomfort in a 'prisoner of war' cage, before being released to continue.

After a week on the run, the candidates are taken to a holding centre, where expert interrogators use very sophisticated techniques to induce – or force – candidates to give more than the 'Name, Rank and Number' that the Geneva Conventions permit captors to demand from prisoners of war. The details of how these inquisitions are conducted are highly classified. For the individual, after a week of starvation, cold and lack of sleep, the training exercise seems almost real. The questioning becomes a highly personal, individual battle with the interrogators, who although they seem to be holding all the cards, can be misled (or even tricked) into making incorrect assumptions. Keeping track of time becomes of critical importance to counter the deliberate disorientation being induced by the interrogation process. One glimpse of a careless guard's uncovered wrist watch through a chink in the blindfold can (as I experienced) restore a subject's equilibrium. As with all previous tests, candidates are free to give up at any time – a constant temptation to which many succumb.

All the selection processes used by elite or special force units achieve two purposes. Firstly, through applying strict entry standards they maintain both the quality of the unit and its perception of itself; and secondly, the highly realistic and testing experience gives successful candidates a tremendous and enduring self-confidence that enables them to overcome seemingly impossible situations on real operations. Although most of the tests involve hard physical activity, the real emphasis is actually psychological – on producing men who know they can continue to operate well beyond the normal limits of endurance, by controlling their own fears and weaknesses. Such men have become aware of their limitations, and through necessity have devised ways of working around them – or of forcing through and beyond.

In peacetime, the danger and difficulty of special forces exercises can be even more severe than they might be on a live operation, and men are killed. Members of these sorts of unit – like fighter aircrew – live constantly in the shadow of war, training in the expectation of having to use their skills in real combat. People don't survive for long in special forces units unless they are totally committed to their jobs. Every man is expendable, either in peacetime if he fails to achieve the required standards, or in war when dangerous jobs must be done. When coupled with the tremendous mutual respect (and affection) that exists within special forces units, this expendability generates a feeling of selflessness and so becomes part of the strength of the unit, drastically increasing the individual commitment of each man.

In comparison to ordinary military units, the inner discipline, individual sense of purpose and expert dedication of special forces troops combine to become almost monastic. The SAS memorial at their base in Hereford, which bears the name of every man to die on active service with the regiment, has the following inscription:

> We are the Pilgrims, master, we shall go
> Always a little further: it may be
> Beyond that last blue mountain barred with snow
> Across that angry or that glimmering sea . . .[2]

This memorial used to be under a clock, which gave rise to an SAS expression 'beating the clock' – avoiding having your name appear on the memorial by surviving.

Humility is not generally regarded as a special forces' trait, so perhaps 'We are the Pilgrims, master . . .' sounds a little strange for such a capable and ruthless organization as the SAS. Their capbadge motto 'Who Dares Wins' sounds more like it. However, in the face of a military task, humility is vital to the making of a logical and accurate assessment of options and plans.

Despite US Special Forces modelling themselves on the British SAS (the initiator of Delta Force, US Army officer Charlie Beckwith, served on secondment to the SAS in the 1960s when he was a young captain), they seem unable to shake off the 'gung-ho' attitude that has been at the root of their more highly publicized disasters. Reticence is a particularly British trait; exuberant confidence is the corresponding American national characteristic. Unfortunately for Special Force operations, this otherwise attractive and very positive attribute can become a serious disadvantage, giving rise to over-estimation of their capabilities and under-estimation of the enemy and the task. The US Army calls it the 'can do' philosophy, in which nothing is too difficult and all things are possible, an illusion that can easily become dangerous.

This same 'can do' attitude also plagues the peacetime British Army, where it is referred to as being 'wilco' (from the radio jargon for 'will co-operate' – which translates into English as 'Yes'). A 'wilco' person is eager to please, positive at all times, and makes the life of his superiors as easy as he can. Instead of raising difficulties and problems, he will get on and solve them (or gloss them over). 'Wilco', 'can do' people see themselves as epitomizing the best face of the peacetime military: the image of the self-assured, confident professional to whom all problems are a welcome challenge, who it is assumed will take to the real problems of war like a duck to water.

The reality is that few people can be 'wilco' to everyone. In peacetime armies, most are unquestioningly co-operative only to their immediate superior and upwards. Every task they accept from superiors has usually to be carried out by somebody else – usually their own subordinates. 'Wilco' unit commanders can cause serious problems in peacetime armies, wasting valuable time in being co-operative, while leaving insufficient time for the real military essentials. This process tends to affect units right across the board – because no one commander is prepared to stand out as the one unco-operative individual amongst his peers in the formation.

In special forces, whose tasks are complicated, difficult and dangerous, attitudes are very different. Tasks are not simply accepted, but closely examined to see whether or not they can be done. Operations that seem impracticable could be refused, or changed radically into something more sensible. Orders for special force operations are therefore generally non-specific, stating the required result rather than the detail of exactly how it is to be achieved: for example, 'rescue the hostages' rather than 'attack the embassy'.

It is policy to leave as much as possible of the planning of a special force operation to the men who will actually have to go and do the job. During preparations, a special force commander may actively seek the ideas of his men (the SAS call this holding a 'Chinese parliament' – a process that would be derided in ordinary units). A special force commander may end up adopting the 'Chinese parliament's' plan if it looks better than his own. Once a special force operation is in progress, the first and most basic axiom is that 'the man on the ground is always right'. If, for example, a four-man reconnaissance team reports that it has been compromised and asks to be helicoptered out in two hours' time, then that is what happens. Any questions as to whether the team commander made the right decision would be deferred until after the extraction. Similarly, if a recce team reports sighting a squadron of enemy tanks, then the rest of the operation in which they are involved is planned accordingly. Special force commanders of every level are free to change their plans as they proceed, confident that their HQ will back them up. Normal troops in combat do not always enjoy such trust and support.

In peacetime, armies attempt to find forms of training that will put their soldiers under pressures comparable with those of war. As a rather extreme example of this, Iraqi officer cadets are required to cross a high gorge by a single fixed rope. While the others watch, each crawls across, some slipping under the rope and having to continue hand-over-hand. Inevitably some fall – and are killed.[3] There is a very fine line between realistic training that familiarizes men with battle conditions and encourages them to believe they will be able to cope, and training that is too frightening to be useful. In the British Army, 'adventure training' (rock climbing, fast-water canoeing, sub-aqua, mountaineering, etc.) is much encouraged as a method of challenging soldiers in training without putting them off. 'Outward Bound' activities are now widely accepted as being character building for civilians as well as soldiers.

Military parachuting is one peacetime military activity that succeeds in introducing a realistic taste of the anxiety and danger of combat, making men feel and react together as they might in battle. Military parachuting is far from being fun or enjoyable. No paratrooper enjoys sitting for hours feeling airsick in troop-carrying aircraft flying just above tree-top height, turning, pulling up and descending with stomach-wrenching force. Paratroopers are always relieved to jump – unstoppable in their desire to get it over with. David Cooper, the Chaplain of 2 Para throughout the Falklands War:

In war, however, there is always the unknown, and no guarantees. Even the most realistic training has limits. With 1 Para, we had a high rate of parachuting incidents, deaths and injuries, due to [having a lot of] young soldiers and having become inexperienced [at parachuting while] in Berlin. Most people reacted to the accidents philosophically, saying that it was bad luck – even though the more imaginative would certainly have reflected on it.

When you become a paratrooper, you accept that at times your life may be in the hands of someone who is not as careful about it as you are. In war, however, somebody is trying to kill you.

Military parachuting as a means of getting to work could be likened to travelling on the London Underground at the height of the rush-hour carrying suitcases weighing around 200 pounds. Apart from the weight of his 'chute, a parachutist's equipment weighs a hundred pounds or so (radios, ammunition, weapons, food, etc.), carried in a bergan strapped to his front. After jumping, he waits until he is clear of the aircraft and his 'chute has safely opened. He then unclips and lowers the heavy bergan on a fifteen-foot nylon cord to land slightly before he does. Most jumps take place at night, when the procedure is the same except that the exact moment of impact with the ground comes as a surprise.

When an entire unit, from commanding officer down to the laziest storeman, cook or lorry driver, has to be fit and determined enough to do at least six parachute descents each year, its lowest common denominator of fitness, motivation and esprit de corps will be high. Although experienced paratroopers lose some of their fear of parachuting, every single man is frightened, and has to will himself into jumping when the time comes. Some paratroopers lose sleep on the nights before jumps, and worry incessantly that their 'chute will fail to open. Although 'balloon training' (jumping from a tethered barrage balloon rather than an aircraft) is much safer than jumping from an aircraft flying at around 200 mph, for some reason it purifies and concentrates the fear. Jumping from a small wicker basket suspended under a tethered barrage balloon requires a totally cold-blooded leap, as if from an 800-foot cathedral spire into the perfect quiet of completely still air. Some less imaginative souls do enjoy it, and others have done it so often that the fear loses its edge.

While I was doing my basic parachute training (as a captain), a young private in my section who I was worried might be about to commit the unforgivable crime of refusing to jump, confessed to me that he was 'shit scared'. We'd done a couple of jumps already, but bad weather had cancelled several sorties and everyone was feeling the strain. I told him I felt the same way, which he refused to believe: 'You must be joking,' he said. 'You wander round chatting to everyone as if you haven't a care in the world.' As an officer, on our next sortie I was due to jump first. I told him how worried I was at the prospect of having to stand in the door peering out into the slipstream waiting for the green light. He believed me and was genuinely amazed to find he wasn't the only person feeling scared, a realization that gave him renewed confidence. We sat together in the aircraft, and although he was pasty-faced with fear, he followed me out of the door.

For the next jump, because his weight was similar to mine, he drew the short straw of being the first to jump. I offered to take his place but he shook his head – to my relief. Again we sat together, shouting comments to each other as the Hercules banked over the sidings at Didcot in Oxfordshire on the short hop to the drop zone at Weston-on-the-Green. We stood up and rigged ready for the jump. With a few minutes to go, as the air load master beckoned him forward to the seething maelstrom of the door, he paused and turned towards me. I was very worried that he might be about to refuse. Instead, he grinned and slapped me on the arm, shouting something like 'See you on the ground.'

This time, greatly boosted by his example, I followed *him* out of the door.

The safest parachutists are those who force through their fear to concentrate on what they are doing. A nerveless individual with no fear would be dangerous to both himself and those in the air around him. However, many young paratroopers (and those who haven't jumped for a while) become switched-off by their fear, jumping as if in a daze, incapable of steering away from others in the air, only returning to their senses after landing. A similar paralysis of thought is experienced by troops in combat, which must be overcome if they are to be effective. Parachuting may therefore be compared with combat, providing a very real sense of danger under circumstances that allow units of soldiers to practise overcoming their fears in relative safety. This process is of course a very private business, and paratroopers would not normally admit to being frightened of parachuting to outsiders. The airborne attitude is tough and uncompromising. Paratroopers are less than respectful towards their non-parachuting comrades. Some would call this arrogance. British Army paratroopers refer to non-parachutists as 'crap hats', and their United States brethren talk disparagingly of 'leg units'.

Although a paratrooper's sense of self-knowledge does not extend as far as humility, it does include a genuine respect for paratroopers in other armies – the so-called 'Airborne Brotherhood'. Airborne troops often feel a great affinity with the enemy paratroopers against whom they are fighting, as happened in the Second World War: in North Africa, Italy and Sicily, when British airborne forces came up against German Fallschirmjäger. At times, paratroopers can feel they have more of an affinity with the enemy airborne soldiers they are fighting against than with the line infantry of their own side.

The US Army's airborne – XVIII Corps, with one airborne division (the 82nd, of around 16,000 men), a heliborne division and the 101st (Screaming Eagles) air assault division – is around half the size of the entire British Army, and the 82nd (All American) Division is three times the size of all the British airborne units together. British paras find the scale of this operation very impressive – to the point of being green with envy – but have reservations about the toughness of US airborne training, and the hardness of the paratroopers it produces.

Some armies train in order to develop a strong esprit de corps, rather than having this spirit emerge as a natural by-product of operational efficiency. British Army parade ground drill, in which the battlefield manoeuvres of a century and a half ago are used to instil the sense of discipline that enables men to continue functioning on the modern battlefield, could be seen in this way. US airborne training is characterized by running and singing (airborne versions of the US Army's traditional marching songs), rather than the heart-bursting efforts, usually in full marching order, required of P Company candidates. (The French Army, especially the Foreign Legion, also set great stock by their traditional songs.) US airborne running is a mass shuffle in step, with singing, company banners and unit chants, with the aim of instilling an airborne ethos into the students, rather than testing them or getting them to fighting fitness.

The parachute training itself, held at Fort Benning, Georgia, involves the usual ground training and lectures, but like the running is carried out en masse – as an enormous group ritual. Much other US Army training is done in this way, with one instructor on a dais at the front demonstrating using a microphone and PA system, and the assembled troops following his actions in unison. For parachute training, which seeks not only to train men in vital drills, but give them the confidence to jump, mass indoctrination does not allow for the personal attention given to British students by the RAF's parachute jump instructors.

As part of the confidence-building process, British paratroopers used to be taken to the RAF's parachute packing depot at RAF Hullavington in Wiltshire during their basic parachute training course. As well as the paratroopers gaining confidence from seeing the care put into the packing, the packers (young women from the RAF) met the men whose lives depended on their skills – and many friendships resulted. US Army parachute packers are encouraged to take care with their work in a rather more direct manner; as an added incentive to making sure that they do their jobs properly, they have themselves to use the 'chutes they pack – on compulsory parachute courses.

*

Outside the ranks of elite units, motivation is very different. In peacetime, self-interest is high on the list of motivating factors. This starts in the recruiting office.

Joining the armed forces in peacetime, with no immediate prospect of having to go to war, is presented by recruiters as a career like any other. They offer training that will be of use in 'Civvy Street'; trades like heavy goods vehicle driver, electronics technician, avionics fitter, telecommunications expert. (Soviet Army pre-entry programmes, known as DOSAFF, were exactly this.) The military side of service life is presented as an adventure; where else could you be given a trade, and have all the excitement of weapons training, sport, Outward Bound activities and foreign travel? As if all this were not enough, the forces also pay good salaries, regular money that is better than a young man could expect from most employers on leaving school.

The US Army's recruiting slogan (1989, so post-Vietnam) 'Be All You Can Be', appealed to the American dream of self-improvement and self-advancement in a very individualistic and mobile society. The long-running British equivalent was 'Join the Professionals'. Both advertising campaigns emphasized that recruits will be transformed by their military experience into better individuals, that joining the army will be to their own personal advantage. Neither slogan contains any notion of service to the country or commitment to fighting. The British Army campaign portrayed soldiering as a 'trade', and the 'Professionals' as the best you could join – a cleverly acceptable (in the 1970s) shading of the army's real purpose.

Professional volunteer armies are raised from a population that has to be persuaded to join, so recruiters have no choice but to present the armed forces as a career. Conscripts however can be rounded up and made to serve. Conscription in peacetime is regarded as part of the duties of citizenship – even in countries like the former Federal Republic of Germany where there is little enthusiasm for the military. The purpose of a peacetime conscript army determines the attitudes of its pressed members. The Bundeswehr was an impressive, efficient and highly motivated organization, each man serving for two years as part of NATO's deterrence of potential Warsaw Pact aggression. In pre-unification days, the threat to West German territory was very real. The Swiss take their military service very seriously, too, in defence of both national borders and their long-standing neutrality. If threatened, they aim to become an entire nation under arms. Few Israelis have doubts about the need for their compulsory conscription, regarding themselves as a nation under permanent siege.

In war, or under the threat of imminent war, recruitment turns strongly to the realities of the situation, invoking both patriotism and a sense of shame. The classic 'Your Country Needs You' posters of the First World War had Field Marshal Lord Kitchener's eyes and pointing finger following the viewer wherever he stood. In what could perhaps be the perfect recruiters' pitch, Islamic countries declare their wars to be a 'jihad' – a holy war in which all their dead go immediately to heaven.

The lesson of both the Falkland and Gulf wars is that in future crises there will be no time to call up or conscript troops. If large numbers of men are needed they will have to be trained already, either as members of large standing armies, or as part-time soldiers with civilian jobs, well-trained enough and motivated for a sudden call to fight. The build-up to the Falklands operation allowed invaluable preparation time in which to make the vital transition from peacetime attitudes to those of war. The circumstances were remarkably helpful; 3 Commando Brigade had just returned from an arduous three months of arctic and mountain warfare training in Norway and were ready to fight, and there was time for the follow-up formation 5 Infantry Brigade to train together in Wales before setting sail for the South Atlantic. In the Gulf, vital preparation time was created initially through effective bluffing of the Iraqis by the Americans. The air campaign then created further preparation time for the land armies, in the end leaving them with little more to do than occupy the ground.

In the process of getting ready for the Gulf War, the British Army created its one operational division (1st Armoured Division) by literally stripping out most of its other units, both in Germany and in the UK. Only one-third of the Gulf War combat units were from the regiments listed in the order of battle, the other two-thirds being an amalgam from other regiments. Spares were taken from the units left behind, rendering many of them immobile. Tank regiments and artillery in Germany and the UK returned from leave to find their tank parks broken into and engine power packs literally ripped from the chassis of their tanks – as spares for Gulf combat units.

It is very unlikely that 1st Armoured Division would have succeeded in its highly effective blitzkrieg advance had it been required to come straight from Germany and fight. The troops had to acclimatize and get themselves fit, as well as transform their vehicles from the unreliable peacetime mode to well-maintained combat readiness.

A strenuous programme of military training in Saudi Arabia had also to be completed before the division (actually only two brigades, with extra artillery) could be declared ready for war.

In the future, soldiers are likely to find themselves translated abruptly from the routine of peacetime into the realities of combat. Unless they have trained realistically, preparing themselves mentally as well as physically for the fight, they will suffer severe psychological problems, both during combat (becoming psychological casualties) and afterwards, perhaps permanently. Combat effectiveness and the number of psychological casualties are directly related to the standard and realism of training. Realistically trained units like special forces do very much better than less well-prepared units.

3

FORCING THEM TO FIGHT

For an army to be successful, courage in battle is an essential quality for its soldiers to possess. Individuals whose behaviour in combat falls below the level of the rest are labelled cowards – which, setting aside the punishments that military discipline might impose, in the closeness of a military unit and under the extreme pressures of war, is a terrible burden to have to bear.

Military attitudes to behaviour in combat have been formed through bitter experience, over a long period of time. The concept of courage and cowardice is deeply rooted even in peacetime military men, who, although they might have no experience of coming under fire themselves, have very definite views on what constitutes cowardly (and heroic) behaviour. Military law is equally clear on the subject. In the past, battlefield discipline has been ruthlessly maintained through the application of military law. Today western armies rely upon the personal discipline of their soldiers. In modern battle, the individual is often fighting on his own, in the darkness with nobody to know whether he played safe and kept his head down, or pushed on. Some armies, however, have maintained a severe code of military law on the battlefield, including the Red Army during the Second World War, and Saddam Hussein's Iraqi Army.

As part of understanding the pressures placed upon soldiers in modern combat, this chapter looks at how modern Western concepts of cowardice and heroism developed, and some of the ways in which military discipline has been used to force men to fight. Military law embodies the official view of how soldiers should behave in combat, prescribing punishments for those whose nerve fails. We will also look at the evolution of this official view, and how peacetime military perceptions of the correct way to behave in combat have become unrealistically formalized. Whether or not soldiers agree with these concepts, most are influenced by them in some way or other. The long-term effect of combat on individuals is in part determined by how they themselves rated their performance; whether they believed they acted honourably or felt they were cowardly when nobody was looking. It is very difficult for the individual to take an objective view, particularly if he considers he behaved badly on the battlefield. In reality every individual behaves in a mixture of ways – both hero and coward combined.

Even in war, the number of military people who personally experience combat is often much smaller than one might think. Those who really have been in combat know that the difference between heroism and cowardice can be a hair's breadth, in response to an extreme situation that brings out extremes of human behaviour. Military history provides many examples of cowards who became heroes and heroes who inexplicably turned yellow, because every soldier is part-coward, part-hero. After combat, self-esteem based upon each individual's perception of how he behaved can often be low, even in highly decorated individuals. Being honest, most combatants have something which they are secretly ashamed of or unhappy about.

The yardstick by which heroes are decorated is completely arbitrary, determined by who was present to see the person in action (and the quality of the reports and recommendations that were subsequently written). The concept of cowardice is an equally arbitrary assessment; those who did not experience combat judge those who did, and such a verdict is even more damaging than the actual combat to individual self-esteem. When cowardice is the subject of a court martial, judgement is usually given by a panel of officers who neither knew the accused nor were within miles of the action he was involved in.

Combat places tremendous psychological strains upon the individual, and certain psychiatric conditions can prevent men from behaving as they are expected to behave. But although battle shock is a medical problem, military law plays a complicating role part here too, putting doctors into a difficult position. On the battlefield, doctors become judges, issuing both psychiatric diagnoses (a medical reason for cowardice) and, by default, white feathers. Fighting men, knowing that everybody seeks some way of avoiding danger, mutilation or death, are inevitably suspicious of those who leave the battlefield apparently unscathed. Regardless of what military psychiatrists might say to the contrary, as far as fighting men are concerned, only actual physical injuries provide an honourable exit from the battlefield ('a Blighty one'). Psychological 'wounds' are still regarded with scepticism. This scepticism is ill-informed, derived not from war experience but from unreal, ignorant peacetime concepts. Like many other forms of ignorance, it spreads readily, from the military to their families and friends, and is swiftly adopted by the media, who bandy emotive words like 'hero' and 'coward' quite freely. The concept of 'heroism', with its strongly implied masculinity, is deeply rooted in the military psyche, and strongly supported by the full power of military law.

The attitudes of military commanders to individuals less brave than their fellows has varied greatly throughout history. According to Herodotus, Leonidas, King of Sparta, in 480 BC dismissed troops he believed 'had no heart for the fight and were unwilling to take their share of the danger [in the defence of Thermopylae]'. The Duke of Wellington, a severe disciplinarian, observed that: 'All soldiers run away. The good ones return.' During the First World War, more than 3000 British soldiers were sentenced to death for crimes committed in combat, mostly desertion and cowardice. About ten per cent of these sentences were actually carried out. Back home, few people knew of the executions, and the proceedings of the courts martial were not released. In France the death sentences were announced – and sometimes carried out – in front of troops on parade. These harrowing ceremonies were supposed to deter potential offenders, and keep the divisions fighting.

It is clear in retrospect that many if not most of the executed men were suffering some form of battle shock. Some were second offenders, sent back to the front line to redeem themselves, which (unsurprisingly) made their mental state much worse and they repeated their offence. Army doctors at the time commented upon the condition of condemned men when they committed their offences. Questions were asked in Parliament about their psychological condition, their ages and immaturity (most were under 25, with a number of teenagers), and the hasty judicial procedures that preceded their executions. The Secretary of State for War's answers were evasive.

Today, these men would have been treated as psychiatric battle casualties, rested a short distance behind the front line, given hot food, then returned to their comrades to continue fighting. For many, such immediate treatment would have restored them to normality. Unforgivably, the psychiatric principles underlying such treatment were known, understood and practised by battle shock recovery units in the First World War. It is believed that front line army doctors successfully treated tens of thousands of more fortunate battle shock casualties in this way.

'Battle shock' has been defined by the British Army Director of Psychiatry, Brigadier P. Abraham, as an 'inability to fight which does not result from major physical injury or disease'.[1] Statistics collated from the Second World War onwards show it to be the largest single type of battlefield wound. In Northern France between July and September 1944, over 20 per cent of all wounded in the British Second Army were battle shock victims. The 6th US Marine Division suffered 2662 wounded in ten days of fighting – and also 1287 psychiatric casualties. Overall, battle shock accounts for one-third of all wounded.

The symptoms of battle shock develop over a period of time, and vary from one person to another, depending to a significant extent on the support they are receiving from their comrades. Ordinary fear can develop into a crippling over-activity, and consequent physical and mental exhaustion. Bereavement gives rise to depressive reactions, and some experts believe that endorphins generated by the body in response to stress may seriously inhibit the central nervous system, possibly for long periods. 'Fugue states', in which men retreat inside themselves to escape from unbearable memories (and reality), and 'conversion', in which fear causes incapacitation, are the most bizarre battle shock reactions. Men lose their sight, hearing and the ability to speak, or the use of limbs – often their trigger finger, hand or right arm.

Even though subconsciously their minds are inventing this incapacitation in order to avoid combat, the 'injuries' are genuine in so far as the individual has no control over them. Russian battlefield treatment during the First World War was based upon inflicting pain and fear greater than that causing the paralysis, achieved through placing electrodes on the throats, eyes, ears and affected limbs, then increasing the current until the pain was unbearable and the paralysis was 'cured' – logical, but hardly humane. British Army Director of Psychiatry Brigadier Abraham, discussing the treatment of conversion:

Incidentally shooting, or the threat of it, is a method of suggestion often tried, particularly for those who have opted out of the battle in a more obvious way by drug abuse or desertion. It has, however, never really been shown to succeed in promoting fortitude, as opposed to preventing flight, and it is certain that those shot will not renew the fight against the enemy.[2]

After the First World War, Britain reduced the number of combat offences that could be punished by death. It took until 1930, and several heated debates in which generals rose to defend the use of firing squads, before the threat of judicial death was removed from

British soldiers in combat – and certain offences (spying and inciting mutiny, for example) still qualify as capital crimes at the time of writing.

The First World War was in many ways too devastating and traumatic for the British Army establishment to comprehend fully. The generals were from another, more genteel, Victorian, horse-drawn age. They were unable to understand how to treat volunteer private soldiers who were better educated than many army officers used to be.[3] The terrible savagery of modern machine gun warfare could only be experienced by those who lived, week in, week out, in the front-line trenches. The generals and their staff were not able to do this, which created an unbridgeable divide between divisional headquarters and everyone else.

The use of the death sentence to motivate troops is the ultimate essence of how military law functions in combat conditions. Fear of an inglorious, sordid and shameful death was thought to keep men at their posts in the face of another variety of death – unknown and unseen. In the First World War, not only did men live in fear of the Kaiser's military machine to their front, but also knowing that to their rear another equally ruthless apparatus waited, to snap up those who fell by the wayside. The only refuge left to the individual, in such a depressing and hopeless environment, was the camaraderie of his own small group of soldiers – the infantry section, the artillery gun crew. The approbation of this group is more important to the individual than the strictures of a code of military law supported by the threat of a firing squad. The First World War marked the end of set-piece, parade-ground battles and a sordid beginning to the massed armies and totality of modern warfare. In modern combat, men are dispersed over large areas, split into small teams. Discipline has to be self-imposed and informal, based on the attitudes of the small groups of soldiers that do the fighting in modern battles. Formal military discipline exists to ensure that each small group knows what is expected of it, and that those who fail to pull their weight do not get away with it.

The evolution of British military law has been a continuous process since 1385 (when Richard II set down regulations for his army). Unswerving discipline is the vital product of military law, an absolute code designed to keep soldiers fighting and the war machine working smoothly. In combat, when legal formalities seem a million miles away from the grim realities of the moment, leadership and the accompanying power of personality actually motivate the unwilling or the frightened, not rules and regulations. In extreme situations, leaders may be forced to use violence on their own soldiers to prevent a retreat or to keep an attack going forward – breaking military law themselves. Such actions are well documented, particularly in the First World War; the French artillery regularly fired on their own troops to keep them from fleeing their trenches, and the British Machine Gun Corps had Standing Orders to fire on friendly troops to stop any retreat. In the Second World War, officers and NCOs fired on men to prevent them retreating under enemy fire.[4]

For individual soldiers in combat, military law gives a foundation to their determination to stick it out, being perceived by them as either a threat or a code of behaviour. In applying equally to everyone, military law can be a subconscious source of stability, and therefore a comfort when things get really grim. Threats of undefined future legal action cannot, however, overcome the fear reactions of individuals in extreme danger. Motivation is a complicated process, in which carrots and sticks are wielded simultaneously. In battles fought by small teams of men, often in complete isolation from anyone else, the sticks are not the rules and regulations of military law, but a code of behaviour already defined and accepted within each group. The leader defines, interprets and imposes this code, to which the members submit in order to remain in the group.

In a hostile and dangerous environment, rejection by the group is the worst fate of all. Comfort, reassurance and protection from danger are available only from the group. For each lonely individual, earning and retaining the approval of comrades is the single most important motivating factor of all. At this level, military law has no significance – unless the leader needs to invoke it for his own purposes. Official regulations may also have no relevance to the group, on occasions being ignored or 'overlooked'. A team operating away from its parent unit can do as it likes. Serious misinterpretations of orders or regulations can lead to dangerous situations – and perhaps to criminal activities. A formed unit of soldiers, with vehicles (and petrol, which is unlikely to be available to civilians in a war zone), weapons, ammunition, food and organization, is well-equipped for racketeering, extortion or violence against civilians and even fellow-soldiers. In some circumstances, the team may be unable to cope with enemy prisoners of war or casualties. It may only have enough food or medical supplies for its own use. From the group point of view, in an extreme situation far from help or censure, massacring the prisoners might be the logical solution and perhaps the only option. When such a group rejoins its parent unit and official reports are written, the unpalatable facts can be adjusted to couch the group's aberrant logic in terms acceptable to military law. In any case, without having lived through this kind of experience, how could an outsider make a valid judgement?

That is a deliberately extreme (and theoretical) example of the way group perceptions dominate the combat zone, but official military histories and war diaries do offer versions of events that the actual participants know to be at odds with their memories. Proud regiments with fine traditions stretching back hundreds of years may prefer to overlook the platoon that tried to withdraw under mortar fire after their lieutenant was killed, and the sergeant who stopped them by shooting one of the section corporals. They all committed the most serious crimes under military law, but, in the circumstances, no charges would be laid and the record would not mention the incident.

Queen's Regulations and the Army Act 1955 are the body of law that governs the British Army. The Manual of Military Law is the user's guide to the application of this law, giving the most common examples of the actual charges that might be formulated from the various regulations. Like British Army traditions, Queen's Regulations have evolved through the experience of centuries of wars, campaigns and skirmishes. They are based on laws originally used to discipline the lowest, roughest, most ill-educated individuals in the land – many of them convicted criminals escaping judicial punishment. The evolution of these laws into the code that governs today's British Army parallels the development of modern professional armies.

Punishment for soldiers has always been severe. Flogging, shooting and hanging were common in most armies until the beginning of the twentieth century. Oliver Cromwell's New Model Army Ordinance (1645) attempted to use harsh but fair discipline to create a strong esprit de corps. Sir John Moore's troops required savage punishment to keep even a semblance of discipline during the Peninsular War, and Wellington imposed regular public demonstrations of flogging, hanging and shooting to keep them under control.

Battles in those days were short and bloody, each man supported and encouraged by his comrades. The performance of each soldier could easily be seen, heroes and cowards alike. The infantry square as a formation held men together in moments of great danger, solidarity being the only defence against the slashing blades and stabbing pikes of the cavalry. Although punishments for poor combat performance were severe, enforced by sergeants and officers who stood behind to ensure that none fell back, self-discipline was essential. Rifleman

Harris of the 66th Foot gained the admiration of his comrades by telling another soldier that if he saw him flinch in battle he could shoot him out of hand, and it is clear from his account of his army service that he regarded his reputation with comrades and his status within the group as of prime importance.

The men themselves were Wellington's 'scum of the earth', commanded by often absurd aristocrats and housed in appalling conditions. After Waterloo, the British Army was at a very low ebb and the forty years of peace that followed were disastrous as far as training and the development of tactics were concerned. The débâcle of the Crimea, and disasters such as the rout at Majuba in 1881, during the Boer War, showed that a formal reorganization of the army was long overdue. In the latter decades of the nineteenth century, the administrative foundations of the modern British Army were laid, and a code of laws established for enforcing certain minimum standards of conduct in battle, based on the unfortunate experience of the Peninsular War.

These were the rules applied to volunteers and conscripts alike in the First World War. The imposition of a standard set of rules on the various and aggressively individualistic regiments that make up the British Army tends even today to make each regiment more determined to do things in its own fashion. The enormous casualty figures of the Great War, however, diluted the regiments with poorly trained conscripts, weakening the regimental system and increasing the power of the headquarters staffs. The war was fought on an enormous scale, with little scope for tactical initiative below brigade level. Terribly costly attacks (in terms of lives lost) often achieved absolutely nothing. Headquarters staff were based well away from the trenches, planning the slaughter from well-appointed châteaux while living well-regulated, comfortable lives. On occasions, they were actually ordered not to visit the front line; General Haig feared that if they saw too much, they might lose their appetite for planning further operations.

From the staff point of view, maintaining the morale of the troops and their desire to continue fighting was paramount. In a defensive stalemate, the first side to crack would lose the war, wasting the hundreds of thousands of lives that had already been expended. There was no room for sentiment or humanitarian considerations. The regiments had to hold the line as fodder for the artillery, or plod forward in ponderous offensives as the high-rolling General Staff gambled in their attempts to break the stalemate.

The regiments provided a tribal identity for groups of soldiers –

and convenient organizational blocs so that the Staff could rotate men in and out of the line, supply them, and organize the attacks. The regiments were also the means by which the Staff judged morale and combat effectiveness, using composite unit personas created (and even invented) by their individual commanding officers. (The Staff would return from liaison visits to make reports like: 'The 1st Blankshires were looking a bit down in the mouth today, but the Loamshires are in splendid fettle.') Beyond regimental level, interest in the individual did not exist, each officer and man buried within whatever companionship and camaraderie the fortunes of this brutal war allowed. Whole regiments were wiped out in hours, friends and comrades being replaced by strangers.

As far as the Staffs were concerned, the determination of the troops to fight had somehow to be guaranteed – or enforced. The legal code inherited from the Peninsular War had used fear of death and disgrace to deter offenders. In an environment as dangerous and unpleasant as the First World War trenches, only the death sentence could provide a meaningful punishment – and only if it was well publicized. Other nations came to similar conclusions. Although with the Bolshevik Revolution in 1917 the Russian Army abandoned the death penalty, the Soviets were to execute more of their own soldiers in the Second World War than even the Nazi military authorities did. In the First World War, however, the British Army seems to have shot more of its own soldiers for combat-related offences than did its allies. The way the regulations evolved to allow this, and how after the war these regulations were amended, shows the birth of an awareness in the army of how modern combat affects combatants. For the soldiers themselves, fighting under the fear not only of death (or mutilation) from the enemy, but of well-publicized executions to 'encourage' them to continue, the threat of an unworthy, disgraceful, but at least postponed death was yet another burden.

The judicial code of the First World War was instituted during the Duke of Cambridge's long and significant period in command of the army (1856–95). The buying and selling of commissions and peacetime flogging were abolished in 1871 and ten years later, the Army Act laid down the military law that in amended form survives today (as the Army Act 1955). The Duke's legal changes were matched by useful campaign experience and the development of new, sound tactics. In the ten years following the Boer War, the army was re-equipped and reorganized. By 1914, the British infantry in particular were the most capable and well-trained in Europe, and probably the world.

The Manual of Military Law was in its sixth edition by the time the First World War started, military discipline rigidly and ruthlessly spelled out in its pages. The Victorian army, and the volunteers and conscripts of the Great War, were very different from Wellington's 'scum', but this edition reads not as the progressive regulation of the new army, but as the harsh law of the Peninsular War, making savage examples of individuals in order to discourage the similar offences. The highly disciplined, efficient and well-trained army of that first decade of the twentieth century did not actually need to deter its rank and file by horrid example. The Victorian army had a well-ordered lifestyle of its own, its soldiers had their own codes of behaviour. Looting, rape, pillaging and cowardly behaviour in combat were rare occurrences. Nevertheless, the Manual of Military Law stipulated 25 active service offences for which the punishment was death by shooting (or hanging, 'according to the exigencies of the service'). These offences ranged from 'Desertion on active service' to the 'Diverting of supplies intended for another unit'. Although some are obviously the most serious offences that men in combat could commit (for example, 'took service with the enemy having been made a prisoner'), others are exactly those crimes for which Wellington had employed his 'iron hand' of exemplary punishment in the Peninsula: 'Attacking anyone bringing up supplies or damaging property of the country in which he was serving'; 'Housebreaking for plundering purposes'; the peculiar: 'Leaving his commanding officer to go in search of plunder'; and: 'Breaking into a military store . . .'

The imposition of the death penalty on soldiers in combat derived partly from past practice and also from the Articles of War first issued in the mid-17th century, during the Commonwealth. Their severity had provoked controversy, especially after the execution of Admiral Byng in 1757. He was shot on his own quarter-deck, having failed to make what he judged to be a forlorn attempt to relieve the British garrison on Minorca, under siege by the French.[5] (This was the incident that prompted Voltaire's famous comment that the English 'kill an admiral every now and then to encourage the others'.) Byng's fate is an extreme example of how ridiculously (and fatally) inappropriate peacetime notions of heroism and cowardice can be when applied to the actions of real people in real battles. Military law is not concerned with obtaining justice for the individual, but with the maintenance of military discipline. In the years that followed, British admirals did very much better; perhaps they really were gingered up by the example made of Byng, which in turn could have reinforced the Admiralty's belief in severe punishment for errant behaviour in combat.

Over a century later, the enforcement of standards of behaviour in combat was formalized in the Manual of Military Law with a ruthlessness equal to those applying to general behaviour and discipline. The specimen charges for capital offences leave little scope for judicial interpretation (or amelioration), and the details laid down for the implementation of the regulations were meticulous. The offences themselves were highly subjective, and open to terrible misinterpretation:

Shamefully abandoned or surrendered a garrison, place or post to the enemy, or compelled another soldier to do so.

Shamefully cast away their arms, ammunition or tools in the presence of the enemy.

Treacherously corresponded with the enemy or 'through cowardice' sent a flag of truce to him.

Behaved in a cowardly manner or induced others to behave like cowards.

And there was a catch-all clause to cover just about anything else that a soldier might do:

Knowingly, while on active service, committed any act calculated to imperil the success of His Majesty's forces or any part thereof.

Drunkenness when a soldier in combat was on sentry duty was singled out as being particularly deserving of execution. Death was also prescribed for sleeping on sentry duty, in an attempt to frighten exhausted men into staying awake. (Keeping sentries awake is a common problem when soldiers are tired.) The two offences were lumped together: 'Being asleep or drunk on sentry duty or leaving the sentry post without being properly relieved.'

All recruits joining the army before 1914 were issued with the 'Small Book', which listed all 25 capital crimes, plus the warning that deserting whilst only under orders to go on active service also risked the death penalty.

It seems odd that such a savage legal code should have been imposed upon an army that among European nations at the end of the nineteenth century was the model of good behaviour, training, morale, experience and valour in combat. Military laws, like military traditions, evolve, often changing only in the light of war experience. Before the First World War, few of the specified capital offences seemed to be committed, so few men had been executed. The severe legislation had therefore remained on the books, unused and so unquestioned. During the First World War, however, soldiers were executed for every one of these offences: of a total of 3080 men sentenced to death between 4 August 1914 and 31 March 1920, 312 were actually executed (277 being British, 3 of whom were officers) for purely military offences (rather than civil crimes like murder). Compared to the overall casualty figures, these numbers seem insignificant, particularly as around 90 per cent of the death sentences were commuted. However, the executions took place throughout the war, averaging out at around six each month. Sentences and executions were announced to soldiers on parade, and in some cases senior officers ordered public executions.

Desertion was the most prevalent offence, and 268 died for it, followed by 18 executions for cowardice. These two offences were in fact synonymous, although cowardice required a witness while desertion was proved merely by evidence of absence. They were considered to be the same thing – deserters were cowards and vice versa – and both were capital offences.

The generals who authorized each execution were part of an efficient legal system that could try, sentence and execute a man in a few days. The first, on 8 September 1914, was one of the fastest of the war: a nineteen-year-old deserter convicted two days earlier. Field General Courts Martial, with simplified wartime procedures, did not consider the individual circumstances of an offender, in many cases merely matching the man's actions to the wording of the Manual's sample crime, then passing the maximum sentence. The selection of the unlucky 10 per cent that actually went before the firing squads was a lottery, made by a chain of staff officers with only scanty documentary evidence, none of whom had any knowledge of either the crime or the condemned man. The Commander-in-Chief made the final decision.

As far as the 312 who were executed are concerned, justice was not done. The full records of their courts martial will not be released until the second decade of the next century, ostensibly to spare the feelings of relatives of the 'disgraced' men. However, published works by William Moore and by Julian Putkowski and Julian Sykes[6] reveal the shocking haste with which trial and sentence were carried out. Doctors' reports were ignored, legal representation for the accused was non-existent and over ten per cent were not represented at all. They were not told of their death sentence until around eight hours before the event, thus being denied any opportunity to appeal. Their average age was 25, and many were under 21.

When the Army Act was debated by Parliament it was revealing that, in the main, senior officers and MPs who had not fought in the trenches were the ones who believed the death penalty to be essential to military discipline. Ernest Thurtle MP, who had served in the trenches as a captain, championed the abolition of the death penalty. He saw how the old military law, in the first total war fought by the British Army, had been turned into 'the power which enables non-fighting people, the majority, to send fighting men, the minority, to be killed or maimed in any cause the majority may decide proper. And the fighting man may not refuse on pain of death, or, at least, penal servitude.' The old, harsh discipline, designed to keep control of the 'scum' who fought in the Peninsular War, then formally codified by the Victorians, had been applied to an enormous army of comparatively well-educated and highly motivated civilians. In the chaos of the Kitchener volunteers and conscription, and the arrival of the Commonwealth expeditionary forces, the old regular army had struggled to impose its standards on the masses and thus maintain its identity.

The generals were of the old army, unable to change, and the savage imposition of old-style discipline was often the only way they felt they could impose themselves on their formations. Lt Colonel Hugh Mowbray Meyler MP stated that many courts martial were specifically ordered to impose the death sentence regardless of any mitigating factors, so that the General Headquarters could make the decision of whether sentence should actually be carried out. He was among many front line commanders who came forward in opposition to the death penalty, expressing concern at incidents in which they had been involved; he was quite clear why senior officers supported the death penalty, and that they were wrong in believing their leadership (exercised from afar) affected the psychology of the soldiers: 'It was only those who lived cheek by jowl with the soldiers who knew their real psychology. You train your soldiers not to be impressed by fear, to despise fear, and then you go and bring out . . . this death sentence which is supposed to improve their discipline by means of fear. The whole thing is illogical.'

During the Army Act debate, an impasse was reached when the army refused to submit the records of courts martial, claiming that only the accused were permitted to see them. Thus, as the accused in question were dead, the cases could not be examined individually, nor could injustices be corrected. Since then, there have been many calls for convictions to be quashed and pardons given – to no avail.

These regular and apparently well-publicized executions (six per month) must have had an unfortunate effect on the hundreds of thousands of soldiers struggling for sanity in the nightmare world of the trenches. At home in Britain, news of the executions was suppressed. Parliamentary answers to wartime questions were deliberately evasive, as the shootings were hardly likely to attract more recruits. In reality, were soldiers deterred from capital crimes by the death sentence, or was the threat of such an unfair death an extra stress factor, increasing the likelihood of nervous breakdown or battle shock? The actual deterrent effect of the regular and well-publicized execution of soldiers for offences committed in combat was never determined. The British military establishment felt that the record proved it to have been effective because, they declared, no British offensive was ever postponed because of fears that the troops would refuse to go over the top. The German Army had the death sentence, although it was rarely used, and the German High Command echoed the British view; General Ludendorff complained that German deserters were being treated leniently by judges and that many 'lived happily at home, tacitly tolerated by their fellow citizens'. The German belief in the efficacy of the death sentence is not borne out by the experiences of the Russian, French and Italian armies; they carried out frequent death sentences, but, particularly towards the end of the war, found they could no longer guarantee the obedience of their troops.

Under the Australian Defence Act, Australian forces in France were exempt from the death penalty. Much was made by General Haig of their poor discipline and unruliness, comparing them unfavourably to the New Zealanders, South Africans and Canadians, who were all subject to capital punishment (25 Canadians and 5 New Zealand soldiers were executed during the war).[7] However, apart from some criminal 'bushranger' activities, the desertions and indiscipline of Australian troops that made General Haig so hot under the collar were in fact a reaction to being misused – to Australian formations being split up and used piecemeal to patch up the front, to the unexpectedly tough winters,[8] and to British Army discipline, which seemed to the Australians on whom it was imposed, with very little warning (on their arrival in theatre), alien and unnecessarily rigid.

The American Expeditionary Force arrived in France in 1917 with a very different history, and therefore with very different attitudes towards desertion. The Civil War had given the Americans ample experience of large-scale modern warfare using both untrained volunteers and conscripts, and the legacy of a well-developed court martial procedure. Both Confederates and the Union had used public executions in attempts to quell a massive desertion problem. Flogging and hard labour had also been used. Politicians of the day had intervened in much of this, urging lenience and amnesties, to which the generals trying to fight the war had objected. As the Civil War dragged on, cold, heavy losses and homesickness overcame fear of punishment.

In the First World War, death sentences on American soldiers had to be approved by the Commanding General of the Army. Of 44 handed down, 11 were actually carried out. Every man accused of a crime for which he could be shot was examined by the divisional psychiatrist and then by a consultant. The US Judge Advocate, in his final report from AEF headquarters, August 1919, stated that: 'Murder and rape were the only offenses for which the offender suffered death in the American Expeditionary Force.' Malingerers and those suspected of self-inflicted wounds, were retained in the combat area for examination by the divisional psychiatrist, one of the earliest examples of modern PIE (Proximity, Immediacy, Expectancy) battle shock treatment.

The US Army Medical Corps doctors working with British and French infantry battalions concluded that war neurosis sufferers were indeed shot as malingerers and that men diagnosed as suffering from clinical hysteria were falsely accused of malingering and committed suicide. 'Mistakes of this kind are especially liable to occur when the patients have not been actually exposed to shell fire, on account of the idea so firmly fixed in the minds of most line officers and some medical men that the war neuroses are due to some mechanical shock.'[9]

As far as the soldiers themselves were concerned, the supposed deterrent effect of the death sentence seemed irrelevant. In practice, the executions were not as widely publicized as perhaps the headquarters staff thought was the case, some taking place in virtual secrecy. Although on occasions the firing squads did operate in front of divisions paraded in hollow squares, and eyewitnesses report being marched past the bloodied corpses, at other times the men were turned about, hearing only the rifle volley and the pistol shot of the coup de grâce. The death sentence could only work as a deterrent if offenders were seen to be charged and sentenced, and if every sentence was seen to be carried out. Perhaps, beyond the marbled corridors of divisional HQs, it was realized that although the sentences had to be carried out, the job should be done as quietly as possible, to maintain morale. The firing squads and the military policemen involved in the executions were deeply affected, and doctors had to be ordered to attend, sometimes giving a condemned man morphia before using their anatomical expertise to place a white card over the heart. Despite standing only feet from condemned men, firing squads often missed, requiring the doctor or officer-in-charge to put the wounded man out of his misery. One doctor reports nearly being shot himself in the process.

Making examples of offenders in front of their own units was thought likely to cause mutiny, and occurred only rarely. Ernest Thurtle, as part of his campaign for abolition in 1929–30, had included an eyewitness account in his pamphlet *Shootings at Dawn* of the execution of a lance corporal from 1 West Yorkshire Regiment. The effect on firing squad members was severe:

I was ordered to pick the two worst characters in my platoon . . . The two men I selected for the firing party went with the adjutant. When they came back, tough characters though they were supposed to be, they were sick, they screamed in their sleep, they vomited immediately after eating. All they could say was: 'The sight was horrible, made more so by the fact that we had shot one of our own men.'

There were very close shaves with the letter of the law; for example, the soldier of the Duke of Cornwall's Light Infantry accused of 'shamefully casting away his arms (bayonet and pouches) in the face of the enemy' at the battle of Le Cateau in August 1914. Luckily his officer had survived the battle and was able to save the man's life by explaining that he had ordered the soldier to leave his equipment behind as it had become inextricably caught up in barbed wire. Officers overlooked sleeping sentries rather than throwing them to the legal lions, and in ruthless contrast, men were executed at the insistence of divisional commanders keen to be seen to be doing something about discipline.

In short, those who were executed were scapegoats, and their deaths cannot be said to have served any useful purpose. Their comrades were shocked, revolted and saddened by the deaths, but there is no evidence that the remarkably high standard of combat discipline in the British Army was due to those 312 sickening examples. The soldiers seemed simply to absorb this self-inflicted sadness and pain as yet another of many tragedies of a terrible war. It is amazing that the regiments were able to continue year after year, obeying the suicidal orders that emanated from the staff HQs.

In the years that followed, Britain wanted to forget the Great War. Parliament finally abolished the death penalty for all military offences except those that were treacherous or mutinous, and the bill received royal assent on 29 April 1930. The army, trying to get back to some kind of peacetime normality, was doubtless thankful to throw the court martial records into archives. With the Army Act modified, there was no political incentive between the wars to re-examine the individual cases. In France, meanwhile, under pressure from relatives and war veterans, the government investigated, rehabilitated and in some cases heavily compensated the dependants of victims of what the court described as 'the erroneous application of the regulations'.[10] None of this was reported in British newspapers.

After the slaughter of the trenches, the British Army's position in 1920 was particularly difficult, a prelude to the stagnation of the thirties and Britain's initial unpreparedness for the Second World War. Tactics of stout denial employed by the War Office with respect to those shot for military offences were probably a very necessary defensive measure. As far as the British Army was concerned, the one outstanding question from the Great War that had to be resolved satisfactorily was the debate over whether 'shell shock' was a physical disease or perhaps an injury – or merely human weakness. If 'shell shock', or 'neurasthenia' as it had been diagnosed in many courageous officers (like Wilfred Owen), was a disease, then the doctors had to be able to diagnose and if possible prevent it. The best of all solutions would be if 'shell shock' could be proved simply not to exist.

To the senior generals of 1919, whose military careers had started in the late 19th century, the degeneration of the cavalry and infantry manoeuvres with which the war opened in 1914 into an Armageddon of tanks, machine guns and the trenches, was too much. Modern warfare had produced a stalemate, and in the war of attrition that followed, the generals had imposed upon their forces the time-honoured values and standards that they understood. As far as they were concerned, their values had withstood the ultimate test, and won the war. As they saw it, the army could not enter another modern war believing that modern weapons, artillery in particular, could induce a breakdown in military discipline without injuring anybody. To reach that conclusion would provide a cowards' charter, an easy way out for everyone which would make future wars impossible to wage.

This view paralleled that of many civilians; that 'the War to end all Wars' had been too terrible for any person or nation to risk repeating. However, in the same way that civilian wishful thinking of the 1920s failed to realize that modern warfare was only in its dreadful infancy, so the generals underestimated the capacity of the civilian population to fight for their own survival, and endure on the battlefield. The future generals of the Second World War, including one Captain B. L. Montgomery, had emerged from the trenches. Although they were still very junior officers, they had seen for themselves how civilians fought alongside regulars. Their strong views on leadership and battlefield motivation were to overcome calls for the return of the death sentence for military crimes in the Second World War.

The report of the War Office Committee of Enquiry into 'shell shock' appeared in 1922 and supported the military view that cowardice should be subject to the death penalty. A rider stated that cowardice might be beyond an individual's control, so specialist medical opinion, 'the best possible expert advice', was essential in doubtful cases of 'war neuroses'. It was 'extremely difficult to distinguish cowardice from neurosis since in both fear is the chief causal factor'. The report recommended that men of already proven courage should receive special consideration in cases of a subsequent lapse. The recruiting system was criticized for not checking men's mental and nervous stability although, 'During the final year of the war . . . the administration was placed on a much sounder basis.' Drink was also mentioned, one medical officer stating that without 'the rum ration I do not think we should have won the war'. The Black Watch were known to have always tried to give their men a good meal and double ration of rum in coffee before they went over the top. Conversely, some teetotal generals had banned the daily issue of rum in their formations. The enquiry decided that drunkenness had not been a problem.

The conclusion of the enquiry was remarkably forward-thinking, the precursor of modern battle psychiatric treatment. Slight cases were not to be allowed to leave the battle area, but should be treated by 'rest and comfort for those in need of it and to hearten them for return to the line'. It also stated that soldiers were not to regard nervous problems as an honourable means to escaping the battlefield. During the enquiry, front line officers and doctors had been sympathetic to the effects of combat conditions on soldiers, talking particularly of heavy mortars and artillery, and of static periods in the trenches when men could do nothing but endure the deaths of their comrades. Others, with no personal experience of combat conditions, were not sympathetic at all. A Ministry of Pensions neurologist opposed giving wound stripes (a medal award) to men who 'had simply broken down mentally' rather than being blown up or buried. A consultant neurologist to the French Army, Professor Roussy, declared that:

Cowardice, I consider, is a lack of self-control of the individual in the presence of a situation in which there is an element of danger and in which there is an element likely to cause fear. The man who flees the battlefield as a result of not exercising sufficient control is a coward.

The medical findings of the enquiry were perhaps presented so as to placate the generals. There was no such thing as 'shell shock', which, they said, was 'a costly misnomer'. The stresses and special conditions of modern warfare had merely exaggerated the usual sorts of neuroses seen in civilian life. The enquiry identified three categories of what today we would call battlefield stress: concussion (relatively rare); emotional shock from prolonged strain, with perhaps a terrifying experience, triggered off by something trivial; and mental exhaustion from great strain and hardship over a long period.

Whatever the politics of the enquiry, the doctors seemed quite clear that cowardice was a form of human weakness: 'Cowardice I take to mean action under the influence of fear and the ordinary type of shell shock was, to my mind, persistent and chronic fear.' Another believed that 'loss of sleep and inadequate rest' was the main cause: '. . . nervous energy varies in individuals just as bank balances do. Some become bankrupt and succumb . . . Most real men take a lot of depressing . . . and so they draw on an overdraft and manage to carry on.'

Although the latter doctor had front line experience and there is much in what he says, he implies that 'real men' do not suffer from shell shock. This unfortunate attitude persists today, plaguing the long-term treatment of psychiatric combat casualties, and is still at the heart of many deeply rooted and damaging guilt complexes suffered by combat veterans. Modern military men are as much at fault as this First World War doctor. Trained to overcome fear, they tend to despise anyone who might succumb to it – particularly themselves. Furthermore, fear is unquantifiable. No one can assess how frightened an individual may become in given circumstances, nor understand how other stresses may have affected him. Therefore, no one can assess whether a man 'broke' before he should have done – or indeed what the 'correct' breaking-point should be.

Penalties for desertion have been clearly shown not to be a factor in controlling men's adverse reactions to combat. During the First World War, despite the executions, 10.25 British soldiers in every thousand deserted, while in the Second World War, after the death sentence had been commuted (in 1930) the average was 6.88 in every thousand. The highest desertion rate in the Second World War occurred in the Middle East in 1941 (10.05 in every thousand). Once the problems of poor-quality reinforcements, inadequate welfare, poor leadership, boredom, and inadequate training were corrected by good leadership and administration, the Middle East desertion rate fell by half.

The essentially civilian armies of the Second World War came under regular army discipline, which many felt was unnecessarily strict. No differentiation was made between men who had volunteered for war service, and those who had been compulsorily called up. As in the 1914–18 war, when some of those who had volunteered found themselves facing capital desertion charges, a blanket imposition of military law was not felt to be in keeping with the spirit of a volunteer, civilian army keen to do its duty. Many Second World War soldiers thought of themselves as civilians throughout, 'Hostilities Only' stamped on their documents, saying modestly afterwards that they were not 'proper soldiers'. Some regiments made special efforts to keep their regulars together in separate battalions to avoid conflict with conscripts – and possibly also to minimize the erosion of regular army 'good order and military discipline'.

Major General Julian Thompson, the Royal Marine commander of 3 Commando Brigade in the Falklands, believes that for modern troops imposed discipline is only really necessary during initial training and possibly at other critical times. If invoked, he believes that its actual application is important. In some situations however, he cautions, discipline may not be enough:

The last British soldiers to be shot for cowardice were in the British battalion of the International Brigade in Spain in the 1930s – because their own discipline was insufficient to hold them together.

British parachute and commando training courses provide both strong discipline and bonding, which once applied to men during those courses, always remains. There were discipline problems in the Falklands before and after the fighting – but never during. For example, at Ascension Island on the way down, Lt Colonel Mike Holroyd Smith, CO of 29 Commando Regiment, dealt with two soldiers who had beaten up a bombardier by sending them home. The two men were in tears, and begged him not to send them home – but he did. It was the most severe punishment anyone could give at that time.

2 Para suffered a serious breakdown of discipline at the end of the war – which after all they had been through was a very normal thing to happen to them. The ceasefire removed their whole raison d'être at a stroke.[11]

Their stealing and indiscipline did not concern Julian Thompson: 'Taking things that don't belong to you, under their particular circumstances, was neither here nor there.' He was nevertheless very concerned to prevent the development of any real trouble:

I had to get the COs in and line them all up to read the Riot Act. Careful and diplomatic work by 3 Commando Brigade's police sorted it out – MPs from outside would certainly have caused a riot. I banned everyone from the streets of Port Stanley – including myself! The idea of five battalions ending up trying to get a drink in the Upland Goose [Port Stanley's only pub] didn't bear thinking about.

A strict curfew was imposed:

So no one was allowed outside the houses. They could drink what they liked indoors. We sent out patrols to keep our guys off the streets – not the Argentinians!

As people began to relax, the effects of the tremendous strain they had been through were starting to emerge:

A morale problem at this time was inevitable. We had 2500 men crammed into a town with a normal population of 800 – in which 25 per cent of the houses had been destroyed. It was all part of the same path, albeit in a slightly different direction. Punishment was not uppermost in anyone's minds, but the strong desire not to let down one's chums was. In Vietnam and Korea men didn't know who their chums were, so some ran away because a warm cell seemed more alluring.

I don't believe in the death penalty, although I can see that you might have to shoot somebody at the time to maintain discipline – to stop a rape for example. I'd have shot men in that platoon at My Lai [Lt James Calley's platoon, of Charlie Company of the Americal Division] in order to stop them massacring the villagers. The death sentence, however, does not deter.

Most soldiers, unless they have been in combat themselves, are in the strange position of being experts in something that they do not fully understand. Their attitudes to battle and, particularly, to cowardice and heroism, are not based on personal experience, but on what they have learned from others. The British Army has a vast reservoir of experience from which its expertise, traditions and attitudes have grown. Military law comes from the same source. Peacetime soldiers are given very clear ideas on what constitutes heroism and cowardice – also drawn from the reservoir – whereas soldiers with combat experience, who have seen it for themselves, are not always quite so certain.

Behaviour in combat is a very basic, primitive, almost taboo subject, often spoken of by soldiers using clichés – or not spoken of at all. The reservoir from which modern military attitudes towards behaviour in combat derive, contains water which is centuries old, and flavours and influences the thoughts of soldiers today. In one sense these very traditional attitudes could be regarded as inappropriate, because modern warfare has changed so much. In another sense, however, as men continue to try to kill each other, warfare over the centuries has not changed at all. Military training, despite its increasing technological bent, must still condition men to kill and to withstand the brutality of an environment totally different from anything they might experience in civilian life.

Every soldier has been a civilian, and brings into the army the values and attitudes of civilian life. Some of these values are good, but many are negative and have to be changed through training. British Army training establishments often complain that 'recruits these days are softer [physically and mentally] than they used to be'. Training depot staff feel they have to mollycoddle the youth of today to get them through the rigours of basic training.

As the Commandant of the Royal Military Academy, Sandhurst, confirms, soldiers today are also better educated than they have been in the past, which makes them more questioning of authority. Although they are still trained to obey, the complexity of modern warfare has made mindless obedience too dangerous. Soldiers are now expected to question and clarify their orders, often deciding for themselves what must be done. Orders backed up by military discipline still remain at the nub of all military activity. The demands of the job have however increased dramatically, with new pitfalls for the unruly (and the thoughtless). Contravening the 'Yellow Card' in Northern Ireland, for example (which contains the complicated orders governing when soldiers may open fire), can lead to a soldier's arrest, trial and imprisonment on a civilian murder charge.

Better educated, thinking soldiers, highly motivated through training and by esprit de corps, are very much more effective than men who simply obey orders. Several paratroopers who fought in the Falklands, asked to comment on the remarkable lack of Parachute Regiment casualties compared to similar operations in the Second World War, attributed this to their training, equipment and education. Excellent field craft and lighter weapons that encouraged men to crawl along the ground rather than walk forward played a part in reducing casualties, but the significant factor (they said) was education.

RQMS 'Mac' French fought in the Falklands as platoon sergeant of A Company HQ, 3 Para:

Without intending any disrespect to the Second World War soldiers (I'm very grateful to them for all they did), today you've got a better educated, more intelligent soldier, who you can't just order to take an objective as quickly as possible. He's got self-preservation and is too well educated to just stand up and get killed. He'll look at the objective and work out his own way to get there and kill the enemy – which might mean crawling for another hour or more. He'll only change his mind when there is no other way to take the objective. We had this happen in the Falklands, Sergeant McKay was a prime example.

(Sergeant I. J. McKay won a posthumous Victoria Cross on Mount Longdon, attacking machine-gun positions by himself, using grenades.)

On 17 June 1991, in a free vote of 228 to 124, the House of Commons struck out an amendment clause to the Armed Forces Bill that would have abolished the death penalty throughout the services. Six capital offences still remain today:

> Serious misconduct in action.
> Communicating with the enemy.
> Furnishing supplies or aiding the enemy having been captured.
> Obstructing operations.
> Giving false air signals.
> Mutiny, incitement to mutiny or failing to suppress a mutiny.

With the exception of the last offence, all these capital crimes are vague enough for convictions to be largely dependent upon the interpretation of courts martial. Unauthorized communication with the enemy, even to evacuate wounded or to effect a surrender (theirs or one's own), is technically punishable by death. One hopes that a court martial would weigh the effect and circumstances of a capital offence before pronouncing sentence, but as we know from the First World War, in extreme situations, extreme judgements are made. As the law stands, courts martial have only to prove the charge.

In the 1991 Commons debate Armed Forces Minister Archie Hamilton stressed that the death penalty 'would not be carried out in peacetime', although no formal declarations of war were required to trigger the law. 'It is a question of being in armed combat' like the Falklands or the Gulf. Of Britain's allies, America, Canada, Belgium and Italy retain the death sentence for servicemen. Mr Hamilton stated that the services themselves wanted the death penalty: 'The death penalty should be available as a deterrent in a situation which involves armed operations and acts of treachery which could have serious implications for the outcome of an operation of war.'

The case for the death penalty as a deterrent to civilian crime has never been proven. Michael Shersby (Conservative MP for Uxbridge), having argued for the death penalty for the murder of policemen: 'I will find it difficult to support the proposition that we should retain capital punishment for offences committed by some young soldier, sailor or airman who may be terrified in the heat of battle about what he or she has to face in an armed situation.' In a comment remarkably reminiscent of the post-Great War debates on this subject, Sir John Stokes (Conservative, Halesowen and Stourbridge): 'I don't believe that we can or should let down our fighting troops by any sign of weakness or any theoretically liberal or pacifist arguments.'

It seems that even today legislators do not understand the true nature of combat. In the heat of battle, with death all around, nobody needs capital offences – to motivate them, to deter them, and certainly not to reassure them that the iniquities of others will be justly punished. In combat, you can get away with most things. If you and your fellows feel strongly enough about the treacherous behaviour of a particular person to wish him dead, then you have the means, ample opportunity and scruples blunted and deadened by killing the enemy. Soldiers have no need to be protected from treacherous people by legislators.

In high-tech warfare, in the air or on board ship far removed from the bloody basics of land fighting, it could be argued that the deliberate, premeditated treachery of an individual could cause thousands of deaths – and so deserve the death penalty. But war is not unique in the opportunities it gives to such people. A madman with knowledge of explosives working night shifts in a nuclear power station could be equally destructive. What is the difference? In any case, capital punishment does not deter criminals, and certainly does not inhibit the insane. Why then does Parliament still retain the death penalty for servicemen (and women) in war?

The illogicality itself provides an answer. Servicemen and women are set apart from the rest of society, governed by different rules, having volunteered away many of their basic rights as citizens. They are expected to do their duty and serve without considering their own interests. They are told that their superiors will look after them (take care of their families, make decisions about their careers, comprehensively decide what is best for them). Thus free of the normal worries of civilian life, service personnel are able to devote themselves wholeheartedly to their military duties. Provided the individual does not develop ideas of his own as to how he would like to live his life, he has a trouble-free existence – as a fully committed member of the wolf pack.

Capital punishment has two deeply rooted, long-standing (and unnecessary) psychological effects. It reassures military and civilian authorities (who feel they must control the wolf pack), while strengthening the identity of the wolf pack through knowing it can kill those that break its basic behavioural code.

4

COMMITMENT TO FIGHT

British servicemen have been killed on operations every year since the end of the Second World War (with the exception of a 12-month period between 1967 and 1968). British soldiers have therefore always had the thought and likelihood of combat in the forefront of their minds. Even though, from the soldier's point of view, anti-terrorist duties could not be classed as war, they do serve to focus men's attention on the true implications of joining the army. Like men training to enter a war zone, peacetime soldiers are committed by Northern Ireland training to the possibility of real combat – of being shot at or blown up, and having to shoot back (see Appendix II, p. 411).

Since 1969, when permanent army garrisons were established in Northern Ireland, over 600 regular and UDR soldiers have been killed. The campaign has settled into a regular chore that has the advantage of giving junior NCOs invaluable training under realistically stressful conditions, and enough excitement amid the hard slog and boredom to keep junior soldiers interested. Training units for Northern Ireland has been developed to a fine art, using only the most experienced Northern Ireland experts, who continue to visit the Province to keep their knowledge up-to-date.

The 'Commanders' Cadre' part of the Northern Ireland training package prepares the people who will have to take the decisions on the ground, aimed squarely at the young NCOs. The lectures are effectively presented, using huge video screens with high quality sound tapes, films, slides and so on. Much of the historical and political background to the 'Troubles' is put over using past television documentary programmes. Each lecture ends with a video compilation of whatever has been discussed; a lecture on riot control will end with a long clip of Belfast riots, the sounds of mayhem slowly fading into the wistful gentleness of Irish music, conveying a very strong sense of the sadness, waste and ridiculous dichotomy of Northern Ireland.

Once there, British soldiers are expected to operate in a very sophisticated fashion – in many ways going against the instincts drummed into them by normal military training. In the early days, British Army riot control tactics resembled 18th-century infantry drills, variants of those used decades earlier in the Malayan emergency when, after warnings, marksmen would shoot the ringleaders. The army learned rapidly in those early days, particularly from its mistakes. It has always been sensitive to the reaction of its soldiers to serving in Northern Ireland. For almost twenty years the Irish regiments (the Irish Guards, Queens Royal Irish Hussars, Inniskilling Dragoon Guards and the Irish Rangers) were barred from anti-terrorist tours there (to their chagrin). However, individuals become able to disociate themselves from the upsetting scenes of civil disorder they see. Instead they look in on themselves, identifying strongly with their unit, their platoon and the four-man teams in which they perform their tasks. Although individuals can be touched by particular events, the greatest trauma comes from successful terrorist strikes that kill their friends.

For those involved in terrorist incidents, the shock can be severe. A mundane, boring four months can suddenly erupt into terrifying violence, which just as suddenly vanishes. Soldiers who complete full 22-year careers in the British Army invariably have several Northern Ireland tours under their belts. In later tours, they find themselves returning to the same areas they patrolled decades earlier as young soldiers, to encounter gunmen they arrested now walking free having served 'life' sentences.

Over the years, serving in Northern Ireland has changed radically. In the early days, the urban areas were relatively safe, with only 'cowboy' gunmen who fired at a patrol, then ran off. The rural areas were much more dangerous. In the mid-seventies, WO2 McCullum (then a junior NCO and later to be a Platoon Sergeant in A Company, 3 Para in the Falklands) found Armagh (a rural area on the border with the Irish Republic) very different from urban Belfast:

Working in four-man patrols, watching known IRA members' houses, knowing they could hit you with fifteen men was much more scary [than the city streets]. Although we knew their capabilities and weaponry, in our small patrols, surrounded by enemy sympathizers, we were very vulnerable.

Over the months of the tour, the tension would build up:

We'd smoke all the time, go off our food and start drinking, worrying that we were going to be hit.

McCullum's first contact was on the South Armagh border in 1975, against a well-organized fifteen-man IRA ambush.

We were walking along the road and had stopped to observe – then they opened up, with automatic weapons. There was nowhere to run, nothing we could do, just lie there and take it.

And you're talking about fear. The fire was coming from about 250 yards away, from the treeline on the horizon. With only the grass for cover, we couldn't get off the road because of thick gorse on both sides.

The IRA had automatic weapons and the chances of being hit were very high.

I started thinking about my wife, family, mother, kids . . . What the fucking hell am I doing here?

A Garand round (from a 7.62mm rifle) hit the grass a foot from McCullum's head.

I knew he was after me, and had me in his sight so I crawled backwards. The next shot came straight away to where I'd been, so immediately I knew that if I hadn't moved, I'd be dead.

After the initial shock, McCullum's training took over:

I started thinking of everything I'd been taught, camouflage and concealment . . . 'Shape, Shine, Silhouette', and took off my gold ring. It wouldn't have been visible, but in my mind's eye it was. I pulled my red beret off too, and tried to squeeze further into the ground.

I then tried to work out how to fire back, thinking through the different fire positions, the thoughts coming as quick as you like. When you've got no cover, there's nothing you can do except try to get behind blades of grass. The rounds were cutting down the branches of the trees and bushes overhead, and this shit-head was still trying to get me. Rounds threw dirt into my eyes, which I had to wipe clear in order to be able to see. I kept on slithering backwards, and six more rounds followed my progress. I could see their furrows, pin-point all the way. That's what I call fear.

The incident lasted about fifteen minutes, with around three thousand rounds being fired by the IRA, and eighty-nine returned by the Paras. The IRA were in a half-moon ambush, using automatic weapons (apart from the Garand).

We only had three SLRs and a Bren gun, so our fire power was very limited. They missed us. We missed them. But *we* suffered from the fear factor. We were really taken to bits. It was a hell of a nervous thing to have to go through, which I wouldn't like to have to do again.

McCullum remembered this incident seven years later as he sailed south to the Falklands War. Although he didn't consider himself to be a combat veteran, after this incident and several Northern Ireland tours, he found he wasn't suffering any of the fearful anticipation he might otherwise have felt, 'because I'd already been baptized to it. But I did think that there could be nothing as bad as being caught out in the open like that, waiting to get taken out . . .' Northern Ireland had also been a more individual experience, facing danger in groups of four, and working mainly away from the rest of the unit. This isolation had heightened the anxiety and fear: 'Being with the platoon – as a part of the company – I wasn't on my own like we were in Ireland, so the fear [in the Falklands] was very much less.'

On 27 August 1979, at Warrenpoint in Northern Ireland, two bombs exploding in succession killed sixteen members of 2 Para as they travelled in the back of a four-ton truck. The battalion had spent two years in Northern Ireland, suffering another four dead in shooting incidents. Their chaplain in the Falklands was David Cooper:

After losing sixteen at Warrenpoint, then another four – two of whom we managed to shoot ourselves – we were used to death in the battalion. In something like the Falklands, however, the risk of death was different.

Military training makes men used to death, helping them to accept it under active service conditions. Part of this acceptance involves an emotional de-sensitization, that allows individuals to shrug off the deaths of friends and continue with the job in hand. Nick Taylor, a private in Support Company of 2 Para:

Our company were hit at Warrenpoint, and several people I knew were killed. Afterwards, we had little time to think about it. It never hit me emotionally; I was sad, but never anything more. Nobody took any of that down south [to the Falklands] with them.

War veterans feel troubled by their own lack of emotional response to events like the deaths of members of their family, or the memory of the deaths of close friends in combat. Their wives complain that they seem cold, uncaring individuals. Combat veterans from wars as disparate as Vietnam and the First World War frequently describe themselves as 'dead men' – that is, emotionally dead. The process of deadening the emotions of soldiers starts during basic training and is perpetuated in the way people talk and relate to each other in the day-to-day inter-relationships of military life, as well as in the shared group philosophy of units. Between soldiers, the expression of emotion is very limited – the 'stiff upper lip'.

Soldiers themselves, however, fail to see it like this. In committing themselves to do their duty and go willingly and with determination into combat, they clear the decks of distracting emotions. They do have emotions, which they share with each other – and 'have a good laugh'. Looking back, old soldiers invariably remember the happiest times of their lives as being with 'the lads', usually in terrible conditions or even in danger, laughing it off as a group. Nevertheless, buried beneath the group perception, each individual does experience emotions, which he keeps to himself – a repression of emotion that becomes a habit. 'Group' emotional perception is created in recruit basic training as part of a process of turning each recruit into a team member. Each is subsequently able to transfer himself into another group, and plug into its 'group' perception. Being a military unit, the group commits itself to combat easily, each group member being committed in the process. The repression of individual emotions (and so each man's individuality) is an important part of the commitment each man makes to actually enter combat himself, take part in the fighting and everything else that entails.

Unlike a real war, Northern Ireland is a comparatively predictable environment for soldiers. Chaplain David Cooper:

In Ireland, you knew the terrorist's tactics and so knew what to avoid. If you copped it [were killed], people thought it bad luck – that it was just not your day. It helped knowing that there was also a lot you could do to make it difficult for the terrorist.

However, in somewhere like the Falklands, as an individual there's not much you can do to put off the enemy if you're being shelled or shot at. Being infantry, there is at least some consolation in knowing that at the end of the day you will actually come into contact with him.

Although a tour in Northern Ireland provides good training, the risks there are still not the same as in war. In war there is no respite – like you get when you return from patrol to the Crossmaglen concrete submarine,[1] or 'Endex' [end of exercise] when you go home [from work] like anybody else. After Goose Green, when we were resting after the battle patching up the battalion, within minutes of an Air Raid Warning Red we found ourselves digging out mangled bodies from the *Sir Galahad*. Aircraft would just appear completely out of the blue. There was no recovery time, no time to relax knowing the threat is at a distance.

Real war is on a completely different scale. One paratrooper described Northern Ireland as 'a sort of everyday life, with the odd shot' that couldn't be compared with the Falklands. Having experienced the real thing, hard-bitten Falklands paratroopers were often not prepared to talk about it. David Cooper: 'After Northern Ireland tours you always get the "old-warrior-sandbag" stories – but after the Falklands there weren't any. One young lad joining the battalion from the Depot said he wished he'd been in the Falklands. The Colour Sergeant told him, "Thank God that you weren't."' Other soldiers, who appeared not to be bothered in the slightest by what happened or what they did in the Falklands, nevertheless appreciated the tremendous difference between Northern Ireland and real war. Platoon Sergeant McCullum of 2 Para: 'For them it was like having played reserve team football in Northern Ireland, then playing in the first team for Liverpool.' Helicopter pilot Major Jeff Niblett, speaking of his feelings on the evening of 21 May 1982, after only the first day of the landings at San Carlos: 'Nothing in the past had prepared me for this level of violence. The cumulative action of three tours in Northern Ireland was nothing like the violence we'd experienced in this one day.'

The value of having served in Northern Ireland is however generally acknowledged by all who served in the Falklands. Despite the battle for Goose Green being totally different from anything the men of 2 Para had ever encountered before, their Northern Ireland service at least provided a foundation of personal experience from which to react to the confusion and fear of a real battle. Those older section corporals who had led the patrols and been directly responsible for the welfare of their men in Northern Ireland, again provided the robustly reliable framework that kept the battalion going throughout the Falklands War.

Sailing south towards the Falkland Islands in the spring of 1982 was a period of transition, from the carnival atmosphere of the Task Force's departure from the UK to a sober realization that some sort of military action was going to take place, and that men were going to be killed. For a time the tribal reactions of troops were hyped up in parallel with the media's enthusiasm for military action, exemplified perhaps by the Royal Marine Band's version of Cliff Richard's song 'Summer Holiday':

> We're all going on a summer holiday,
> We're all gonna kill a spic or two . . .

The chaplain of 2 Para, David Cooper: 'Most Toms [the Parachute Regiments' abbreviation of Tommy Atkins] wanted a fight, but didn't think that anything would happen. They'd trained as soldiers, yet because they hadn't been in a battle, as paratroopers they felt a bit emasculated.' Each man was curious about how he would react in combat, but largely unaware of the levels of violence that war would actually generate. Despite their intensive training, most had no real understanding of what war was really like. 'It was a naive and innocent attitude, [the future battle] seen as something like a live firing exercise with any bodies being Argentinian. As we went south and ships were sunk, everyone sobered up a bit.'

Until the first casualties, a war is uncannily similar to a large peacetime training exercise. For each individual, this unreality continues until something happens that affects him personally. Some individuals may completely escape such an experience, and return home at the end of the war untouched and unaffected by it. WO2 Bill McCulloch, a Platoon Sergeant, B Company, 2 Para:

Until the *Belgrano* was sunk everyone thought there would be a political solution. After that, and when the *Sheffield* was sunk, we knew it was serious. We were in waters with sightings of enemy submarines, Russian spy planes and [signals intelligence] ships shadowing us, and then suddenly we were surrounded by vast amounts of our own shipping. It all became very serious.

Up until the last twenty-four hours before we disembarked, we were training professionally and intensely in the usual way, keeping busy, with no time to dwell on what might happen. We then got things like the padre's service – whose message was something like 'God bless you and I hope your head stays on your shoulders . . .' People started thinking that it was all going to happen.

In well-trained sub-units (their members closely bonded together before they enter the combat zone), although the group attitude may become more serious and inward-looking, each individual nevertheless remains detached – a spectator rather than a player, shielded by the strength of the group. The moment of realization occurs at different times to different individuals, involving an acceptance of the situation and (in well-motivated troops) the commitment to fight. Private Mark Northfield, a GPMG (general purpose machine gun) gunner of 4 Platoon, B Company, 2 Para: 'The Falklands was my third exercise with the battalion, since I finished basic training.' (Several paratroopers made this slip, referring to the Falklands operation as an exercise. For the SBS SC3 (Swimmer Canoeist Grade 3) trainees, whose selection and training was complete except for a gruelling final exercise, the Falklands War in fact became this last stage, the trainees joining SBS teams under experienced NCO commanders.)

We were very cocky. It was good fun shooting at planes, they couldn't hurt you. In San Carlos, I saw *Antelope* go up, and we thought submarines had got it. I realized it wasn't an exercise when one of the other platoons had a contact with an Argentine patrol and we heard the firing. At that time I had full confidence in what we were doing. Later, at Goose Green, I began to wonder.

David Cooper:

The landings went all right and firing at the aircraft was seen as a bit of good fun, like the fairground. Waiting before the attack on Goose Green, we all became apprehensive. I decided not to brood on it, and just go for it. For us the reality came as we got stuck-in at Goose Green.

Nick Taylor, a private in Support Company of 2 Para:

No more fun and games after Ascension Island, even though the hierarchy were saying that it would be called off at the last moment – they were playing it low key. We were all looking forward to it, no qualms at all. Our curiosity about combat was very innocent; I was 19, after three years in Ballykinler Camp [Northern Ireland]. On the way down we trained dead hard, didn't drink – ironic really as we were very fit anyway. We had lectures in the evenings and a lot of work on the kit, but it did get boring, so maybe we did the fitness to stop from feeling bored.

After Ascension we were certain, despite what we were being told, that we were going to war. The fitness training stopped and we worked on the equipment. The whole battalion went to the padre's service – all voluntary, yet we all turned up.

The Scots Guards and Welsh Guards battalions, sent south as part of the ill-fated 5 Infantry Brigade, came directly from public duties in London and so at that time were more used to polishing boots, brushing bearskins and being photographed by tourists than operating as infantry. Tim Spicer (as a captain) was the operations officer for the Scots Guards:

The battalion was completely unprepared for going to war. We'd been doing public duties from Chelsea Barracks for five years, and were exhausted by it; it is very tiring and mind-bendingly dull. We could shoot straight and were fit, but our tactics were very rusty. Some of our officers were uninterested in military matters, used to coming in at ten in the morning, leaving at three in the afternoon, living the old-fashioned guards officer lifestyle. They had become social soldiers, and needed motivating. Two officers were just not interested any more.

This sorry state of affairs was fairly normal for a public duties battalion, in which an officer's professional experience may be limited to ceremonial. A short-service (three years) guards officer can finish Sandhurst training, then do very little further military training for the remainder of his commission. Many then slip sideways into jobs in the City of London where the distinctive Brigade of Guards tie can still open doors. Regular, career guards officers whose battalions are at public duties whenever they return from other postings to regimental tours, can similarly fail to gain the same level of real military training and experience of their fellows in other infantry regiments. Tim Spicer: 'Public duties is a killer – of military skills and group cohesion. I was surprised that we were sent, and not two of the many available UK infantry battalions – or the Grenadier Guards who had just returned to UK from BAOR.' The official reason was that by sending the two public duties battalions, the Army's Arms Plot (a complicated ten-year plan by which units rotate to and from foreign postings) would not be upset. Nor would two mechanized battalions have to be withdrawn from BAOR, reducing the size of Britain's NATO contribution below the minimum demanded by the Treaty.

I was captain of the London guard when the Argentinians invaded [the Falklands]. The soldiers were phoning in from the sentry positions asking when we were going. I told them we wouldn't be going, but I had a premonition that somehow we would be involved.

The Scots Guards realized their shortcomings and worked hard to overcome them:

On hearing that we were going to war, everyone pulled together – on admin, tactics and fitness. There was a lot of ground to make up. We were lucky to have the breathing space of an exercise in Wales and the sea voyage in QE2 and *Canberra* for preparation and training. No one knew what to take. I had to write out a kit list, then re-write the SOPs [Standard Operating Procedures] overnight for the 2ic, because the ones we had were useless. I was working twelve- to fourteen-hour days.

Spicer also realized that his military knowledge was greater than many of his fellows'. 'Like a weight on my shoulders, the responsibility was mine to get the show on the road.'

In war, the battalion operations officer is the CO's confidant, one of the few people with whom a CO can discuss things frankly and in confidence. The Scots Guards' CO, Lt Colonel Mike Scott, well aware of the inexperience of his battalion, discussed his ideas and decisions with Spicer, who found this added to the weight of his responsibilities:

I grew concerned that as the CO's sounding-board, whatever I said was likely to be implemented. Although I had the right experience and the others in the battalion deferred to me, I had to be very careful. On the Wales exercise, when all the usual training rules were waived and I saw how much live ammunition we had been given, I realized that this was serious stuff.

The burden of advising the CO increased.

I started to work out who [of the officers] would be the reliable guys and those who in our command structure would need watching. We [Colonel Scott and Spicer] decided early on that we would have to fight; the rumour [at the time] was that we were going down as a garrison force only.

Commanders, staff officers and administrators, who had never themselves experienced war, were moving from the familiar routines of big exercises into the unknowns of preparation for combat. Dog tags were already issued (two discs, stamped with name, number and religion, one to be left on the body at burial, the other to be taken for records). Soldiers en route to war are permitted to make their own wills – legally binding despite only being witnessed by a mate. Units coaxed the men to ensure that each had made a will, the unit chaplains finding themselves looking after motley collections of notepaper and envelopes for safe keeping. David Cooper: 'The Toms were very superstitious about this, as if making a will was somehow inviting death.'

Unit paymasters urged men to join an official life insurance scheme called ADAT (Army Dependants Assurance Trust), buying units of cover over the counter without the need for medicals, at a time when other insurance companies had imposed war exclusion clauses. Each man also filled out a white Prisoner of War Geneva Convention form, which he would have to carry at all times in case of capture. Platoon commanders went through the various clauses of the Geneva Conventions with their men, clearing up (to the best of their ability) misapprehensions about the legal niceties of war fighting. Most took the view that if you knew the rules the enemy *should* be obeying and kept within them yourself, then at least you'd see where you stood. The Part One Order that formally declared the Falklands operation (Operation Corporate) to be a live operation was issued, yet another strangely unfamiliar part of the administration of a real war which further heightened everybody's expectations.

The Scots Guards were pleased with the preparations they had made, and the training standards they had achieved. Tim Spicer:

There was excitement without apprehension and a tremendous feeling of self-confidence. The team had gelled and we were confident that we would uphold the traditions of the regiment. That sounds rather pompous, but for a regiment like ours with such a long history, it is an important part of our motivation. Each section felt part of a well-trained, happy outfit with traditions. All ranks admitted afterwards that they were proud of the regiment, and glad they'd done well – although in action they felt their friends were more important.

Regimental traditions are said to be less important in combat than loyalty to one's friends. In preparing for battle, however, knowing that others of the same tradition have prepared in the same way in the past (and done well) makes men feel less isolated.

Before going to the Falklands, 2 Para had the interesting experience of a reunion with veterans of the major parachute battles of the Second World War. Members of 2 Para in the Falklands felt a very strong pressure to do as well, to justify themselves as paratroopers in the same tradition as the men they had actually met. They were also comforted by the knowledge that their tribulations were similar to those successfully endured by their forerunners.

To Tim Spicer, the Scots Guards' more historical regimental tradition seemed less important to his guardsmen (the private soldiers) than to the officers and NCOs:

I felt it to be like handing on a baton in a relay race, with the fear of dropping it; not wanting to let either the team down or yourself. Fear of failure was a stronger fear than fear of being shot. At least if you were shot it would hurt, but afterwards you'd have nothing to be ashamed of – you'd be proud. I couldn't have faced life if I'd run away. Some men fold in battle with battle shock, but they get treated and return for a second chance. Officers couldn't do that. I was worried about one particular officer, who in the end didn't run, although the others were very disparaging about him. I assumed that our soldiers would do it. I wouldn't like to dwell on the thought that they might have run – they were well trained and well led, good sorts and it never worried me.

RQMS 'Mac' French was the Platoon Sergeant of A Company's headquarters, in 3 Para. For him, the anxiety he felt during the voyage south to the Falkland Islands was the same as if the war had already started. Right up until the very end, he was plagued by constant fear and curiosity about being shot, and dying: 'Would it be painful? Would I see my wife and my daughter, and the son she had inside her? There was still a bit of bravado left in me then, which has all gone now. But the fear and worry was with me throughout.' Even as a highly experienced Parachute Regiment NCO entering his first real war, French discovered gaps in his professional knowledge:

I didn't know what to do if someone comes out with a white flag [to surrender]. We'd never done it in training. I was trained as part of a close recce party, to go out and capture Argentine sentries for interrogation as soon as we landed. I remember thinking how easy it would be, but as we started practising on each other, I realized that it wasn't going to be as easy as people would have us believe. You can practise as much as you want, but when you get an actual human being to start throwing around and a licence to do him physical damage, to kill or maim him, it's a whole new ball-game. There's no blanks [blank ammunition] involved. At the end of the day you're going to leave someone behind, and you hope it's not going to be you.

The first United States soldiers to go to Vietnam went as trained formations, with the invaluable advantage of knowing each other before entering the war zone. The troops had trained together in the United States, and knew the capabilities and personalities of their leaders – who in turn knew their men. To most, including the troops, Vietnam was an alien, unknown country, and the reasons for America's involvement there were shrouded in anti-communist rhetoric. For professional soldiers, however, geography and politics are only important in so far as they affect the military operation. Many British troops thought the Falkland Islands were somewhere north of Scotland, an ignorance that did not affect their performance in the war.

America's Vietnam War started with trained, formed units, and ended with often disparate, disenchanted conscripts. The draft and a rotation system known as DEROS (Date of Expected Return from Overseas) completely changed the psychological and social structure of America's army, from properly integrated units into disparate bands of individuals trying to survive. Once the war got under way and the draft began in earnest, draftees knew that they were likely to have to fight. Even the many reluctant soldiers realized that recruit training was giving them skills that they might have to use against a real enemy. For most, a sense of self-preservation made them learn – a desperate form of motivation that the instructors encouraged. For draftees, basic training was a nightmare of imposed military behaviour from which life-saving nuggets of knowledge had to be extracted.

Members of the Israeli Defence Force, which has fought for the nation's survival repeatedly over the last forty-five years, surrounded as it is by hostile Arab neighbours, are totally committed to the concept of having to fight. The IDF is fully integrated into Israeli society in a way that is unique. Being a truly citizen force, this integration is so complete as to make Israel effectually a nation under arms. School pupils look forward to conscription as part of their civic duty – and also as an adventure. Conscientious objection is rare, and draft-dodging almost unheard of. Although the unpopularity of the Lebanon campaign did cause some motivation problems, the obvious and continued external threat to Israel's survival ensures that most young Israelis fully accept the necessity of military service. In direct contrast to American youth in the 1960s, Israeli school-leavers are committed to fighting even before they start military training. Schoolboys train to be selected for one of the elite combat units; running with weighted rucksacks, practising map reading or training in swimming pools to stay underwater for the periods required of commando divers.

Conscription in most armies takes place during the critical age period between 15 and 20, when physical development is well ahead of emotional and intellectual maturity. Adult bodies can be trained for strength and endurance, while immature minds are conditioned into military ways. This is a formative and vulnerable time of life, when adult personality is shaped. Military training invariably has a great impact on this developing personality. Under a regime of conscription, every teenager must serve in the armed forces, and so in national life these vital formative years become the responsibility of the forces. Supporters of conscription as the means to 'putting some backbone into the youth of today' seek to impose onto the military an awesome responsibility which has nothing to do with defending the nation.

Israel's small population makes combat readiness and conscription their only means of self-defence. The IDF have therefore become involved in the psychological development of their teenagers – starting with pre-induction tuition at school to prepare them for military service. Israeli teenagers are made to feel a vital part of a youthful, adventurous and ideological mission, that tries to channel their enthusiasms into military life rather than stifling them. Jewish history (modern and biblical) provides plenty of motivation. The collective memory of six million Jews killed in the Nazi Holocaust is a strong incentive to military defence.

In the 1960s, as the Vietnam War proceeded and more soldiers returned home, veterans with personal experience of the war were increasingly appointed as the drill sergeants and officers training fresh intakes of draftees. In every army, recruits are invariably in awe of war veterans – individuals who have survived an environment that the recruit believes impossibly demanding and difficult. Until the very end of basic training, when miraculously the recruit makes the grade and becomes a soldier, constant doubt is heaped upon his ability to do anything – let alone operate efficiently and survive in combat. Hearing and seeing combat veterans, who have actually done the things they themselves are being trained to do and coped with seemingly impossible circumstances, is an encouraging experience. The advice and instruction of veterans, accompanied by personal anecdote, is received with rapt attention – particularly concerning conditions, survival techniques and the reality of combat. Vietnam draftees were told first-hand stories of the ill-treatment of Vietnamese, and of military necessities like the application of artillery fire on to villages – often with photographs taken by the vets.

The message that accompanied many of these personal war stories seemed to be that, although US forces were only permitted to attack military targets, because of the anonymity of the Vietcong and because virtually all the rest of the civilian population were implicated in the VC's network, it was permissible to kill just about anybody. The common usage of disparaging words like gook, zipperhead, slant, dink and slope encouraged this belief by reducing the Vietnamese people to a sub-human species, that Americans were entitled to destroy without compunction.

Most soldiers are xenophobic. By identifying closely with their own group, unit or regiment, they inevitably discriminate against outsiders – usually with a keen sense of humour. In the training of Vietnam draftees, however, the sense of balance that accompanies most soldiers' humour was absent. Naive, home-town American boys were in effect programmed with what they took to be the official message. Few understood the politics of Vietnam or even the reasons for US forces being deployed in south-east Asia. The seriousness of their psychological corruption becomes even more apparent when the nature of military basic training is understood.

Military basic training works by first breaking down the civilian identity of each individual, before building him back up again as a soldier – in a continual slog of almost unendurable pressure. In the 1960s the American approach took this process a stage further, relying not on breaking down the recruits' civilian identity, but on forcing them (partly through humiliation) to *reject* that identity and assume a new totally military persona. This made their return to civilian life after one year in Vietnam very difficult, even without the severe anti-veteran reactions of the American public.

The first part of US forces' recruit training, 'Boot Camp', grinds down individuals so that they accept both the total power of military discipline over their lives, and the futility of resistance against it. 'Hazing' by instructors, in which recruits are continually verbally abused, is supposed to make them unflappable, and is the start of the emotional deadening that leaves war veterans seeming cold and uncaring. In most armies, 'hazing' contains some element of sexual innuendo to personalize the insults – based on male-dominated heterosexuality. US Army training in particular emphasizes masculinity and macho ideals – far more than British Army training (which puts more emphasis on self-reliance and initiative), although both stress what might be called 'supermasculinity', supposedly unique to trained military personnel. In raising men's self-esteem, 'supermasculinity' correspondingly reduces the status of women to that of either civilian camp followers or second-class soldiers.

The now disbanded British Women's Royal Army Corps (WRAC) wore either unflattering female uniforms or ill-fitting men's combat uniforms and large boots. US Army women soldiers work hard at being exactly the same as the men – something they clearly are not. However, in the Israeli Defence Force, which depends for its numbers on women taking an active and important role, the femininity of women soldiers is actively encouraged. A 1980 IDF pamphlet urged women soldiers not to be 'Amazon-type warriors wearing ill-fitting male uniforms and toting sub-machine guns' but 'trim girls in uniforms that bring out their youthful femininity'. They are expected to bring 'homeliness and a softened, family atmosphere to military units'. They wear make-up, nail polish and jewellery while on duty, which British WRACs were forbidden to do. Soldiering may be 'men's business', and masculinity an important factor in motivating male soldiers, but in the IDF the femininity of Chen soldiers does not threaten or reduce the macho atmosphere; it has the opposite effect – of further emphasizing the supermasculinity of male soldiers.

Sex is an important tool in recruit training. As only trained soldiers can achieve 'supermasculinity', recruits are made to feel they belong to a lesser species of uncertain gender. In the breaking-down process, they are often degraded through being feminized by their instructors they will become 'men' only on successfully finishing the recruit course. For US Marine trainees, being a US Marine and being a man are the same thing. Vietnam recruits were referred to by instructors as 'snuffy', 'pussy', 'women' and 'girls' ('You can't hack it, little girl'). The Marine Corps itself was 'the crotch', while other branches of the military were 'the sister services'. Women were referred to as 'Susie Rottencrotch' and women in the Marines were considered to be like some kind of sub-species.

Most recruits feel better, bigger and stronger with their masculinity boosted. The new-found self-confidence is however closely and deliberately limited to their new identity as soldiers. In willingly accepting that military training has made men of them, they have linked their

enhanced masculinity with their performance in the military environment – and more importantly in combat. They remain men only if
they keep the faith – a creed that Rambo could have written. The
constant references to sex and masculinity during basic training (a
three-to-four-month period of sexual abstinence) could be disturbing
to anybody with sexual uncertainties or problems – especially for
civilians drafted to serve in Vietnam. Armies are by tradition supposed to rape as well as pillage, and rape was a common aspect of
the Vietnam War – by the Viet Cong but also by GIs.

Military training does not turn men into rapists, murderers or
psychopaths. (Some deranged individuals will rape women or kill
indiscriminately anyway if given the opportunity.) Military training
is designed to make men fight, and cope with combat. In the most
extreme circumstances, some men cope in extreme ways, that afterwards are incomprehensible and abhorrent to those of us who were
not there. Such things happen in every war. In psychological terms,
rape in combat (the sort of incident that the My Lai massacre brought
before the world) must be a part of the mechanism for easing fear –
a way for the frightened individual soldier to win and dominate.
Rape is generally thought to be a form of domination practised by
otherwise sexually inadequate men, their way of achieving some sort
of victory over women. In a battlefield rape, a soldier reaffirms his
maleness in the most undeniable fashion. Because his masculinity has
been made integral to and dependent upon his ability as a soldier,
for a frightened, frustrated and inadequate individual, performing a
rape must seem to improve (or at least reaffirm) him as a soldier.
Although perverted, in the extremes of combat this rationale is logical, however hard it may be to imagine the desperation that drives
men to rape women (then shoot them in a final act of domination).
The ability to achieve an erection in such circumstances is particularly
hard to fathom, let alone the using of it to rape a whimpering grand-
mother trying to protect her meagre rice store.

When freshly trained draftees arrived in Vietnam, they discovered
that their unofficial and essentially dishonest concept that killing
Vietnamese was 'okay' had the tacit support of the whole military
structure – including the chaplains and psychiatrists to whom many
went for help and moral guidance. Chaplains heard confessions of
murder, rape and atrocity, and rather than instructing men to report
such actions to superiors, offered absolution on the basis of repent-
ance only. Both chaplains and psychiatrists worked to keep men
fighting – their military function – giving advice to deeply troubled
individuals that would be both morally and psychologically harmful

to them afterwards. In the process, these caring professionals further reinforced the unofficial, immoral line. The psychologist Robert Lifton called the whole combat environment of Vietnam a 'counterfeit universe', of false values created and generated by military authorities so that the soldiers could continue fighting the war. By the time recruits reached the end of their basic training, their new military personalities were co-existing under tension with the repressed remnants of their civilian personalities, and were already numbed and desensitized. On arrival in Vietnam, by accepting the ersatz moral rules of the 'counterfeit universe', individuals survived their tours but created the inner tensions and conflicts that subsequently made so many of them mentally ill.

Enlisted men knew they were going to Vietnam for one year (13 months for the perversely elitist US Marine Corps), whereas the officers served only six-month tours in command. Good combat reports were essential for promotion, so to double the numbers of officers earning them, their tour lengths were halved. Officers were thus totally set apart from the men they were leading.

Some draftees decided to go to Vietnam rather than burn their draft cards, in order to find out what the war was about. They had no military experience and, faced with the growing public opposition to the war, went out of an altruistic sort of curiosity. The altruism stemmed from a much older social concept – that of the young man doing his duty to the society that raised him. Partly in a repaying of dues, and as part of the process of proceeding to manhood, many young men ended up in Vietnam expecting to be military heroes and real-life John Waynes. The shock of battle soon destroyed those misapprehensions.

Basic training provided the first challenge to such men, who did well because they wanted to do the job properly. The more altruistic, those who disapproved of the war and the military, were determined that the army should not get the better of them and so worked extra hard. They found themselves experiencing an unexpected pride in gaining the approval of their instructors. However, by competing against the instructors, they had missed the point of their basic training – that it was preparation for something even more unpleasant and difficult. When they arrived in Vietnam, the sudden unsavoury reality of the war hit such men very hard indeed. As public protest at home against the war increased, draftees in basic training became committed to their own survival, which was very different from the commitment of most soldiers going to war, who merely hope that they will survive. Personal survival became an overriding desire that had serious implications, for the draftees as individuals, for Vietnam and its people, and for the prosecution of the war. Nobody was going to take chances. Firepower was the thing to use – rather than risk your arse.

On the last day before leaving for Vietnam, many thousands of Marine Corps recruits were given the 'rabbit lesson'. Throughout a lecture on escape, evasion and survival in the jungle, the instructor held a live rabbit. As he proceeded, the audience became interested, intrigued, then rather fond of the rabbit. At the end of the lesson, the instructor 'cracks it in the neck, skins it, disembowels it . . . and then throws the guts into the audience'. One marine commented: 'You can get anything out of that you want, but that's the last lesson you catch in the United States before you leave for Vietnam.'

A version of the 'rabbit lesson' is common to many armies, but as the final message from the instructors to draftees en route to war, it had a powerful, violent and dangerously ambivalent message.

Commitment to survival was reinforced on arrival in Vietnam. Many GIs were briefed by their new officers in the following terms: 'I don't know why I'm here. You don't know why you're here. But since we're both here, we might just as well try to do a good job and do our best to stay alive.'[2]

5

FIRST BLOOD

Even after decades of military training, no career soldier would honestly admit to really knowing his profession unless he had been in combat. Several of Britain's most senior generals of recent years have had no personal experience of live operations, and one in particular (a tank soldier) was concerned for his personal credibility with the rest of the army as he took over its top job. Without having experienced the enormous pressures of 'the real thing', peacetime soldiers can only hope that they would be able to cope. More significantly, some senior military men come to believe that, having studied history books and spoken to war veterans, they know what real war is about. Like a pilot who has never flown outside the flight simulator, they cannot know how they will perform in real life but they have evolved very definite ideas as to how the job should be done.

Being blooded in combat is an initiation rite, a graduation ceremony for soldiers that has no equivalent in any other walk of life. It affects them for the rest of their days, and separates them from the rest of humanity. It is a growing up; a loss of innocence and virginity; a realization of naivety, immaturity and incompetence; and even an acceptance of weakness, fear and inadequacy. A few individuals may manage to avoid an honest self-appraisal in the process, but for most, combat is the time when they come face to face with the reality (and fragility) of their lives.

In Vietnam, because each draftee was on his own, personal 365-day tour, and joined a platoon of other individuals all at various stages of their own tours, blooding in combat was a totally individual experience. The old hands dreaded having to look after rookies, whose mistakes could get them killed at the end of their tours. Many raw recruits found themselves on their own, avoided by the experienced soldiers until either they learned the ropes and were accepted, or they got killed.

The transition from rookie to vet in Vietnam involved first-hand experience of death:

There was a silence, and ... a dread thought that the games were over, that there was death lurkin' in this country.

Then, after further deaths, men start to search for some meaning for it all:

The guys said 'If he'd stayed lower that wouldn't have happened', and it was a good excuse because no one had any other reason why he was dead. But he was. So they decided to stay lower; that was the answer ... I wondered why he died, why him and not someone else. Maybe it was his background, maybe because it was his time to go ... but then after a short while there were men dying and being wounded and being maimed and there was no common factor. They were short and tall and black and white from all parts of the country. And when I finally gave up looking for a reason why one became a victim while another didn't ... that there was no answer ... no easy way to go through the rest of the day ... I started to wonder why anyone was dying.[1]

A Marine Corps infantryman:

Like a guy would get hit in the chest – if he'd buttoned his flak jacket, he wouldn't have got it you know. If he had stayed in the stupid bunker where he belonged, he wouldn't have got killed ... We were always dealing with it on that level ... Which was the same thing they'd programmed into us from Boot Camp. You know the only times I really thought about death ... only ... for a couple of minutes because ... it was too overpowering ... was when nothing was happening, when it was quiet.

Another was surprised at the amount of damage his rifle caused to a Viet Cong he shot from a range of thirty feet – in awe and horror at finding himself the instrument of so much destruction.

The banality of the official perception of Vietnam service is indicated in an article by Captain Jack K. Tarr in a US Army publication of 1968. The men were not briefed on what to expect in Vietnam he said, often bringing with them 'personal weapons that are forbidden'. 'Often a soldier will not be able to go on a combat mission because he has brought only his prescription dark glasses with him, but didn't have the regulation two pairs of clear glasses. Some arrive with plenty of civilian clothing, but not enough military uniforms ... [this wouldn't happen] if Stateside commanders had done their job.'[2] More to the point, Captain Tarr felt that the army did nothing to prepare men or their families for the personal aspects of going to Vietnam. In Fort Campbell, Kentucky, in 1965, the widows of men killed in action in Vietnam had no idea of the benefits and allowances to which they were entitled, or much about their husbands' financial affairs.

Men too young to vote often go to war; the average age in Vietnam was 19. And as the most junior soldiers are the ones at the very front doing all the fighting, they also suffer the largest numbers of casualties and deaths. For teenage soldiers, the trauma of going to war overlays the trauma of leaving homes and families, and being flung into the adult world. As well as becoming combat veterans, they have also to make the difficult transition to manhood – in very masculine company. Private Graham Carter, in D Company of 2 Para in the Falklands War:

I joined the battalion straight from [recruit] training, as they were unpacking their gear from a cancelled trip to Kenya. As they handed back their tropicals and drew thermals, they were all saying that it would never happen.

I had to make my reputation in the battalion as well as get used to the idea of going to war. However, my section commander, Corporal Sullivan, took me under his wing, so in fact it was quite easy.

Corporal Paul Sullivan was a very experienced NCO who understood the pressures facing Carter as a freshly fledged paratrooper. In preparing for war, every man in the section was under considerable personal pressure, and knowing that Carter might not get from the others the help and almost paternal supervision that he needed, Corporal Sullivan adopted him as his 'oppo' – in what the US Army calls the 'Buddy' system. Despite his duties as section commander, Sullivan looked after Carter in a minute by minute fashion. In battle this very close relationship would develop further until as a pair, they would operate as one man, watching each other's back, four eyes instead of two. Private Carter: 'My first "exercise" with the battalion was landing at San Carlos, where, being short, I got totally soaking wet going ashore. We were apprehensive before the landing. Then we saw aircraft being shot down.'

The landings at San Carlos were part of the build-up of political pressure on the Argentine government – a bluff-calling demonstration of force. Even as the landings took place, many members of the Task Force still believed that the Argentine forces on the Islands would 'see sense' and give up without a fight. The orders given to the troops before landing, particularly for opening fire, were clouded by this political ambivalence. Many individuals, both because of what they had been told and also through being unable to assimilate the wildly unreal and almost film-like scenario that was unfolding before them, were uncertain of what to do. Most watched the first

Argentine air raids with astonishment and almost schoolboyish glee, before seeing smoke rising from British frigates and realizing that men were being killed. Few people in those first seconds shouted the opening fire orders that would have galvanized everybody else into action.

I remember a Super Etendard flying over our position that we could easily have taken out. We didn't because our orders were not to open fire – something about us being a political threat still ... This was naive, and now [with hindsight] we would have blasted away regardless.[4]

Platoon Sergeant 'Mac' French, A Company, 3 Para:

I'll always remember to this day going through the ship [HMS *Intrepid*] down the various decks, picking up ammunition before the landings; two grenades here, two greenies [green plastic containers, carrying two mortar rounds each] there ... It was still an exercise at that stage, although the fear was at the back of my mind.

We laughed and joked even though we were digging in and the Skyhawks were attacking. We learned quickly. If they came at you at an oblique angle, then [it meant] he was squirting his load at somebody else. If it was a full frontal silhouette however, you hit the trench.

For the Paras, the Royal Navy and amphibious operations generally were completely and in many ways disturbingly different to everything they were used to. Private Taylor, Support Company, 2 Para:

Getting into this poxy little landing craft in the darkness was scary, despite our having practised it. We'd not practised however with heavy bergans, and there was a swell that meant you had to time your jump really well. Nobby Stiles managed to fall in and so missed the long tab up Sussex Mountains – although he arrived in time for the rest [of the war].

I couldn't believe that in the first moment of the operation we became completely soaked. After waiting an hour or so on the beach, many blokes were gibbering with cold. We wanted to get on with it. When we saw the ships being sunk, we dug a trench so deep we could hardly see over the parapet. It filled with water, so we dug it even deeper and threw in sods of peat to stand on.

Corporal Kelly, section commander, 3 Para:

When we moved on to HMS *Intrepid* [from the passenger liner *Canberra*], it was rather a culture shock. We were tired after a sleepless night. After drawing ammunition, everyone knew it was very different, and we were a bit irritable. We landed in broad daylight, having been greatly delayed, and could hear all the firing from Fanning Head. We were dry-shod, but many of the others were totally soaked, chest-deep. Having landed we heard of the first casualties – two helicopters shot down near us. We had to move fast three or four kilometres up the hill. Two Pucaras flew overhead, then everybody started to take it seriously.

Sergeant McCulloch of B Company, 2 Para:

... tension rose greatly at having to hang around for a couple of hours before landing. The navy were very unimpressive. They were shouting all their orders so that anyone on the beach could have heard them, and then when we walked down the ramps, we found ourselves in four feet of water. We all had to wade ashore, and some men fell and were totally immersed. Starting off soaked in sea water caused most of the serious foot problems and frostbite that were to develop.

Corporal Tom Howard of the Field Surgical Unit:

The first moment in my military career that I thought I could be killed was as we landed by landing craft at Ajax Bay. We were homing in on the SBS's red light, then the landing craft came to a halt in the darkness. The coxswain announced that we were in the middle of Argentine floating mines. We stayed there for over two hours and became freezing cold and very pissed off. Eventually the coxswain started up [the engine] and just drove into the beach. We were all right, and everyone got on with the work, and forgot about it.

The Parachute Regiment train much of the time in the rain, wind and sleet of the Welsh mountains. Getting soaked in the first hours of the operation was not the end of the world. Corporal Kelly:

We're very good at accepting our lot and getting on with it. However, having just landed in the Falklands, we couldn't start changing our socks or powdering our feet on the beach. The opportunity for this came only after we'd carried everything to the top of Sussex Mountains – a very hard slog that took several hours.

By the time we reached the top and went firm, for some it was already too late. Many of the soldiers, particularly the coloured lads, really suffered from severe frostbite. From my platoon, one had to be casevaced [casualty evacuation] then, and a good two-thirds of the remainder of the platoon were suffering.

For 2 Para, 'blooding' included physical pressures and demands equal to those imposed in training and during their P Company parachute selection course:

At four in the morning, after we'd taken Goose Green, I looked around the barn we were sheltering in, to see everyone lying on their backs with their feet in the air. In the relative warmth, the circulation was returning to their feet, causing unbearable pain which could only be relieved in this way.

In peacetime, there is great pressure on the recruit training establishments to produce enough trained men to man the units. Men who fail to reach the required standards are often kept on the course, to the extent that most recruit trainers become very cynical about the quality of trained soldier they are producing. In peace, once the borderline cases reach their battalions, they either survive and make the grade, or leave. The onus switches to the unit to get rid of them, a difficult, bureaucratic procedure designed to keep up the numbers. Private Northfield, 2 Para:

One of our soldiers was left on the ship because he was hated by the platoon. He'd had a severe attitude problem since he first joined the platoon, and was known to be a thief. He should never have got through his training. Once we knew that we were definitely going into battle, he seemed to cause more problems – as if he was trying to get himself pulled out. He eventually came ashore, but was kept in the rear areas. He ended up getting his medal – and even had his picture in the papers.

When 2 Para reached the start line for their advance to Goose Green, each man was engrossed in the comforting familiarity of routine battle procedures practised many times on exercises – except that now they were loaded with much larger quantities of live ammunition than they had ever been issued with in training (or in Northern Ireland) and faced an enemy that would fire back. Private Northfield: 'It really sank in to everyone on that start line, anyone who hadn't *yet* realized what it was all about. We were on an advance to contact, to take out every enemy position all the way to Goose Green. Everyone had grenades . . . My section commander Mick Connor saved a lot of our lives with his experience.'

The naivety of soldiers going into battle for the first time is partly due to their inability to understand the harsh realities and unforgiving rules of the combat environment, but also because, as a psychological defence mechanism, they prefer to remain ignorant. Chaplain David Cooper of 2 Para:

And even at Goose Green, there was innocence. On the approach march, as the Argie artillery were shelling an area to our right with airburst and PD,[3] one of the soldiers in front of me turned round and said, 'We're giving them hell aren't we?' I had to tell him that they were firing at us!

OC B. Coy, [Major] John Crosland told me that on their start line, his soldiers were completely incapable of detecting which rounds were incoming and which outgoing. They assumed it all to be outgoing – not realizing it was the enemy firing at them. The level of our training was such that they'd never seen artillery firing. Only when they were on the receiving end, did they begin to realize.

The paratroopers were tense before going into action, but settled quickly. Sergeant McCulloch:

Most of the lads had already experienced being under pressure, several having been under fire in Northern Ireland. After crossing the start line [at Goose Green] there was great tension, but once we hit the first enemy positions, after about ten minutes, we just went into our drills.

Learning drills for every combat eventuality pays off in battle. Men frozen with fear, or uncertain what they should be doing start going through the drills they have been taught, reacting without thinking. In the process they regain themselves, pushing fear aside.

We saw an Argentinian wandering around, about twenty metres away, who was ordered to halt but ran. Someone took him out with the GPMG, a burst of five or ten rounds – our first contact.

The paras learned rapidly as the battle proceeded. 'Effective enemy fire' is a phrase drummed into every infantryman during training. During an advance, troops need to keep going unless they are actually being fired upon. 'Effective enemy fire' is defined as fire directed at you and injuring those around you, at which you are permitted to take cover. In battle, discriminating between the noise of all the different sorts of gunfire is difficult, but essential if an attack is to keep going. Troops learn very rapidly: with bursts from automatic rifles, after the first few rounds, the recoil pulls the enemy's weapon upwards, spraying the subsequent rounds safely into the air. After first diving all over the place taking cover, troops soon learn to ignore this sort of fire.

Initially, at Goose Green, 2 Para wanted to start the battle, a desire that had evaporated by the time they lined up for their second encounter at Wireless Ridge. David Cooper:

The soldiers were so eager to get going that we had to restrain them on the start line, the platoon commanders telling them to wait. After Wireless Ridge, one man told me that he would never have got up from that start line if his platoon commander hadn't moved off and shouted 'Follow me'. They had grown wiser and knew how unpleasant it would be. You don't put your hand back into the dog's mouth after he's bitten you.

For the painfully young and inexperienced Private Carter, his blooding at Goose Green was to be a particularly traumatic experience. Before the battle started, his platoon (12 Platoon) had been caught up in a typical round of military 'buggering about':

We'd gone south to take Camilla Creek House [a march of several hours over rough ground], then been recalled back up to the battalion [climbing back up Sussex Mountains]. We'd then been sent *back* down to retake Camilla Creek House, before finally being ordered to return yet again to the battalion.

This performance had taken three days, during which the platoon had been operating with only their light 'belt order' equipment (without sleeping bags or shelters) and no rations.

We ended up having just enough time to replen [replenish] before the attack, before going back out to Camilla Creek House yet *again*.

Camilla Creek House was the rendezvous for the whole of 2 Para, the place from which at first light they would mount their attack on Goose Green. As the rest of the battalion arrived, it became very crowded:

The whole of 12 Platoon ended up crammed into the bathroom trying to get some sleep, with the whole house jammed with hundreds of people. Everything then happened so quickly, especially when their artillery got our range and rounds started landing close by.

D Company set off in darkness:

We didn't know where we were going, or anything about the enemy, and had only a short briefing on our axis [axis of advance: the line or bearing along which an attack is to be made]. We couldn't see a thing, so we didn't start shooting until quite late in the advance. 10 and 11 Platoon in front were taking casualties, but even though we were stumbling on trenches with dead Argentine soldiers, not much happened on our central axis. We found the first enemy position when one of the lads actually fell into the trench. There were weapons and ammo, all covered in mud, just left there. They'd all bugged out, so we never saw anybody. After an hour or so, we began getting effective fire on to us. We started taking cover when we heard rounds whistling around us.

As it got light, we saw who was firing at us and fired back – usually at ranges of around 300 metres. Paul [Sullivan], the section commander who was behind me, was hit in the knee and screamed out, and then took two more [bullets] straight through the head and was killed. I got on to the radio to bring up some reserves into the dead ground to the left – to go through the enemy position. When they arrived, their sergeant sent me back to see if Paul could be helped. It was no use. He'd gone.

Carter was awarded the Military Medal for this episode, which with characteristic modesty he describes in only the sparest outline. He had been involved in a savage ambush which, as the paras regained their initiative and fought back, turned into a vicious gun battle. His platoon commander had been killed, and his section effectively put out of action, with section commander killed and section

2ic seriously wounded. Despite being the most inexperienced man in the platoon, Private Carter had fought off the enemy, attended to the wounded, then got control of the section and called up the rest of the platoon to make a counterattack – all under continuous fire.

In all this, he had lost his close friend and mentor, Corporal Sullivan:

Losing Paul hit me that night as I dug in on my own for the first time. I spent the whole night worrying that there should have been something I could have done. Someone came up to me a little while after the incident and said that Paul was still warm, so if he had been dead when I checked, why was he still warm?

Paul was the first dead person I'd ever touched, so I still can't say definitely that he was dead. However there was no way . . . the whole of his face was gone. From the nose downwards had disintegrated, two bullet holes through the head . . . actually gone through to the chest. There was no breathing . . . checking him out came fairly naturally, doing it the best I knew from the drills I'd learned in training. Rounds were still coming at me, so I had to keep my head down, continuing doing the drills . . .

The fact that he was the only person who had befriended me didn't hit me at the time, only coming to me that night and the next day.

The Goose Green battle was a shocking, mind-numbing experience for every member of 2 Para. Chaplain David Cooper:

Beforehand, they were innocent of what it was like to be part of such violence, and afterwards it took a lot to recover. Elation and surprise were the first emotions when Goose Green ended. We were then concerned to find out who had survived.

Nobody had any idea of what had happened outside their section or platoon. They heard rumours over the radio or from the next platoon by word of mouth. Brothers didn't know what had happened to each other. There was great anxiety to know – and some never heard about deaths until I told them at the church service two days later. We also never heard what happened to the casualties – we just had to say that they'd left the RAP [Regimental Aid Post] alive.

I asked the RMO Steve Hughes about the CO ['H' Jones]. He told me that he was dead, along with Dave Wood and Chris Dent. I remember that this made no impression on me whatsoever, which was very strange. I knew all these men very well; we'd been on holiday with Dave Wood a few weeks before coming south. I'd been quite close to 'H' as well, as probably the one person in the battalion in whom he could confide.

That night [before the final end of the battle] I just lay in the gorse and tried to find some warmth. A realization of what had happened began to come to me. The death of Dave Wood started to dawn on me, but I didn't lie worrying and went to sleep. I woke up. It was still dark. It was cold. I was hungry and thirsty. Some of the soldiers had made a fire further down, so I joined them, trying to make a brew. We were dazed and shocked, with no humour, nothing to say. Our feelings were numbed, no feelings amongst us. Shortly after daylight a company of marines walked by, having walked the length of the battlefield. Not a word was said to them. I didn't want to talk to them. We regarded them as aliens.

In this first battle, David Cooper experienced a fundamental change in the priorities by which he lived his life. He sees in this change the source of many of the long-term psychological problems that afflict combat veterans:

When you think you are going to die, things like financial problems have no relevance. Human relationships are more important. The problem comes when you return, and bank balances, recessions and the pressures of normal life reimpose themselves. You end up going back to live just like everyone else. You can remind yourself that it wasn't always like that, on the battlefield – but you still end up living like the rest of the world does. Perhaps the change of priority in battle is simply a response to the circumstances?

Going back to living the way the rest of the world lives gives combat veterans serious problems. Other people have not had their experience. In being blooded, the soldier has become a member of an exclusive club, which has very high membership fees.

To be involved in a war is not enough, because many people [soldiers] experience war without being anywhere near the fighting. Being involved in the fighting marks the soldier off as having gone through an experience that can't be explained. It doesn't matter how eloquent you are, you can't describe it, and civilians can't understand it. A soldier finds it very frustrating trying to explain. This is why many people after the Falklands found themselves getting inordinately angry and short-tempered. They would be very easily angered, then equally easily depressed as well.

After the Goose Green battle, a 'them and us' feeling developed with HQ, through the headquarters not being able to understand what the battalion had been through. 'HQ would say things like: "Don't give us that. We know you've been through a battle, but it wasn't all that bad."'

For Sergeant McCullum of 3 Para, and more particularly for his young platoon commander, the blooding of their platoon was a particularly tragic experience, a classic 'blue-on-blue', where friendly forces fired on their own side:

It could have been avoided. The story never came out, so we don't know what actually happened. Our platoon had sent out a patrol, commanded by the platoon commander, to investigate intelligence reports of an ammunition dump in the Findlays Rocks area. I also sent an experienced section corporal to look after him – the officer was only a young lad, inexperienced. With two engineers to examine the ammunition, they were thirteen strong. They went out at night, and as it got light, they found themselves on the Alpha Bravo line, between A and B companies.

There was confusion as to where the patrol was, where it thought it was and the grid references sent by the various parties concerned to the mortars and the artillery. Sergeant McCullum worried that his platoon commander might have been to blame in this:

I never spoke to my platoon commander about this aspect of the story, either at the time or after the war. If I had, I'd have started to blame him, and I wasn't interested in doing that in these early stages. He was obviously going to have to carry on with the war, and even at the end I never asked him. People had been hurt. They were his own boys – and my boys as well – and if I'd found out that he was to blame, I'd have looked at him in a different sort of light. We had a job to do together, we didn't need that kind of hassle.

What we do know is that the other company opened fire on us as we were returning from a patrol. They thought we were part of an Argentinian company that was known to be on the run in the area. People say that the mortars stopped firing after the artillery realized what had gone wrong and checked its own firing. Then the other company stopped firing too.

McCullum's platoon commander was badly affected by his experience:

He'd been caught on a forward slope with a section and shot to bits. Nobody had been killed, but seven were wounded. When he came back, explaining to me what had happened, it was obvious he was very shocked. He didn't mention the blokes, about how we'd lost a section . . . all he could talk about was how all these rounds were flying at him, making whistling noises.

Now, from that ambush in Northern Ireland [described in Chapter 4], I knew exactly how he felt. His radios had been shot to pieces, there was nothing he could have done about it. All he could try was to get up the slope and away from the firing, which is what he did.

The two other men, a machine gun team, who came out of it unscathed were equally affected by the experience. Their baptism of fire, after only two days ashore, had been severe – a protracted ambush that neither should really have survived. The two men realized this, but despite being described as 'nervous wrecks', obviously had to carry on. Platoon Sergeant McCullum watched them carefully.

When C Company heard that they had been firing at their own men, the news was 'the worst thing that happened to them . . . their world collapsed'. They did not know whether anybody had been killed, and after their deliberate attempts to make sure of their kills ('we could see people wriggling, so we'd give them another couple of bursts'), for several days assumed they'd been responsible for the deaths of many of their own people.

Most live operations, despite being meticulously planned, change radically almost from the onset. The Goose Green battle started as an advance like many others made in training. Private Northfield:

It started off textbook, then went for a complete ball of chalk. Mick [the section commander] knew that this was likely to happen . . . I had a stoppage [on the machine gun], and the first fire control order I had from Mick in the battle wasn't like in the textbook. It was, 'Get that fucking gun working over there!'

We made a mistake in all walking [together] over the top of the [Darwin] ridge. We could see their bunkers on the forward slope of the next ridge. Then another mistake was made by someone in deciding to move to the left. Taff Hall was shot in the back and went down, Sergeant McGerarty was hit in the face, and Tim Street ('Strasse') was shot in the leg. They were moving forward when they were hit. Strasse's leg was swung up into the air by the impact of the bullet, throwing him on to the ground.

Steve Illingsworth and another guy went back for Strasse and dragged him away – then went back for his fucking webbing. The fire was heavy, including .50 calibres. Steve took a shot in the neck and was dead as he hit the ground. He should never have gone back for the webbing . . . I wouldn't have.

When the guys were hit I didn't react or think about it. Others tended to them, so I thought they were okay. Being on the gun, I had to continue laying down fire. After we'd got away off the ridge out of the firing, and sorted out the casualties, we sat down and I saw a mate of mine crying. He said 'Steve Illingsworth's dead.' He was Steve's best mate, and had seen it happen. He snapped out of it after that very quickly, and I didn't see any more grieving – although people may have done inside, in private.

For many during that first battle, all naive notions of fair play evaporated quickly on hearing that Lieutenant Jim Barry, platoon commander of 12 Platoon, D Company, 2 Para, had been killed while taking the surrender of a group of Argentinians showing the white flag: 'When we heard about the young officer being taken out by some surrendering Argentinians, that pissed us all off. We thought sod it, we're not going to take any prisoners.'

There is little chance to assimilate the experience of being in combat for the first time. Private Taylor's war was over sooner than he had thought it might be. Support Company's advance to the Goose

Green start line in the darkness was in single file – the so-called 'company snake':

Company snake, five minutes walking then stop. It was hard to get going again, with the warm bits of your soaked clothing beside your skin, and the rest freezing wet and cold.

Not much foreboding, but a good sense of humour, everyone laughing when people fell in water or slipped over, or when kit fell out of their bergans.

We carried easily over 100 pounds [each]; Milan rockets and firing posts, ammo, two days' food, little personal kit, poncho, socks, sleeping bag. The bergans were horrible shapes. They got caught on the banisters and hatches of the ship before we disembarked.

The BBC announced that we were advancing to Goose Green – I thought, 'Jesus, unbelievable that somebody could have done that.' It made us apprehensive that the Argies knew we were coming. Knowing we were on the way, they could have dug in better and fought a better battle.

Mega amounts of tracer flying in and out at Goose Green in the night – which looked quite pretty.

As it got light we were ordered forward and saw the trenches that B Company must have taken out. HQ Company were sorting out the prisoners, and there were dead Argies on the ground. It was the first time I'd seen anything like this, but as we ran past, all I was interested in was getting to the top of the hill to start firing.

They had big bunkers, and we fired into the slots [with Milan anti-tank missiles]. There was artillery coming over our heads most of the time, landing 15 or 20 yards away. They say you never hear the one that gets you. It's true. My one [a shell] landed in the back blast area of the Milan and took three of us out – which was the end of my war.

For the aircrew of the light helicopter squadrons, the first day of the landings at San Carlos (21 May 1982) was traumatic. They flew ashore knowing that their tactics and the basic role of light helicopters in conventional war were as yet unproven in full-scale battle. The learning process was to be swift and bloody.

The troop and cargo carrying Sea Kings and Pumas are 'medium' helicopters, able to carry a section of men or a 105mm artillery gun, while the twin-rotor Chinook is of an even greater order, able to carry guns, vehicles and half a company's worth of men. Over years of peacetime exercises, light helicopters had come to be used for forward reconnaissance, as a secure eye-in-the-sky from which artillery could be brought down on to enemy positions, and even to control operations. Northern Ireland and earlier jungle anti-terrorist campaigns had confirmed their effectiveness in these roles. Light helicopters are however desperately vulnerable to small arms fire from the ground. Until the Falklands, British light helicopters had never been exposed to the high volumes of hostile gunfire that are the norm in conventional war. Although individual pilots realized that aircraft were going to be shot down, the operational planners continued to think of the light helicopters as an inviolate airborne observation platform – and tasked them accordingly.

During the voyage south from the UK, 3 Commando Brigade Air Squadron had taken their vulnerability seriously. The air observers (crew-men) trained to do emergency deck landings in daylight, in case their pilots were wounded, and impromptu GPMG mountings were rigged for the self defence of the aircraft. SNEB rockets were also ordered. Flight Commander Lieutenant Nick Pounds:

Proof firings were carried out at Ascension, every Gazelle pilot firing a couple. The rockets were accurate for line but were designed to be fired in a dive from at least 150 feet, which is far too high for a helicopter. But they had smoke and woof and so would do for self defence.

Once dawn broke over San Carlos, the whole venture would be at the mercy of the Argentine air force. By daybreak, the Rapier anti-aircraft missiles had to be in position and working, ringing the hills over which the enemy jets would come.

The landings became delayed, bogged down by accidents on the landing craft, undetected sandbanks off the landing beaches and the discovery of enemy at Port San Carlos. In the meantime C Flight of 3 Commando Brigade Air Squadron were tasked to recce the Rapier sites, then escort the Sea Kings from 656 Squadron when they flew in the missile launchers – as vulnerable, underslung loads. Because the timetable of the assault had got out of sequence, the aircraft would have to fly over ground not yet secured by ground troops. Nick Pounds:

The Gazelles were flying ahead of the Sea Kings proving the route – in pairs, a strict rule because lone aircraft are very vulnerable. However for some reason one of the pairs had split up. Sergeant Andy Evans and his crewman Sergeant Candlish were then shot down by machine gun fire, although nobody knew about this to start with. I reckoned that a few rounds had damaged the engine, which ran away up [revved violently out of control] so Evans had to ditch it [into the sea].

The second aircraft, with Lieutenant Ken Francis and Lance Corporal Bret Griffin, must have come looking for them and was shot down too. No one knows exactly what happened as they were both killed.

M Flight were in reserve on board RFA *Sir Percival*, following the action over the radio net. Lieutenant Robin Makeig-Jones was sent to investigate. He was not helped by hearing one of the Sea Kings give a grid reference that was 2000 metres wrong, and by not knowing that the Gazelles had been shot down. Nevertheless Makeig-Jones realized there was a problem and was very cautious. In spite of this he was also shot up, but survived to make the first clear report of what had happened.

Radio communications were difficult in San Carlos Water because of the surrounding ridge of mountains. Realization that something serious was wrong, then piecing together what had happened, took time. The violence was sudden, and because it took place over a radio net, terribly remote. Nick Pounds:

The light helicopters had never been in a war before. It was a lovely morning, there was a gradual feeling of relaxation on the radio net, everything was going really well. Once it got light it had been just like a big exercise. Then suddenly there was death. The loss was very sudden, instant reality – the two aircraft down, and one badly shot up. We suddenly realized what going to war in a helicopter was all about. The learning curve became very steep – the first British light aviation experience of war.

The helicopters had been intended to operate from the flight decks of the ships – a naive hope in view of the Argentine air threat. Because of the air raids, the ships sailed that night from San Carlos Water and the helicopters were disembarked at very short notice; Pounds had time only to grab his pack and radio. He slept under the aircraft that night:

It pissed down with rain. There was no hot food, no tents. We were all very low that night. I thought to myself – 'sleeping bag soaked on the first day, what a terrible start to the exercise!'

Morale was a problem that night. Everyone was dwelling on the disaster of the first day. The next day we all seemed to have got over our mental doubts. The next morning everyone was raring to go. C Flight [which had suffered the losses] had gone on the piss. The next day they were all right too – and up to strength again, having received one aircraft from each of the other flights.

The Scots Guards and Welsh Guards battalions arrived in the Falklands battle zone as part of 5 Infantry Brigade, desperately keen to take part in whatever action there was to be had. The commandos and paras seemed already to have taken the lion's share of the glory and they wanted some for themselves, to prove that guardsmen were as good. The Scots Guards' Operations Officer Tim Spicer: 'In the waiting, we were naive about combat. We wanted to be in there.'

After the landings, and the successful attack at Goose Green, everyone was looking forward to advancing on Port Stanley and the inevitable attack on the Argentine garrison there. However, one of the battalions was going to have to stay behind, guarding the anchorage at San Carlos against Argentine counterattack.

Morale [in the Scots Guards] would have plummeted if we'd been ordered to guard the beach-head. No one wanted that job. The COs were competing [for their battalions] to be in the front – with a sort of controlled motivation and aggression. But the CO [Scots Guards] waited his turn and wouldn't push the battalion forward.

Having just arrived, 5 Brigade units felt most likely to be left behind as the rearguard, which soon changed as 5 Infantry Brigade commander Brigadier Wilson planned his 'great leap forward' down the southern flank. Wilson gave orders for this move on 3 June. As a preliminary, CO Welsh Guards Lt Colonel Rickett was told to march fourteen miles over Sussex Mountains to High Hill, five miles northeast of Darwin. However, after a tractor carrying heavy equipment was bogged in, the march was cancelled some fifty minutes after it started. Their recce platoon had already flown by helicopter to Goose Green. The battalion returned to its defensive positions, recce platoon becoming 'lost'. With Tim Spicer and army pilot Sam Drennan, Lt Colonel Rickett flew over the mountains to find them. They then carried on eastwards to Bluff Cove, doing the reconnaissance for 5 Infantry Brigade's move there. Spicer:

I was uncertain about what would be at Bluff Cove. Thank God we saw red berets on the ground. The return flight was a real horror – appalling weather that brought home a touch of reality about the environment; and I wondered what it would be like being shot at as well . . .

The Scots Guards were taken round to Fitzroy (near Bluff Cove) by ship, transferring into landing craft – a very unfamiliar mode of transport:

The boat move that night was more frightening than the whole of the Tumbledown battle. The entire battalion was jammed into four LCUs, everyone sitting on boxes of mortar and GPMG ammunition. *Intrepid* had dropped us off in the LCUs about ten miles further out than planned – due to some naval problem. The waves were crashing over the sides of the landing craft and everyone got soaking wet.

The Guards were not properly equipped with waterproofs, and, having had no experience of amphibious operations, had no idea what to expect.

Star shell burst overhead, then we saw a frigate bearing down on us from the darkness. I grabbed one of the machine guns. I don't know what I was going to do with it. Luckily it was one of our gunships [a Royal Navy frigate] returning from the gun line, and after an Aldis lamp conversation with the Royal Marine crew of the LCU, we were left alone. We had no immersion suits, and were therefore helpless if anything were to happen to the craft. There was nothing we could do. We had no control over the environment or our situation.

The Scots Guards arrived at Bluff Cove soaked and shivering with cold. One of 2 Para's company commanders took pity on them and ordered his men out of the sheep sheds in which they were sheltering. Lieutenant Peter McManners, a parachute engineer:

They had just finished slaughtering sheep so it was resplendent with entrails and blood. Seeing the state of the Guards, 2 Para gave up the relative comfort of the sheep-shearing sheds. He [the company commander] led his men out to live in the hills as he knew they could look after themselves.

Half of the Welsh Guards were shipped from San Carlos in RFA *Sir Galahad*, a welcome break from the inhospitable mountains. Unfortunately, Fitzroy, rather than their destination, Bluff Cove, was the ship's first port of call. Lt Col Rickett: 'The distance on foot to their intended destination was estimated to be over thirteen miles — at least one day's march given the conditions and kit to be carried.' There is in fact a seven-mile route they could have taken, across Port Fitzroy. However, unwilling either to wait on the beach while the RFA was unloaded, or to walk, officers refused to obey Major Ewen Southby-Tailyour's order to leave the ship.[5] They wanted to get to Bluff Cove, where the other half of their battalion had already landed, and believed, despite the danger of air attack, that remaining on board was the best option. Trying to persuade them to disembark, Southby-Tailyour promised to get them all ashore in two or three runs, after which they could walk to Bluff Cove by nightfall.

The unfortunate Welsh Guards (and other units still on board the *Sir Galahad* and *Sir Tristram*) then suffered a sudden and savagely effective bomb attack which killed 32 of their men (of a total of 48 dead), wiping out the mortar platoon. The first battalion Welsh Guards was effectively finished as a fighting force by this attack, losing many more wounded as well as much of their personal equipment and most of the battalion's stores.

After the Bluff Cove disaster attempts were made to rally the remnants of the Welsh Guards and restore the honour of the regiment. In the process, the battalion escaped becoming the beach rearguard.

British special forces wearing diving equipment, parachuting from a C-130 Hercules into the sea, following a pallet containing inflatable boat, outboard engines, fuel, ammunition, radios and other heavy equipment

Iraqi soldiers undergoing 'battle inoculation' training. Live ammunition is fired a few feet from their heads, but the critical lesson of keeping as low as possible is clearly not being learned here

Israeli Defence Force women soldiers – 'Chen' – are encouraged to wear makeup and jewellery and to be as feminine as circumstances allow, giving their units more of a 'family atmosphere'

LEFT: Mass being celebrated by a crop-haired US Army chaplain in the field during the Vietnam War. Both chaplains and Army psychiatrists found themselves torn between their pastoral duty to each individual and their military duty to help keep men fighting

BELOW: Members of a US Airborne patrol, walking along a wide track, have just been ambushed by Viet Cong only feet away in the undergrowth; they are kept alive by the shocked survivors. Those killed are being covered with ponchos (top right)

RIGHT: 'Dustoff' helicopters were strictly for casualty evacuation, the dead only permitted to fly if there was space among the wounded. In Vietnam, helicopter casualty evacuation established overly high expectations of medical support that could not be provided in a more intense war

A remarkable photo sequence of US Airborne infantrymen coming under fire in Vietnam. As the machinegunner (centre) fires back, the soldier on the left cringes away from the noise, trying to ignore what is happening

Then, as the machinegunner is hit (the impact knocking him upwards before he falls forward), the soldier on the left, who hasn't moved, looks on with studious detachment – despite heavy enemy fire all around him. Such 'freezing' is common to most soldiers, particularly when in action for the first time. (After these photos were taken, the Viet Cong overran the American positions. In escaping, two further men were wounded and the camera was dunked in water during a river crossing)

A US Airborne officer (101st Division) in
tears as he attempts to radio for
casualty evacuation after a firefight in
Vietnam in 1966

(The short straw was drawn by 40 Commando, who to add insult to injury also had to provide replacement companies to the Welsh Guards.) The Welsh Guards were then kept back in reserve for the attacks on Tumbledown and Mount William. One officer commented bitterly: 'The majority of people seem to get killed in war through incompetence and idleness.'[6] This fails to understand the confusion and chaos through which wars are fought. The Bluff Cove tragedy illustrates this very well, being preceded by misunderstandings between the Royal Navy Task Force Group at sea, amphibious operations staff, and the RFA and landing craft captains. Such confusion is however a normal part of amphibious operations, and has to be sorted out through experience and common sense. Transplanted into the midst of an already difficult situation, an Army battalion with no experience of amphibious operations, plus an assortment of other equally inexperienced sub-units, refused to take the orders and advice of experts, making the tragic mistake of staying put when they should have disembarked and dug in. To members of 3 Commando Brigade, there would have been no option but to disembark – which is not to be wise after the event, but proves the inestimable value of commando training, and troops and units dedicated to amphibious operations.

In war, inexperience can lead to the same tragic ends as incompetence and 'idleness'. As in any human activity, some military units are better at doing what is required than others. This is not to say that the others are any less keen to do their duty, nor is it to demean their efforts. It is a simple fact of life. Any fault lies with those responsible for posting inexperienced units into theatres of war. That said, the Argentine Air Force bombed RFA's *Galahad* and *Tristram* . . . Regimental pride can determine how people within military units react. Some justifiably proud units may not always entertain realistic (and necessary) self-appraisal before they go to war (see p. 28). Some officers attached to the Welsh Guards, for instance, noted an arrogance among Welsh Guards officers not evident in the more realistic Scots Guards. War brings everybody face to face with reality, and is particularly severe on the psychologically unprepared.

6

DOING BUSINESS I –
WAR AT SEA

It is difficult to find out exactly what actually happens in combat. Regimental histories and war diaries can gloss over unsavoury details, and the usual correlation of historical records is not possible as few records exist to be compared. Only the memories of those who have survived are of any use, and they must be treated with caution.

Memories are tempered by time, and also by a psychological mechanism that filters out the worst parts. Old soldiers actually prefer not to remember many of their most unpleasant experiences. The pain of what happened is still with them, and telling the story hurts – with the additional risk of bringing more hurtful memories to the surface. Also, combat looks very different when seen at different levels, from the perspective of private soldiers or through the eyes of their leaders. A keen young private straight from basic training is primed with everything he has been taught, but has no personal experience with which to temper his training. A more experienced private will understand what is going on far better, and see different aspects of the behaviour of his fellows. The more senior the leader, the less contact he has with the soldiers who do the actual fighting. He commands through leaning on subordinate leaders rather than working directly with the fighting men themselves. The perspective of battlefield leaders is therefore different again, and varies greatly, from that of a section corporal looking after eight men to a platoon commander in charge of three sections, and so on up the chain of command.

The recollections of old soldiers correspond very closely to the different perspectives of their age and rank at the time of the combat they are describing. Each individual sees things differently anyway, but memories of the same episode of a platoon sergeant, his lieutenant, the section commanders and the privates will not be the same. The platoon commander will remember how the sections fought, and the way the section commanders led them; the platoon sergeant will remember his platoon commander's performance, the casualties and morale of the whole platoon; and the section commanders will remember how each man performed and what they actually did to the enemy. The men themselves will remember a severely localized part of what actually happened, tempered by their own understanding, perhaps embroidered by stories they heard afterwards – and limited by what they actually want to remember.

This last limitation, however, applies to combat veterans of all ranks and ages. Senior officers can be particularly politic, especially in remembering events that are not entirely creditable to those concerned, and may be the least reliable of all when it comes to describing the horrors of war (which they may not have experienced personally) and its emotional impact on the individual.

War at sea is very different from combat on land or in the air. As in an aircraft, every member of a ship's crew is literally in the same boat, exposed to exactly the same tension and dangers from which, until the ship docks at a friendly port, there is no respite; aircrew are exposed to danger in short, very concentrated bursts. The captain of a ship, with his officers and departmental 'sub-commanders', shares the same dangers as every other sailor on board; army commanders are often much more remote from their men in battle, the more senior perhaps a kilometre and more away from the fighting, monitoring and controlling events over the radio. Naval officers man their action stations alongside the sailors who do the actual fighting, enjoying uniquely close relationships between all ranks in each ship's company. Bill Matthews, a Royal Navy Petty Officer during the Second World War: 'In a small ship, you can hate the sight of everyone else. All sorts of things happen – fights, scratching, picking quarrels, but in action everything is so interdependent that it's all scrubbed out.'

In the Royal Navy, ships' captains live a strange, deliberately isolated life, separate from the rest of the officers. They are not members of the wardroom, and will only be invited there on specific occasions. They live, eat and sleep in their own quarters, coming up on to the bridge, or into the operations rooms whenever needed. A ship is its captain's tool, a weapon of war that he has honed to fighting fitness, and which he fights almost single-handedly. He stays separate from his crew in order to be able to carry out his solitary battle. The ship's

officers run the various branches of the ship, co-ordinated by the
First Lieutenant (known in the Royal Navy as the 'jimmy', in the US
and other navies as the 'XO' or Executive Officer).

In combat, although crew members know their captain is physically near to them, they will only see him if they happen to work on
the bridge or in the operations room, or when in moments of reduced
tension he comes round to see how everybody is faring. The ship's
Tannoy system, used constantly to make 'pipes' to the whole company giving the many necessary orders, becomes the captain's one-
way means of communication directly to every member of his crew
– if he chooses to command his ship in this way. Different captains
play this in very different ways; some are deliberately remote, staying
away from the men and leaving pipes to their first lieutenants. Others
are continuously doing the rounds of their ship's company, and give
constant, blow-by-blow accounts over the Tannoy.

Naval warfare is remote and nerve-racking, but exactly the same
as peacetime exercises until the moment the ship is hit and men are
killed. Fire is the greatest fear in most men's minds, followed closely
by the primeval, unthinkable dread of a watery grave in the dark
depths of a cold ocean. Only a handful of men on any ship fight the
enemy directly, the remainder supporting them as engineers,
storemen, fire-fighters, stewards, seamen, radar operators and so on.
The First Lieutenant of HMS *Avenger*, a Type 21 gunship during the
Falklands War, Lt Commander Tony Bolingbroke:

Down below the tension was always the greatest. The worst stress was
endured by those whose action station jobs entailed waiting. The engineers
– although in the very bowels of the ship – had work to do which took
their minds off it. The NBCD and technical repair teams, the general support
(cooks and stewards) and first aid parties had nothing to do except wait for
the first action damage to occur with the accompanying fires and casualties.
It was very quiet between [Tannoy] broadcasts, the claustrophobia of incarceration – and very frightening.

Modern technology makes even the direct engagement of the
enemy by the handful of weapon operators a remote and disturbingly
unreal business. The ship is fought, not from the bridge as in the
Second World War, but from the velvet darkness of the operations
room, in the middle of the ship. Indistinguishable, white-shrouded
figures hunch over radar screens and back-lit plotting tables, muttering into throat microphones. Coloured lights flash on and off, as
ashen-faced operators tap computer terminals. In moments of severe
danger, as the ship is attacked, the fate of captain and crew are in the

hands of teenage ratings, using amusement arcade skills to destroy incoming missiles and fighter aircraft.

War on board a ship is so unreal almost to be unbelievable – until the ship is hit. On the voyage south to the Falklands, which took anything from 25 days (the fastest transit) to well over a month, Royal Navy ships' companies trained very hard, partly to improve their ability to do such vital things as close down for action, but equally so as to bring everybody to terms with the seriousness of the situation. The ships were stripped of all peacetime comforts; wardroom carpets, beer coolers, pianos and even sacred trophies like HMS *Antelope*'s antelope head, were torn from the bulkheads and thrown over the side – in a spiritual girding of loins ready for the fray. Tony Bolingbroke:

We spent the time practising the Closing Down for Action routine to get it faster; it went from fifteen minutes to about two. We had to establish set routes through the ship for all those running to their action station posts – one way systems to avoid congestion. By Ascension this had improved immeasurably.

Sam, the Chinese laundry man, a locally contracted civilian from Hong Kong, stayed with us on board the ship – somewhat against his better judgement. As the likelihood of action increased it became harder for him, not because of fear but because his laundry profits would plummet. He knew that when on defence watches, the crew would not change out of their blue cotton denims and woolly-pullies.

Avenger's company used to joke about checking the ship very carefully after special forces had been on board – having been dropped off on covert raids – for missing fittings and bits and pieces of dubious or dangerous equipment left behind. This turned into a serious occupation after a primed fragmentation grenade was found in the sickbay – a deckspace regularly used as overflow accommodation.

Some ships kept varying degrees of normality despite the war raging around them. The senior ship's officers of LPD (landing pad dock – the amphibious operations command ship) HMS *Intrepid* insisted on dressing for dinner each evening – in white 'red sea rig' shirts, cummerbunds and mess dress trousers. There was a heated row one evening in San Carlos, after one of the air raids, as to whether or not the ship could be said to be in port. If so, custom dictated that plates of fried chips and dishes of tomato sauce should be set out on the bar before dinner.

Avenger also maintained some semblance of normality:

We kept trying to show this particular movie (a western) during quiet moments, to give everybody a break. Every time it came on, we went to Action Stations. The wardroom would be plunged into darkness as the projector was knocked over in the rush to get to the door. We felt that we were simply not meant to see that film.

Everything on board ship becomes geared for war; the clocks are changed so that, after reveille and breakfast, everyone can be at their action stations by first light – when the enemy air force arrive. The time to which each Falklands ship worked (and to which the crew set the clocks) was often different, depending on how they had arranged their routine.

All cookers, ovens and water boilers are turned off during the times of possible air raids to minimize the fire risk. The crew are fed 'action snacks' of sandwiches and 'nutty' (sweets), and warm brews from thermos flasks. The corridors become an obstacle course of fire-fighting equipment, and the recumbent bodies of sweating fire-fighters in asbestos suits and hoods trying to read well-thumbed paperbacks in the red gloom of the emergency lighting.

There was much macabre joking about the engineers and Exocets [missiles]. One of the anti-Exocet drills was to turn in such a way as to present the engineers' machinery space to the incoming missile. Bets were laid as to who would be the first out of the small hatch in the roof bulkhead – and who would be next.

To help minimize the tension, people like the stewards (in non-combat jobs) were allowed in turn to go on deck and man small arms. Firing small arms at incoming air raids was only a token gesture – but gave invaluable psychological release and a degree of physical exercise, providing excitement and some relief to wound-up crew members.

Outside the corridors and steel-grey working spaces, it might be night or day. Only the bridge crew get to see daylight. Rough seas are apparent to everybody, however, and the nightmare of seasickness affects many sailors, some severely. In rough weather, buckets would be placed strategically (for example) round the bridge so that an afflicted officer of the watch, between peering into the radar and checking the course being steered, could vomit without making the floor dangerously slippery. Although less affected sailors might make the odd disparaging comment about a seasick officer or rating, the sufferer must carry on. When weather gets really rough, particularly on smaller ships (like long, thin Type 21 frigates that roll very sharply sideways with a slow bucking from bow to stern) everybody becomes nauseous. The whole ship's company might retire to their bunks, strapped down to prevent injury, leaving a skeleton crew to run the ship.

When a ship is hit and men injured and killed, the whole company are deeply affected. Modern ships are very tightly crewed, with the minimum numbers needed to man the three eight-hour watches, all crammed into the smallest possible space. Everybody knows everybody else, and losses are keenly felt. Saving a stricken ship is a firefighting battle – of well-trained crews carrying on despite the danger of explosion and further flash fires. Warships are floating bombs, filled with fuel, ammunition and highly toxic substances, that leak, smoulder and burn with a vengeance. Modern aluminium alloy hulls, that actually burn when temperatures get high enough, laced with miles of plastic sleeved cable serving electronic equipment, have proved terribly prone to fire – the cable burning to create toxic fumes. Older ships are designed to cope with being hit, constructed rather like a row of buckets connected by water-tight doors, sealed down when the ship goes to action stations. One or two buckets might be holed, and even fill with water, but the ship remains afloat. Decades of peacetime had led naval architects to believe that modern missile systems could guarantee that ships would not be hit. The newer Type 21 and Type 42 gun ships proved to be nothing like as robust when they were hit.

Ships only sink once, so their crews have no chance to gain real experience of fire-fighting. Whether they save the ship or not depends on their standard of training and whether any key pieces of firefighting equipment have been damaged. The bridge has to coordinate the effort, sealing off parts of the ship (which can mean condemning men to die in air-tight compartments in order to stop the fires spreading). Inhalation of the fumes causes many casualties and experienced hands soon learn to crawl along the deck with their faces as close to the ground as possible, breathing air from the thin layer that usually remains below the smoke.

The wardroom usually becomes the emergency sickbay, the oxygen cylinders, ventilators, stretchers and first aid boxes already placed there ready. Smoke inhalation injuries, broken limbs and skull fractures are common, with severe burns – often from flash fires and fuel vaporization explosions. Moving casualties around a stricken ship is very difficult. Stretchers are hard to manoeuvre down steep companionways (stairwells) or through hatches. When a ship is battened down for action, it may be impossible to move a stretcher through. Abandoning ship may be easier said than done, when routes are blocked by fire, smoke and damage and the wardroom is full of serious stretcher cases. The only solution is for helicopters to risk themselves by hovering over the burning vessel so that stretchers can be winched up – a time-consuming, nerve-racking and dangerous process.

When a ship goes down, it creates a severe sense of loss and grief among its company. This sense of bereavement is most keenly felt by the captain (known as 'Father' on some ships), who carries the added burden of knowing that he alone is held responsible. A good ship's company is as close as a family – and once the ship is gone, because it has no further job to do, it is split up. In the Falklands, the survivors from sunken ships were sent back to the UK via the *Canberra*. Their ship was gone, their mates were dead and injured, and their war was over. Some felt that in their rapid and degrading transition from being the crew of a highly-trained warship of the line, they had somehow let everybody else down – a guilt that caused problems after some sailors arrived home.

The task of rescuing shipwrecked sailors is disheartening for other ships' companies, who see themselves in the faces of survivors. Fire at sea causes terrible injuries, which are always shocking – particularly at night when visibility is poor. Petty Officer Bill Matthews:

The most horrible sight I ever saw was in April 1940, in Scapa Flow after a number of our H boats [destroyers] had been ambushed by German U boats while on their way out of Narvik.

We fished out the survivors as best we could. They had been floating in the freezing water for some time and were covered in fuel oil. Two seamen stood down the bottom of each net to grab them as they went past. The fuel oil had been burning, and many were burned when their ships were hit. You could see the skin swollen over the top of their charred uniforms.

One man's head had swollen up to the size of a large beach ball. He was begging for a cigarette, and when I touched the skin of his face with the cigarette, it all came away in my hand. As we pulled them up the scramble net, red bloody gashes would appear as their cooked skin came apart – on their backsides or chests – anywhere. It was ghastly.

Thank God none of 'em lived for very long.

In the Second World War, while the land armies were recurrently winding down from one campaign or preparing for another throughout the six years of hostilities, the Royal Navy was constantly involved in combat with no respite. Similarly the naval war was constant throughout the Falklands crisis, a continuous period of high tension, broken with bursts of severe anxiety and danger.

For most sailors there was none of the physical relief of the land battle – of hard physical effort, shooting at aeroplanes, the savage release of tension afforded by gun battles and the sense of getting to grips personally with the enemy. War at sea is a technological team game, each individual a small cog in a large machine, with only the captain able to exercise any personal influence over events. Each man is the hapless victim to stresses and tensions caused by events over which he can have no control. His land fighting colleagues have at least an illusion of being able to determine their own fates – through exercising personal combat skills. This illusion greatly reduces the tension they suffer. The reciprocal is also probably true; that in combat sailors endure a more stressful environment than either soldiers or airmen.

The remoteness of the naval war, and the accumulation of sailors' stress and anxiety, created (unfounded) fears among the fleet that the land war was being lost. Sailors understand very little of what soldiers do – and vice versa. (Nobody understands the air force!) This basic ignorance made it very difficult for Falklands sailors to understand what 3 Commando Brigade were doing on land – why they hadn't simply marched to Stanley and taken out the Argentinians. In ships bobbing helplessly on San Carlos Water, enduring day after day of highly effective Argentine air force raids, particularly in the Royal Fleet Auxiliaries, crew complained (some bitterly) at the lack of progress being made by the soldiers ashore.

The lack of understanding between land forces and the navy was significant at higher levels in the waging of the Falklands War. As an example, Task Group commander Admiral Woodward believed his task was to ensure the survival of the shipping – which he referred to as the 'return ticket home' if the land battle was lost. For this reason, he gave a lower priority to the importance of releasing gunships in time to fire for the set piece land battles for Stanley, to the considerable concern of land commander General Moore. For soldiers, the gunships' fire was wonderful – when (and if) it arrived. On most nights HMS *Avenger*, a Type 21 gunship, would leave the safety of the Task Force to the north-east of the Islands to come inshore and bombard land targets in support of ground troops. Away from the rest of the fleet, usually on their own, often acting as air defence 'goalkeepers' by day, gunships like *Avenger* were very vulnerable and took heavy casualties.

The Falklands naval war was dominated by fear of the French-made Exocet missile – an aircraft-launched sea-skimmer that the British media claimed was invincible. The *Avenger* survived two Exocet attacks, so clearly it was not. Although the lethal reputation of Exocet was a constant worry to sailors, it did not generate the all-consuming fear suggested by the media. Exocet's strengths and weaknesses were well known, and the navy had plenty of other equally lethal threats to worry about as well.

In action, *Avenger*'s Captain Hugo White fought his ship from the ops room – amidships, below the bridge and in darkness except for the glow of radar screens. On the night of 27 May, in her first operation of the campaign, after firing at shore targets, an Argentine artillery battery started ranging in on them. In the sombre quietness of the ops room, the exploding shells could clearly be heard on the underwater phones. In the engine room below the water line, the exploding shells could be heard even more clearly. Engineering officer Lt Commander Nick Harry and his crew, with nothing to do except wait for something to go wrong with the engines, had intellectual discussions, 'animated debates about whether or not the Royal Navy was a terminal experience'. First Lieutenant Tony Bolingbroke:

On that first night on the gunline, from the bridge you couldn't see any of the fire coming in. You could hear an eerie hissing sound on the underwater telephone of the shells hitting the sea. The flight deck occasionally reported gun flashes.

Captain White made jokes over the Tannoy about poor Argentine shooting, to cheer everybody up:

We were aware that we were handing it out for the first time ever but also that there was a risk of receiving some back. The ship ran itself and all I had to do was play Russian roulette with the shells landing. Did I go towards where the last one landed, or away?

Avenger's first day in action was traumatic. They had heard Type 22 frigate HMS *Broadsword*'s running commentary on the demise of HMS *Coventry* (a Type 42 frigate sunk by Skyhawks dropping 400 kg bombs) and learned of the loss of merchant cargo ship *Atlantic Conveyor*. They felt like new boys, in an alarmingly uncertain environment. Captain White:

No one knew even a third of what was going on, or where other ships were. After entering the TEZ [Total Exclusion Zone] we saw two heavies on radar and because no one had said what they were, we assumed them to be Argentine. We didn't fire because of the first of many hunches.

In the event these two very large radar blips turned out to be the *Elk* (a merchantman taken up from trade) and *Canberra*. We learned the lesson that intuition would be so important in the days to come.

On the night of 27 May, from the bridge of *Avenger* Lt Commander Bolingbroke could see flashes from the guns on the shore. He saw *Avenger*'s gun firing – a bright flash – then the shells landing on the targets.

It was an eerie detached feeling, in the warm, calm and quiet, except for the bang of the gun. On the shore there was the glow of starshell and the flash of the HE exploding. It was more like a night NGS [naval gunfire support] exercise — except that we could hear the incoming fire.

'Goofers' from below frequently lurked on the bridge watching night firing:

... seeing the fireworks and the red lines of tracer. It was odd watching people killing each other, with a hot cup of coffee in your hand. Between broadcasts it was very quiet, the claustrophobia of incarceration — and frightening. The fear was the worst on that first night because no one knew what to expect.

In the first Argentine air attack of the war, HMS *Sheffield* was sunk by an Exocet on 4 May 1982. Thereafter the Exocet missile acquired a sinister reputation, its supposedly infallible electronics making it seem invincible. By late May, Argentine forces in Port Stanley were equipped with Exocets mounted on the backs of lorries parked in the south-east part of the town. That night (27 May) they fired the first at *Avenger*, and missed through a fortuitous error in their firing drill. To prevent the missile locking on to friendly targets close to the launcher, each missile is set with a minimum range. After reaching this minimum range, the missile begins to scan for targets. On this occasion, *Avenger*'s distance off-shore was overestimated, and an over-long minimum range set.

From his action station in *Avenger*'s ops room, Captain White heard: 'A woosh — then a strangled cry from aft over the Tannoy.' Sub Lieutenant Carl Walker (the flight deck officer and Captain's Secretary) announced that a 'bloody great missile' had just flown over the flight deck. His voice was raised in pitch and loud. By contrast, every one in the ops room was working hard at seeming calm and professional.

Walker and his flight deck crew had seen 'a hard, white light', getting brighter and larger by the second, coming at them from Port Stanley. They had thrown themselves to the deck. They estimated it had passed five feet above the flight deck and fifteen feet aft of the hangar under powered flight — dead level and going hard, skimming the surface of the water and vanishing to seaward. Inside the ops room, despite the noise of the missile being audible even without headphones, they assumed it to be a shell — and that the flight deck crew were panicking. Captain White was annoyed and said sharply: 'Tell the flight deck not to worry me with such silly reports. We are fighting a war up here.' Afterwards he was amused at his own response to this near miss: 'Because it was our first night in action we were keeping a furiously stiff upper lip and thought that Exocets over-flying the flight deck were par for the course!'

Avenger's second escape from an Exocet was less dependent on luck, as I had the dubious distinction of seeing for myself. On 29 May I was a member of a Special Boat Squadron team flown on to *Avenger* to be taken south for insertion into an area just north of Stanley. By the time we had arrived with our equipment it was too late to make the landing before first light, so we stayed aboard as passengers. The next day was choppy and I was seasick – staying horizontal on a bunk except for meals. We were out in the Total Exclusion Zone with the *Hermes/Invincible* group of warships, which we would leave after dark to steam south to our drop-off point.

The atmosphere on *Avenger* was tense. Throughout the day there were constant air raids, the ship's company continually going to Air Raid Warning State Red, racing from mess decks to action stations pulling on long white anti-flash gloves and hoods and strapping respirators and 'once-only suit' packs (immersion suits) around their waists. The engineers in the bowels of the ship were making macabre jokes about being hit by an Exocet; the stewards were making interminable rounds of the ship carrying 'action snacks' of sandwiches, sausage rolls and flasks of hot, sweet tea to fill the plastic mugs that everyone carried tied to their respirator belts. The Action Station of the surgical team was the wardroom, with oxygen bottles, stretchers and boxes of surgical instruments. Prudently, I was there with them. That afternoon was quiet and Captain White was walking round the ship chatting and joking with the sailors. He was in the main passage when he heard the 4.5 inch gun start firing.

PWO (Principal Warfare Officer) Lieutenant Richard Simmons's first reaction during air attacks on the ship was to fire Chaff Delta (tinfoil to confuse the radars of the attackers) before hitting the 'Action Stations' buzzer. Everybody quickly learned to close up the hatches and go to their Action Stations when they heard the whoosh of the chaff – before the sound of the buzzer. Captain White ran up to the bridge and quickly assessed the situation. The raid was two Super Etendards and four A4 Skyhawks. They had reached their turn-round point south of the Task Force and had banked north to go home. One Super Etendard went to the east in a last effort to locate the fleet. He turned on his radar and got a blip, which was *Avenger*. Then all the aircraft turned right and attacked.

HMS *Exeter* picked up the first sweep of the Super Etendard radar and reported 'Super Etendard radar bearing two zero.' *Avenger* was ten miles south of *Exeter*. The reported bearing was misheard on *Avenger* as 'Bearing something zero zero' and was assumed to be 'Three zero zero' because of the location of *Exeter*. Chief GI Taylor (Chief Petty Officer Gunnery Instructor) fired chaff for an attack from the south. PWO Richard Simmons quickly swerved the ship away from this attack bearing.

When Captain White reached the ops room he realized the bearing was wrong, but there was no time to present the broadside of the ship to the attack (its many radar reflecting surfaces help confuse the incoming missile). He slowed the ship right down to present a slim target to what they now thought were two Super Etendards. On the bridge three smoke trails could be seen – wisps on the horizon coming towards the ship. In the wardroom, the surgical team and I listened to terse piped reports from the bridge: 'We have just detected the signature of a Super Etendard doing a single sweep on his radar.' The ship swung from side to side and the gun overhead pounded out chaff rounds.

In the ops room they heard the change of mode on the radar which indicated missile release and assumed two Exocets to be on the way. The radar picked up some small blips which were assumed to be Exocets (but were probably Skyhawks). They watched the Super Etendards, their jobs done, peeling away right and left, to cut north-east back to Argentina. The attack was now coming in – one Exocet and four Skyhawks. *Avenger* fired chaff which just had time to bloom in a full pattern all around the ship. Captain White declares he 'had got over any feeling of need to economize'. A further complication in this time of extreme stress was a Wessex helicopter trying to land aft on the flight deck.

They waited for what they still thought were two Exocets to come within gun range. In fact the guns were probably locked on to the two Skyhawks. Then, late into the attack they saw three or four more contacts coming in – more than just the two Exocets they thought they had identified. The helicopter quickly left *Avenger*, flying through the cloud of drifting tinfoil. The first lieutenant kept us informed over the Tannoy: 'We have detected an Exocet launch, range 28 miles – on a bearing directly for us . . . the bearing is confirmed.'

At Mach 0.9 it doesn't take long to travel 28 miles. In the wardroom we were lying face down on the floor. The next pipe was horrifying: 'Impact imminent 12 seconds. Brace, brace, brace.' We closely examined the weave of the wardroom carpet, trying very hard not to think of *Sheffield* and of the point just along the corridor which the missile was programmed to hit – amidships and nine feet above the water line.

The bridge reported a fireball on the horizon and three aircraft coming in low. The gunners had been told to shift from the Super Etendard on to the Exocet, then fire when the targets came within range. They therefore assumed that they had shot down the Exocet. (When the fireball was reported, the contact being fired at had faded from the screen.) In fact *Exeter* had fired a Sea Dart missile over the top of *Avenger* and hit one of the Skyhawks. It was assumed on *Avenger* that her gun, which was firing every couple of seconds, had splashed the second Exocet. This left one Exocet and three Skyhawks still coming in. The danger had increased rather than receded. Captain White continued to pore over his radar screen, trying to cover all the alternatives. He started an ops room count-down to impact. On the green screens they watched as the Exocet blip homed on to *Avenger*'s chaff, then very slowly, 'so slowly that it seemed like an age', bearing to the right, running out of fuel and dropping into the sea – having been successfully seduced away.

In the ops room Able Seaman 'Buster' Brown was on the MGDBD (Missile Gun Director Blind's Display) keeping its radar locked on to the incoming aircraft and tracking the missile. (The tracking of the target has to be dead accurate in order to get a good radar lock so that the gun can hit it.) *Avenger*'s gun was now pumping out airburst HE shells exploding 4500 yards from the ship, creating a flak barrage through which the A4s would have to fly.

Avenger was going very slowly, trying to stay within the pattern of the chaff, swathed in gun smoke. The sea was calm – with good visibility. Ideal conditions for the attackers.

The raid, three Skyhawks, was getting closer.

Then the gun stopped with a minor fault. A crowd of sightseers had gathered on the bridge. The incoming aircraft were now very big and very close. The gun started firing again.

The first lieutenant was worried that the Skyhawks would open fire with cannon and kill everyone on the bridge. He piped 'Brace Brace Brace' and dived to the deck. Action Officer of the Watch Lieutenant Simon Wall remained on his feet throughout.

There was a tremendous 'whoosh' as two aircraft went either side of the bridge, both at the same height, flashing across the width of the ship. The third was hit by the 4.5 inch gun and cartwheeled into the sea off the starboard bridge within 100 yards of the ship. As they leapt to their feet on the bridge, there were fountains of spray to either side of the ship where the bombs had gone off, straddling the bow. The two surviving aircraft wheeled hard left for Argentina.

There was a huge sigh of relief. Tony Bolingbroke recalls:

The whole thing took about two minutes but it seemed like ages, with lots of time in which to get frightened. I could see the enemy pilot's face and had the sudden feeling that one could never survive such a close contact.

Captain White's pipe broke the unbearable tension being suffered by those of us not directly involved with the defence of the ship. He quickly reported what had happened and added:

I told you when we left Guzz [Plymouth] that I was lucky – well here's proof of it. Well done to you all for a very cool and professional effort.

There was debris off the starboard bow so *Avenger*'s sea boat was launched to investigate. They found a metal box, a Lox bottle (aircrew oxygen cylinder), a human leg encased in flying boot and overalls (with a book in the pocket), and what looked like a pilot's sheepskin seat cover – which on investigation turned out to be a human lung turned inside out.

Repelling the Exocet became very important for the crew of *Avenger*: they had beaten the great scourge of the campaign. They were also fortified by their captain's panache and good luck. White could easily have been a pirate captain, quiet with a wicked sense of humour, cool and professional. His brain instantly absorbed information and his unerringly rapid reactions to events gave his crew the confidence to do instantly what he said. His first lieutenant: 'He had an aura and was much admired. It was not hard to convince people that his ship was going to be all right. His luck was a talisman that seemed to protect the whole ship.'

Although the gunship crews were closely involved in the land battle and committed to risking themselves every time they were summoned to take position on a gun firing line, few sailors understood the land battle – or knew how it was going. Because of this, each gunship took on board an artillery special forces liaison officer every time they fired, to explain the purpose of the night's firing and give advice. These liaison officers were the vital bridge between the very different perceptions and operational aspirations of army and navy (and have been a feature of naval gunfire support since the Second World War).

Captain Bob Harmes was one such liaison officer (from 148 Commando Forward Observation battery), and holds the dubious Task Force record of having been sunk three times:

On a ship you can't run away from it like you can on land. I got to know quite a lot about the quality of different wardroom carpets. During attacks, the Tannoy gives you a blow by blow account when you would really prefer not to know.

I reckon that if you work it out there were more men killed on gunships that were firing in support of troops in the ground battle than anywhere else – certainly more than in any one major unit in action. They were pretty gallant little ships.

Harmes became an expert in fighting ships' fires, and on abandoning ship. His first sinking was HMS *Ardent*, on the first day of the landings, 21 May:

She'd fired for one of our teams during the SAS raid on Goose Green, hitting the airstrip with airburst every time the Argentinians tried to line up a Pucara for takeoff.

The feeling of unreality among the crew in what they were doing was apparent to Harmes – himself an experienced, slightly cynical paratrooper: 'It was like a game – and several aircraft were destroyed.' On the gunline, in Falkland Sound to the west of Goose Green, *Ardent* then came under attack herself by Pucara, which she shot down using the 4.5 inch gun:

It was like an amusement arcade game, lining up the cross-wires and shooting down the space invaders. Then without any warning, an aircraft appeared from out of nowhere and dropped bombs which overshot us by only a few metres.

Ardent left the gunline at mid-morning on completion of firing and went north up Falkland Sound to be an air picket guarding San Carlos against air attack. The Argentine air force's route to the San Carlos anchorage was from the south, flying up Falkland Sound. As a 'goalkeeper' (air defence ship), *Ardent* was the first target they would see.

In the confines of San Carlos Water, there were air raid warnings throughout the day. *Ardent* was attacked by Skyhawks and Daggers, often several times in any one-hour period. Then came the fatal raid, five aircraft with two bombs each:

The first aircraft dropped two bombs and both hit the ship. One went through the main aircraft hangar, exploding as it went, causing most of the deaths. The helicopter was destroyed and the avgas [aviation fuel] caught fire and burned. The hangar was completely gone, blown away in the explosion.

Harmes went aft to help: 'I had the feeling that I didn't want to be caught out being useless!' The lead aircraft's second bomb went into the ship but did not explode, lodging in the aft auxiliary machine room. The other six bombs all missed.

The attack left *Ardent* without power and with only the mechanical Oerlikon cannons for self defence – a sitting duck. Five to ten minutes later, 'it seemed like no time at all', the inevitable second raid came in. Although Harmes's proper place of action was standing-to with the ops room crew, he decided to escape from its claustrophobic darkness on to the deck outside.

There were six more hits which left two unexploded bombs. The aft end of the ship was on fire and there were many casualties, so there was lots of rushing around. Two further raids came in after the first. A total of seven bombs hit the ship – plus the two that hadn't exploded. The noise of each explosion was very loud. There were Tannoy announcements throughout telling everyone what was going on. With every hit I felt myself go up and down.

In between the raids everyone got up and carried on with their jobs. With [the arrival of] each new raid, everyone hit the deck and waited until it went away.

After the first bomb, he went aft:

There were many bodies on the flight deck so I went back to the sickbay to tell the doctor. I remember that he had a very bad stutter. The doctor went aft [to the flight deck] just as the second raid came in. I assume he was killed.

It seemed to go on for ages. After the first bomb, she wallowed in the water. The next bombs hit in the same place – aft and amidships. Luckily after the first one everybody was forrard of that. She became terribly bent and buckled up.

Harmes was eventually taken off the crippled ship by HMS *Yarmouth*, back to San Carlos with the rest of *Ardent*'s crew to SS *Canberra*. The survivors of sunk ships were often wet through, with nothing except whatever they stood up in. On *Canberra*, after medical checks, they were issued with a 'survivor's pack' of blue trousers, white wool polo-neck sweater and plimsolls. They were then moved from San Carlos out to the Task Group for passage back to the UK in the first empty ship. Their war was suddenly over – a bitter blow to add to the shock of losing the ship.

Bob Harmes was however not one of the evacuees, which he had trouble explaining to the handling staff on *Canberra*:

I had a row with a keen Royal Marine officer who insisted I'd been sunk and so had to return to UK. That's what the regulations said and that was that. In the end I persuaded him that he was wrong by arguing that the regulations related only to RN personnel and as I was in the army they didn't apply.

Harmes returned to San Carlos on a fueller ship in time to watch *Antelope* blow up. Then, on the night of 11/12 June, HMS *Glamorgan* was hit by an Exocet missile, with Harmes on board.

Captain Nigel Bedford, a special forces forward observer located on Mount Harriet, saw an SSM (surface skimming missile) launched from the shore and attempted to warn the ships by radio. He timed this at 0647. Lieutenant Simon Wall, the Action Officer of the Watch on *Avenger*, reported a 'fast, bright, white light from the north of Stanley. Looks like a missile.' It had streaked south, a blip on *Avenger*'s ops room radar, stepping remorselessly down the screen towards *Glamorgan*, closer with every sweep of the dish. *Glamorgan* saw the missile coming and fired a Sea Cat. They sped towards each other and as the echoes merged on the screen everyone prayed that they had hit. Then the Exocet trace emerged from the blip, carried on south and was absorbed into the point of light that was *Glamorgan*.

Bob Harmes had been in the ops room, making out the post-bombardment report with David Tinker – the Captain's Secretary. Tinker's other job was Flight Deck Officer, so having finished drafting the signal, he went aft back to his flight deck.

I left the ops room five minutes after David Tinker. As I was opening the side hatch from the ops room, I heard a loud crash. It was just the noise – no shudder or vibration – just the noise of the crash. I thought, 'I want to see daylight and smell fresh air.' It must have been about 4 a.m. local time.

David Tinker was killed in the explosion. Hugo White, captain of HMS *Avenger*, watched grimly. 'I had a sudden cold feeling in my heart. If *Glamorgan* was in trouble I knew that I would have to risk my ship and help.' This time the Argentinians had got their Exocet launch drills correct. It seems that HMS *Glamorgan* strayed into the Exocet danger zone plotted after *Avenger*'s narrow escape two weeks earlier. It was the same 'hard white light' that had skimmed a bare ten feet above her flight deck. Exocet travels at Mach 0.9 so this whole episode took about 30 seconds.

On *Glamorgan*, Harmes forced his way out of a side hatch and on to the deck where he found a scramble of people. A petty officer shouted, 'We've been hit by an artillery shell.' Harmes replied, 'Their gunners might be good but they're not that bloody good.' (The ship was steaming along at 20 knots and was well off shore – an impossible target for artillery.) Harmes went aft to work with the fire-fighters. Fires were blazing on the port side aft, and the flight deck's fuel was spilt and burning. The helicopter was burned out. When the flames looked like getting near the Sea Cat missiles the bridge decided to fire them – but forgot to warn the people working aft on the fires: 'The sudden launch of the Sea Cats was the most terrifying bit.'

HMS *Avenger* approached *Glamorgan* to render assistance. First Lieutenant Tony Bolingbroke: 'I watched the fire-fighting with particular sadness and déjà vu. As part of my job immediately before coming to *Avenger*, I'd trained them in just this skill.'

Because the ship was steaming as fast as it could the flames and fire went aft, preventing much worse fire damage. *Glamorgan* limped back out to the fleet towards HMS *Invincible*, which sent its Sea Kings across at first light to remove the casualties. Harmes left *Glamorgan* on the second casevac helicopter, to return to *Invincible* for retasking to another gunship: 'It was a very gallant effort to keep *Glamorgan* going. The fires could easily have got completely out of control and the ship been lost there and then, that night.'

When HMS *Coventry* was hit by three 1000 lb bombs (on 25 May), all power and communications were lost with immediate fire and flooding. Twenty minutes later the ship was upside down, her keel a few feet below the sea level. Captain David Hart-Dyke still finds it hard to believe that 280 of his men escaped (19 were killed in the bomb blasts):

It was 6.20 p.m. when my world stopped. I was aware of a flash, heat and the crackling of the radar set in front of my face as it disintegrated. As I came to my senses nothing could be seen, except for people on fire, through the dense black smoke, but I could sense the total devastation of the compartment [operations room].

Those who were able took charge calmly and effectively . . . I could see no way out and was suffocating in the smoke. Ladders were gone and doors blocked by fire. I was calm, rational in my thoughts and quite prepared to die: there seemed no alternative. When eventually I got to the upper deck, as the ship was beginning to roll over, I saw the ship's company abandoning ship. It was remarkably calm and orderly. I'm still trying to find out who gave the order! Perhaps no one did. People just very sensibly got on and did it. It was the only thing to do.

Half an hour later, Hart-Dyke watched *Coventry*'s last moments:

Less than an hour earlier my ship had been an efficient fighting unit complete with brave and cheerful crew. I could hardly take it in.

The whole company stayed together on the voyage back to the UK.

As a ship's company we kept close together and dreaded leaving each other for good. I was unsmiling, preoccupied with my thoughts and still emotional.

By his own admission, it took Captain Hart-Dyke two years to get over the shock of losing his ship.

Second World War sailors suffered (and survived) several sinkings. In 1940 Bill Matthews survived the near sinking of his ship, a destroyer, off Norway in a very cold winter, after being seriously holed by a rock. Then, as a member of the prize crew that took the German merchantman *Alsta*, he survived being torpedoed by a British submarine. (It was an understandable mistake on the part of the submarine captain, as *Alsta* was still flying the German flag.) Matthews also survived several bombing raids, in which ships all around were sunk.

The helplessness of being on a ship being attacked from the air affects all sailors in the same way. Matthews:

The raids were petrifying. We hid under the 18-inch-thick galley table. The first were Stukas and Dorniers. We ended up being the only ship in the harbour [Tromsø] not to be hit. We were surrounded by huge fish, dead from the explosions, their guts hanging out in the water.

Destroyer *Eskimo*, who had been picking up survivors, was torpedoed and her fo'c'sle dropped down onto her keel, trapping everyone under the wreckage. We went on board to cut them out, and the noises they were making were terrible. In the end it was decided to leave them as we couldn't do any more.

In 1942, Matthews joined the Fleet Minesweeper HMS *Blackpool*, working out of Harwich:

Minesweeping was very dangerous – but the danger of it was part of a highly standardized practice. On a minesweeper it was all or nothing. If you hit a mine you'd all be killed. If you didn't, it was a non-event. You dropped marker buoys, swept between them, then reported the area clear. I didn't realize how bad it was until after I stopped doing it. Habit is a wonderful thing.

Petty Officer Matthews believed he was doing something useful and positive with a touch of humanitarianism about it. His views on the land battle, and all the savagery that he imagined it involved (compared to what he had experienced) are typical of the views of many wartime sailors:

It seemed a good job to be doing – saving ships by sweeping mines. It was a happier thing than massacring somebody. An errand of mercy rather than an errand of murder. Those army soldiers could tell you a thing or two . . .

7

DOING BUSINESS II –
LAND FIGHTING

When all the theorizing and jargon is removed, land combat more than any other form of warfare, is about killing other human beings. Military people cushion themselves by talking of 'taking out', 'zapping', 'blowing away', which they do to 'the enemy' – a sub-species who must be destroyed. Soldiers often fail to realize the humanity of their 'enemy' until they come face to face with him to find they have been killing youngsters, and fathers with wives and children, just like themselves. These terrible moments of realization rarely affect airmen or sailors – who fight one step removed from the enemy, machine against machine.

However, most of the time land warfare is deadeningly and uncomfortably boring. The elements play a great part in determining the condition and morale of each man. Living conditions for soldiers are at best very basic, and usually dreadful. Historically, more men have died through sickness and disease than through enemy action. An important part of military training is therefore to be as hygienic as possible, so that despite living in appalling conditions, casualties from sickness and disease are minimized. In combat, soldiers' hygiene is traditionally closely supervised by NCOs and officers. In the British Army, daily shaving and washing are usually insisted upon. During the Second World War, according to platoon commander Sydney Jary, the Germans on the Western Front were plagued by lice – which the British avoided through their constant insistence on good hygiene, regardless of surroundings or situation. Lice were everywhere, and all manner of insect life. Keeping on top of the problem was vital to military efficiency, particularly in jungle theatres, where insect-borne disease can easily claim more lives than enemy action. According to another Second World War veteran, fleas were the worst.

Living in trenches for long periods is particularly conducive to disease if hygiene rules are ignored – as the Argentinians in the Falklands discovered. When captured most of them had some form of dysentery. Defecating has to be done at night outside trenches, or into cans and newspapers inside the trenches. Falkland troops attacking Argentine trenches, after taking cover or crawling towards the Argentine positions, frequently found themselves covered in human excrement.

In the prolonged operations of the Second World War, British logistic services made great efforts to supply clean socks, underwear and shirts regularly to front line troops, and at least one hot meal a day. There were Mobile Bath Units, which also provided clean clothes. This sort of service was not possible in the Falklands, although had the war continued any longer, something like it would certainly have become necessary.

Jary notes the effects of cold on his platoon, in Holland on 11 January 1944:

The cold was penetrating. The oil in our automatic weapons froze and until anti-freeze lubricants were issued, our Brens were useless. Holding a wide front, with large gaps between company positions, necessitated putting out many standing patrols, particularly at night. The privations of these small patrols, usually a corporal and three or four men, were greater than for the rest of us. Some had hallucinations and a few were evacuated suffering from exposure. Keeping fit, warm and clean became a great effort.[1]

There was no escaping from the conditions – they must simply be endured. Jary had the sensitivity to leave them to it: 'Conversation dried up . . . They just wanted to be left alone.'

There is no balance in war between the rare moments of danger, fear and high excitement, and days of nerve-racking waiting, often in very uncomfortable conditions. The land battlefield (unlike the clear blue skies and stormy seas) is littered with the remnants of battle, a constant reminder to every tense and waiting soldier of what may at any moment happen to him. Sydney Jary made the mistake of investigating a group of three stationary but apparently unmarked tanks that his company commander was worried might still be able to fire at them. After an anxious sprint across open ground in front of their trench positions, he reached the first vehicle:

Climbing up above the tracks, I put my head into the cupola which was open. A familiar and terrible stench hit me. Inside was a charnel house. Six inches away, a set of bared teeth, set in an unrecognizable black lump, grinned at me. Beside it a charred and bony arm reached up in agony. Spread on the floor like a pool of tar, lay the melted remains of the driver.

I had entered Dante's Inferno. My head reeled and, with my mouth, nose and lungs filled with the stench of death, I fell back to the ground.

Although unmarked by fire on our side, all three assault guns had brewed up and were blackened on the sides which faced the enemy . . . Never again did I look into a knocked out tank or self-propelled gun.[2]

In comparison with earlier wars, particularly the Second World War, the numbers of casualties suffered in the Falklands seem very low. As an example, during 2 Para's battle for Darwin/Goose Green, when the battalion fought across open moorland with inadequate artillery support and only their own mortars to bail them out, 16 men were killed. Casualties from Argentine artillery were to an extent minimized by the battlefield itself (water-logged peat) absorbing explosion and shell splinters. Even so, 2 Para's casualty figures for such a battle are surprisingly low, for reasons that are not immediately apparent. In general, Falklands troops were attacking heavily defended positions in good locations, against a well-equipped and competent enemy who was using modern weapons.

The low figures cannot simply be attributed to the poor morale of some of the enemy. The Argentine Army ranged from tough, highly motivated marine units and commanders trained by the British Army, to bewildered young conscripts. The appalling Falklands weather and terrain did however favour the British, who were well used to training in similar conditions. Another reason for the apparent disparity in casualty figures lies paradoxically in the increased danger of the modern battlefield.

If attackers in a modern war used First or Second World War infantry tactics, they would be slaughtered in large numbers. Modern weaponry has made new tactics and improved fieldcraft essential. Today each infantry section has its own fire team, with at least one machine gun. Although it takes time and patience, the careful use of both cover and covering fire, with the fire and movement of pairs of soldiers working together ('pepper-potting'), allows men to move towards a defending enemy without being mown down wholesale. Sergeant French:

With the firepower of modern weapons and night surveillance devices, you have to assume that you can always be seen: in fog, mist, darkness or whatever. You therefore have to crawl, and when someone fires at you, work out a different direction from which you can kill him, working round using every bit of available cover to get him.

When it comes to fighting, you can either stand up and walk forward in formation, as taught in the text-books – and get killed; or play it dirty and sneaky. At the end, the dirty sneaky person will survive.

Falklands battles, particularly 3 Para's battle for Mount Longdon, were a succession of concurrent, individual fights, between small groups of attackers and desperate defenders, both sides struggling to work out where their enemy was:

In the Second World War, with the weapons they had and the lack of night viewing devices, they might have got away with getting up to walk. We had no option but getting on to our bellies and crawling. If it extends a battle from two hours to eight hours of crawling, then so what? Being alive at the end of the day is obviously better.

The 'start line' in a battle is the critical point on the ground from which an attack is launched. It must be a safe place in which the attacking force can organize itself without harassment from the enemy. At a given time, the start line is crossed and the attack starts – each man fully conscious of walking into something very different from anything he has ever experienced before.

We walked in single file across the start line, which is always out of sight to the enemy. Once you come under incoming effective enemy fire – when people around you start being hit – you break down into individual fire teams.

We'd got it down to a fine art. You'd stop for a few seconds, taking cover while working out how to take out the [enemy] bunkers that are firing. Everyone lays down suppressive fire on to the enemy positions, while you move in by the easiest route. We'd go through it bit by bit, taking out bunkers and trenches one by one.

If they'd had the same equipment and weapons as us, I think the Second World War guys would have done it the same. Having a shorter, lighter weapon makes you feel smaller and more sneaky, whereas a .303 with a long bayonet gives you a false sense of security, makes you feel you can walk in there, bold and brash. It's also harder to crawl around with a long, heavy weapon.

In basic training, today's soldiers observe their fellows through night vision goggles. They realize that on the modern battlefield, night has become virtually the same as day, and that to survive fieldcraft must be used at all times.

In the past, large battles were fought to strict timetables, with men having to move forward in keeping with a timed schedule – almost regardless of the tactical situation. This pressure to get on made it difficult for these battles to be fought carefully, with subordinate commanders under great pressure not to hold up the attack. Many casualties were undoubtedly the result of this pressure. Battles are still fought according to timetables – the co-ordination of artillery support and the movement of large numbers of men and vehicles make it impossible to do otherwise. However it does seem that there is a change in the attitude of today's professional soldiers: they are simply not prepared to become cannon fodder – to be mown down in the fulfilment of somebody else's timetable. Platoon Sergeant French:

When you are pushing forward, under pressure to keep going but continually bouncing off the door, what can you do? You try everything. If you can't get through the door, you find another way round. We're not simple natives. The modern soldier doesn't keep running in the same direction. There is a time and place for heroism, and I don't think the person that actually does it, knows beforehand that he will be capable of it. Until you get into that tight corner, you don't know how you'll behave.

This modern insistence on self-preservation and minimizing casualties (which characterized Montgomery's campaigns) was illustrated particularly well by US General Norman Schwarzkopf's planning of the land campaign of the Gulf War of 1991. Two decades earlier, his generation of US Army officers had seen their men cut down and mutilated in Vietnam, and were resolved that this would not happen in the Gulf. There was also considerable political pressure to minimize casualties, so as to retain public support at home for the war.

American commanders were haunted by the spectre of Vietnam, having personally seen lives lost because of the stupidity of self-serving officers there – and through vague political objectives coupled with the limited provision of military means. Schwarzkopf himself had returned from South-East Asia in the 1970s to say publicly: 'I hate what Vietnam has done to our country. I hate what Vietnam has done to our army' and that he was unsure whether he would ever go to war again.[3] The Gulf War was fought by professionals at every level, with very precise objectives and maximum firepower. Allied lives were at a premium.

In the recent past, when human life was perhaps not held to be so important by military commanders, amateurism may also have been a factor in the high casualty toll. Sydney Jary:

The problems for the first two months in Normandy [summer 1944] were a lack of comprehensive, imaginative training, and personal experience of battle. We were also seriously handicapped by our casual attitudes, lack of thought and persistent reliance on the dogmatic teaching of the Battle Schools.

The Battle School staff permitted no discussion and argument, and were themselves lacking in battle experience. The regular soldiers were experienced only in policing the Empire, and as keenness and innovation were not encouraged, nobody had spent time thinking about new tactics.[4]

Perhaps because many of the men in the D-Day armies were conscripts obeying orders in a very alien environment, rather than thinking soldiers, people just did as they were told without too much questioning. In any case, questioning doubtful orders was considered insubordination in those days – a serious offence. Although oldschool army officers might still agree with that, many younger officers and NCOs today would see it as their duty to question orders that might lead to unnecessary deaths.

Patrolling is a nerve-racking and demanding infantry activity that nobody in combat welcomes – especially when it seems to have no particular purpose. In the Falklands patrolling was carried out by parachute and commando units for very precise reasons – to find out where the enemy's positions were located. In the Second World War, however, as in the Great War, patrolling was at times an antidote to military inertia – with no specific aim in mind. Jary: 'Patrolling was often carried out because someone at Brigade thought the troops needed to be kept busy. "Dominating noman's-land" is a dubious aim in the absence of any other purpose, especially when it means losing the lives of the good officers and NCOs.'

Falklands troops were generally given clear aims for patrols. With the pressure they were under just from the appalling weather, patrolling for no purpose could have damaged their fighting capabilities – lowering morale as well as making men colder and wetter than was necessary. British infantry patrolling in the Falklands (as distinct from special forces' harassing operations) did have the almost incidental effect of intimidating the Argentine troops.

Argentine snipers were particularly effective during the Falklands attacks, using sophisticated night-scopes and very accurate weapons. Often the only way for the British to deal with them was to use covering fire to close to within thirty metres, and then kill them – using 66mm anti-tank rockets or hand grenades. Sydney Jary does not consider snipers had much military relevance in the Second World War:

I had little stomach for sniping. More often than not it was a cold and calculated way of killing which achieved no military advantage. It did not take ground nor did it stop an attacking force. I suppose it lowered the morale of poor troops, but I have little evidence that it did.

Getting anywhere near the enemy is often a long, hard slog carrying loads a Sherpa would sensibly refuse. Peacetime exercises never replicate the extreme physical hardship of these conditions (let alone the fear and danger) – particularly as live ammunition is rarely issued in sufficient quantity to make realistically heavy loads. Before attacking Mount Longdon, for their one night of actual fighting, the men of 3 Para had to endure three weeks of severe Falklands weather, with constant air raids, as well as walk across East Falkland – plus a detour north to Teal Inlet. By the time they closed with the Argentinians they were exhausted. Corporal Kelly of 3 Para:

We marched to Teal Inlet in mid-afternoon, tabbed [tactical advance to battle] all night, laid up the next day [hiding from enemy aircraft] and arrived the following night. We were carrying heavy weight and kept having to cross waist-deep rivers. We were in loose file and not stopping, so nobody wanted to fall behind. It was dark, so there was no worry about enemy aircraft or attack. We were carrying as much ammunition as we could manage. The radio operators were the heaviest, carrying radios and batteries. In fact, their loads were considered so heavy that they'd been given spare drivers [as porters] just to carry their batteries.

Being continually wet caused serious foot problems, and the cripplingly heavy weights took their toll:

You just don't carry the correct weight in peacetime. At the end, everyone was going downhill with bad backs, knees, illnesses like tonsillitis, heavy colds. Three weeks more and we'd have been down to three quarters or less.

We ran out of rations [on the march] as we'd only been given one day's worth. One young lad, aged 17, was sitting around oblivious to everything. We made him brews and got him a ride to Teal Inlet on a tractor carrying ammunition.

They knew they were marching towards a possible engagement with the enemy, although most hoped this would not prove necessary:

We'd seen a lot of aircraft, and most people wanted to do something [attack the Argentinians]. But when we were told Teal was clear, we felt relieved ... We'd been without our packs and sleeping bags for three days ... We were happy to be able to shelter inside the houses.

However, on arriving at Estancia, Corporal Kelly's platoon (4 Platoon) went forward six miles or so to secure the ground ahead of the battalion, into what at that time was no-man's-land between British-held Mount Kent and the Argentine main defensive positions. A sudden injection of danger was to seriously upset their equanimity.

Arriving at Estancia we were sent further on to secure the Murrell Bridge. For the first time we saw evidence of Argentinians – fag packets, tins and rubbish.

They prepared a defensive position with trenches either side of the Murrell river:

We had two sections dug into the peat on the far side of the bridge, about 150 metres either side the track. The next day, the Argentinians on Two Sisters [less than 2000 metres away] started off with their .50 cal machine guns, taking great chunks out of the peat banks we'd made in front of our positions.

The platoon commander was 300 metres the other side of the bridge, about 600 metres behind us. When I asked him to get us out he refused, saying that the enemy fire was not effective! I told him he should get his fucking arse over our side of the river and try it because it looked pretty effective to us.

I had a standing patrol 500 metres away in dead ground. The Argentinians started mortaring them, chasing them back to our positions. Then their artillery came in. We threw smoke grenades and legged it to some rocks. The firing continued for several hours until it got dark, when we were able to withdraw across the bridge. It was sheer luck that nobody was hit.

Once the artillery started, the platoon commander believed us! They dropped some very large rounds about 100 metres away – probably 5.5 inch – each one making a huge hole that would completely take out any trench complete. Forget the standard 18 inches of overhead cover!

After the weeks of waiting and their long march, 4 Platoon were in battle, under fire but unable to do anything in response, or to help themselves. They were completely isolated from the rest of their company and battalion, in a dangerously exposed position for no apparent reason or purpose – which made them think: 'We were unable to do anything about these enemy, and nobody could help us. We realized that trenches were not safe places, and that survival depended on luck.'

The platoon withdrew back to Estancia to their company, where they settled down to recover physically from their experience and await further orders:

We were quite well off living in a peat-banked, mud hut shelter, which was dry inside and lined with cardboard from ration boxes. We'd been on the go for six days, and our feet were getting pretty bad, but it was quiet and we were able to get some sleep and rest. Wearing trainers, and drying out our boots, our feet were able to recover too. It was a bit boring, but we were glad of the rest.

They were shaken by the heavy machine gun and artillery fire of the Murrell Bridge incident, which had been 'pretty hairy'. They assumed (wrongly) that their unpleasant experience would qualify them to be in reserve for the planned attack on Mount Longdon:

When we found we were not to be reserve [but in the lead] it shook us up quite a bit. However, after briefing the section there was no problem – everyone just got on with it.

After formal orders for the Mount Longdon attack, Kelly had returned to his section. In their peat and cardboard hut, they'd been braising a leg of lamb which he was looking forward to eating. Fresh rations become increasingly necessary after weeks on dehydrated and tinned Army 'compo' rations. In his absence, human nature had overcome military discipline:

When I got back, I found they'd scoffed the lot, which concerned me much more than whatever we were supposed to be doing on the attack. In fact they'd done this before – with some bread. We'd been given apples too, which I still had in my pocket, so when I found it was all gone I refused to share the apples out.

The roughness of the terrain and the appalling weather were a constant challenge in the Falklands. Getting to within striking distance of the enemy with the necessary ammunition and equipment to do the job took enormous effort and occupied most of the time. Platoon Sergeant McCulloch of 2 Para:

The whole thing was very physical. Because of the weights we carried and the miles we tabbed, a good percentage of the lads came away with back problems. We all carried the same weight, so when people felt sorry for themselves, I told them that if I could do it at my age, they should have no problems.

Constant uncertainty gave some relief to the discomfort and monotony, as well as the sense that what they were engaged in had a purpose – means to a very definite end.

Sometimes on exercise, people get a bit bitchy, but this never happened – probably because we kept them very well informed. With well-educated soldiers, if you tell them what's happening they understand and will live with it – whether they like it or not.

In order to move quickly, the battalions often left their heavy bergans behind, carrying only ammunition and food for twenty-four hours. Even so, 'light order' (belt order) meant carrying around 50 pounds weight. Although essentials like spare socks and foot powder, and a few comforts like poncho shelters could be strapped to belt order, the basic luxuries of military life like sleeping bags, cookers and food were often lacking for several days, until helicopters could be spared to bring the bergans up.

We never went in with our bergans, and we learned after waiting 72 hours for an attack, to live off our belt orders. It got the buddy-buddy system working well. When we got on to an enemy position we'd use enemy rations – and in the case of young Carroll [who after falling into a river during the Mount Longdon attack, developed cold exposure] we dressed him almost completely in dry Argentine kit. I remember thinking that he'd be taken for a prisoner back at Ajax Bay!

Platoon Sergeant McCullum, of 3 Para:

It was difficult keeping the boys going during the 70-mile march. You know who the weak links are, who you need to look after, and keep an eye on them. If I saw one of my section commanders loading up one of the less fit lads with piles of ammunition, I'd have a quiet word: 'Take that weight off him. Give it to somebody else. He's only a tosser, and he'll fall behind, slow everybody down and give me problems.' I did lose one man on the march, with a back injury when he fell onto his radio.

The confusion of combat (often referred to as 'the fog of war') is impossible to imagine. When stories are recounted after battles, of heroism and exciting action, the terrible uncertainty is usually omitted. During the battle, there is only the hope of survival, and therefore little of the sense of continuity that creates an identifiable story-line. Nobody knows when it will end (for them personally or for their unit).

The significance of events on the battlefield only becomes apparent when it is all over, revealing whether the operation was a victory or a defeat – or that it had evolved into something completely different from what was planned. Individuals proceed minute by minute (sometimes second by second) without really knowing what they are doing. In the first hours of a battle, inexperienced troops try to remember what they have been trained to do, at the same time trying to work out what is going on – plus continually hoping they are doing the right thing so as not to let their comrades down.

The confusion of modern battle puts the onus on each individual soldier to make his own decisions. Battle plans change the instant contact is made with the enemy, often leaving each small group of soldiers to work out their own method of achieving the military aim. In the Second World War, the German Army was particularly good at fighting independently in small groups without direction – a philosophy based upon each man knowing the aim not only of his own unit, but of formations two levels above. This philosophy (or principle) is taught to all NATO commanders today under the formal title of *Auftragstaktik*.

For 3 Para the attack on Mount Longdon started with a long diversionary move before last light, walking north for two or three hours (to encourage the enemy to expect an attack from the north) before coming back east again after dark. 4 Platoon were not impressed — and then the fog of war descended. Corporal Kelly:

The thought of walking north for no reason was a bit of a crack-up. However A Company had a ladder and plank, which we all used to cross the Murrell river — rather than getting wet. Then in the darkness one of the platoons cut across another platoon, people following the wrong file and getting mixed up. In the process, our company (B Company) got split up, and for over an hour there was complete and utter chaos. Once we got it sorted out, we had to run to get to the start line in time. As soon as we arrived, we were off, moving forward in the actual attack — which at least prevented people from thinking too deeply about it.

Having regained their composure and crossed the start line in good order, the clarity of the plan was quickly replaced by chaos and confusion:

Everything was going to be so simple. As the initial assault platoon we were going to take the first part of Mount Longdon, and then the other two platoons were going round to clear another bit. However, after 50 metres we walked into a minefield, which changed everything.

It wasn't pitch dark. Once we got out of the shadow and on to a slight ridge line, we could see Longdon. We knew we were in a minefield because Corporal Milne (One Section commander) stood on one. The noise wasn't so bad — just the very bright flash. He started screaming about the pain in his leg. We all went down, then someone crawled forward to give him first aid and morphine. (He lost the leg all the way to the top of his thigh.) The Argentine sentries opened fire, but the fire went over our heads. We didn't know how Milne was because we then advanced, leaving him behind.

Navigation in the featureless terrain of the Falklands was a constant problem for artillerymen, helicopter pilots and even ship's navigators (using radar to determine their position off-shore). Trying to navigate accurately as well as keep men together in the darkness was a nightmare. Sergeant McCullum, a platoon sergeant in A Company of 3 Para:

On the way to our start line at Mount Longdon, my platoon had become disoriented in the darkness. We were in a box formation and somehow our left-hand and right-hand men lost contact with the rest of the company. I knew we'd gone wrong when from my position behind the front sections,

I saw the light of pencil torches as the platoon commander and the section commanders looked at their maps, trying to find out where they were. We were now out in front of the rest of the battalion, who were about to start a night attack, so another sort of fear hit me, sending me sky-high. I rushed forward saying [to the platoon commander]: 'What the hell are you doing? We could be advancing towards the Argentinians! Get a grip!' When we actually arrived safely on the start line, a new sort of fear [of the actual attack] came over me.

The soldiers however were mentally prepared for the confusion that would ensue. The success of the battalion would be determined largely by the decisions *they* made, and by *their* determination. Private North-field of 2 Para, at Goose Green: 'Mick knew what was likely to happen . . .' Having explained the actual battle plan to his section, the experienced section commander had added his own, very basic version of what he wanted from them: '[Mick] told us that regardless of what happened, we were to walk from point A to point B and kill everything in between.' Each man kept inner thoughts, fears and anxieties to himself, concentrating on the job that was about to begin:

We never discussed things like incoming fire, fear or getting hit. I think he [Mick] expected us to do our jobs regardless. If we took casualties we were supposed to carry on to the objective . . . but in fact, if your mate goes down, you go to him.

Before an attack, a unit needs to know the opposition's locations and strengths, both for planning the operation, and more importantly so that they can find and kill the enemy. However, on 26 May 2 Para went south to Goose Green with no accurate intelligence about the enemy they were attacking, plus some information that was wrong and dangerously misleading. The confusion in the mind of every soldier in the battalion was considerable. Chaplain David Cooper:

The intelligence we had about the enemy was minimal – and too highly graded [classified for security purposes] to be given to us! We couldn't patrol forward ourselves [to get our own information] because the SAS were supposed to be in the area. Before we advanced down from Sussex Mountains a patrol of SAS came through from the [Goose Green] area and told us that it would be a piece of piss as there wasn't anybody there!

This incorrect information was duly passed down the chain of command and reached the other ranks in modified form. Private North-field: 'As we marched towards the Goose Green battle, word came down the line that it had been taken by the Royal Marines, and that there were hardly any enemy left. We were just to clear the bunkers and make sure it was all mopped up!' This false information in the event made little difference. The men were well trained and very highly motivated. After all the waiting around, they wanted to get to grips with the enemy, and when that happened, they knew what to do. Accurate information would nevertheless have helped.

Sergeant ———, then a corporal in 2 Para, had been told that civvies from the settlement walked their dogs in the morning, and that if he saw anyone wandering about, that was who they would be. When he came to the base of Darwin Hill, people were visible wandering about, but as there were fifty and more of them, all supposedly walking their dogs, he became suspicious. On reporting he was told, 'No, they're civvies with their dogs.'

Now what would fifty and more blokes be doing in the early hours walking their dogs? I couldn't see any dogs, so after getting as close as I could and seeing that they were wearing military uniform and speaking Spanish, I decided they must be Argies.

Having been scouting in front of his company, the Corporal was concerned about what he should do. The official word was still that they were dog-walking civilians, so he was left to make up his own mind. Some of these men were coming very close to his section position, and two were taken prisoner – they were definitely Argentinian. A third attempted to escape and fight back, so ——— opened fire (the first rounds to be fired in the battle). This caused consternation:

And then I was threatened with court martial for breaking the Geneva Conventions! There was however no doubt about it, and I was the only person in any position to see who they were and what they were actually doing. So it seems like I actually started the battle for Darwin/Goose Green.

Not one of the soldiers who lined up on Falklands start lines had ever been in a similar position before. The experience was totally new and somewhat bewildering. Before setting off, they were at least surrounded by their mates. Once moving, however, they were in unknown territory. They found the battlefield a lonely and strangely unreal place. Private Northfield:

It was dead quiet and dark, drizzling with rain. We lay there waiting for what seemed like hours. I don't remember much until it started to get light. You just couldn't see a thing. It makes it easier in many ways . . . because you can't see anything . . . It's like a blanket. It seemed like for miles and miles, nobody fired anything at all at me. I had no idea of the distance we'd covered. I saw muzzle flashes off to my right, but didn't engage them.

It [the fighting] started off with everyone walking forward in the darkness firing at anything that looked like a trench. I only fired a couple of rounds, and if anything opened up I'd let rip. I have no idea how the platoon was orienting itself [with the rest of the company]. I was aware of L Platoon but none of the others. You're on the ground all the time, so you don't see very far. I just kept in touch with my section, and lost all sense of time, feeling protected by the blanket of darkness – a very false sense of security.

When we reached to the top of the ridge, it was daylight and the shit hit the fan big-time.

Sergeant French:

It's like wearing a blindfold and seeing only orange flashes, some of the flashes firing things at you, and others firing away from you – but you can't tell which. You take any cover you can get, even folds in the ground an inch deep. Stevie Hope was hit a couple of feet away from me . . .

He was the OC's signaller and we'd just crossed the start line. We came under fire and were on the ground. I was lying in this tiny stream, about an inch deep, which was running down my collar, across my chest and out down my legs. It was freezing cold, but at the time it was fucking lovely. No one was going to see me and the fire was going over my head.

I heard these strange sounds; one was like a dentist's drill, and the other like a very fast zip noise – lots of them.

French did not recognize the significance of these noises and so did not understand what was happening:

It was several years later before I realized just what danger I had been in at that time. In battle you don't hear the crack of rounds being fired at you – all you get is the thump as they hit. Two years later, I was an instructor at Brecon, pulling targets up for a demonstration of machine gun fire. From the safety of the butts [below ground, beside the targets] I heard exactly the same sound as that night – the drilling and zipping noises. I then realized that Stevie Hope and I had been in the middle of the beaten zone[5] of a machine gun – with lots of rounds very close to our heads.

The drilling sound was a round entering the ground, and the zip was the displacement of air around our heads. It gave me a wave of fright to think about it – although on the night, I didn't know what it was.

French and Hope were a pair, moving together, covering another pair as they moved forward:

It was our turn to move but when I got up, Stevie stayed down. There was only a small trickle of blood on his face, nothing else. Corporal Lovett (who was later killed) urged me on and said he would look after Stevie. I took the radio off him then moved on. I thought he was all right – just a graze – but he died eight or nine hours later.

Falklands battalions crossed their start lines in an 'advance to contact' – a speculative and cautious closing on the enemy in a well balanced formation from which attacks can be made. The enemy's locations were usually not known in any detail beforehand, so until they opened fire (or men stumbled across them in the darkness) complicated attack plans were a waste of time. Each company and platoon advanced along a given line (at night a compass bearing), keeping within boundaries based on the line of advance. Anybody straying outside the boundaries or off the line could expect to be shot by neighbouring platoons. Once 'contact' is made with the enemy (when he opens fire), the leading sections assess his strength and decide whether to make their own attack. The rule of thumb is that a section may attack a single trench, but if there is an automatic weapon firing, the rest of the platoon must make the attack, with covering fire from the leading section.

It should be explained that an infantry section contains around eight men, including a machine gun team, commanded by a corporal. Three sections working under a platoon headquarters section make up a platoon, and in an ascending pyramid of threes, a company is formed from three platoons, a battalion from three companies (plus a support weapons company that is often split up in war between the rifle companies). Three battalions make a brigade, three brigades a division and so on.

In the Goose Green battle, 2 Para's B Company had to attack a number of Argentine outposts before hitting their main position at Boca House. Platoon Sergeant McCulloch:

Their positions were foxholes rather than proper trenches or bunkers, and the section commanders got on with clearing them out. The weather was bad, wind and driving rain, some support fire was coming in, and the Argentinians held their fire until we got on to them. Their positions were not in depth, so we were able to roll them up. We couldn't work out the layout of the enemy positions, because we could only move within our [platoon and company] boundaries. We came upon dark mounds, with them lying behind firing.

We worked in pairs, clearing anything that came up in front, a few hand grenades and a bit of M-79 [a grenade launcher held rather like a shotgun]. Section commanders controlled it by voice, and I could see it all from 30 yards behind. The PC [platoon commander] was between the front two sections, keeping everyone in line.

We got 'Check Firing' [so as not to be firing on the other platoons as they advanced], then had to wait while the other sections did their stuff. Then the whole company advanced again. There were a few more small pockets of enemy, then we hit their main position at Boca House.

The numbers and disposition of the Argentinians were simply not known. Military arithmetic says that an infantry company can attack a platoon (the attacker requiring a 3:1 superiority), but anything larger, according to the book, requires a battalion.

We'd been told there was a platoon, but then they opened up with .50 cal machine guns which left the GPMGs [only 7.62mm] standing. We had to go to ground, and without mortars or artillery we were stuck for several hours.

Company commander Major John Crosland, knowing that he had to find from somewhere the firepower to defeat the much heavier calibre Brownings, decided to 'misuse' the battalion's Milan anti-tank missiles. Designed at great expense to penetrate Russian tanks head-on, Milan proved ideal for 'bunker-busting'. Sergeant McCulloch:

They were very effective – the enemy producing white flags and running. We then advanced towards Boca House over hilly, undulating ground, two sections in front, one to the rear. The point sections were on top of one ridge, and the others back in the dip, out of sight to each other.

The platoon was effectively split, unable to communicate with each other, pinned down by enemy fire and unable to move:

We were under fire on the ridge while the others were trapped down in some gorse in the dip – for about two hours. We needed smoke [from the mortars] to get them out, and one of our corporals was shot in the face and shoulder. Baz Bardsley won the MM for getting him out. The rear platoons, behind us [exposed] on the open ground, also suffered killed and wounded.

   The Argentinians were using a mixture of Brownings and GPMGs, but were inaccurate. However if their fire came in close you had to get down – you had no choice when the ground was being chewed up in front of you.

   Although we were outgunned, they withdrew and abandoned their weapons, which we found were in very poor condition – rusty, poorly maintained and dirty. They must have had quite a few stoppages. The time they spent getting their weapons firing after stoppages undoubtedly saved us many casualties.

The enemy positions were difficult to locate, and incoming (enemy) fire concentrated on the forward platoons. Private Carter, D Company, 2 Para:

10 and 11 Platoons in front were taking casualties, but even though we were stumbling on trenches with dead Argentine soldiers, not much happened on our central axis. We found the first trench when one of the lads actually fell into it. There were weapons and ammo, all covered in mud, just left there. They'd all bugged out, so we never saw anybody. After an hour or so, we got effective fire on to us. We started taking cover when we heard rounds whistling around us.

As it got light, the paras were at last able to identify the Argentine trenches: 'We could now see who was firing at us and so fired back – usually at ranges of around 300 metres.'

Dawn also enabled Argentine artillery and mortars to bring down observed fire:

There was a vast open space DF'd[6] by the Argies, which everyone had to cross. We tried to stay in some rocks to one side, but when a sniper started on us we had to cross the open bit. Luckily they didn't get their mortars on to us in time and we got across without injury.

We heard that lads in the other platoons had been hit and killed. Then one of our lads tripped over some wires, discovering in the process that we were in the middle of a minefield. It was like a lattice-work of string, connected to anti-personnel mines. We could see them all in the darkness. This lad Spencer was hefty and a bit clumsy, and blundered around tripping over these strings and setting mines off. There were several explosions, but somehow neither he nor anyone else was hurt – we called him 'Boomer' Spencer after that.

They came across the results of the Milan strikes on Argentine bunker positions, and spent time giving first aid to enemy wounded.

The men slipped smoothly into the jobs they were accustomed to doing from peacetime exercises. The real thing was sufficiently like past exercises for everybody to know what to do, but certain habits and misconceptions from those peacetime exercises had to be altered. Private Carter:

Guys found themselves taking cover behind galvanized tin walls – until they realized the bullets were going straight through. On exercise, you get used to walls and fences being good cover, whereas in fact rounds go straight through them.

In training, practising throwing grenades even on a carefully constructed grenade range is a dangerous, fraught business, and can lead to casualties when soldiers panic and drop them. Grenades that fail to explode must be safely detonated using plastic explosive – with the risk that they will go off as the PE is being attached. A battlefield is very different from the controlled safety of a grenade range. In the darkness and among rocks, grenades can easily bounce downhill back onto attackers. On Mount Longdon, the Argentinians were able to roll grenades down natural chutes in the rocks without exposing themselves – chutes which also delivered 3 Para's own grenades back to their throwers (fuses smoking). Getting close enough to bunkers in order to slip grenades through the slots, or throw them through the rear doors requires much more confidence than could ever be generated on a grenade range with peacetime safety restrictions.

Unrealistic practices learned from training exercises persisted; for example Private Northfield:

... like a good mate of mine who threw a grenade into a tent, then tried to hide behind the door. The explosion took his hand off. Now that was funny – throwing a grenade into a tent!

Sergeant French:

We carried grenades fully primed with the fly-off levers in, a couple in each pouch. We also tried out the Argentine ones when we found them. They had a timing thing underneath, so we'd alter it then throw them and start counting, to find out how they worked. I never got it right myself!

The unaccustomed freedom to use any one of a wide selection of weapons led to Argentine weapons being adopted:

We also used Argentine magazines and ammunition [which fitted British self loading rifles], and some of the guys picked up FNS,[7] because you could fold the stock down and fire it on automatic. Me and the OC even tried to get this Browning going, to fire at these bunkers. It was on a louch pole,[8] and we couldn't get it sorted out – thank goodness, because thinking back, there was all hell going on around us, and God knows what sort of reaction it would have caused.

Losing a weapon in peacetime is possibly the most heinous military offence of all. On the battlefield, however, weapons were just tools of the trade – expendable:

I had a 66mm slung over my shoulder, and realized that the strap had broken and it wasn't there any more. In peace, you'd have panicked about losing it, but I thought 'Oh, so what'. Somebody behind me picked it up.

2 Para's doctor Captain Steven Hughes:

I had an SMG which was useless [doctors may carry weapons to defend their patients]. I really should have had a pistol. The battalion had left all the pistols behind [in UK] – something to do with Bisley! I kept trying to lose the SMG – deliberately leaving it lying around, not picking it up. But someone invariably picked it up and returned it to me. Eventually David Cooper got me a .45 pistol from the Argies. All the guys got rid of their SMGs and acquired folding butt FNs – and one guy acquired a GPMG.

Learning about artillery was also a rapid process; on peacetime exercises few infantry ever see it in action, or understand its uses and limitations. One of the harsh realities of war is that artillery shells cannot differentiate between friend and foe, and that in the confusion some inevitably land among friendly troops. The attack on Mount Longdon by 3 Para was planned with artillery on call if needed. Sergeant McCullum:

We were shocked to find that we were being put into a silent attack [without the artillery firing] on what turned out to be an enemy battalion position. We did expect there to be at least a company, but it was a shock to see how well-defended they were.

The silent attack worked well – until a lad trod on a mine and woke them all up. Then all hell broke loose. We were caught in open ground, stuck while B Company took lots of casualties. We couldn't fire because nobody knew what was happening, or where anybody else was.

Fatal mistakes are inevitable in the confusion:

At some stages I think we did fire on our own troops, trying to follow the tracer, the lights . . . and over-shooting. We got stuck too, in a gully with lots of Argentine bodies. Argentine special forces snipers came in with night sights and pinned us down, which is when our artillery came into play with the mortars.

As many soldiers have experienced, the sudden arrival of friendly artillery, although very dangerous, is a godsend:

It was brilliant, not frightening, coming in as close as you could get, almost on top of us. We couldn't tell whose tracer or whose artillery was ours. When the bullets are whistling, rounds are rounds – but it cleared the way, enabling us to go over with very little opposition. I think that's where A Company were let off lighter than B Company, who didn't have the fire support we had.

I had an argument with a marine who'd been on the Two Sisters [45 Commando's battle, 11/12 June]. He reckoned we'd done it all wrong. They'd pounded it with artillery before going forward, taking it with few casualties. Then again, maybe there were less enemy on Two Sisters and Tumbledown [the Scots Guards' objective]? And if we'd used the artillery first, maybe we'd have walked into a really wide-awake enemy, losing more men trying to get to the bottom of the feature? Who knows? That's what the colonel gets paid for.

Everybody was making mistakes – and learning rapidly, in an environment where any error could be fatal. Private Northfield (on Darwin Ridge):

We made a mistake in all walking over the top of the ridge [together]. [When we got over the top] we could see their bunkers on the forward slope of the next ridge; then another mistake was made by someone deciding to move to the left.

Northfield's section came under fire. Three men were hit and seriously wounded. In the process of rescuing them under fire, a fourth man was hit in the neck and killed.

Northfield remained on the crest of the hill, lying behind his machine gun providing covering fire. It was now daylight and he was able to see what was happening around him. For the first time in his military career, he watched a real assault being made by fellow paratroopers on the Argentine bunkers:

I first became aware of the other platoons then, as they assaulted the Argentine trench positions. It was done by the book, three blokes moving up, working together as an assault team.

Without receiving any sort of orders, he prepared to give them covering fire:

It was obvious what they were about to do, so I laid down suppressive fire into the bunkers as they pepper-potted all the way there, covering each other. As they came into the area of my machine gun fire [from the left], I moved it off to the right.

One of them crawled up the side of the first bunker with a grenade, pulled out the pin and from less than five feet away, dropped it into the firing slot. After the explosion, the two others got up and started emptying their magazines into the doorway round the back.

The bunkers were in lines, each one unable to fire in support of the one next door. The paras were therefore able to take out each bunker one by one, rolling them up from the left, coming under fire only from the bunker they were attacking. Slick, well-practised battle drills ensured that once the paratroopers identified an enemy position, everybody knew exactly what they had to do. On this occasion the enemy were not so well-trained: 'We were able to get so close because the defenders were sixteen- and seventeen-year-old conscripts who were keeping their heads down.'

Once the paras entered the enemy defensive positions, they clicked into closely choreographed battle drills. Still under small arms and shell-fire and taking casualties, they were in full force, working with a terrible momentum. Having endured hours of shelling and sniper fire on their laborious approach without being able to respond effectively, it was their turn. They also knew that this was the most decisive and dangerous moment of the attack – when enemy resistance, shell-fire or a counterattack could destroy their cohesion. Maintaining the momentum of the attack and pushing on as quickly as possible was vital.

We didn't take any prisoners, you can't at that stage, they're just a liability. You'd take prisoners later – if there's any still alive. [During the assault] you just have to shoot them . . . You're too busy in combat, in an attack. The adrenalin is going and you push, push, push forward all the time. You haven't got time to think, 'Is this right, is this moral?' The machine is going forward and can't be stopped.

Each trench was grenaded then cleared with rifle fire, killing all the occupants. Although the drills were slick, the paras were surprisingly aware of the human dimension of their actions:

I remember a phos [phosphorus] grenade going into a trench and there was quite a bit of screaming, and I remember thinking, 'That doesn't sound nice'. But war's not a very nice thing and shouldn't happen. When you shoot people they don't just jump up in the air and die. They have a habit of screaming for hours before they die. To hear people screaming and dying . . .

Private Carter:

As we went through their positions we ended up leaping in and finding we were sharing it with Argie dead. We didn't think about this as there would be live rounds coming at us. We'd throw grenades in regardless, so there might easily have been wounded in there already, then we'd get into the trench and if anything moved or moaned you fired until the moaning or movement stopped. It was a pitch black night, we couldn't see a thing, and we worried only about our own section, the safety of our own little team.

During the battle, attitudes towards shooting and killing the enemy were of necessity heartless and pragmatic. Sergeant McCulloch:

We never saw our dead man after he was shot. We saw him get hit, knew he was dead, and then got on with the job. You couldn't sit there and dwell on it as there was too much else to do. We treated the enemy dead with indifference, just dumped them under the hedges for collection.

Men were nevertheless deeply affected by what they did in the heat of battle. Sergeant 'Mac' French:

You cannot possibly imagine the depths to which you descend in war. I shot a man at close quarters on Longdon and in the split second before I pulled the trigger, I wondered if the round would go through him, ricochet and come back to hit me or someone else? And would my comrades recognize the gunflash as me firing, or think it was an enemy gunflash? I even had time to decide that the SLR was too powerful to use – among the rocks. In all this, there was absolutely no question at all about the morals of anything, of taking this bloke out.

It was getting light, a sort of grey dusk, and we were getting towards the end of the battle. He had crawled out of a cave and was no more than three or four feet away. It was close quarter combat, and I had a 9mm pistol as well as my rifle. I decided to use the pistol.

The Argentinian wasn't even a human being, he was an enemy. It was only afterwards that I thought of him as human.

My thoughts at the time, their speed, and my thoughts afterwards and now were completely different. I'm older now, more mature, I've seen my children grow up . . . you can ascribe it to whatever you want. Since the conflict, I've come to realize more that I was wrong to kill people, because killing people isn't particularly very nice whether I do it, or somebody else does. Having said that, if the government sends me somewhere, then I'll do it, but I won't enjoy it. I can live with the conscience, but I'll think long and hard about it and certainly have no bravado . . . I'm not turning into a religious freak; I've always been religious, but I think long and hard now . . .

When he shot this particular man, Sergeant French had been with his company OC, and their signaller had just been killed:

We pushed on, and I came upon the Argentine bloke coming out of the cave. After I fired, I shouted to the OC, 'It's okay, it's me. There's a bloke coming out of the cave.' Too late now, but once again the question comes back to me, was he trying to surrender? I don't know. He was scurrying out, and that's all I saw.

One thing it did tell me, if you are going to surrender, do it before the fight through [the hand-to-hand combat as attackers fight through a defensive position] – or run like fuck! Once you start wading into each other, I think it's too late – no matter how careful of other human beings you are.

Surrenders on the battlefield are tricky, dangerous and fraught with misunderstanding. Sergeant McCulloch:

You had to disregard white flags, because some were surrendering while others continued firing. We shifted fire to the other trenches, but when it came to actually clearing the trenches, you had to disregard the white flags.

Word soon got round the battalion that they were still shooting after white flags. However, after the white flag, they were usually away and running back, so you didn't have to shoot somebody who was trying to surrender. They solved the problem by running away.

They were a funny mixture of determined guys who stayed to fight, and others who just didn't want to be there. At the time, this was perfectly understandable.

In 2 Para at Goose Green, the bush telegraph flashed one particular message to most soldiers with great speed. Private Northfield:

When we heard about the young officer being taken out by some surrendering Argentinians, that pissed us all off. We thought sod it, we're not going to take any prisoners. My own personal opinion is that prisoners should be shot – it's what I would expect if I was surrendering.

Lieutenant Jim Barry had been killed while taking the surrender of a group of Argentinians at the school house – a misunderstanding rather than any particular treachery on the part of the enemy. Private Carter:

10 and 11 Platoons were attacking the school house, and it seemed quite funny at the time. It looked as though they were playing cowboys and Indians, running round the house throwing grenades and shooting anything that came out.

Our platoon commander [Lieutenant Barry] with our section went forward to take the surrender of some Argentinians. When we were twenty metres away, some other enemy opened up with machine-guns, hitting Lieutenant Barry. He fell across the barbed wire fence. Then they used him as a target, cutting him to bits. We tried to use the GPMG, but we were in a dip and couldn't bring it to bear. Paul, the section commander, who was behind me, was hit in the knee and screamed out, and then took two more straight through the head and was killed.

Our 2ic Smudge [Lance Corporal Nigel Smith] then tried to fire a 66,[9] using his left shoulder as the fence was in the way. Although he got the rocket off, its backlash took him in the face and chest, so he was in a bad way. I tried to go back to give him first aid, but was hit in the helmet, so I scurried back into my little hollow. Up front the medic and signaller were flapping, and we had a bit of mucking about . . . Brummy and I tried again to use the GPMG.

A sniper was doing all the damage, from a dip in the ground about 200 metres away. He moved and we saw him. I put half a magazine into him and he curled up like a cat. I knew I'd hit him, so I finished him off with the rest.

I got on to the radio to bring up some reserves – to come into the dead ground to the left, then go through the enemy position. We started getting everybody sorted out, then a Pucara came across. Geordie'd been hit by rounds ricocheting off his GPMG, and had bullets in the back and up his backside. He was bandaged, with his trousers down and a drip shoved up his arse. [When the Pucara arrived] he leaped up and ran for it over a barbed wire fence, shouting that they weren't going to get him this time.

The bush telegraph also broadcast news of the death of Commanding Officer Lt Colonel 'H' Jones. (Even today, his death is spoken of by members of 2 Para using the euphemism 'to go down'.) For the battalion as a whole, the news seemed not to have had much impact. Those few soldiers with access to the battalion command net (the radio frequency on which the battle was fought) heard Colonel Jones at work commanding his battalion and controlling the battle. Most soldiers however were unaware of anything beyond their own platoon or section. Private Carter:

Before the CO went down, he'd been shouting over the radio at A Company to get on with the job. It was expected that he would go over and do something with them, so we weren't really surprised at what happened. Anyway, after what happened to us, we didn't have time to think about his death until the battle was over.

Platoon Sergeant McCulloch:

I told the lads about the CO going down. At the end of the day, the Parachute Regiment is well used to death at all ranks. You just get on with it, and someone else takes over.

Chaplain David Cooper:

A parachute battalion is a bit of a democracy and most of the soldiers felt that the CO should take his chances along with everybody else, that he shouldn't be exempt from the risks. When 'H' copped it, I don't think the soldiers were really affected as whatever happened to him had little bearing on them. They certainly did not feel suddenly leaderless, as their section commanders and platoon commanders were within sight. It made more of an impact on the company commanders, making them realize that it was all getting rather serious.

'H' Jones was posthumously awarded the Victoria Cross for his decisive intervention in the impasse to which 2 Para's A Company had succumbed on his left flank.

A posthumous VC was also won by 2 Para's sister battalion 3 Para, earned by Sergeant Ian McKay when B Company became tied down by a series of well-sited Argentine bunkers and heavy machine gun posts. The confusion and uncertainty of this action is typical of combat situations, and made McKay's bravery and single-minded determination particularly worthy of a VC.

Shortly after crossing their start line, B Company had been halted when Corporal Milne trod on a mine. The men went to ground under heavy fire from fully-alerted Argentine sentries. Corporal Kelly was in charge of the leading section, and found himself standing in the middle of the minefield. There was no choice but to stand up and continue walking, regardless of the incoming fire and the likelihood of treading on another mine. If the lead man was blown up, the next man would have to take over. There was no time to clear a safe route:

We were ordered to continue the advance. As lead section commander, I had to stand up and get going. I tried to see what was in front of us, keeping my head down. Then I looked behind, to the next man. He didn't want to move, saying that he couldn't go on. So I just walked on, and everyone followed in my footsteps.

There was terrible noise, heavy machine guns and so on from the [Argentine] sentries firing, which in fact helped. Had it been silent, walking through the mines would have been terrible.

Military text-books teach that minefields must always be covered with fire, to kill attackers as they pick their way through. The Argentinians' commander had set his defences according to the book — and so forced the paras to change their plan:

From the moment we crossed the ridgeline, we had been in open ground [exposed to the enemy]. They would have mined only the open ground, so I guessed we would be safe (for the time being) once we reached the edge of the rocks. As I crossed the minefield, I knew we had to get into those rocks.

This change of plan came not from the company commander or the CO, but from Corporal Kelly, the NCO there on the spot:

The platoon commander wanted to carry on with the original plan, but I could see that had gone for a ball of chalk. There were bodies all over the rocks; people were taking cover rather than pushing on . . .
   The platoon commander then agreed to get the platoon into cover, so we tucked ourselves into the side of the rocky area and waited while the PC talked with the company commander over the radio. Nobody was firing at us and we didn't know what was going to happen next.
   We met another platoon who told us they'd been taking casualties. Then the PC came back: 'We've got to advance slowly along the side of the rocks, keeping in line with the platoons in the middle.' We [2 section] were to continue as point [the leading section]. He then took me forward to show me the route to take. Then the PC was shot — through the leg.
   Because he was on the slope, the bullet knocked his legs away and he fell over then slid down the slope. He wasn't too bad; nothing had been smashed — just a flesh wound — but high up in the thigh so he couldn't walk. He was in pain. We got him back, sorted out his wound, then I crawled forward again to have another look. There was a lot of fire. I got a gun team forward, but all you could see was muzzle flashes — nothing definite.

This was a moment for inspired determination — firstly to work out what action should be taken (which in the confusion was not at all clear), then for somebody to have the guts to actually do it.

Our sergeant [Ian McKay] had taken over command of the platoon. There was a 25-metre gap which we had to cross. After ten minutes or so, he set off [with four others] to find the way. He never came back.

McKay was killed attacking enemy trenches.

That left me and one other section commander with the rest of the platoon this side of the gap. We tried all ways to contact McKay — radio, shouting . . . then decided that he wasn't coming back.

One man did come back after about half an hour. He'd taken cover behind a rock, knowing Argies were still in the trenches, keeping quiet when we called, then eventually crawled back to us in a state of shock. He thought he'd seen McKay go down – away on the right-hand side. The enemy trenches were in shadow, dug in at the base of the rocks so he wasn't sure. He said that the first time the enemy had opened fire they'd not seen them. They'd waited until the last second [still trying to locate the enemy positions] as more fire erupted from the darkness in front of them.

Of the others with Sergeant McKay, Corporal Bailey got through, past the trenches into a small gully – and was wounded. Another 'Tom' (Private James) got through, but became stuck in a cleft in the rocks between the trenches and us. There were five or six trenches occupied by enemy near and above him – so close he could hear them talking. He knew that we'd be coming through, so he kept his head down and hoped for the best.

The company commander sent up another sergeant to take over the platoon, then we formed up and went across the gap together. Another platoon fired in support of us – the fire co-ordinated over the radio. They were above us, firing at the heavy machine guns, the rounds coming in over our heads. We were able to shout to each other, it was so close.

We ran as fast as we could move. It was light enough to be able to pick your way across. I was now doing the platoon sergeant's job, so was in the rear of the platoon. We'd by-passed the trenches, but as we went by they opened up at us side-on. Most people were hit at that stage, [ending up] lying within about ten metres of each other. I was coming across last, with nobody to either side. Our machine guns were firing, with lots of fire coming from all directions – and loads of noise. After twenty or thirty metres, a man went down in front of me so I went over to grab him – to keep him in line with the rest. It was dark, and I didn't realize that he'd been shot. As I got to him, I felt as if I'd been kicked in the back and side. I tried to stand up but my legs just gave way. I rolled down, and thought 'fucking hell' and then it started burning . . . inside us. I lay there for a bit . . . everyone had realized we were being hit and that we had gone to ground.

The heavy machine gun was the main problem. It was dug into a really well-made sangar [fortified trench position] about 100 metres away and we just didn't have the fire power to take it out. Our GPMGs didn't make any effect on it and we'd used all the 66s [anti-tank rockets] on sangars we'd already taken out. The platoon commander was trying to find out what was happening and where the fire was coming from. Once he'd done that, they went off to take the trenches out. There was no problem. The enemy trenches were in a line and so all they had to do was roll them up, one by one.

In the moment he was shot, Corporal Kelly ceased to be an effective soldier, and became a casualty – a liability. He could not walk, and his war was definitely over.

Battles have strange lulls and seem illogically paced, so that individuals are never certain even at the end, whether the action is over or not. Tiredness affects everybody throughout, subtly reducing their effectiveness; at the time high adrenalin levels may make individuals unaware of this. The desire to sleep only really catches up with people once their adrenalin levels have dropped – when the battle (or at least the danger) really is over. Hunger, however, can overcome better judgement. Private Northfield's section believed the Goose Green battle over:

We'd found a tin of Argentine spaghetti, and after sorting out some enemy ammunition [to use], we were sitting on a bunker eating this can. A sniper started up on us, so although we were more interested in the spaghetti, we had a look round. There was movement in a nearby bush, and a long hedgerow to the right.

Our section commander walked straight out towards the bush, covered by me [on the machine gun]. He ordered the figure in the bush several times to put his weapon down and come out. There was more movement so the sniper got blown away with the GPMG. There was further movement in the hedgerow, so I fired in there too. Afterwards we counted fourteen stiffs . . . We were right beside the main gate to Goose Green. After the firing, a lot of artillery and other fire came down on us, and we realized that, contrary to what we'd been told, there was a lot of Argentinians in the place.

The OC asked me if I could locate another sniper that was pinning us down, by sticking my head out of cover to see. I said, 'No fucking way' – a 7.62mm round really ruins your day.

We'd heard rumours of napalm being dropped by the Argentinians. Just near us, a Pucara piled into the ground – strangely with no flame or explosion. It just crumpled into the ground, as if in slow motion. I was supposed to be watching my arc with the gun, but I couldn't keep my eyes off it. I wondered whether he'd ditched his napalm first.

The battle then suddenly seemed far from being over:

We were hiding behind some bunkers and the Argentine 105mms [howitzers] didn't seem to be able to go low enough to get us [firing at minimum ranges], their shells exploding over the top [behind us]. Two Chinooks and seven Hueys [Argentine helicopters] flew over the mountains behind us. We'd been told that there were two thousand Argies in Goose Green, and I knew that there could be a company [80 or more] in each Chinook and fourteen men in each Huey.

For the first time, Private Northfield felt fear:

The rest of the time the battle was too fast-moving for me to be worried, but I'd just had a letter telling me my wife was pregnant. I thought then, that being in the middle of this lot, I wasn't going to see the child . . .

Once the battle really was over, people had the time to start the process of assimilating what had happened to them. It would take time even to begin to understand the nature of the experience they had just survived. Private Carter: 'We had time just to sit and think it through . . . to get used to what had happened. It really hit home, the friends we'd lost.' The section were mostly dead or wounded. The commander (Carter's mentor and friend) Corporal Paul Sullivan was dead. Carter had to find another unattached soul to be his 'buddy':

I teamed up with another guy, and we persuaded ourselves that we'd get through alive. The platoon had to be reorganized, by our platoon sergeant. A new second lieutenant came in [to replace Lieutenant Barry]. In fact the sergeant looked after the platoon, which was reduced [from three] to two sections. I found again, that I didn't know anybody.

Padre David Cooper: 'We were dazed and shocked, with no humour, nothing to say. We were numbed, no feelings amongst us.'

Even after battle, the danger remains. For 2 Para, cleaning up the battlefield and getting Goose Green back to some semblance of normality was a dirty and at times distressing task. A serious accident with a dump of artillery ammunition (see Chapter 10) – brought death once more. They were vulnerable to Argentine air raids, and after moving to Fitzroy, they were witness to the bombing of RFAs *Sir Tristram* and *Sir Galahad* – then rescuers of the maimed and severely burned survivors.

The experience of 2 Para in the Falklands is unique in that they alone of all the units fought two consecutive, full-scale battles. No British unit has done this since the Korean War. Their Falklands campaign has been compared with the levels of fighting seen in Normandy in 1944, before and during the fight for Caen. Whether or not their experience (with modern weapons etc.) can sensibly be compared with anything in the Second World War is debatable. Nevertheless, their attitude towards going into battle a second time, and their performance in that second battle are of very great significance. After Goose Green, 2 Para expected other units to carry on with the fighting. Chaplain David Cooper:

Still being a part of the battle, our feelings were numbed. We were tired, happy to see friends, very close to each other – but with an increasing foreboding. I told the 5 Brigade commander [Brigadier Wilson] that it was somebody else's turn other than 2 Para to earn medals. Before the *Galahad* was bombed [conveying the Welsh Guards from San Carlos to Bluff Cove], there was a marked reluctance to do anything else until some other unit had done their bit. After the *Galahad*, everyone became very impatient to get the job finished, to stop hanging around . . . messing about. Left to the crap-hats, it would never get finished. It seemed at that stage as if nobody else had done anything much. And *Galahad* was clearly an Argentine victory.

2 Para's doctor Steve Hughes:

After Goose Green everyone was pretty shot away. The whole battalion had been through an experience that they'd never expected. For three or four days everyone was just ticking over, the battalion's lights were on with nobody much at home.

Then we started snapping back into a more normal semblance, realizing that we'd been through an experience that very few others had been through. There was a very close feeling about the battalion, of being tightly bonded together by the experience.

The whole battalion became xenophobic, mistrustful and almost antagonistic towards others:

Outsiders could come and visit, but they were made to feel that they were intruding on the family – be they brigadiers or whatever. We were polite, but you were either part of the battalion, or you were an outsider. There was 'Them', and 'Us'.

The military machine had come to a stop, then with time, it got going again. Discipline never broke down at all, but was much more relaxed and informal – except to outsiders.

Julian Thompson, 3 Commando Brigade's commander, recalls visiting the battalion at Goose Green, to be greeted by a loud and challenging shout from the far side of the settlement from a member of the battalion who was not prepared to be ignored: 'I am saluting you, sir!' Thompson commented that he was under no illusions as to who in fact was doing the saluting as he returned the compliment: 'I'd never seen such a gungy, scruffy, dirty group of individuals – but they were all seven feet tall.'

Hughes realized that the war was not yet over. The battalion moved to Fitzroy:

. . . where the real medical problems started – due to diet. D & V [diarrhoea and vomiting] became common, and people went down with trench foot – who had to be bedded down. People were seriously and noticeably losing weight and the lack of fresh rations was causing skin infections. The attitude was very much that, 'We've done our bit in this war. It's somebody else's turn now.'

Then when the *Galahad* disaster occurred and all these burned guardsmen were brought off, the guys realized that the guards did not know what it was all about – innocents in a theatre of war . . . They just didn't know the rules. The innocents had paid the price – it wasn't their fault, but that was what had happened. A resolve came over the battalion. They were the ones who knew how to do it. Because they knew the rules of the game, they felt it was up to them to finish it – even if it meant paying the price a second time.

This new-found resolve restored the battalion's sense of purpose. After the Goose Green battle they had been coasting, cushioning themselves with the idea that they had done their bit, a nice thought which, deep down, most of them knew was not going to work out.

They knew exactly what to expect. They'd stuck their fingers into the electric socket once already and knew what it felt like – and now it was up to them to do it again. It was in the 2 Para mentality to accept that a dirty job needed to be done, that they had better get on and do it. Everyone became moulded back together again, to get the job done with quickly and get off home.

Private Carter:

When we heard we were going back in again, morale took a bit of a dive, but it all went so quickly that we didn't have time to think. We were shitting ourselves from diarrhoea, and I was so tired they nearly left me behind sleeping under a covering of freshly fallen snow.

Sergeant McCulloch:

We were surprised that 2 Para were pushed back into it so quickly – before other units had done anything. Again we just cracked on.

The battalion started preparing for another battle, going through the routines yet again:

We had people with frost nip [mostly in their toes]. Guys had been taking boots off Argentine dead to replace their own crap British boots. We zero'd our weapons – and found ourselves collecting up the brass afterwards! – a conditioned reflex from peacetime training [when spent cartridge cases are handed back into the stores for re-use].

They had learned an enormous amount at Goose Green:

Second time round we were much more relaxed. What you get taught in training are just drills only, to be massaged to suit the position you are in. On the first start line, before Goose Green, we were very quiet, not a word, very serious. On the second start line, before Wireless Ridge, I sat and had a cup of coffee and several of the lads had a fag. We were in dead ground to the enemy, so nobody was getting excited about it. It was very relaxed, but efficient, with everything happening as it should. We knew what was coming, like once you've jumped from a balloon the first time, you know what to be scared of the second time.

Sergeant 'Mac' French of 3 Para watched the show from Mount Longdon:

They tried going over the top first, but the incoming fire was too heavy, so they went back behind the peat banks and waited for more artillery to soften them up. All along the peat bank, little lights came on as the lads made a brew while they waited. Compared with what you get taught at Brecon, no smoking, fires or lights at night, here was the reality. Battle-hardened troops knowing that their lights would not be visible to the enemy, human beings deciding to take every opportunity to have a brew.

Private Carter:

We didn't know what to expect at Wireless Ridge. All they said was that we were attacking an unoccupied side of the ridge that needed to be secured. One lad fell into a stream that night, and it was so cold we all huddled together. Two of us spent the night running up and down a hill to keep warm.

The next day, we couldn't actually see Wireless Ridge. We had Orders, then marched forward. We were told there were trenches with enemy, but were given no idea of how many. We were a depleted unit, but much better than we'd been at Goose Green. We were more confident, plus we had two light tanks and the mortars had been replenned.

It was freezing on the start line. Everyone was jumping up and down to keep warm, looking at the lights of Stanley. We assumed that we'd have a clear-up job to do, against conscripts; that it would be easier than at Goose Green. The Argies would know what had happened at Goose Green, and so we thought they would kick-out fairly early. [After crossing the start line] we moved into a rocky area, shouting each other's names as we went round corners. We found an enemy radio on channel, still talking. Grenades then [small arms] rounds went into each trench, Argies cowering in the corners.

At Wireless Ridge, 2 Para had full artillery support, which greatly reduced the enemy's resistance. Unfortunately, in the latter stages, confusion over locations led to disaster:

We asked for [artillery] support, then got four artillery rounds amongst our own lads. We heard the fire orders, then the FOO [Forward Observation Officer] scream 'Check Firing'. All we heard was the whistle as they came in. [One man was killed.] They then put up a load of illum [illuminating rounds: flares under parachutes], so we had to walk across open ground with it burning overhead. The FOO was public enemy number one.

That was when Fred Slough, my mate, was hit, rounds in the body and out the back. He was alive, got first aid from our medic and the stretcher bearers took him away, so we assumed he was going to be all right.

(Private Slough in fact died.)

The confusion extended also to the paras themselves:

We were out in the open on a limb, and it looked like 10 and 11 Platoons were shooting at us. We asked the OC to come over and check our position. He bimbled across seeming oblivious to tracer all around him, then wandered back. We thought, 'Silly bugger'.

Then our platoon commander stood up, shouted to everyone to keep down and was knocked over himself, hit in the leg. He was screaming and shouting, but when the medic stripped him off there was no wound, just massive bruising where the round had hit his ammunition pouch.

Sergeant McCulloch found the Wireless Ridge battle more straightforward than Goose Green:

Once we got the word to move, we got on with it and the time went very quickly. Second time, we were attacking a feature we could actually see, with much better visibility. It was a noisy attack. They'd been hammered by the artillery for quite some time before we went in, and having seen the conditions they lived in, we knew they wouldn't be very efficient. We sat and watched it go in, ground burst mixed with airburst, which we wouldn't have liked to be under. It gave us a lot of confidence.

We could see some of the enemy positions, but because others were dug in under peat banks, and so were not silhouetted against the sky, we didn't see them. We had to sweep back to find the ones we'd missed, which gave us the most dangerous moments of that attack.

Once we'd gone firm, the Argentine artillery started firing at us. Their groundburst shells went into the peat about nine feet, absorbing most of the impact. For D Company up in the crags, the rounds exploded on the rocks, which was very much worse.

We took one casualty on the attack – an exposure case. We had to cross a stream, and one young lad, Carroll, slipped in. I looked round to find him vanished, submerged up to his helmet. Lucky he didn't drown. We couldn't do anything for him, so by the time the battle had finished he was a serious exposure case – and we casevaced him. Falling in the river had seemed amusing at the time – but actually wasn't very funny.

When their battles really were over, everybody was deeply affected by the experience. Private Carter:

After a whole night of thinking about it, the next morning we walked into Goose Green. The carnage I saw that morning really brought home to me how awful war is. Coming through the positions that had held us down, you could actually see Argentinians with half their heads missing, arms and legs off. They just stare at you, as if they're not dead – only they are. All the way, bodies were littered everywhere. The troops had got a tractor and were slinging them on to the back, guts hanging down . . . without actually being there and experiencing it, you can't actually describe how terrible it is.

The most terrifying moments were hearing artillery rounds coming in, and knowing that there was absolutely nothing you could do about it. You tried to find some protection somewhere, a rock or whatever, everyone leaving their weapons everywhere. Nothing else mattered, you couldn't do or think of anything else. Regardless of what was happening, you had to get into cover. Tracer fire coming towards you at night is frightening too, it looks like it's all coming for you.

There were many amusing times too, some of them completely crazy, in the middle of a battle . . .

Sergeant French:

It was very interesting seeing how everybody turned into machines after crossing the start line. It's not a natural state to be in — when you start killing. We're not put on to this earth to do that sort of thing. Anybody who tells you it is natural is either lying or they've got something wrong with them.

Once we'd got the taste and flavour of the battle, we turned into different people. And once it was over, we came back out of it again. The pitch of excitement is high, and some people didn't really come out of it fully — even months or years later. Several left the army and became mercenaries in Africa, to try and get the taste of it back.

Private Northfield:

Some people act over the top, even in the context of war, with unnecessary waste of life — like putting a 9mm pistol to the head of a sixteen-year-old boy and pulling the trigger. This extreme sort of thing didn't happen very much, but it wasn't simply caused by the death of the officer [Lieutenant Barry] — it was there in some people anyway.

I was eighteen years old, straight from training, very Parachute Regiment, filled with aggression — and *at the time* it didn't bother me.

8

DOING BUSINESS III –
AIR WAR

War in the air is a purely 20th-century phenomenon, which has in many ways remained unchanged since the beginnings of the Royal Flying Corps in the First World War. One particular aspect, the disparity between the small number of aircrew (mainly the officers) who fight the war and the large numbers of ground crew who service the aircraft, is even more pronounced today. Most people in flying units are not therefore risking their lives in combat, nor are they being exposed to the horrors of the battlefield. They live busy and sometimes nerve-racking lives, particularly when waiting for aircraft to return from missions, but unless their airfields are attacked, they remain remote from the fighting.

Throughout the Gulf War, RAF Tornado squadrons flew missions deep into Iraq. Initially these missions were flown low-level at night, skimming under enemy radar to attack strongly defended air force bases. Many of these missions delivered JP 233, an airfield denial weapon containing cratering bomblet charges and anti-personnel minelets that can only be delivered from low-level. These missions proved terribly vulnerable to anti-aircraft attack ('triple A') and aircraft were shot down whilst running a gauntlet of dense and terrifying flak.

The Tornado ground crews, however, were living lives that, after the first four days of the air war, were physically very much easier than on peacetime exercises. As the war proceeded, they found themselves doing exactly the same work, but at a greatly reduced rate – and a degree of boredom set in, particularly for the ground crew. The disparity between the aircrew's almost daily exposure to intense danger, and the experience of their ground crews left behind at base could not have been more pronounced. In the early days of the deployment to the Gulf, three British crews were lost in quick succession while training. One Tornado crashed into the sea, two on to the land – which had the salutary effect of focusing everybody's attention. The training itself was virtually identical to that of peacetime, with the exception of air-to-air refuelling, which had to be practised – along with electronic warfare drills. Most of the physical flying around the countryside was what they had been practising anyway in day-to-day training.

Aircrew went to the Gulf expecting to fly low-level at night – which is virtually a solo mission, each aircraft flying on a separate route, only grouping together over the target. Even during the war, night low-flying practice was not permitted in the UK, so crews relied on the experience of previous training stints in Canada – particularly their annual three weeks of night low-level practice at Goose Bay, Newfoundland.

The Tornado is an 'electric jet' with complicated electronics that do not like water. The extremes of desert climate provided dust, sand and heat and torrential rain. Each aircraft was well-protected from enemy attack as well as the elements in purpose-built shelters. When waiting on the ground, blistering summer heat warped Perspex canopies and made life very uncomfortable for crews. In the first weeks of August 1990, in temperatures of 30 and 40 degrees Centigrade, pilots were unable even to walk to the planes wearing NBC (nuclear, biological and chemical) kit – one at least collapsed on the tarmac – but by January, when offensive operations started, the weather had cooled down considerably, to something like pleasant British summer temperatures. (Once in the air, Tornado's air conditioning allows pilots to set any cabin temperature they like.) So during the actual air war, which took place in the winter months, heat was not a problem, although the ground crews (particularly the armourers) had hard physical work to do in preparing the aircraft between missions. However, compared with a peacetime Europe Taceval (tactical evaluation exercise) in which aircraft must be completely turned around at least three times a day in three hours, the Gulf work-load was light. After the first four days of the air war, ground crew were doing only one turn-around a day.

Living conditions between the different squadron locations varied. Some airmen returned from 'work' wearing their civilian clothes, to four-star hotels and sun loungers beside the pool. The Scud missile threat kept others inside their hotels, while yet others lived in the desert, in Portacabins that flooded when it rained. Going to war each day from a hotel was generally regarded as a bizarre unreality that further exaggerated the strangeness of what they were actually doing.

When RAF personnel were initially sent to the Gulf they had been promised three-month tours. One month before the 15 January deadline imposed on Iraq by the Allies, most of the experienced people were sent home and replaced by an almost entirely new batch of ground and aircrew (who then fought the war), upsetting both training and the expectations of everybody concerned.

During the initial deployment, the first batch didn't have much time to worry, but the second lot, having been warned off for the changeover several months ahead, had plenty of time to get anxious.[1]

There was also a group of people in the UK designated as Battle Casualty Replacements, to take over from those killed and injured in the war. These people were continually on stand-by, going in to work each day not knowing whether they'd be back home in the evening or going to war, a process they had to endure three times a week. 'At least in theatre [of war] you knew where you stood.'

For every person involved in the Gulf crisis, the threat of chemical and biological warfare was a constant nightmare. The failure of this threat to materialize did not reduce the stress and anxiety it induced. Units reassured themselves that they were both well-trained and well equipped. Good NBC environments were set up – in some locations freight containers with air-tight 'Porton liners' in which aircrew could live between missions if their aircraft site were to be contaminated by chemical or biological strike. Intelligence assessments of the capabilities of Scud missiles with chemical or biological warheads were reassuring: 'Each Scud would take out a tennis-court-sized area. As the airfield consists of lots of tennis-court-sized areas, we reckoned that the incoming threat was not great.'

The actual experience of working in NBC equipment in an imagined contaminated environment was very familiar from peacetime exercising; every pilot and navigator had flown in the AR-5 ('rapist's hood') respirator, preceded by many sweaty hours of practice in the simulator. Flying in full NBC protection equipment was very uncomfortable, and very different from normal flying: 'like running up hills carrying a sack of potatoes'.

Before the air war actually started, the locations of targets deep inside Iraq were withheld from all but the few specific people who actually needed to know them in order to do their jobs. At Tornado location Tobruk only four people knew what was going to happen once the deadline was reached. The rest simply were not told.

Freed of worrying about specific targets or missions, aircrew spent the waiting time learning the evasion tactics for every missile that the Iraqis were thought to have, and the drills and counter-manoeuvres if 'locked up' by their various air defence radars. There was surprisingly little low-level night flying practice, probably because at night in the computer-controlled Tornado, pilots are able to do very little throwing around of the plane – making night low-level dull by comparison with day low-level. Apart from practising anti-radar and missile evasion, flying training consisted of simulated bombing missions. The F3 Phantom air defence aircraft at Dahran, however, did continuous operational combat air patrol from the beginning of the RAF's deployment until the end of the war. This entailed having four aircraft in the air for twenty-four hours of every day – all without firing one single shot in anger. Not surprisingly, 'The F3 crews got very pissed off.'

As in any war, uncertainty played a major part in the psychology of every airman. Even after all the practising and intelligence, nobody knew what was actually going to happen. Naturally everybody had their own ideas, but nobody knew anything for certain. In particular, the expected threats to aircraft turned out to be entirely different in reality. The surface-to-air missiles that were expected to cause problems were taken out by the early raids, leaving only SAMs that everybody understood how to deal with. 'In the end it was triple A – a very old-fashioned threat that nobody had thought would be a problem. Bullets were no longer supposed to be dangerous!'

Around 12 and 13 January aircrew were told of some targets, and how the strikes were to be made. On the Sunday (13th) the complete air strike plan was revealed to squadrons. Also on the Sunday, Dahran Tornado base lost a crew while training in the desert in Oman:

In a way it was the best thing that could have happened. Everyone rode straight through it – emerging from being told about the disaster as if they'd just been told the tea money was going up. It prepared them mentally for what was going to happen – and when we later took losses over Iraq the aircrew coped with it very well.

The deadline for Iraqi forces to withdraw unconditionally from Kuwait expired at midnight on the 15th – the Tuesday. Everyone was ordered into the squadrons at 0900 that morning. The crews were briefed, drew their maps, read through all the intelligence reports related to their routes and target locations and the planes were prepared. Then the crews were stood down, but told to be airborne by midnight.

On the night it was a cock-up. Some crews were not due to fly until 3 and

4 in the morning. By the time they were stood down it was too late for any of them to take sleeping pills – so the war started with everyone shattered.

The first few missions took the Iraqi air defence by surprise. Iraqi planes were seen crashing and on fire, and some aircraft were 'locked-up' (tracked) but not actually hit by Iraqi missiles. When some raids arrived at their target airfields, they found landing lights still on and Iraqi aircraft on the ground taxiing. They dropped their bombs, the lights went off and the anti-aircraft fire started. The last few aircraft in some raids had light triple A coming up at them, but as each of these earlier missions was of only four aircraft, this was minimal. On their return, the aircrew were 'euphoric but shagged-out, saying that it was easy'.

The second wave went off an hour or two later. The Iraqi air defences were fully alert, so they were shot at and returned to base talking not about how easy it was, but about triple A. At first the Iraqi fire was inaccurate, but they learned fast, to the extent that on the evening of the 17th (Thursday) the early evening wave returned from their sorties saying it was 'horrendous'. Several squadrons noted a marked difference in attitude towards triple A between the crews who had flown missions and been shot at, and those who had not yet been exposed. After three days' intensive flying, tiredness was affecting everybody. One typical squadron leader confessed that 'by the end of the third day I was completely shattered, having flown three missions with another three aborted.' At another base: 'On the first day, my boss, after being dragged in at 0900 the previous morning, flew a straight 38 hours. By the third day he was knackered but wouldn't sleep when he should have done. I was a bit disappointed at him for that.'

After the first four days (17–21 January 1991) when everybody flew every day, it was realized that the British Tornados were flying more than anyone else in the Allied air force. The Tornados were told to back off, going into a comparatively relaxed routine in which crews flew every couple of days, 'which pleased them because they didn't get shot at so much, but led to the ground crews getting bored.' The Tornados were flying at night, so the plane would be serviced on landing by the night shift, leaving the day shift with literally nothing to do – which they became unhappy about. The boredom forced some squadrons to change the shifts round for the sake of their day shift ground crew's morale, which had not been the original intention.

The daily routine for aircrew was much the same as for peacetime flying – except that they spent longer planning their missions. In peacetime they would have come in from the sleeping accommodation three hours before flying, fly for four hours, then after debriefing sleep for twelve hours, time in which they also had to eat, wash and wind down. But because they spent a full eight hours planning their sorties, they ended up short of sleep. Sifting through the masses of rapidly changing intelligence took much of the planning time, which as the triple A threat grew, became progressively more important.

In the planning process, a wing of four aircraft (the 'four ship') would be given an Iraqi airfield as its target; aircrew would select their own DMPI (desired mean point of impact) and work out attack tracks for each plane. The Iraqis surrounded their military airfields with concentric rings of triple A, the prime ring being on the airfield perimeter some four miles across, with larger outer rings of triple A stations. As the planning proceeded, the intelligence changed, sometimes forcing plans to be revised. Each member of the four ship worked on different aspects of the plan, a last detailed briefing session was necessary to then pull the plan together, after which the crews would go to their aircraft – with an hour to spare before take-off. They put on flying kit, and had a last chat with the intelligence staff. In most squadrons, their final preparation was as they left the HQ, in front of the 'War Lord's' desk (the senior aircrew officer, who ran the squadron but did not fly, while its actual commander concentrated on flying missions). The War Lord checked they had their codes, morphine, pistol and ammunition, 'trying to draw them in on themselves to concentrate on the mission. You'd get the odd quip, then they were off, to the bus.'

They had already memorized emergency RVs for helicopter pickups, the times of the Search and Rescue satellite passing overhead and so on. Then they were dropped off along the flight line, where they would sign for their aircraft from the engineer, check its weapon load and get in, a full hour before take-off – twice the usual time. They would start up and do the checks. If the aircraft was faulty, they would be given a spare plane, so that after 45 minutes there would be four planes running with good weapon loads ready in every respect to go. On most squadrons there were ten spare planes for the four that went out on missions. Then they would taxi off, reporting up over the UHF radio link with the words 'Target check one, two, three, four' and be gone into the warm desert night. The next anybody at base would hear from them would be at the very end of the mission, when they radioed in saying, 'Target check' as they landed.

For the aircrew, each mission started gently, transiting at medium altitude to the tanker which was flying an hour or less from the border. They would refuel in mid-air, at the same time moving towards the Iraq border so as to be full at their drop-off points. They would then descend to 200 feet before crossing the border, having checked their low-level flight equipment carefully. If they found that the terrain-following radar or warning gear failed to work they would turn back. In the first few days, the abort rate was fairly high. Transit across Iraq to target was quiet, the route designed to obtain regular updates from known points on the ground so that the navigation equipment would be working accurately once they reached the target. Flying at low-level is entirely automatic, the sophisticated autopilot and terrain-hugging radar doing all the work. Pilot and navigator monitor progress and watch for signs of detection or attack.

The excitement tended to be over the target. The first guy through was usually okay but [aircraft numbers] seven and eight were getting shot at in a bad way. They'd do 450 knots through to the target, then two minutes out put the after-burner on, accelerating up to 550 knots attack speed. They'd turn it off so that as they approached the target they were just beginning to slow down, then release the autopilot and fly manually straight and level for 20 seconds before bomb release – which is when they got seriously fired at by the triple A.

This 20 seconds flying manually straight and level was a serious problem – which had been known and talked about in crewrooms and bars for years. The bomb aiming system will not work unless the aircraft is flown in this fashion, exposing the crew to maximum danger at the most vulnerable point of their mission. Iraqi triple A had tracer rounds alternating with ball, so the bullets' trajectory could be clearly seen:

The crews were frightened fartless by being able to see the triple A coming up at them, and to an extent it put them off their attacks. But the tracer also marked the interlinking of the Iraqi anti-aircraft defence, revealing safe corridors down which they could fly – enabling them to change their approach to the target at the last minute.

Once they had made the bombing run and dropped their bombs, they ran away low level on autopilot again, calming themselves down before crossing back into Saudi Arabia and pulling up to the tanker for a refuel.

Each sortie worked out as being two and a half minutes of complete panic surrounded by four and a half hours of calm.

In the last minutes, the concentration required to make the drop to an extent cancelled out much of the fear of the triple A fire through which they had to fly.

Tornado is a 'Greenpeace' aircraft; you need 126 switches to be in the right place before the bombs will come off the rails. They're actually designed not to drop in peacetime. If you've been training in peacetime for a practice attack, you've trained not to make that [final] switch – if you do the bomb will come off. So for real, when you do drop the bomb, you've broken the routine, and so stand a good chance of breaking other routines too.

Crew were more worried about getting the switch settings right and successfully dropping their bombs than about the Iraqi air defence or the missile alarms.

It's a big job getting the switches right. During that final run-in, you'd be looking out for visual signs of triple A and the navigator would be watching for missiles and indications of radar lock.

On returning to base, debriefing took 90 minutes, a detailed account of the mission to intelligence staff right down to the colours of the tracer bullets, strobes and any radar illumination they had experienced, the missiles and guns fired near or at them, and the locations and directions of fire. They then completed mission reports, before going back to the living accommodation to sleep. They worked a total of between 12 and 14 intensive hours every day.

They shared villas – two per bedroom, two sleeping on the balcony and two in the sitting room . . . Sleeping was difficult. I'd give them some pills to sleep for five hours or so. Even so, people complained about not being able to sleep.

Two sorties left each location each day – the evening mission returning at 1 a.m., getting to sleep at dawn. They would start work again planning the next mission at around ten the next morning. The early morning sortie would get back in at midday, then sleep through the afternoon before waking in the early evening to start planning.

The 'War Lord' was a key individual in each of the squadrons, ensuring every aspect of the smooth running of the war on behalf of the commander who is actually flying. War Lords are always aircrew themselves, temporarily grounded for the duration of their tour. They know most of the aircrew, and have earned reputations as aircrew themselves that give them credibility with those flying, and the ability to understand the stress under which the flyers were operating.

We knew most of the guys, and had our own reputations from the past. We'd done some hard peacetime training – losing crews in the process which had hit me dreadfully hard at the time. We did worry about them, but you have to roll with it. We lost friends, and didn't even know how many until the prisoners of war were returned. While the war is going on, you can't dwell on it.

I felt dreadfully bad that I wasn't flying, that I'd missed it. They were feeling hard things without a doubt, so my whole object was to make life as easy as possible for the aircrew as I could. If they were being a pain in the arse, the rule was that only me or the detachment commander could tell them — nobody else.

Some aircrew took advantage of this, ordering people to do things, pushing their luck, even being rude. After missions, War Lords would take such individuals aside and 'sort them out'. 'But I felt an over-whelming need to take every care of them that I could.'

The ground crews were in a very different position, almost spectators of the war. They became very sensitive about not being told what was going on:

They thought that one Scud going off at twenty thousand feet would kill them all — which wasn't true. Being deeply involved with intelligence for planning the missions, aircrew were well briefed. It was our fault that we didn't pass intelligence down to the ground crews as we should have done. We were too worried about the tactics and fighting the air war.

One of the main problems with the Royal Air Force in war is that the officers are fighting the war and the boys are only supporting that effort. In the army, the boys are the weapon and so must be kept briefed up.

On one Tornado base, the ground crew became particularly worried about being attacked by Palestinian terrorists. Their living accommodation was on the far side of the airfield, which the Saudi airport authorities refused to allow them to drive across. The result-ant round trip was about ten kilometres, past the local town. The airmen became worried that by regularly driving past this potentially hostile residential area, they were encouraging a PLO reaction — which never materialized. 'In the end we had to issue small arms, which, despite the fact that they wouldn't have been able to use them to fight off a bomb attack, did make them feel better.' Despite facing the same daily journey, the aircrew at this base were not at all concerned with being bombed or shot on the airfield. Compared with the danger they were exposed to on missions, they felt completely safe on the ground. Perhaps the ground crew's feelings of vulnerability stemmed from a subconscious desire to share in the dangers being faced by aircrew?

Ground crew sensitivities required very careful handling:

We had to be very careful what we said — no funny asides, or expression of opinions when someone else was within earshot. The rumours really flashed around the place because of the boys' constant thirst for information.

CNN [Cable News Network, the authoritative American television service] was on all the time, which was a mixed blessing as on the one hand it started rumours, while on the other it scotched quite a few too. Rumours were a real killer.

Once the war started ground crew became too busy to worry — except over whether their crew was going to come back. Each ground crew was allocated to its own aeroplane, around seven men per aircraft with separate day and night turn-around teams of three, plus specialist weapon-load teams to rig the bombs. They looked after their crews really well — having cups of tea ready for them immediately on landing, then as the war progressed, painting the noses of each aircraft (with shark's teeth, names etc., normally a forbidden activity in peacetime).

Fear on the ground varied between individuals and between different groups of people. It was illogical — and because the bases were never hit in any enemy attack, it was not based on any sort of personal experience:

The only frightening thing in war is the unknown — things that you've been unable to think through. The noise of the Patriots turned out to be the most frightening. We knew all about the Scuds — that they were only a limited threat, but nobody knew what Patriot sounded like coming off the rails — and it made a bloody great bang!

I had two girl operations sergeants who were brilliant throughout. Some others [men] were very nervous; for example the clothing store people would be in their respirators if you slammed the toilet door. We had to split them up after a while.

There had been early publicity given to RAF air defence fighter crews' concerns that their F3 Phantoms were older, less sophisticated, vulnerable to the new MiG fighters that the Iraqis were thought to have. In the event these MiGs made no challenge to Allied air superiority, largely because of the initial four-day blitz of low-level, airfield attacks by the Tornados using JP 233 mine and bomblet munitions. After the first four days, Allied air tactics changed. Iraq's MiGs were not engaging incoming raids. A combination of the low-level bombing plus electronic counter-measures (ECM) escort aircraft on each mission had removed the SAM threat. Iraq's medium-level SAM system was discovered to be no better than SAMs used in the Vietnam War; the Russians had clearly not supplied their more sophisticated low-

and medium-level equipment, nor any of their high-altitude SAMs. Raids could therefore fly at medium and high level with impunity.

The stress of low-level bombing and the threat to aircrew from triple A was very great, and during the first four days caused serious morale problems. Having disabled the Iraqi airfields, however, total air superiority had been achieved, and it was no longer necessary to fly low-level towards targets. Crews were spared running the gauntlet of crude but effective gunfire. 'Flying low-level the guys became obsessed by triple A and after four days needed a rest. If we'd carried on we'd have had to slow the sortie rate and change our tactics.' The Iraqi air defenders were only firing at sounds. Every time they turned a radar on, it was blasted by radar-seeking weapons. Nevertheless their triple A was very effective.

They seemed to have unlimited ammunition. [Intelligence calculated that] one airfield on one night fired over 40 tonnes of ammo against four aircraft using 16 guns in the middle of the airfield blasting away to create the comic book 'wall of lead'. It looks terrible at night, coming up at you.

The squadrons were so concerned at the effect of the triple A on aircrew that they completely re-thought their bombing tactics in case airfield denial raids again became necessary:

We could go in small packets [of aircraft] or as ones and twos [rather than eights or more], as well as lobbing in thousand pounders ['stand-off' bombing] on to the anti-aircraft sites to keep their heads down. The Iraqis had listening posts at the border and so after the first days, planes could find themselves under fire all the way in.

The question whether the Tornado crews would have (or could have) continued making intensive low-level attacks remains hypothetical:

By the time we'd thought all this through, they'd stopped us going low-level anyway. The guys were relieved. They'd done around three low-level missions each. The recce crews, however, flew the whole war low-level, on their own doing five hour missions across Iraq. And later in the war we went back to low-level against some targets.

The second phase of the air war was not unlike the Second World War bombing of Germany: freefall bombing of larger targets from medium altitude, around 20,000 feet. The actual accuracy of this effort was little better than that achieved by Bomber Command half a century earlier; 8 bombs dropped from 20,000 feet on to 20 square kilometres of oilfield might hit only one part of the objective, causing an enormous fire out of all proportion to the one or two bombs that happened to fall on to the target. American-supplied laser guided bombs (LGBs) solved the accuracy problem — and constituted the third phase of the air war. LGB sorties had to be planned by 6 p.m. on the day before to fit in with the Americans' administrative requirements:

You could plan the previous day, then come in for the mission four hours early, check the details, brief up afresh then do it, flying at medium level at night. The work rate went down, flying every other day. People relaxed and actually slept. We knew the targets well in advance and it was an easy regime, plus we weren't being shot at. After doing a lot of LGB, the guys got very blasé about SAMs coming up at them, until a number eleven [the eleventh aircraft in line across a target] got shot down, the nav killed and the pilot captured.

The complete absence of any threat, and the relief of the low-level having ended made it difficult to motivate aircrew to the same extent as they had been at the beginning of hostilities:

Changing from the intense environment of low-level, LGB was very benign. There were no enemy planes to shoot at them, and we had a great problem to get the crews wound up into the right frame of mind. This incident did the job for us.

Had the war continued, the weather would have become a serious problem. Winter rain and cloud created difficulties both on the ground and in the air:

The rain made ground work hard, plus in the air having to tank in cloud. And for LGBs, if you can't see the target you can't drop, and for several days they had to return, which got them really bunched up. Two and a half days of solid rain caused lots of problems, particularly at Dahran.

The smoke from oil fires started by the retreating Iraqi Army also restricted visibility and caused all manner of flying and target acquisition problems.

The psychological condition of aircrew in both peacetime and war can often be measured by the number of times they return without dropping their bombs or attacking the target. Because judging whether an aircraft is unserviceable is entirely the responsibility of its crew, unserviceability offers an opportunity to avoid going on a mission: 'This is common even in peacetime — some guys just don't want to fly, and can abort as many as 90 per cent of their flights.' Differentiating between genuine unserviceability and reluctance to fly is never easy. In the Second World War the damning phrase 'LMF' (low moral fibre) was used to label anybody suspected of avoiding operational flying. This was a concern to War Lords in the Gulf:

The crews wouldn't take a plane that had anything wrong with it. Their lives were on the line. When they had to turn back, they were very fed up, especially if it happened a few times on the trot – and I'd find myself wondering if we had a case of LMF.

Later when we started doing the LGBs, we'd have guys who kept missing the basket,[2] and you'd wonder if they were actually capable of doing the job. We did a quiet survey of all the crews, and found out that with this one particular guy it was just bad luck, only three times on the trot. The guy himself was feeling under pressure – missing his one shot at the target at the end of a whole day's work from a lot of people.

I had one guy, however, who kept aborting through aircraft failure – and in the end I had to get rid of him. He did return to the squadron after spending some time with the psychiatrists, and flew medium-level missions all right – although I have to say that I didn't want him back.

Serviceability records indicate that aircrew were very much more inclined to abort the more stressful and dangerous low-level missions than they were later in the war for medium-level missions. On the less dangerous missions, aircrew entered Iraq carrying more aircraft faults than they did in the low-level phase – which makes sense from a practical point of view. Low-level flying leaves virtually no margin for error, especially in navigation and terrain-following systems. Medium-level bombing in the company of other aircraft does not require anything like the same system reliability.

The accuracy of bombing missions was also a cause for concern:

We got paranoid about defending the guys from our superiors, who analysed where each bomb was falling. The crews were very aware of this analysis, and in the LGB phase, debriefs were very different from before. Whereas you could have said what you liked in debrief about your low-level sorties, after saying your piece about the enemy's ECM [electronic counter measures], LGB debriefs consisted of watching the actual film of the attack, and seeing exactly where each of your bombs went.

Despite being able to see exactly where each LGB landed, the process of evaluating the actual damage caused by the raids took a long time. And once the evaluations were made, the time it took to disseminate this information meant that the squadrons only found out how they had done several days after the event:

We got no information about battle damage so we didn't actually know how we were doing – which the guys really needed. And when they did get feedback, they didn't always believe it.

The free-fall bombing phase from medium level caused spectacular oil fires which at night were visible to the crews, who assumed they'd dropped smack on target. In fact the fires were proved to have been caused by only one bomb hitting part of the refinery, with the other seven or so missing — and these were twenty-square-kilometre targets. The crews were not prepared to accept that they were as bad as actually they were — and even now they feel like that.

Throughout the Gulf War, the attention of the senior command (and so everybody else in the Allied air forces) was concentrated on where each bomb landed, the effect of individual weapons and the 'collateral damage' (which might include civilian casualties) that resulted. The aircrew were thus always aware of the effect on the ground that their raids were having — which in past bombing campaigns has never happened. The psychological reactions of the crews to this knowledge was very important:

One crew dropped bombs on to an Iraqi market place, which made me worry that they were going to be upset. We watched it on the film; afterwards it had become a meat market. I was also worried about flak from above. However, in the event there was no reaction at all.

The psychological effect of going to war in a modern jet is minimal — until something dangerous happens.

From inside an air-conditioned Tornado, flying it just like in training, wearing the same kit you've worn for the last fifteen years, you feel very safe and secure. It's your own little comfy environment that you take with you. If you can't see the damage, you can't be affected by it. It's the same flying any aircraft. You lose yourself in the job, doing it as you have done in the past, day in, day out. You know exactly how to do it. In war the aircraft is exactly the same — with very little difference to peace flying. After the second and third days of low-level we started to worry that the aircrew were becoming too tired — and we [on the ground] were also becoming tired. Then we stopped doing low-level and the war relaxed.

Losing a crew was a fairly straightforward business:

After crossing the border, they'd call in on the radio; if they said 'Mission successful all aboard' we knew they were all right. This time they said 'Mission successful, no contact with leader', so we knew something was wrong.

At other bases, there was no radio contact at all with missions after take-off. Ground staff had simply to count them all back in.

Once they landed, I isolated their four ship from the others for a few hours while we did the casualty procedure. We'd work out where the missing crew had gone down, then wait until the time they would have run out of fuel [had they survived] before alerting the search and rescue cell and telling them where the fireball had been seen. The admin was equally simple — a phone call to get the Noticas [casualty notification] system going.

On this occasion the night sortie was cancelled so we were able to go round to the four ship's accommodation for a few beers – the traditional method of seeing them on their way. The replacement crew arrived the same day, and we had the next missions to plan, so life and the war went on. It was fairly certain to us all that they were dead, but until the prisoners were returned nobody knew for certain. None of the squadrons dared to think that their lost aircrew were anything other than dead until the prisoners walked off that plane – like returning from the dead.

The bodies were brought back home and the funerals took place during leave – quite quickly.

I still get very emotional about it even now. If I hear certain music from those times, I still get choked up. The funerals were like normal squadron funerals [when aircrew are killed in peacetime training] – really powerful.

After everything that had been learned from the experience of the Falklands War, Gulf combatants were supposed to have been prepared for the detrimental psychological effects of combat. Senior officers in the RAF do not seem to have taken this aspect of battle preparation seriously:

There was no preparation of any sort for battle shock. My boss (an air vice marshal) actually said, 'Oh, we don't bother with that sort of thing.' I nevertheless tried to prepare myself for whatever might happen – thinking it through so that it wouldn't come as a shock.

We expected to lose an awful lot more men than we did. After the first Scud raid we had a serious de-brief, pointing out who would have died had it been for real. We'd been panicking and got things in our NBC drills wrong. The next time, having been told to slow down and get it right, everybody was perfect. We then kept the men in the picture all the time. They're very intelligent technicians, sharp people who can think it through provided you give them the info. If you don't, rumour takes over.

Before it started I didn't think I'd be going home. Once we gained air superiority, however, we knew we were going to survive. It was very like an exercise, and also almost totally unreal – even when we lost a crew.

When aircrew are shot down, hundreds of miles from their base, the only manifestation of their fate is their absence. There is no twisted, smouldering wreckage or charred bodies to show what has happened:

. . . they didn't actually come crashing through the ceiling in front of us. It was nevertheless hard waiting to lose the first crew. We wondered every night who would be the first? And as the nights went by and it didn't happen, the tension built up.

Another vital lesson of the Falklands was ignored. Young, inexperienced aircrew were weeded out of their squadrons and replaced by older, more experienced officers from other units. Stable, well-practised crews were thus split up at the very time they most needed stability — breaking a cardinal rule of military leadership. The Air Staff's motivation for this is understandable; they hoped to ensure success by using only 'first-team players'. This blinkered attitude denied vital operational experience to young aircrew, but worse, it expressed a totally unjustified lack of confidence in their ability.

As the war proceeded, and particularly after the initial low-level sorties, crews became more cautious. When crews were lost, and battle casualty replacement crews arrived from the UK and Germany, 'The replacement crews were noticeably more prepared to push it at low-level than the guys who'd been shot at already.' Care had to be taken to ensure that crews were not exposed to more danger than they were capable of coping with: 'I decided to rest one crew that had been shot at during the medium-level bombing phase. They had been a bit twitched by a very close missile. I stood them down for a day.'

And as crews flew increasing numbers of missions, some became sensitive to the relationship between the danger they were exposed to and the value of the targets they were being ordered to attack:

Towards the end of the war they were complaining that some of the targets were a waste of time — which as we got to the end of the [priority] target list was inevitable. We'd question the choice of target with HQ, who'd tell us just to get on with it.

The crews would whinge and complain, and when they got back they'd give you rocks [moan] — 'and even the weather was shite, just as we said it was going to be . . .' At the end we were knocking out the secondary airfields that the Iraqis might use if they decided to put in some kind of attack — relatively unimportant targets. If anybody complained we'd tell them that if a few soldiers' lives might be saved by their mission, they should just get out there for four hours and do it.

The stress and continuous tension created different reactions in different people. Irritability was common, as was complaining:

They were very critical about everything; very quick to pick up mistakes by anyone on the ground, by engineers or intelligence. They could make mistakes themselves, but it was never their fault. One or two were particularly barbary [difficult], but you just had to let it ride. You couldn't bother the OC because he'd got his own war to fight.

I told the guys on the ground that the crews would be rude, difficult and unreasonable — but they had to bite their tongues until they'd gone, then curse them all they wanted. As they weren't the ones being shot at, they'd got to make allowances. We'd follow the crews all the way through the flight process to ensure that there wasn't actually any trouble.

The threat of chemical and biological attack never materialized. The fear that certainly existed in the early days of the deployment was neutralized to a large extent by good training in NBC drills, and then by the realization that the feared attacks were simply not going to happen: 'They'd spent Christmas in and out of NBC suits. But by the end people weren't even bothering to put the suits on.'

Throughout the campaign RAF chaplains were in regular circulation. By contrast, although field psychiatrists were in the theatre of war, they appear to have had little to do with the fighting squadrons:

The padres were brilliant, working mainly with the ground crews rather than aircrew. A psychiatrist came once to see us. The padre in Bruggen [back in Germany] for some reason sent us a thousand bibles, which were used to prop up the desks. You can't expose the men to that sort of thing!

You also couldn't help but be moved and lifted by the response of the British public – who sent letters by the thousand, cakes, sweets, footpowder, and even 2000 free Mother's Day cards for us to send home, Valentine cards ... We did manage in the end to answer every letter we received.

Once the war was over, and the need to remain in the desert was gone, there was widespread impatience to pack up and get home as quickly as possible: 'At Endex [end of exercise] plus 30 seconds they all wanted to know "When are we leaving?"'

Air force personnel are only rarely on the receiving end of bombing raids. Phantom navigator Dennis Marshall-Hasdell watched the Argentine air force bombing British shipping in San Carlos Water with professional interest.

I was with the Blowpipe [anti-aircraft missile] operators who couldn't take cover. Understanding how a fast jet attack comes in, I was able to watch the bombs coming off the rails and see the retard chutes deploy before I ducked into the sangar.

In the first of the air raids on land targets, bombs intended for the Ajax Bay and San Carlos Settlement supply dumps landed 40 metres from Marshall-Hasdell's sangar. The attackers were a pair of naval Skyhawks (whose crews he evaluated as 'very good') which flew at fifty feet directly overhead.'The bangs were never as big as I had imagined they would be – perhaps because the soft peat absorbed much of the force. The holes were not as large either.' The All-Clear was sounded by banging tin cans together, and Marshall-Hasdell got out of the sangar into which he had thrown himself and wandered across to where the bombs had fallen to inspect the damage.

Lots of people were milling around and a warrant officer had taken charge. One soldier seemed to have gone batty – and was shouting. As I arrived, a body was being pulled from a trench. A bomb had landed 20 feet or so in front of the trench, and the shock wave seemed to have rattled him around inside it. There was blood coming from his mouth and ears, and he seemed to have become like a piece of jelly – as if every bone in his body had fragmented.

At this point in his narrative, Dennis suddenly cut back over ten years to the first air crash he saw, to tell me about the body of one of his air force friends who had managed to eject from a Phantom as it crashed into a German village (see Chapter 2). It seemed as if he had suppressed that memory until reminded of it by the body of the dead Falklands soldier. Now the two memories existed side-by-side in his mind. He had looked at his friend's body dispassionately: 'I never thought how awful it was – mine was just a reaction of interest. The horror of it didn't really register.' His reaction to the death of the soldier from the explosion of the bomb was very similar; he saw the finality of death, but it was not a horrific thing: '. . . it somehow didn't look that bad.'

Marshall-Hasdell's interest in the activities of the Argentine air force was very strong – seeing the things he'd trained to do himself being put to the test in combat: 'A professional, detached feeling . . .' While walking back from discussions at 3 Commando Brigade HQ on a lovely clear day he watched a pair of Skyhawks drop bombs which landed on the sangar he knew to be occupied by the other members of his FAC team. He was protected from the blast by rising ground, and as the aircraft were 300 yards away, he didn't bother to take cover, watching the bombs being released, then landing and exploding:

As the aircraft came in, I carried on walking, observing with great professional interest. I accepted what was happening, and once I'd seen where the bombs landed, got back ASAP to see if the boys were okay. I found a hole in the front of the sangar, and inside the nearby wool shed, huge bales of wool were blown all over the place. The blast had thrown them about, but thankfully no one was injured.

The reality of the war had not yet touched many members of the ground forces. Only those who had seen what the bombing could do, or had friends killed or injured by it, realized that the bombs could kill them as well. Until that happened to people, the bombing was a diversion from the grim conditions under which everybody ashore was living:

I still felt excited about the whole venture, as probably most others did. Everyone was busy being terribly normal – going about their daily business. Once the trenches are dug, how do you keep people amused and dry? The air attacks were almost an entertainment.

When aircrew are shot down, one particularly traumatic aspect of their experience is to come face to face with the damage and death that their bombing has caused. At high altitudes, bombing has no discernible result and becomes an exercise in accurate navigation and optimistic bomb aiming. The killing that is the essence of all warfare is not apparent, and certainly is not a factor in the perception of aircrew – who concentrate on the demanding technicalities of their job. Air force killing occurs with what the psychologist Robert Lifton refers to as 'near-total separation of act from idea'. Lifton sees weapons technology as being the means by which the American military get round the problem of guilt at killing, keeping the realities of combat and killing at arm's length – the essence of what he terms 'numbed warfare'.

In Vietnam, members of air crew did not experience the 'searing inner conflicts' of ground troops. 'I don't feel like a war criminal. What I was doing is like screwing fuses into sockets.' The air war in Vietnam, against primitive early versions of Russian SAM systems, was a one-sided fight that extended across South Vietnam:

Anywhere in Vietnam is a free drop zone. There were no forbidden targets. If you didn't find any particular targets that you wanted to hit, then normally you'd go ahead and just drop your bombs where you wanted to . . .

This war, from the pilot's standpoint, is a very impersonal war. You go over there and whether or not you believe the goals that the government prescribes for us to fight for or whatever, most of the pilots just go along and figure, well it's a job. You fly. You see flak at night. That's about as close to war as we get. Sometimes you get shot down, but you don't see any of the explosions. You can look back and see 'em, but you don't see any of the blood or any of the flesh. It's a very clean and impersonal war.

You go out, fly your mission . . . come back to your air conditioned hootch and drink beer or whatever. You're not in contact with it. You don't realize at the time . . . what you're doing. It dawned on me . . . from reports of 13-year-old NVA [North Vietnamese Army] soldiers being captured . . . that they had young girls driving most of these trucks that we were destroying up north.

And as far as damage reports that were put out by the pilots, it was a kind of standard joke . . . among the officers . . . this was just a place to advance your career. They tried to get everyone a command of some sort. They made sure everyone pretty well got a medal . . . In my unit . . . it was a Distinguished Flying Cross.[3]

Pilots immersed themselves in the technicalities of their trade, keeping guilt at bay. As professionals, they regarded bombing with professional pride, which they used to overcome their fear of being shot down.

A correlation has been identified between guilt and the altitudes at which pilots bombed. High-level B-52 crews spoke of exercising professional skills and of their technical performance; the suitability of the targets was not something that they would ever question – or even be aware of unless they were shot down and confronted (as many were) with the reality of what they were doing. Low-level fighter-bomber crews like this F-4 pilot, who glimpsed the villagers as they came in to attack, rationalized what they were doing in racist terms that denied the enemy any sort of humanity: 'My way of killing is better than their way [the ground troops]. The Pathet [Lao] and North Vietnamese are a plague. We have to eliminate them. They have no regard for human life.'[4] At the other end of the spectrum of guilt, helicopter gunship crews, who saw the effects on the ground of what they were doing, experienced the same kinds of emotions as ground troops, with some added passions and conflicts.

Airfields for fixed wing aircraft are heavily defended and located well behind the front line. In comparison to the living conditions of soldiers on the front line, life on air bases is relatively normal. For aircrew, flying light, medium and heavy lift helicopters and vertical take-off aircraft like the Harrier in support of the ground battle, however, base locations may be much closer to the front line. More significantly, their operations are integral to the fighting of the ground war, so they are exposed to both its dangers and its horrors.

Helicopter pilots flying casualty evacuation missions have a significantly different perception from that of ground troops. In the confusion of the battle, pilots cannot know where the front line actually is, and the noise of their engine and rotor blades drowns the sound of gunfire. They therefore rely totally on the assurance of ground troops that the landing sites are not under hostile fire. When their mates are dying, ground troops will give such assurances in order to get their wounded flown out without delay. Casevac pilots often land at the front line to find themselves surrounded by shell fire, becoming riddled with bullet holes, while in the air, they are under the constant threat of ground fire and from enemy aircraft attack. All pilots have the additional problem of flying into the war from secure rear area bases. Casevac pilots fly from a relatively safe and normal environment in and out of severe risk, seeing and carrying the carnage of war, forced to trust those on the ground, but nevertheless continually fearful of landing.

The helicopter is the newest and possibly the most significant piece of technology in modern warfare. Flying 'battle taxis' is a correspondingly new dimension of combat experience, as aircrew and air cavalry infantry troops discovered in Vietnam. The speed of Vietnam air assaults (often ten minutes from the receipt of orders to the first troop-carrying 'slicks' touching down at the other end) plucked men from peaceful base locations, pitching them without warning into uncertain and often violent battle. Helicopter warfare was exhilarating as well as frightening and dangerous, an unreal, rotor-buffeted experience. Decades later, thousands of vets still find the distinctive, deep beat of Huey rotor blades evocative and disturbing.

Helicopter warfare was developed by the Americans in Vietnam as the alternative to fighting the Vietcong on their terms. The use of helicopters and heavy fire-power were synonymous, both ways of using technology to fight the war for them. An example of this sort of operation was published in a contemporary internal US Army pamphlet under the heading 'Lessons Learned Vietnam'.[5]

Outside the village of Dien Troung in Quang Ngai Province on 22 May 1967 at 0600 hours, enemy fire pinned down the leading platoons of an infantry company as they attempted to enter the village. The company commander's group, in particular, spent four hours trapped in a peanut patch. It took four hours with heavy helicopter gunship fire support for the company to withdraw, then a further 32 hours of fire from helicopter gunships, plus 13 air strikes, 2000 artillery rounds, and the reinforcement of three more rifle companies before the village was taken.

These operations would go according to the enemy's plan – until the gunships arrived. Firing 20 metres ahead of friendly troops, they were able to suppress enemy fire to allow withdrawal. After dark, continuous illumination and 'Spooky' C-47s with Gatling guns allowed the ground troops to press a close, tight cordon around the village. CS gas was sometimes used mixed with VT[6] for the assault.

During the Falklands War, the extreme shortage of helicopters made Vietnam-style air mobile operations impossible. Entire units walked across the islands, leaving the few helicopters to bring artillery guns and ammunition forward, then evacuate casualties from the front line back to the rear.

The helicopter war was very different from that fought by other arms. Totally individual and uniquely intimate, each helicopter crew covered the whole battlefield, crossing open and therefore high-threat country in daylight – even if not actually involved with a battle. Beyond the anchorage at San Carlos, where the Rapier missile sites protected shipping and the vital logistic units, there was no effective air defence to protect the helicopters from enemy aircraft, and in some forward troop areas only the shoulder-launched Blowpipe missiles.

The helicopters were vulnerable to both the enemy and a harsh environment. The weather changed constantly, and the bare and featureless terrain offered no cover from either the wind or enemy fire. Frequently the winds were too strong to allow aircraft to land, and peacetime safety rules were ignored. Even without the enemy to contend with, flying in these conditions was dangerous and stressful, particularly as helicopters had to keep below fifty feet, above which fixed wing jets operated.

Operating from rear areas up to the battle front, and with the noise of the engine, helicopter crews felt detached from events outside – as if exercising on Dartmoor. They were very well trained and practised in these sorts of operation, but even so, in battle, coming in with vital supplies and flying out with seriously wounded casualties the pressure was great.

The light helicopters' first major battle was in support of 2 Para at Goose Green. The paras attacked on the night of 28 May. At first light the next day M Flight of 3 Commando Brigade Air Squadron were tasked to go down to help. Early morning fog over Sussex Mountains held up their arrival for an hour.

The battlefield was very confused. The OC of M Flight, Lieutenant Nick Pounds, was uncertain of exactly at what stage he came on the scene. It looked as though A Company had just been pinned down at the foot of Darwin Ridge. After a time, when the expenditure of mortar ammunition began to exceed the rate of resupply, M Flight (in Gazelles) delivered ammunition direct to the mortar lines. Only two mortars were firing, the crews of the remainder busy unpacking and carrying ammunition. The mortars were on the brink of running out of ammunition throughout the whole day.

At around 1000 hours the casualties started. The helicopters flew forward to pick them up, in the process bringing ammunition to the forward company locations, then delivering the wounded to Camilla Creek House a few kilometres to the rear, for pick-up by heavier support helicopters for the flight back to the Main Dressing Station at Ajax Bay. Serious casualties were taken to the Ajax Bay MDS direct. They were totally defenceless. Machine guns and SNEB rockets had been fitted to the Gazelles, but were never actually used. Crewmen were too busy helping to navigate to operate these weapons, which in any case obstructed the rear doors, reducing the space for stores and making it difficult to load casualties. After losing two Gazelles to ground fire on the first day, it was realized how useless these weapons were. Jeff Niblett of the Royal Marines never bothered to fit them on to any of his flight's Scouts. For him, this first ground battle was both traumatic and tragic:

We lost Dick [Lieutenant Richard Nunn] during the Goose Green battle, as our two aircraft were crossing a no-man's-land between the forward operating base at Camilla Creek House and the paras' A echelon [rear] area. Two minutes later we'd have been safe at Camilla, and two minutes earlier the paras could have seen them off.

The attack was so violent and fast, with no time to think about it. We came out of the cloud base – which was uniform at about 300 feet – and saw the two Pucara descending from right to left, about half a mile away. As we saw them, they saw us and turned, coming straight towards us over completely bare-arsed, featureless terrain. We were straight into it, with no chance to evade or hide behind anything.

I was very surprised at the speed at which they could turn. All the previous fighter evasion practice I'd done had been against jets that cannot fly slower than around 400 knots. The Pucara could do less than 200 knots, and these were flown by very good pilots. Standard fighter evasion tactics were useless, and we couldn't just land and run for it. We'd have lost the aircraft, and probably have been shot up ourselves.

They engaged at about three to four hundred metres, coming in very close. I watched the cannon flashing orange light as they closed. They could stand the aircraft on a wing tip, flip it round, keeping us in sight as they came back for another solution. A fast jet would have shot off, taking valuable time to get back for another go. The Pucara could keep their attack going continually.

I felt absolutely determined that I would get out of this and not be shot down, using every bit of experience I had to overcome the situation – to my own and the aircraft's absolute limits. They were free-playing with us, in clear sky beneath the 300-foot cloud base, and we had absolutely no means of self-defence. It's impossible for me to judge how long the attack took.

Luckily my crewman John Glaze was not strapped into the co-pilot's seat. If he had been, we would be dead now. He was able to dodge around in the back and tell me where they were, giving instructions. We were right down in the weeds, flying for our lives. You can't appreciate how it was unless something similar were to happen to you. John would shout, 'Coming in from the left,' and 'Wings level at six o'clock' meaning they were straightening up to open fire. I'd then throw us to one side or the other.

Once they'd shot down Dick, the second Pucara joined in attacking us, making it a bit more exciting.

The first Pucara made several attacks, using rockets, cannon and 7.62mm machine gun. Despite the extreme danger, Niblett was reacting logically. He remembers both the Pucara and their fire coming very close indeed to the fragile Scout. The enemy, anxious to make the kill, came in too close for one of the rocket attacks, the ripple passing in front of and behind the helicopter, none actually hitting. Being so close to the ground, on impact the rockets threw up a spray of muddy peat which splashed the windscreen.

I responded by reaching down and turning on the windscreen wipers, thinking that we'd better be able to see by the time the next attack came in. The 7.62mm machine gun and cannon attacks had no great effect on us — no noise, just a small ripple of puff impacts on the ground. It was like watching TV with the sound turned off.

Nick Pounds watched from the ground, first seeing the two Scouts crossing the open ground, and remembers thinking that 'a quick dash was required' for them to escape. He was able to piece together the whole incident.

The two Pucaras had seemed to be heading for 2 Para's mortar line. They saw the two Scouts, then changed their attack profile. Coming in between one and two hundred feet above the ground, at two hundred knots, they were impossible to avoid. Over the UHF radio Niblett ordered the two Scouts to split left and right, and they dodged and weaved, trying desperately to escape back into the cover of the rough, hilly ground to the north-east, and the air defence screen of Camilla House.

The Pucaras had taken one helicopter each. After avoiding the first attack, in the second Richard Nunn was hit, a rocket smashing Sergeant Belcher's leg, rendering him incapable of helping as a lookout. The Pucaras realized the Scouts were not armed, and pressed home their attacks. On a third attack, Nunn was machine-gunned, killed instantly by a 7.62mm bullet through the head. Sergeant Belcher was hit a second time in the legs. As their Scout ploughed into the ground it swung round, throwing Belcher out. Although the Scout landed intact on its skids, the fuel tanks ruptured, spraying avgas over the red-hot engine cowl. The aluminium and plexiglas caught fire and burned fiercely.

Jeff Niblett achieved the safety of Camilla Creek House, but Dick Nunn had been caught on a spur and hit just as he reached cover. The Pucaras departed, seeming to Pounds to have been 'driven off by the bad ground'.

The attack had been sudden and very determined. The Pucara pilots were very good indeed, slowing right down to stalling speed, with flaps and wheels down as air brakes, in order to get at the much slower flying Scouts. Everyone on the ground was firing up at them and Pounds was amazed that they were not hit.

Pilots' helmets contain ear defenders, which double as ear pieces for the several radio nets that they must monitor. The muted scream of the helicopter turbine and the static of the radios is all they can hear. Although able to see what is going on outside the plexiglass bubble, not being able to hear creates an illusion of somehow not being part of it – a feeling of dislocation from reality. This illusion can be very dangerous. Niblett: 'During the Pucara attacks we were never more than feet off the deck. The unreality of the situation, and the loss of a sense of involvement with what was going on outside made it very easy to have flown into the ground.'

Today, aviators often ask Niblett why he didn't just climb into the cloud, where he would have been safe.

I made a decision not to go up into the cloud because in the suddenness of the attacks, their frequency and closeness together, there was no time to think that option through. My heart rate was very high and I was under great stress. I didn't want to punch up into the cloud in such a high threat environment – from the weather and terrain as well as the enemy – because I had no recovery or navigation aids, no stabilizers and I was low on fuel.

Niblett also recognized what he calls the 'panic factor':

With the fear I was experiencing, I would have got it wrong. We'd have dropped out of the cloud and been killed. Second World War pilots who tell me that they always used cloud, don't realize that it's just not a viable option in a Scout. At least by hugging the ground, I could deal with the situation.

The climb to 300 feet would have given the time and airspace the Pucaras needed to finish off their helpless victims. Even if the helicopters had reached the clouds, getting back to base and landing safely would have been nigh-on impossible. 'By chance John Glaze and I got back to Camilla Creek, spotting the farm roof and turning towards it.'

The paras reported shooting one of the Pucaras down, and thought that the other, being fired upon from Camilla Creek, had broken off his attack and taken the escape option that Niblett had rejected – vanishing into the cloud base. War is filled with half-truths and varying versions of incidents. Claims for kills – by ground troops shooting down aircraft, fighters in air-to-air combat, and even infantry engaged in a fire-fight – are always exaggerated, different units claiming the same aircraft. The confusion over the fate of the two Pucaras in fact started three hours earlier, at midday, when one aircraft of a three-ship mission (flown by Teniente Arganaraz) was hit by a Blowpipe SAM, fired by an artilleryman attached to 2 Para. Pilot Arganaraz found himself upside-down and delayed ejecting. To his surprise, the aircraft righted itself and he was able to limp back to Port Stanley. The paras confused this earlier hit with the second and (for the Argentinians) more successful Pucara mission.

In fact, after attacking the Scouts, the two Pucaras left the area together. However, while transiting back to Port Stanley, they lost contact with each other in low cloud. Teniente Giminez, in A-537, vanished and was never heard of again – until 1986, when the wreckage of the plane was found crashed into high ground north of Mount Pleasant, his body still strapped to the ejection seat.

Safely back at Camilla Creek House, Niblett did 'the fastest-ever shut-down' and rushed over to join crewman John Glaze in a trench, to try to calm down and recover from their experience.

Nick Pounds arrived in his Gazelle, and one of the paras pointed out the smoke from where Dick's aircraft was burning. I didn't know what had happened at that stage – it took some time to piece it all together.

The watchers on the ground had lost sight of the two Scouts, then saw the plume of smoke as Richard Nunn crashed. Pounds flew to investigate, finding the burning aircraft with Sergeant Belcher beside it. Having been thrown clear, Belcher had been left sitting on the ground, both legs badly injured (one nearly severed), unable to move. He calmly injected his morphine into the better leg, having decided the other was probably a write-off. Pounds dropped his crewman off to give first aid and went back for Niblett and his stretcher-carrying Scout. Despite being in a state of shock, Niblett immediately got back into his helicopter, an extreme example of immediately remounting the horse that has just thrown you: 'As far as I was concerned, getting back into the helicopter was the best thing I could have done, as it got me flying again. We were still pumping adrenalin as we flashed up [started the engine] and flew down for Billy Belcher.'

Belcher's severely broken legs made it look from the air as though he was kneeling. Dick Nunn was dead, still strapped inside the smouldering wreckage. Niblett flew Belcher straight to the MDS (Main Dressing Station) at Ajax Bay, his wounds too serious for 2 Para's Regimental Aid Post. The whole incident had taken about 10 to 15 minutes and the dogfight much less than that – although to everyone concerned it had seemed an age.

On the casevac flight, as they came over Sussex Mountains, Niblett transmitted a sitrep to his OC Major Peter Cameron, on the Brigade air net: 'We came over the hill from mist and cloud to a glorious, sunny day at San Carlos. Sending the sitrep of what had happened was like telling a story.' Cameron was struck by Niblett's professionalism:

To my dying day I'll never forget Jeff coming up on the radio: 'Hello Zero this is 29. Am returning to Ajax Bay with serious casevac. Over.' And I came up on the air and said: 'Hello 29. This is 9 speaking. Request sitrep. What's going on?' And he came back, absolutely calm, and said, 'Very much regret to inform you 29 Alpha has been killed, shot down by Pucara, but I have his assistant with me and although he's been severely injured in the legs, we hope he will survive.' As calm as that; just remarkable.

Niblett acknowledges that this was a cold, calculated, professional performance:

I appeared to give a very normal radio call – switching from how I was feeling ... it comes from the training ... Now, looking back on it, I feel a sort of frustration. At the time there was no emotion – everything was so factual. And in the back of the cab, Billy Belcher was dying ...

B Flight, with Gazelles from M Flight, had supported 2 Para all day on the 28th, only being reinforced for three hours in the afternoon. The paras were taking casualties and 'H' Jones had been killed, so it had become clear that the two stretcher-carrying Scouts were not enough. Two Army Air Corps helicopters from 656 Squadron helped out for the last three hours before the light failed and the weather closed in.

Some paras subsequently alleged that 3 Commando Brigade Air Squadron refused to fly in to pick up 'H' Jones's body – a sadly ignorant misapprehension that was deeply upsetting to the Air Squadron, particularly to Niblett who took his responsibility to 2 Para very seriously indeed. There was an element of inter-service rivalry in the para accusation: army suspicion of the navy, red berets (paras) versus green (commandos). Some paras preferred to believe that army aviators managed to provide a superior service to that of the Commando Brigade Air Squadron, and that the Royal Marines would discriminate against the army – despite the fact that the

Brigade Air Squadron was staffed by both army and marine pilots.

The reality was that, regardless of how anyone might feel in the tragedy of the moment, 'H' Jones was dead and moving his body could not be given priority over evacuating still-living casualties, or bringing in the vital mortar ammunition that was keeping the battalion alive during the most dangerous part of the battle. Niblett expresses his feelings with reluctance and understatement:

I was quite annoyed at the lack of recognition and the unnecessary criticism of us by 2 Para after the battle. We'd heard over the battalion [radio] net that Jones was down. We were flying back to take Chris Keeble [the second-in-command, who took over] up to the front when we were attacked. They didn't know that we'd been intercepted by Pucara.

For Niblett, flying over the Sussex Mountains and down into San Carlos Water was to leave the hostile battlefield and enter what suddenly seemed to him to have become a beautiful, benign environment. This change in perception signalled the beginning of a change in Niblett's whole outlook to the war and what he was doing. After dropping Billy Belcher off, he refuelled then flew back down to Goose Green to continue evacuating casualties. It was a long day – over seven hours of front-line flying. At the end, Niblett returned to Ajax Bay to see how Belcher was faring and found his brigade commander Julian Thompson waiting for him . . .

He was worried about me. He wanted to make sure I was all right. You only realize how taking casualties affects you [as a leader] when you've actually experienced it for yourself. As the leader, you can't describe how you feel to anyone else – either at the time or afterwards.

I walked to the hospital and asked the medical staff how Billy was doing. He'd just come round from his operation and was okay, although he looked very pale. He was worried about having lost his pipe. I then went to Brigade [HQ] to debrief, before preparing to return to Goose Green the next day.

At the time, I didn't feel too bad about what was happening. That evening, in our Flight CP [command post], with a cup of coffee and the Tilley lamp going, I felt totally physically and mentally drained. I'd never felt like that before. It never happened again; for the rest of the time, I was busy doing things – keeping going because of the pressure of work.

After the surrender of the Argentine garrison at Goose Green (at 0940 hours the next morning, 29 May) Niblett returned to the battlefield with B Flight to pick up their dead.

It was our responsibility to pick up Dick. The standard body [collection] parties were going round that afternoon, but I didn't want to leave him for them. I couldn't bear the thought of him being collected with the rest of

2 Para's dead, dumped in the back of a Wessex with all the others – like a butcher's window. Someone you know well deserves respect.

I dreaded going, but as the flight commander, I was responsible and the duty aspect overrode my personal emotions. Dick was a good friend, my second-in-command and a brother Royal Marine officer. We knew each other well and had a close bond of trust between us. As a commander, you've got a great responsibility to get the job done – and it's very hard to suddenly lose your 2ic . . . one of the liabilities of command. So I got a green body bag, a couple of pairs of plastic gloves and two volunteers, and we flew down to collect Dick.

I was coldly professional about it. We needed to bring back their personal weapons [loss of which entails a Board of Inquiry]. I ordered the Tiffy [artificer] to come as well with his bag of tools, to salvage what spares he could from the remains of the aircraft.

I can't tell anyone exactly what happened. My own morals prevent me; it was too distasteful to talk about . . . The aircraft was completely burned out, so there was nothing for the Tiffy to collect. Dick was still strapped in . . . I realize now, years later, that I should have told somebody about it – and got it off my chest . . .

We flew Dick back to Ajax Bay and were met by [Surgeon Commander] Rick Jolly, who is a close friend to the Nunn family. Rick did the post mortem, and confirmed the cause of death as a 7.62mm bullet in the head.

This confirmation allayed their fear that Dick Nunn had burned to death – alive and conscious when the fire started.

Next, I had to get Dick's kit together, and put it into the FRO ['forces returning from overseas'] system. On the voyage, we'd urged everyone to make wills. I remembered Dick had said he'd put his will into the post box on board *Sir Lancelot*. I sent someone to the ship, who went through the post and recovered it. We made sure it was sent to his family.

Dick's older brother, Captain Chris Nunn, commanding M Company, was still at South Georgia. I had to get a message to him. I arranged for the casualty signal to be sent to him personally, and was assured that it had been sent. A Falkland ship arrived in South Georgia a week after Dick's death. Chris asked them for an update, and was shown a casualty list which happened to have his brother's name on it. My signal had never been sent.

Glancing at a list of dead and wounded to find your brother's name, is a terrible, impersonal and uncaring way to be given such bad news. Niblett's anger at this additional and unnecessary pain is aggravated by elements of self-castigating guilt. Although he cannot be blamed for the Brigade COMCEN's failure, he feels responsible and so is defensive:

In war, you don't have time to go back and check that people are doing what you've told them to do. I was assured the signal had been sent; you can't stand over people ... there isn't time, you have to keep on going forward. You react to events ... you can't go back.

That afternoon, B Flight were tasked back down to Goose Green, to pick up more casualties:

We took a seriously injured Argie who'd been in a ditch for two days — he recovered. We were totally involved in the work — very serious and very unhappy, but we kept on doing the job.

The next day (30 May), we were tasked to help 45 Commando and 3 Para with their move up towards Teal Inlet. It was also the day for burying the Goose Green victims. Dick was buried with all the others. It was like closing a book — a moving service, no hymns, purely a burial. We turned away and carried on with the war. There was no chance to talk it through or reflect on it. I felt so lucky to have survived, I didn't want to talk about it. I had to command the Flight and provide Brigade with helicopter support.

We flew to Teal that afternoon and started operating from there.

As at Goose Green, casualty evacuation was a major part of the Flight's work: 'Having casualties in the back was a distraction when you were flying. We'd land right beside the stretchers so they could be loaded straight on. There were some very bad injuries . . .'

Looking on from the helicopter, insulated from the reality outside by the noise of turbines and radios, these injuries had a visual impact — like a physical blow. Waiting for the stretcher bearers to move clear so they could take off, suddenly amid the mud, slippery green waterproofs and death-pale, rain-soaked faces, anonymous bundles of blood-stained, mud-soiled bandages became terribly, frighteningly injured people.

Emotionally it was all pretty negative. Some of them came on board smiling, giving us the thumbs-up because we were flying them off to be treated. These guys were encouraging and boosted our morale, but I never got used to flying casualties.

The Scouts would be filled with injured men, some lying unconscious, others sitting up — maybe holding a drip for someone on the floor. Argentine casualties were mixed with British, holding each other, keeping the vital drips going.

We never fitted the external stretcher pods on to our aircraft. We'd removed the seats and it was faster just to shove them in. It took too long to get casualties into the pods, and you couldn't do anything with their drips.

External stretcher pods have other disadvantages: men placed in the pod unconscious come round to find themselves sealed into a heavily vibrating, coffin-like container. The stretcher pods of most armies have notices reassuring casualties that they are still alive, and that their journey will end at a field hospital and not the Pearly Gates. Falklands pods were inscribed:

Don't be concerned. You are in a helicopter – you are being Casevac'd!

Niblett's men were very conscious of the dangers they faced in landing close to the front line:

We didn't like being on the ground – it felt much safer to be flying. On the ground, we didn't know where the enemy were – we had no idea at all. We'd land right up where the casualties were lying, adrenalin pumping because we didn't know how close to the front line or the enemy we were. I was bracketed by 105mm artillery – shells landing just in front and to the rear of the aircraft. I heard the thump and felt the shock wave – but there was none of the actual sound of the explosion. We were freer, more confident and felt less vulnerable in the air.

Self-confidence is a vital personal quality for pilots in the harsh environment of combat. Flying to the limits, although a very calculated and careful taking of risks, requires the total confidence of pilot and crew. Hesitation or uncertainty can easily cost the split second that is the difference between survival and death. Integral to self-confidence in war is a belief in personal survival – that regardless of what might happen to others, 'I will not die'. Ground troops can survive moments of weakness, when their individual belief in survival wavers. In the air, such moments of weakness are very dangerous: 'When your mortality is threatened – as it is when you are under attack – you lose confidence and concentration.'

There was tremendous pressure on individual pilots; one pilot from another flight, before he had actually been exposed to bullets or danger himself, refused to fly in the Goose Green operation. He was replaced by someone else, and rested for the day – to recover and fly throughout the rest of the campaign. Apart from the man's own self-confidence, his flight commander lost a degree of confidence too – in a pilot who might refuse to fly in the future.

There was a sense of adventure in leaving the beach-head – of getting on with the war. I felt no uncertainty about it, as I had confidence in our planning and in our ability to do the job. Others reacted differently – which after all the psychological problems I've experienced, I know is only to be expected. We're all human.

The Scouts flew more hours than the rest of the squadron. Niblett was very conscious of the pressure their workload created:

We had only one spare pilot for the whole flight — and none after Dick was killed. I had to fly every day. I did take myself off for one day's rest, four days after Goose Green.

Niblett was in serious need of a break. He allowed himself to stop for twenty-four hours with reluctance, feeling he had for some reason to justify the decision: 'There was very bad weather, and I'd done a very difficult casevac the previous day . . .' This particular casualty evacuation operation was a classic example of skilful, determined and very brave flying:

A Marine from 42 Commando had lost a foot on a mine during the night and was in a bad way. It was a gopping [horrible], no-flying day.

They had to fly between six and ten feet above the ground.

We flew in thick cloud from Teal following a line of telegraph poles — which we knew were accurately marked on the map. We were looking for the point at which [from the map] the telegraph poles dropped over a hill, from where we could maybe fly to Mount Wall [to pick up the Marine]. Unfortunately we remained in cloud throughout and couldn't see a thing, so we had to fly back to Teal along the line of poles — twelve miles or so, flown mostly at walking pace.

We then heard a casevac call from 3 Para at Estancia — a back injury. We followed the wires again, picked up this casualty, then tried again for the Marine at Mount Wall. We had to return for more fuel.

On our third try, the sun had burned off some of the cloud, and suddenly we saw Mount Wall — so we went for it [across country], leaving the safety of the telegraph poles. We brought the guy back to the hill, re-entered the cloud and followed our telegraph poles back to Teal. It was a very hard day.

When I took myself off flying the next day, I felt guilty — that I should explain to my men why I was doing it. I told them I was physically knackered. In fact it was mental too — after Goose Green.

B Flight were moved with no warning from Teal Inlet to Estancia as part of the Brigade's advance on Stanley.

It was particularly depressing, at the end of another long day . . . pouring with rain and we all got soaked through. When the Argentinians started firing 155mm shells, we discovered that we'd deployed to within range of an enemy battery, right behind the infantry with one of our own artillery batteries nearby!

That night, more shells came down, but the next day, after examining the enormous, regularly spaced craters, we realized that this had been an Argentine Canberra bombing raid — the only time they dropped at night.

(Another misapprehension. Argentine Canberras from Grupo 2 de Bombardeo flew regular night missions to bomb British ground forces, mainly on Mount Kent. Their ten refurbished B62s and two T64s were purchased from Britain in 1971.)

Jeff Niblett was conscious of the tension building up inside him. He also did not like their new location. 'It was hard being based at Estancia. It was a very open, bare place, with no cover at all. We were very busy, and in the cold and wet, the aircraft still had to be serviced.'

Although peacetime regulations regarding flying hours and servicing schedules had been abandoned, with the helicopters receiving such a hammering during the day, some sort of servicing became even more important. Ground crews worked all night by torch light under parachute silk shelters, using great skill and improvisation under dreadful working conditions to keep the aircraft flying.

It would have been easy for the ground crews to have justified putting off doing jobs until daylight, but somehow they always got it done by first light. In the squadron, we did over 4000 hours in 15 aircraft, half of those hours actually in combat. We went way over normal rates. It was unpredictable, very interesting, with no pattern to it.

We established a Flight routine – evening briefings so everyone knew what was going on. We had personal routines too – 'bird-bath' washes in tin basins, enforced daily shaving and meals. For aircrew up before first light, and flying until dark, just keeping yourself going was a good test of character. You had to be very flexible in how you ran your life.

During the final two-and-a-half-day push, the light helicopters used SS11 rockets to attack Argentine bunkers. On 14 June, in the last hostile helicopter action of the war, the Scouts took out some 105mm artillery field gun bunkers. 'The aircraft and men were knackered,' so Jeff Niblett flew into Stanley the night before the official surrender to get a good, dry billet for his men and somewhere to park his aircraft. The Argentinians were still armed, and had moved west of the hospital towards the airfield. The British were east of the hospital, both sides abiding by the tacitly agreed line. 'By getting in there the night before, we were able to secure our territory before the grunts [infantrymen] arrived.'

Flying still continued, but from good accommodation, over enemy-free terrain. The danger continued, however. Five days after the surrender, near Murrell Bridge, Niblett had to land in the middle of a minefield to pick up a sapper whose feet had been blown off.

It was silly to land among the mines – but that's what you had to do . . .

9

COMMANDING THE CONFUSION

The danger of war is unpredictable; partly because each individual survives or is killed according to his or her own personal luck, but also because of the deliberate actions of the enemy. Most of the killing in war is impersonal; artillery or machine gun fire observed at long range through binoculars, directed at tiny stick figures that run away like sheep. But physical dangers can reach senior commanders, particularly in high-tech warfare where not even the rear areas are safe. Captain Edmund C. Stone III, us Army, writing of Vietnam in an article entitled 'Small Arms Safety', brings it down to basics:

At least one battalion commander and one brigade commander have been wounded in separate incidents and evacuated out of country due to careless cleaning of 'empty' weapons. On at least one occasion, the evacuation helicopter [taking the wounded commander away] was also hit by enemy small arms fire, compounding the loss . . .[1]

However, despite the actual danger to commanders, when perceived from a staff headquarters combat action is remote, intellectualized into the map symbols and jargon through which the operation is planned and directed. The enemy are coloured red and friendly forces blue, unit positions delineated by 'goose-egg' circles on the (tactical) map. Red goose-eggs are attacked by thick blue arrows, in 'counter-strokes', 'counter-penetrations' and 'diversionary thrusts'. While this is going on, far from lying back and thinking of the motherland, Red forces set up 'blocking positions' and 'killing areas', while organizing a 'counterattack'.

Through the act of plotting the events of battle on to a map, an appearance of order is created from the chaos on the ground allowing commanders to co-ordinate and direct the efforts of their units. However, because it is an intellectualization of the battle this instant map-board order can only be the broadest of generalizations, which may not actually exist in reality. For example, on the ground, an armoured formation making a sweeping left hook attack can be many different things to different individuals; some tanks may find themselves flying along unopposed with the odd shell landing nearby, machine rounds ricocheting harmlessly off their cupolas, while other tanks are smashed and burned by enemy missile attack, forcing the accompanying infantry to stop and assault. A local enemy counter-attack might even force some elements of this sweeping left hook to dig in and defend ground – a totally different battle.

No commander should move a muscle until his logisticians have calculated the implications and brought up the necessary supplies. Commanders earn their pay through attempting to peer through the confusion to what is actually happening on their battlefields. Logisticians, however, must be several steps ahead of their commanders, storing enough of the right supplies in the right places to support future, undefined operations. They impose their version of reality on the intellectualizations of senior commanders, often forcing them to change their plans. Logistical reality is nevertheless another intellectualization – a realistic calculation of what is militarily possible within the resources available. The Falklands War was a triumph of logistical foresight, the supply line running over 8000 salty miles and more than six weeks' freight travelling time.

Battle planning is meticulous and tries to cover every likelihood, but from the onset nothing in combat ever goes according to plan. Anything too complicated rapidly turns into the most impossible mess. Plans must therefore be as simple as possible. The actual value of detailed planning lies not so much in actually fighting the battle, but in working out the implications of all the possible options. Artillery, tanks, machine guns, mortars etc. must be co-ordinated. With different units and flanking formations, a simple attack becomes part of an overall co-ordination of many operations, each unit operating within particular boundaries to strict timings. Detailed battle planning provides only the foundation of information from which the battle is then fought – rather than any cut and dried solutions. Experienced combat leaders absorb the complexity of a battle plan, then boil it all down into the simplest possible message to pass on to their soldiers. In the tension of entering battle, nobody wants to be bogged down with unnecessary detail. The military maxim 'Always expect the unexpected' is particularly apt.

The Second World War infantry officer Sydney Jary found the strictures of 1944 Normandy battle plans unbearable:

I remember with horror being 'locked into' the timetables of meticulously planned large battles ... the preparations for these battles assumed the demented proportion of a Kafka-like nightmare ballet, in which the anonymous 'they' ordained that 'we' must perform a choreographed ritual danse macabre. I felt trapped and helpless.

The junior commander was left with no scope for exploitation ... they put us into a straitjacket.[2]

Jary believed these 'straitjacket' tactics to be the legacy of the Somme, which had deeply affected the hierarchy of the British Army. As junior officers, the senior commanders of the Second World War had seen their infantry mown down in tens of thousands by machine guns, so they tried to protect them using artillery. The infantry were supposed to operate only with pre-scheduled artillery support and accompanied by ponderous, noisy tanks, rather than fighting freely in small, section-sized gangs.

The Falklands was very different – an infantryman's battlefield with artillery on call when needed. In fact 2 Para's battle for Goose Green was fought (through necessity and not choice) with only the battalion's mortars and three 105mm light guns. For the final battles, rather than dictate any form of rigid fire plan with timings to which the units had to conform, Falklands artillery commander Colonel Brian Pennicott was careful to allocate artillery resources to his brigades and let them do the planning for themselves.

In their headquarters, divorced from the realities of the battle they are 'fighting', commanders are faced with difficult, often harsh decisions, giving orders they know will lead to the deaths of their officers and men. Without intellectualizing the battle and being psychologically isolated from their soldiers during the fighting, it is difficult to see how commanders could actually cope. On the battlefield, information is the key to everything. Good intelligence, particularly on vast, fast-moving modern battlefields, is the battle-winner – arguably of more importance than even air superiority (the Falklands War was won without, at times, even air *parity*). As the size of a battle and the numbers of forces involved increase, the confusion also increases – dramatically. The man who rises above this confusion will win the war.

A whole sector of the computer industry has devoted itself to rising above the confusion, known in military jargon as 'C cubed I' (C^3I): command, control, communications and intelligence. The powerful C^3I systems being developed today generate their own computerized sense of the unreality of battle, increasing the isolation of commanders from the reality of the battle they are controlling.

Isolation from reality is normal in many walks of life, comparable with the dissociation (for example) of stockbrokers from the factory floors of the companies whose shares they trade. In everyday life we all wear psychological blinkers that filter the information our senses gather, each of us living our own unique world. Military staff training seeks to homogenize that filtration process by which potential commanders perceive the world, to eliminate individualism and produce reliable staff officers free of idiosyncrasy (even though history proves many of the really successful commanders to have been idiosyncratic in the extreme).

First-hand perception of the battlefield is desperately myopic – severely restricted by circumstances. Even at the very top, commanders know only their own headquarters and its neon-lit map boards, battle progress marked on them in chinagraph by their chiefs of staff. The outlook of everybody in combat, from the tank commander peering through the optics of his cupola to the commander-in-chief in his hardened bunker, is parochial in the extreme. The ability of commanders to make sensible decisions depends entirely on what they know, from their past experience as well as from battlefield intelligence. The paucity of accurate information on the battlefield makes logic on its own an inadequate decision-making tool. A correct and logical decision for one apparent situation can easily become an error (or sheer brilliance) as more information comes in. The best commanders use logic to take well-calculated risks, while hedging their bets – keeping a third of their forces in reserve until they are certain they know what is happening.

Hitherto military commanders have had to make decisions with the help of very little information, sometimes almost improvising. It is hardly surprising, therefore that serious mistakes on the battlefield are common, virtually inevitable, at every level. The combination of isolation and power in men who must win battles through determined thoughtpower and unwavering will is unparalleled in any other sphere of human activity.

War's unique combination of confusion and fear is accompanied by powerful inertia that can bring operations to a halt. Maintaining the momentum (at all costs if necessary) is therefore the single most important function of command. That means forcing men to do things they do not want to do, which can put headquarters seriously at odds with the troops doing the fighting. The human factor is crucial, particularly in commanding very large-scale actions. The commander should have decades of military experience. He knows all his subordinate commanders well, and, before hostilities make it impossible for him to leave the bunker, will have made himself known to his men by visiting all the units under his command. In a well-run army, the commander will learn as much from the reactions of his subordinates (over the radio links) as from the actual information his staff plot on to the battle map. Even in the computer age, personality is the vital spark that keeps men fighting.

The personality of 3 Commando Brigade's commander, Brigadier Julian Thompson, was critical to the success of the Falklands War. Within his brigade, he knew most of his officers personally and many of the soldiers. We in 3 Commando Brigade felt that he trusted us to get on with whatever he asked us to do.

Nobody in the Task Force knew much about the Argentine air force. Armed with HMS *Fearless*'s copy of *Jane's All the World Aircraft*, Dennis Marshall-Hasdell, Phantom navigator turned commando, was given the job of making the air assessment as part of the overall appraisal being done by 3 Commando Brigade staff on how to win the war. He and Arnie Black, a Spanish-speaking intelligence officer who listened to Argentine radio traffic, worked out the flight profiles for the various Argentine aircraft types – how they would best attack the British fleet, and their most likely approach routes to the anchorage at San Carlos. Back in the UK, the Task Force HQ at Northwood were doing the same thing – and interestingly, even with all the resources of the MOD at their disposal, Marshall-Hasdell was amused to see that the quality of their intelligence was the same as the ad hoc stuff produced on HMS *Fearless*.

At sea there were problems co-ordinating the efforts of the various intelligence organizations. Unused to working together, for a time they each kept information to themselves, until 3 Commando Brigade's Chief of Staff, Major John Chester, pulled them all together. Marshall-Hasdell was worried by his new role:

I felt very pressured by it. My intelligence work seemed so amateurish, and I knew that Brigadier Thompson and Commodore Clapp [land commander and Commodore Amphibious Warfare respectively] were basing their plans on what I said. There was total trust from the boss [Thompson], which made me worry about the personal responsibility of it all.

Royal Marine Major Ewen Southby-Tailyour felt similarly pressured, worrying whether the information he was giving on Falklands geography and inshore navigation was accurate and unbiased enough, and about how this would affect the critical decision as to where the landings would be made.

Marshall-Hasdell watched as the ground war was planned:

Julian Thompson was great – but a human like the rest of us. His decisions were based on the efforts of his team, and like all decision-makers, he was very vulnerable to tiredness and hassle – stupid things like the great pressures exerted on him from Northwood. I saw the reality of decision-making; that there is no super-human decider on these momentous occasions.

The confusion and chaos started long before the fighting:

Nothing worked out as anybody expected; [staff officer] Mike Samuelson had constantly to re-do his complicated loading plans as he discovered [when they arrived at Ascension Island] that the ships were packed differently from his expectations. For everyone, it was planning on the back of a fag-packet – and there was no other way it could have been done. You couldn't afford to be rigid in your thinking. The flexibility required was very much an aircrew-type approach, so it made sense to me.

Being there during the decision-making has permanently affected me. Now, having seen all that, I don't respect any person's achievements, their reputation or paper qualifications. I go by my own impressions of them.

Dennis's abiding memory of those days and weeks, was of being levelled – by the task, and by the enormous strain of making everything happen. When the intelligence assessment predicted an unopposed landing, he heaved a personal sigh of relief. Controlling Harrier strikes from a Scout helicopter, as had been planned, would have been suicidally dangerous.

Back at Northwood, it was realized that time was short. With winter fast approaching, after all their calculations had been made there was only a seven-day 'window of opportunity' in which to land on the islands. It was calculated that four weeks would then be needed to win the battle, and that the most vulnerable time would be immediately after the landings. On 19 May land commander Major General Jeremy Moore, tired of staying in the UK, placed himself and his staff on a flight out to Ascension Island, sailing on in the QE2 to the Total Exclusion Zone. Thus, as the headquarters in charge of the war, General Moore's team was out of contact with the battlefield for those first critical weeks after the landings, with no information at all except broadcasts from the World Service of the BBC, and no method of communicating with them.

The command structure of Operation Corporate (like everything else in the expedition to the Falklands) was thrown together in a hurry, with the result that no overall, in-theatre commander had been appointed. Julian Thompson: 'What was needed was perhaps a three-star admiral to co-ordinate between the Task Group at sea, the land battle and the amphibious warfare side.' As a result, he had far more on his plate than if it had been a purely army operation: 'We were in the position of having to run three brigade-sized operations simultaneously – each of which relied on the others for support. One person was needed to draw it all together, allocate the priorities and take charge.' At that stage, Thompson's orders from the UK were far from clear:

There was also the problem of translating political intent into a military mission. What were we trying to do? No one had mentioned Port Stanley as the main objective – you had to work it out for yourself.

Thompson's original intention had been to land and off-load enough supplies for twenty-four hours ashore, keeping the rest afloat at sea. He had made this convenient, but as it turned out totally unrealistic, plan because of assurances from Northwood that the Argentine air force was not a threat.

I was told that the air battle would be won first, before the landings and the land battle. However, it became clear that the air battle was not going to be fought unless the Argentine air force came over to fight it. The other alternative was that something else might be done – bombing the Argentine airfields for example – but I could see that was not likely to be politically feasible.

[Admiral] Woodward was very worried, and tried to hint to Northwood that because of the Argentine air capability, our casualties were likely to be very heavy. In one signal to Northwood, he said something like 'the price of a ticket home on the train from Ascension Island will be very expensive'.

By not first defeating the enemy air force and gaining air superiority, we were breaking one of the cardinal rules [of amphibious warfare]. I informed General Moore by signal that casualties would be very heavy. Northwood's response was to tell us not to worry, that it was all sorted out – which was a lie. It would have been better if they'd told us the reality of the situation. As it turned out, we got through [to San Carlos] the day before the landings by the most amazing luck – with thick fog obscuring all the ships on the run-in.

Again Thompson's lack of firm orders left him to make all the key decisions – and then to take the flak when Northwood complained:

I had no orders to move out of the beach-head. The nearest enemy were at Darwin and Goose Green, and in West Falkland. The question was one of priority – should we get on with the main job of taking Stanley, or should we be diverted by Goose Green?

The essentially naval Task Force HQ at Northwood thought the land war had bogged down. Julian Thompson:

Northwood didn't understand the bread and butter of amphibious operations – ignorance born out of ridiculous peacetime exercising without the extra weight of real ammunition. No one at Northwood had ever actually done it for real. People with no operational experience don't understand what drives real life ops against a live enemy. When [for example] I told them I was flying the SAS forward to do the recce [on Mount Kent, before the rest of the brigade], they said, 'What do you want recce for?' Woodward had similar problems with Northwood on the naval side, and Mike Clapp was generally hassled by them.

Thompson was under great pressure to attack Darwin and Goose Green. His very limited troop and cargo carrying helicopter assets (just eleven for a 5500 man brigade) were needed to off-load supplies from the ships, and bad weather made it impossible to fly artillery south to support such an attack. It seemed that back in the UK, Task Force HQ Northwood simply did not understand Thompson's situation, and certain very senior army commanders were muttering under their breaths about sacking him. 'That caused a wry smile – who would have replaced me?' In the event Thompson was given direct orders to attack Darwin and Goose Green, so the helicopter off-loading of supplies stopped and 2 Para marched south.

Northwood's lack of comprehension is understandable; they were 8000 miles away enjoying an English summer, and largely naval. The co-opted army element had very little understanding of amphibious operations, particularly as all the experts were either with Thompson, or en route to the South Atlantic with Major General Moore. When Moore arrived in theatre, he took over the duty of communicating with Northwood, handling the complicated and sometimes tricky relations upwards, while leaving his field commander free to get on with fighting the battle.

From the rank of major upwards (at the head of companies, battalions, brigades and so on), commanders work increasingly with other officers rather than with the soldiers themselves. Authority is exercised through subordinates down the chain of command, eventually reaching the men who do the fighting. Senior commanders (of battalions and larger) must impress their personalities on other officers who are only one step down in rank – a highly personal and strongly hierarchical situation which can be very much more authoritarian than relationships could ever be with soldiers.

The officers of 3 Commando Brigade at every level knew each other well. Major General Moore and Brigadier Thompson had already worked with their COs and staff officers – on exercises and operations elsewhere. By contrast the army units were an unknown; unfamiliar faces sharing little of 3 Commando Brigade's commando attitude (although the paras worked on the same wavelength), yet nevertheless powerful personalities determined to do well. Keeping them all together was Moore's task – a burden Julian Thompson handed over to him with some relief:

When General Moore arrived, the pressure eased off. I could begin to actually command my brigade, which [by contrast to everything else he had been doing] was a reasonably familiar job.

Once the battles for Stanley started, accurate information was going to be difficult to gather. Julian Thompson had thought this problem through, adopting a well-tried solution:

In the Port Stanley battle, I wondered where I should go. A commander needs to be forward so he can get straight information about what is going on. If it arrives through the usual channels, it's too layered, garbled and altered.

Thompson used staff officer Major Hector 'G', a former SAS man, as his personal liaison officer with whichever battalion HQ was in the thick of the fighting. 'G' would arrive with his own radios, able to monitor the battalion's battle net and broadcast directly to Thompson, cutting out middlemen. His experience enabled him to advise both Thompson and the COs of the battalions he was with at critical moments. For the battalions, far from being seen as the brigadier's spy, he became an invaluable adviser.

Thompson had no doubts that even as the brigade commander, he should lead from the front:

I should have been in the middle of the three units. Had the battle continued in the way I'd planned, I would then have moved forward on to Wireless Ridge. Neither the navy nor Northwood understood this personal command and reconnaissance aspect.

When the final battle started, Thompson felt strangely at home with the situation:

I didn't worry about decisions or about the progress of the land battle. I went into a sort of storm centre within myself to control the battle, as I'd done so frequently in the past [on operations and many exercises]. It was uncannily like an exercise at times, so that feeling was understandable.

I didn't worry because I had confidence in the troops – which hadn't quite been the case during the initial landings because I'd been so worried about enemy air. Once I was started – and committed – I got on with it.

Casualties and those killed were not a weight on my mind. A commander has to erect a carapace around himself when giving orders that will lead to casualties and dead – it's all part of the contract. The commander must however ensure that his soldiers get every possible advantage so they can take their objectives with the minimum number of casualties.

I felt professional anger at various times in the campaign – at Northwood making me do things the wrong way in military nonsenses, getting me to do plainly stupid things. I didn't get any flak afterwards from Northwood – and the flak I received during the campaign was only due to their lack of understanding. Although they didn't understand what the battle was all about, they were good at collecting assets in UK and sending them down to us.

I've pondered on the whole question of the relationship with Northwood, tempering my reactions with the lessons of history. Warfare is such an all-absorbing and important business, it generates enormous heat and emotion. Afterwards, people get wound up by relatively trivial things, winding up not talking to particular individuals or even units. It is possible therefore that I have an over-heated view of Northwood's role in the war.

At the start of a war, there is inexperience at every level. Mistakes are being made all the time. Well-trained troops will push on, despite confusion and error, using their experience and common sense to minimize the effect of these mistakes. With high-grade individuals in the key command and staff appointments, serious mistakes can be rectified before too much damage is done.

Peacetime training does not have the same priorities or emphasis as real combat. In war, the co-ordination of artillery, machine gun and mortar fire, of patrols going out from different units and returning at night, and of the passwords used by sentries to determine friend from enemy, is very different from and infinitely more difficult than the co-ordination practised during peacetime exercises.

When shells, bullets or rockets strike, they do not discriminate between friend and enemy. After firing, projectiles cannot be recalled. The chaos of battle makes co-ordination almost impossible, and the likelihood of friendly forces firing upon compatriots or allies by mistake is a constant threat: indeed, it seems a miracle that such occurrences are not more frequent.

Because friendly forces are shown in blue on commanders' maps these incidents are known as 'blue-on-blue'. There were several 'blues-on-blue' in the Falklands War, the most serious being that suffered by 3 Para in the early days of the campaign, soon after they had landed at San Carlos. Their sister battalion 2 Para had a spirited shoot-out with men of 3 Commando Brigade Air Squadron near Boca House (with nobody injured); and, in a particularly unfortunate incident, G Squadron of the SAS ambushed an SBS patrol, killing the patrol commander Sergeant 'Kiwi' Hunt. One commando ambushed the mortars of their own unit, who were in the wrong place. There were undoubtedly other similar incidents.

I was given a first-hand account of the death of Kiwi Hunt by the G Squadron machine gunner who opened fire on the SBS patrol. We were sharing an observation position during the last few days of the war, and telling the story to me seemed to be a way of getting it off his chest.

Hunt's patrol were not supposed to be in the SAS's operational area. The SAS had seen them coming using night vision equipment, and were lying in ambush. The senior officer present was beside the machine gunner, urging him to wait before opening fire so they could be sure the patrol was enemy – which for some reason the officer had doubts about. A very tense battle of wills ensued, the officer ordering that fire be held, the gunner insisting on letting rip. When Hunt and his three men were within ten metres or so of the ambush, they were challenged – in English by the SAS officer. The gunner said Hunt behaved absolutely correctly, holding his rifle well away from his body and standing stock still. The two men behind him also froze, but the man at the back ('tail-end charlie'), who might not have heard the challenge, tried to creep off into the darkness – a futile effort as SAS night sights were following his every move.

'Tail-end charlie' was perceived to be a threat to the ambush, the SAS officer lost the battle of wills and the gunner opened fire, killing Hunt. The abiding image of this story (as I was told it) was of the ammunition in Hunt's combat vest exploding in the darkness. The SAS man was derisive of what he said were the SBS patrol's reaction to this shocking event; particularly of 'tail-end charlie' breaking down in tears and beating the ground with his fists.

The SAS reaction to this incident (from the rank and file at the time) was that Hunt had strayed into 'their' area and got what he deserved – with the ill-concealed implication that standards of SBS navigation (and professionalism) were well below theirs. In fact it was not the patrol's fault. They had been dropped off by naval Sea King at night, miles from the correct location. Hunt was in the process of trying to establish his position when he was killed. The incident, and the subsequent attitudes to it of those involved, illustrates a fundamental difference between these two super-elite organizations. The SAS are much more likely than the more clandestine SBS to shoot first and ask questions later. They have a restless violence that the SBS, with their diving, demolitions and boating expertise (in my experience) do not share. One SAS man said to me that he felt the SBS were 'better at getting there, but having arrived, didn't know what to do'. Violence is the SAS trade-mark; the SBS stick by their motto 'Strength through Guile'.

Embers of ill-feeling between the SAS and the SBS, which had smouldered at various times on the voyage to the Falklands and during the campaign, were further fanned by this episode. Kiwi Hunt's funeral (during the war) was a sombre affair, with his close friends gathered together by helicopter from operations all over the islands. I attended his wake on board HMS *Intrepid*, at which we attempted to drink some of the emotions away. We were too weak, from poor food and conditions on operations, to cope with more than a can or two of beer each. Hunt's troop commander proposed the toast to 'Absent Friends' with the terse declaration that he'd 'never had to do this before and he hoped he'd never have to do it again', and Hunt's best friend collapsed in tears, overcome by emotion and fatigue.

The most serious Falklands 'blue-on-blue' that I am aware of occurred when C Company of 3 Para fired on a patrol of A Company as it returned to the battalion positions in the hills north of San Carlos Settlement. Nobody was killed but several were very seriously wounded – a miracle caused perhaps by the long ranges at which the small arms were firing.

There had been considerable confusion in the north of San Carlos Water in the first days of the landings. On the night of 20/21 May an SBS operation had neutralized an Argentine heavy weapons company at Fanning Head. Then, later that day (21 May), two British Gazelle helicopters had been shot down by a stray band of Argentine soldiers from the displaced garrison at San Carlos Settlement, and so for some time it was thought that 3 Para's blue-on-blue was a continuation of their activities. WO2 McCullum's platoon commander was leading the A Company patrol:

Our patrol saw over thirty members of C Company coming round the headland, and assumed they were the Argentinians. In turn, C Company saw them and drew the same conclusion. My platoon commander asked for a fire mission, and his grid reference was sent from battalion HQ down to our mortars. C Company also sent a grid for a fire mission, which battalion HQ Ops relayed to the artillery.

Unfortunately, a second grid reference sent by my platoon commander, of his own position, appeared to place him a thousand metres further away than where he actually was. According to his grid, C Company were two kilometres away, out of range and too far for them both to be seeing each other.

In the confusion, nobody realized what was actually happening.

Battalion ops assumed that the situation represented two separate contacts with the enemy. So everyone got on with fighting the 'battle'.

Although the A Company platoon commander appears to be to blame for the confusion, when the battalion mortars fired, their rounds landed squarely on C Company's position – proving the accuracy of the young officer's map reading. Another possibility is that, in a very unlikely coincidence of errors, the mortars happened to be as inaccurately orientated as the young officer. The mortars, however, would already have been carefully checked, revealing such an error.

On reflection it seems that any fault must lie with battalion ops, who were responsible for the co-ordination of all operational activity in the battalion area. It was their job to plot the locations of companies and patrols on their map. Had they been following the situation closely, it should have become apparent that the battalion's mortars were firing on C Company. McCullum:

So there we were, with a strong section stuck on a forward slope with three machine guns, and a whole platoon [of C Company] lined up with at least five machine guns, ready to shoot at them. So you carry on, you go for it! And in the fog of war it was a classic blue-on-blue.

For 3 Para it was their first fire-fight of the campaign, and the platoon from C Company got stuck in. A Company's gunners tried to open up in response, but because of being on the forward slope, in proper firing positions their weapons pointed downhill. They therefore had to sit up to fire, inaccurately from the hip, and were immediately hit – the gunners the first to be wounded.

The ranges were between six and eight hundred metres, and C Company's gunners were pretty accurate. The mortars then came down on top of C Company, but before the A Company platoon commander could order fire for effect, his radio was shot to pieces.

There was no escape from C Company's fire:

C Company's machine gun fire chased the patrol up the hill, wounding nine men. When the patrol reached the top of the plateau, for some reason C Company held their fire.

Hearing the firing, the remainder of A Company came to the rescue from the area of Findlays Rocks, with two Blues and Royals Scimitar armoured recce vehicles. Their now desperate patrol were firing red Very flares, so the Scimitars fired some twelve rounds at C Company – the 'Argentinians'. Then just as the survivors of the fire-fight reached the safety of the top of the slope, the artillery fire ordered by C Company came crashing down around them.

Some forty shells landed beside the patrol, causing two more casualties, both serious head injuries. On the flat plateau top, they were totally exposed to the artillery fire, while down the slope, the wounded were still under accurate machine gun fire from C Company. A Sea King helicopter flew in to evacuate the patrol's wounded, but in attempting to land too quickly crashed, its tail fin and wheel being ripped off. Another aircraft was requested, and the patrol tried to attend to their wounded. Round about this time somebody realized that members of 3 Para were in fact shooting at each other. Corporal Kelly, section commander of 4 Platoon, B Company, believes that the CO himself ordered everybody to stop firing, before investigating the situation for himself.

Finally a second helicopter arrived with the CO on board, and evacuated the wounded. Part of A Company was left to guard the damaged aircraft, while the remainder continued their search for the Argentine ammunition dump that had been the ill-fated patrol's objective. McCullum:

Only five men actually came back from the patrol. They were really frightened and badly shocked. Every time they had tried to crawl towards the top of the hill, the C Company machine gun fire had switched onto them. They said that the best thing to do with rounds coming at you like that was to play dead. C Company's gunners confirmed this, telling of how they'd waited to see movement, then let rip at it, adding a couple of extra bursts to finish them off.

A Company did not blame C Company for shooting up their own men, and when men from the two sub-units met a week or so later, C Company were deeply apologetic. The incident made everyone determined to prevent anything similar from happening in the future. CO Hew Pike strongly supported this reaction, making it clear to the battalion that such disasters were part of the inevitable, sad confusion of war, lessons to be learned and not repeated. The battalion as a whole then put the event behind them and got on with the war.

Corporal Tom Howard was on duty at the Ajax Bay field surgical hospital on 23 May:

They were in shock with multiple gunshot wounds. They thought they'd been fired upon by Argentinians, and told me not to believe reports that the enemy were rubbish. At the time, I was impressed with their opinion that the Argentinians were very, very good – until we found out what had really happened.

Sergeant French, A Company, 3 Para:

I get more angry now thinking back on the blue-on-blue than I did at the time, when I thought of it as part of the fog of war. It need never have happened if certain individuals (not in the patrol or in the defending company) had been doing his job – however who am I to criticize?

Co-ordination of defensive positions is vital. You learn that it is far more important in war than it has ever been on exercise. The effect of the tragedy was to make everyone very much more careful.

Surprisingly, some individuals did not immediately appreciate what had happened:

I was particularly angry when the next day after the blue-on-blue, after a lot of preparation, I handed a detailed patrol plan into the HQ, with my route, FPFs [Final Protective Fires–preplanned artillery targets] etc. all marked – to be told by this person, 'Oh yes, you might do all that at Brecon, but you don't need to bother with it here.' I complained to someone more senior, who sorted this person out with a roasting and a bollocking.

Planning took on a much greater importance for everybody. Corporal Kelly:

For example, the next night, somebody heard helos landing so I was woken up in the early hours to take a patrol out to investigate. We already had OPs forward, so I was worried about another blue-on-blue. I was told to be moving in ten minutes – which I refused. I demanded at least an hour to brief the men fully.

We stayed out until first light, then came back in daylight so that people could see us. We were more frightened of bumping into our own people than the Argies.

The military importance of conformism and 'fitting in' has been discussed in an earlier chapter. The command of a battle involves a tense interplay of powerful personalities, each with his own strongly held ideas. The overall commander must channel these personalities into his concept of operations, and they must limit any criticisms or doubts to within very clearly defined limits. Subordinate commanders can be sacked on the spot for overstepping these bounds.

The chance to do well in a battle does not come to professional military men very often in their careers (if at all), so there is an understandable self-interest in ensuring that they and their unit make their mark. Commanding officers will do their best to get as much support and as many resources for their unit as they can – even at the expense of other units – to give themselves the best chance of success. This self-interest is well understood, and is an important part of the fighting spirit of units. It is also the reason for the very careful terminology used to define (and limit) the role of sub-units assigned to units and formations for specific operations: e.g. 'under command for movement', 'in direct support', 'attached for Phase One only' and so on. Empire-building is common in military formations.

Artillery and fighter ground attack controllers are among the most sought-after people on the modern battlefield as, like Merlin the Magician, they can bring death and destruction far beyond the capability of others. In gathering together the best resources for their particular unit, commanding officers are keen to retain their own artillery observer and forward air control teams. However, from the perspective of these specialist teams, the aspirations of the individual unit commanders to whom they are allocated are less important than the overall formation plan towards which they work. Artillery observers work much of the time towards the brigade commander's plan. Forward air controllers (FACs) find suitable targets for aircraft, then talk them on to these targets in such a way as to avoid enemy anti-air positions and the accidental bombing of friendly positions. They have the very specific job of finding targets to fill the aircraft slot times allocated by higher headquarters that justify risking millions of pounds worth of aircraft (and pilot). Like artillery forward observers, FACs deploy to the front line with other units, but fight their own larger-scale war – rather than the small-scale business of the unit with which they are cohabiting. In practice, however, the parochial interests of units can become a serious complication for FACs and artillery observer teams. As low-ranked outsiders (captains), they can be used ruthlessly by the units to which they are attached – as happened to Dennis Marshall-Hasdell.

D Squadron SAS had established a forward position on Mount Kent, an ideal place for an FAC to do business. In order to get there, Marshall-Hasdell was to fly on to Hill 107 with 42 Commando, then move forward to meet the SAS on foot. With Royal Marine Corporal Dave Greedus, he joined 42 Commando for a night helicopter move in appalling weather with very overloaded aircraft. Having seen how ineffective Argentine cluster bombs were in the wet peat, and how the force of their 1000 lb bombs could be absorbed, he came to the conclusion that risking aircraft on close air support attack missions on Mount Kent was not worthwhile.

As far as the CO of 42 Commando, Lt Colonel Nick Vaux, was concerned, Marshall-Hasdell had been given to him to deploy as he desired – in this instance forward on to Wall Mountain, a five kilometre night march away. Lt Chris Marwood, 42's recce troop commander, was in charge, accompanied by two of his recce sections. Artillery forward observer Captain Nick D'Appice with his OP party were coming too, making a total of some twenty men to occupy what was supposed to be a covert OP. Marshall-Hasdell:

I was never happy with this from the very beginning. From the FAC point of view, Wall Mountain was a pointless place to go. I could see much better from where I was. There was just no decent cover. Although on our own we would have been all right, there was no chance that twenty of us could remain undiscovered.

The patrol were to take the position and then, using artillery and Harrier support, hold it. CO 42 Commando needed to know more about Mount Harriet (his battle objective) which perhaps this forward OP could provide. Unfortunately, as far as Marshall-Hasdell was concerned, this aim was not made clear, and was in the event to be proved untenable.

They spent a night with L Company of 42 Commando, then moved forward through evacuated Argentine positions. All hopes of the operation remaining covert were abandoned when for some strange reason Marwood's recce sections cleared the (empty) enemy trenches using hand grenades and bursts of gunfire:

These silly attacks on deserted enemy positions drew Argentine shell fire, which although not effective, kept our heads down. We dived for cover into cracks in the rocks – which were full of Argie shit. (They shat everywhere.) From the beginning of the operation, I stank.

This was their first experience of shell fire.

Wall Mountain turned out to be exposed, with poor visibility; fog, drizzle and low cloud, and most depressing of all – no radio communications. 'It was a waste of time. There was nowhere to build a sangar or hide an OP, and we couldn't move at all because of the bare-arsed rock.'

On the second day, at around 1100 hours local time, an Argentine patrol of about twelve men came from the front edge of Harriet and split into two sections, one to the north side of Wall Mountain, one to the south. Lieutenant Marwood decided to sit tight, but members of his recce sections insisted they'd been seen – and opened fire. This uncontrolled, rather ill-disciplined action ended all hopes of remaining covert. At ranges of 20 to 50 metres, the British throwing grenades and firing 66mm anti-tank rockets, M16s and SLRs, some of the Argentine patrol were killed.

With no radio communications to call in artillery fire, Marwood decided to withdraw. On the road below, two Argentine trucks appeared and dropped troops off behind their OP position, to cut them off. Captain D'Appice and his artillery team were already moving back towards Mount Challenger in an attempt to get through on the radio, and started bringing down artillery fire.

We were separated from our heavy bergans, with the radios and all our gear. The patrol was spread over quite a large area, with lots of shouting, noise and firing going on. The marines abandoned all their equipment, and although no one told us, it became clear that we were to withdraw.

With no information, and the likelihood of having to fight our way out, Dave Greedus and I decided to abandon our equipment, destroying as much as we could. The two radio sets (HF and UHF) were tough enough, but the HAZE unit of the laser target marker was designed to withstand the weight of a tank!

Abandoning equipment goes very much against the grain with soldiers – even in desperate situations like this one. The laser target marker was a Top Secret piece of equipment – issued in advance of its issue date, specially for the campaign. When he was originally given it, Marshall-Hasdell had actually asked how it should be destroyed – to be told to carry plastic explosive with him and blow it up! So they dug a hole, placed the radios and LTM in the bottom with several grenades, then riddled the equipment with rifle shots, smashing the coding device on the LTM and its lens.

Once we reached Nick D'Appice's position, the withdrawal was under control. I saw that D'Apps had got out with all his gear, which made me want to go back and get ours.

Chris Marwood refused to allow Marshall-Hasdell to go back – a decision taken fast, without discussion.

This was probably the start of my problems; I wanted to go back – but didn't do it. It makes me feel now that if I had gone back, it would have been a brave and heroic thing. Chris Marwood however was sensible and saw the stupidity of it. I fired a few rounds at the Argentinians, then one of the marines said – as a joke, 'It'd be safer if you unload now, Biggles.'

No one had shown me what to do in a fire-fight or a tactical withdrawal. I became an appendage. From then on, I felt useless; I had no training that could help me in this situation, I was of no use to anyone, and I had lost control of the situation I was in. I couldn't see, at the time, why I wasn't being allowed to go back, but accepted Chris's decision because I knew I was in an environment I didn't understand.

I just couldn't see the danger of it then; during the contact I felt cold and logical, with everything happening around me. I felt a strong sense of guilt at not going back for the kit. I feel a sense of frustration about this now; because if I'd gone back, I'd probably have been awarded an MC – but posthumously. No one ever questioned my decision to leave it; the Board of Inquiry after the war was concerned about the LTM's coding device, but agreed with my decision to ditch it.

'H' Jones's death is a telling example of the pressures facing battalion and company commanders. As individuals, through willpower alone they must force and inspire men to risk their lives in actions that nobody in their right mind would actually want to perform. Chaplain David Cooper:

'H' talked to me as a confidant, as a clergyman outside the chain of command. Some would have said that he was unbalanced at times, but I wouldn't agree with that. He wasn't a good peacetime CO. He was an enthusiast and a gladiator and if anyone wasn't of the same type he didn't want to know. We had a young captain who was leaving the army, so 'H' made him Intelligence Officer [the least responsible captain's job in the battalion]. This officer came to see *me* wanting to know what an intelligence officer was supposed to do – as 'H' wouldn't see him.

'H' was very black and white. I liked him, and we got on well. He and his adjutant Dave Wood were a formidable team.

Jones had very clear ideas about the importance of the Goose Green operation:

His assessment of the overall situation was that the Islands had been lost without casualties, South Georgia had been recaptured with minimal casualties, and so if the first contact with the Argentinians was successful, then maybe the same could happen here [at Goose Green]. Conversely if this first battle turned out to be a disaster, then he believed the opposite would be true – and we could [through losing at Goose Green] have lost the war.

Battalion doctor Steve Hughes:

The [Goose Green] attack had slowed down because of the lack of fire from HMS *Arrow* [its 4.5 inch gun having broken down]. We ended up still in open ground as it was getting light – in some confusion. A Company seemed to be making heavy weather of it, then got stuck. Half of them were out in the open, and the others were in cover in the Bower. Casualties were out in the open ground, covered by a line of Argentine trenches, which had to be knocked off.

A Company were bogged down, with no leadership to get them going. They had young, inexperienced officers, who were relying on the NCOs, who in turn were relying on leadership from the company commander. 'H' knew there was a problem, and that his left flank was likely to crumble. There was no point in B Company being where they were if that happened. He had no choice but to go forward and sort the problem out.

Cooper:

It was a major turning point in the battle. But one does keep meeting people who say, 'We employ corporals to do that sort of thing.'

Hughes:

'H' has been maligned by others for being so far forward. He was where he had to be because his whole plan was about to fail through A Company having gone to ground. He was the only man who could get them going again.

Jones and his small Tactical ('Tac') HQ moved into A Company's area, where they were asked by A Company's CSM 'not too politely to keep out of the way while his company commander attempted to sort out the situation'.[3] But Jones was not prepared to wait. He knew the importance of maintaining the momentum of the attack – at all costs. Cooper:

He was pretty psyched up by that time, but I think he knew that the only way he was going to get what was needed was by showing everybody, and doing it himself. I suppose he could have waited for the anti-tank weapons [Milans] to be brought up, but I don't think time was on his side . . . There are plenty of good reasons for not doing anything in a battle.

Hughes:

Because so few groups of people were free to move, Tac 1 split up [to make their attack in two groups]. David Wood and Chris Dent [A Company 2ic] led a group up to the left. They were killed as they tried to go over the top [of the ridge].

'H' had tried to move round to the right, and in running through dead ground failed to see another trench, which picked him off from behind as he came back into their view. He was trying to attack one of the key Argentine trenches. Because of continued firing, nobody was able to get to 'H' until the Argentines started to surrender. A section NCO from A Company, Corporal Abols, seeing a desperate attempt by officers to do something, was stimulated to take on the trenches with a 66 – which was possibly the turning-point in A Company's battle.

Major Chris Keeble, 2 Para's 2ic, took over command of the battalion. The battle was at its critical moment, momentum regained but hanging precariously in the balance. A 'demonstration' of fire power was planned the following morning, intended by Keeble to minimize casualties on both sides. It was not required. Cooper:

A couple of days after the battle I told him [Keeble] that I didn't think the Parachute Regiment would allow a war to affect their promotion plot, and that a new CO would be sent out from UK to take over. Rather than upset the peacetime promotion system, they preferred to send out the next man due for promotion.

After Goose Green, the battalion became almost totally inward-looking, mistrustful, verging on antagonism towards outsiders. Lt Colonel Chaundler arrived at a particularly difficult time. Hughes:

Then suddenly there was this new guy foisted on us from the UK, who arrived and started making stupid comments [at his first O Group] like, 'You're not standing close enough to the razor' – said just after the Blues and Royals had broken the water supply pipe so nobody could get their dehydrated rations cooked, let alone wash or shave!

Chris Keeble nevertheless supported Lt Colonel Chaundler, showing him the ropes, easing him into command.

In combat, regardless of any other consideration, the man holding the rank bears the responsibility – but a wise commander listens to the advice of his subordinates. Cooper:

Chaundler went on to win the Wireless Ridge battle, said to have been the best planned and executed of the whole campaign. He kept casualties low, in the face of enemy positions that were expected to require the operation to continue the following night – for which 3 Para were warned off.

Despite this, Chaundler as the replacement CO received no official recognition. Chris Keeble, having acted one rank up after the death of 'H' Jones, received a DSO, as did the other successful COs. The awards were given [to units] on a ration basis. The VC was more or less forced by the press [on 'H' Jones], and it seemed to boil down to a DSO to each battalion involved in the fighting. In 2 Para, who gets it, Chris Keeble or the CO, David Chaundler? The whole world knew about Chris . . .

The Scots Guards had been honest enough early on to admit their serious lack of military experience. Before the main battle for Stanley, their Commanding Officer Mike Scott had held a brain-storming session between his officers and the experts assigned to his battalion – the artillery battery commander, engineer officer and so on. This session established how the battalion would operate in battle, and keep itself within the bounds of its limited capability. It also established Mike Scott's professionalism with his outsider experts.

Operations Officer Captain Tim Spicer attended the 5 Brigade orders group with his CO, to find that their media-conscious commander had invited television cameras to film the event:

The 5 Brigade O Group had an aura of tension – and BBC cameras. I was surprised and worried about the cameras being there. I thought they might transmit the O Group before we'd made the attack – and no one reassured us that they wouldn't. I felt a touch belligerent towards them, not feeling that we were receiving quite the support we were due.

At the Brigade O Group, Spicer was thinking through how he would allocate the tasks they were being given among the battalion – the so-called 'Task/Org'. He was fully conscious of the importance of the document he was about to write. As at Fitzroy, the CO brought in his experts to help formulate the plan:

It was a proper op order, the real thing, and I went into overdrive. Back at the battalion, we had a Chinese parliament, with the 2ic, the BC and one of the company commanders Richard Bethell (ex SAS, the most experienced man operationally in the battalion).

Moving by helicopter was new to the battalion, and gave Spicer a staff problem that neither he nor the battalion had faced in training:

We had to work out an air movement table – something new for us, which we had to learn how to do. We moved forward to the FUP [forming up point], with a creeping feeling at the thought of impending action. The HQ dug in while the CO held a confirmatory O Group on a hill overlooking the objectives [Tumbledown].

Knowing it was 'the real thing' continued to stimulate Spicer's military professionalism:

It was very interesting eyeballing a real objective – with no four-tonners to take us back to barracks once the attack was over, knowing that some of us would be killed. The artillery rounds started landing . . .

They came under observed artillery fire – the orders group having been seen by the Argentinians:

I could actually taste my fear – like if you lick a battery terminal to see if it still has a charge. The CO dispersed the O Group, leaving us with a strange decision – whether to run away from the artillery rounds, or walk. The BC and I decided to walk – as an example to the soldiers. You couldn't have all the leaders in the battalion running away even before the attack had started. It was a bloody long walk, and I was very glad to get back to my sangar.

As the attack proceeded, Tac HQ monitored progress by radio:

We sat on the end of Goat Ridge as G Company took their objective. It felt much safer at night, with no awareness of the shrapnel coming near to us. There was some tracer on Wireless Ridge, but nothing close to us. There was nothing dramatic, only an air of unreality. Amazingly, comms [radio communications] were perfect and everyone on the net was calm. Brigade harassed us continually for sitreps [situation reports]. G Company sent the code announcing that they'd taken their objective.

Left Flank company came under heavy fire, which Spicer experienced 'in stereo', over the radio as he listened to sitreps, and what he could actually see and hear to his front. Left Flank were pinned down, taken by surprise by the sudden fire – and by Argentine resistance, which the battalion had not expected to have to deal with:

Right from the word go, when we joined the QE2, we thought in our hearts that we'd get down there and there would be no fighting, that they would throw their rifles down. Right up to the last minute we did not expect a fight. We were too confident; I think that fifty per cent of us felt like that.[4]

An experienced and battle hardened naval gunfire team, led by Captain Chris Brown, had joined 2 Scots Guards, fresh from 45 Commando's attack on Two Sisters the previous night (Brown's team had earlier worked with the SAS in their raid on Pebble Island, and taken part in several other Special Force offensive operations and the capture of South Georgia). Brown was extremely concerned that the Scots Guards' Tac HQ, still at the start line, was now 3000 metres behind the battle, incapable of influencing events. Brown:

It was very obvious that this was the Scots Guards' and the battery commanders' first encounter with the enemy. It was another example of the 'silent night attack' which, combined with other circumstances, resulted in unnecessary delay and casualties.

Brown had fired HMS *Yarmouth*'s 4.5 inch gun in support of the Scots Guards' first objective, to good effect. However, he was prevented from giving similar crucial support to Left Flank by battery commander Roger Gwyn, who for some reason, wrongly believed that the naval gunfire would be inaccurate. When Brown was eventually allowed to fire, Scott asked him to 'move it away a bit' as it was 'too close' – another manifestation of the CO and BC's comparative lack of combat experience, which Brown believes resulted in Left Flank Company being pinned down by snipers for over four hours. Having lost radio communications with his own forward observer, rather than use naval gunfire Gwyn himself attempted to bring down artillery very close to Left Flank – which as he was 3000 metres to the rear, was potentially very dangerous for them. Their sensible reaction to this confusion was to get their heads down. Lieutenant Anthony Fraser, commander of 14 Platoon:

The morale of my platoon had been very low. The cold was unbelievable – we had been there nearly four hours and it was taking all our time to keep in touch with our bodies. Most of the men had nothing to do. I felt the combination of cold, uncertainty and the general awareness that we were stuck, led to the group ego shrinking and shrinking and shrinking. At that stage, I thought we had blown it – holding up the whole brigade attack

– and that those people who had said we would be no good, coming off public duties to do this job, were right.

CO Mike Scott felt that as his men were pinned down, it was his duty to go forward to be with them. Brown (who was not consulted) agreed, but Spicer and Gwyn urged him to stay where he was. Spicer:

Roger Gwyn was keen to avoid him [Scott] being killed like 'H' Jones [at Goose Green]. The CO asked my opinion and I advised him not to go up to be seen. He would only be pinned down too. I also told him that we still had confidence in the Company Commander's ability to do the job, and that we should let him get on with it.

So the Scots Guards' Tac HQ waited on Goat Ridge until the second company, Left Flank Company, had moved through towards their objective. They then started moving forward – prompted by enemy artillery fire:

A line of shells burst to the right of us, then a line to the left. The BC had realized that the saddle we were in was probably an enemy DF [defensive fire] which they were now adjusting. We were bracketed and the next rounds would fall among us. He ordered everyone to run forward, up and on to the bottom slopes of Tumbledown, out of the fire. We ran fast, some of us giggling at the incongruity of it – but it was a salutary experience.

This artillery fire was being controlled by an Argentine recce platoon commander, who had stayed behind as the battalion advanced, working as a sniper. Several of the battalion's dead were to have his bullets through their heads. He was eventually captured.

Tac HQ moved forward, reaching G Company, coming under fire from mortars and Energa grenades. For the first time, they saw the reality of the battle – casualties being dumped for helicopter pick-up. As ops officer, Spicer was seeing for the first time the results of his planning: 'Half of me was fascinated by them – I wanted to go across and look at them, talk to them ... but the other half wanted to ignore them and get on with the war.'

With Left Flank pinned down, this second phase of the battle dragged terribly. Spicer felt frustrated that he could do nothing, at the lack of action and his own inability to influence events. He was very tired and cold, eating sweets and desperately wanting a cup of tea. An explosion crashed into the HQ area:

I was blown over by the blast of this artillery shell. I saw a red haze and flashes in my eyes. I checked that the CO was okay, then everyone else. The sergeant major was crawling around on his hands and knees – as if wounded.

Comedy and human necessity overcame the situation:

When the shell came down, he'd been unwrapping a Mars bar (which he'd
been saving for weeks). The shell had blown it out of his hand. He borrowed
my IWS [image intensifier weapon sight] to find it.

   Once the deadlock of the second objective had broken, Right Flank's
attack went like a text-book operation – almost like at Sennybridge [in the
Brecon Beacons]. I gave the code word for 'all objectives taken' to brigade.
Over the radio I could hear them cheering in the background. I felt great
satisfaction that the plan had worked. We then had a row with brigade
about getting helicopters forward to pick up the casualties. They'd been
waiting six hours, and unless the helicopter flew to them, would die.

   The CO then walked the battlefield, and we suffered a big shock when we
came upon the first dead guardsman. He was spread-eagled on the ground,
arms outstretched – like that classic photo from the Spanish Civil War of
the soldier in the instant of being shot. The sniper had drilled him right
through the front of his head. It was a shock because until now we'd been
shielded from the blood and guts. The dead Argentinians didn't bother us.

Argentinian resistance was broken, thousands of their soldiers
streaming westwards from the battlefield, leaderless and without
fight. Spicer:

We walked round the companies seeing that the boys were okay, then joined
in the slaughter of the withdrawing Argentinians. It was like a turkey shoot,
unbelievable. The BC and his FOOs were calling down artillery fire, and our
machine guns were blasting away. I couldn't believe it was happening. My
small scrap of remaining humanity said we ought to stop it, but my brain
said we had to kill as many as possible. The more we killed, the less we
would have to FIBUA [fight in built-up areas] out of Stanley.

The My Lai massacre stirred up enormous emotions in the United
States, both against the war and in support of 'our boys doing their
duty over there'. The investigation that followed showed clearly how
American military leadership worked in such a way as to make massacres more likely. My Lai showed the enormities that can result from
commanders becoming isolated from the realities of the battlefield
and losing sight of the morality of what they are trying to achieve.

   Lieutenant Calley and his platoon were not alone in having carried
out massacres. They were young and inexperienced, needing guidance and mature leadership. Before arriving in Vietnam, as part of
Charlie Company, they trained in Hawaii at a special 'Jungle Training Centre', using live ammunition in a replica Vietnamese village,
complete with booby-trapped huts and slant-eyed, peasant-shaped
targets that snapped up to be shot. The message put over in all their

training was that Vietnamese men, women and children were out to kill them, so to survive, they should kill first.

The British Army uses similar urban replicas (known as 'Tin City') to train every unit that goes to Northern Ireland – replicas inhabited by male and female soldiers acting as a very volatile (although closely controlled) civilian population. It is billed as having 'the most disobedient and violent civil population on the planet', and no British soldier could ever believe that he will experience a similar level of violence in Northern Ireland. The instructors make it very clear to trainees that 'Tin City' is only an aid to training and not in any way a representation of reality.

While still training in Hawaii, Charlie Company's new commander Captain Ernest L. Medina took over. He was popular, but over-enthusiastic to the extent that he was nick-named 'Mad Dog Medina'. The company's first ten weeks in Vietnam were spent patrolling, digging trenches and latrines, setting barbed wire, and becoming enraged at the elusiveness of the enemy. Acts of kindness to the locals, such as the giving of medical help were repaid by sniper fire. Pity for their poverty soon turned into callous brutality. The first death, that of GI Bill Weber, and a series of ambushes and a minefield disaster that killed four and severely wounded twenty-eight, made the survivors feel guilty that they had not been among those killed or wounded.

Finally, when one of the older men, Sergeant Cox, an experienced soldier to whom many had turned for emotional support, was blown up by a booby-trapped artillery shell, a fundamental change took place in the company. Officers and men alike muttered among themselves about 'the only good gook being a dead gook' and of the need to become a savage, obeying only the laws of the jungle. Cox's memorial service was an elaborate military event organized by the chaplain, in which Captain Medina's eulogy became a moving call to arms.

It seems that earlier in the day, Medina had attended a conference at the Brigade HQ at which the new brigade commander had given a pep talk stating that he wanted to 'get rid of [the Vietcong unit located in that area] once and for all', and that he wanted the three companies to 'get more aggressive'. The Task Force Commander was reported to have said that he 'wanted the hootches burned, the tunnels filled in and then he wanted the livestock and chickens run off, killed or destroyed'.[5] Medina's eulogy carried the message down to the troops. After speaking movingly about Cox and the other dead men, he said something like: 'We lost a lot of guys. Pinkville caused

us a lot of hell. Now we're gonna get our revenge. Everything goes.'
The men understood Captain Medina to have also said words to the
effect of, 'Here's our chance to get back at them . . . there are no
innocent civilians in this area'.[6]

Charlie Company were in deep mourning – and very angry. Captain Medina was suffering with them; as commander he would have
absorbed much of their pain. Nevertheless, Medina did not invent
the brutal message he is supposed to have given his men. In fact he
passed on with some accuracy both the words and the inherent message of the brigade and task force commanders. In the light of what
transpired, both those colonels must bear responsibility for not having known the condition of either Captain Medina or Charlie Company, and of failing to realize what effect their orders might have.
Brigade headquarters were clearly too divorced from the brutal realities of the war to understand.

As a ground commander actually fighting the war, Medina would
have known that in order to get rid of a VC unit 'once and for all',
severe measures would be required. In telling his men that there were
no innocent civilians in the area, he was absolutely correct – every
villager would know at least something about the local VC cadre, and
some villagers might be active members. He had been given a firm
and clear objective, at a time when he particularly needed direction.
His company were seething with pain and grief, desperate to be given
something concrete and effective to go out and do. Their comrades
had died worthless, useless deaths, which they wanted somehow to
avenge. Medina's eulogy became the mission that each man needed,
a reason and purpose for their having lived when others died.

The killings at My Lai started at around 0800 hours, as soon as
the men dismounted from the helicopters. The operation had started
with the usual artillery and helicopter gunship bombardment, which
would in itself have indiscriminately killed plenty of innocent people.
Men, women and children were herded together and men fired into
the screaming huddles. Several young women were raped then killed,
animals were shot and huts put to the torch. By 1100 hours, when
the company stopped for lunch, between four and five hundred villagers were dead. That same morning, several hundred Vietnamese
in a nearby village were killed in the same 'combat operation' by
another company. The men acted as if they were in combat, taking
up proper fire positions, kneeling and crouching as they fired at
defenceless people. The villagers looked like the enemy, or at least
what the men had been told the enemy looked like, so during the
massacre they became 'the enemy', and were 'engaged' and 'fought'

in what psychiatrists described as a murderous, play-imitation of the game of combat, a perverted form of the so-called 'baptism of fire'.

During the massacre, some men were business-like and professional, taking breaks for cigarettes, while others were 'wild' and 'crazy', chasing pigs with bayonets, killing, raping and destroying. Many shouted at their victims as they fired; such things as 'that's for Bill Weber'. Some describe a rising of excitement as people were herded together, of hearing a shot and a cry of 'You dirty Vietcong bastard', then of firing into the crowd themselves in horror and excitement combined. There might initially have been mistakes – perhaps even a negligent discharge. Participants spoke of the absurdity of what they found themselves doing, and of doing it again in order somehow to justify it.

Repeating mistakes is a common military method of avoiding blame. For example, one negligent burst of fire from a machine gun is obviously a mistake, but if the firer lets off several bursts he can claim to be 'engaging the enemy in a fire-fight'. When investigating, disproving such a tale could be difficult. More to the point, the discredit on the unit (as opposed to the man) would be great enough to lead to the suppression of the truth even if it were to be suspected.

The inexperience of Charlie Company, and their lack of training and direction, lies at the heart of reasons for the massacre (and other similar events in Vietnam). 'We had only a half-assed idea of what we were supposed to do.' 'The people didn't know what they were dying for and the guys didn't know why they were shooting them.' The men were trying to find some kind of military justification for what they were doing – not only at My Lai, but in many similar units throughout the course of the war. One young soldier remembered thinking that a boy with his arm shot off was the same age as his own sister. As he tried to decide whether to kill him, he thought:

What if some foreign army was in my country and a soldier was looking at my sister just as I'm looking at this little boy. Would that foreign soldier have the guts to kill my sister?

The young soldier made his decision: 'If he'd have the guts, then I'd have the guts,' and pulled the trigger.[7]

Others spoke of the desire to kill being like 'scratching an itch, it's going to drive you nuts unless you do it'. They compared how they felt with Second World War soldiers:

When they used to have those battles I imagine a lot of the guys were really tremendously relieved . . . [at My Lai] they could just sit there and mow them down. And that's what I guess they wanted to do.

There was also fear that the VC would counterattack. One of Lieutenant Calley's platoon, testifying at his trial:

I assumed at every minute that they would counterbalance [counterattack] ... [by means of] some sort of chain or a little string they had to give a little pull and they blow us up, things like that.

The massacre seemed to this soldier to be 'the natural thing to do at the time'.

In Charlie Company nobody sought to cover up for what they had done. The men compared notes and boasted of the numbers they'd personally killed that day. They discussed the technical merits of their weapons, the relative damage caused by artillery shells, .45 calibre pistols and hand grenades. They talked as if My Lai had been a military victory or an acceptable act of war. After the massacre, Charlie Company thought of themselves as 'more relaxed' and 'loosened off'. They justified what they had done by noting that afterwards they suffered less casualties and that the VC threat 'dropped off'. The killing of children was justified because they would 'grow up to become VC anyway'.

Some men had decided not to take part in the killings. The strength of perverted leadership that had encouraged the rest of the platoon to open fire, made them feel that they were the unhinged, unstable personalities. One said: 'I wasn't the only nut [that didn't fire] ... I wasn't really crazy. [Condemning what happened] was the right thing.' However, refraining from taking part in the killings did not absolve such men from the terrible effects of guilt – that led a psychologist to describe the men from Charlie Company that he visited eighteen months after the massacre as 'frightened, conscience-stricken, terrified kids'.

Between 1971 and 1972 the Vietnam War began to wind down. The lack of purpose and moral military leadership was replaced by a widespread nihilistic desire to survive – described by journalist Donald Kirk as:

not so much a test of strength under pressure, as it often was a few years ago, but as a daily hassle to avoid patrols, avoid the enemy, avoid contact – keep out of trouble and not be 'the last American killed in Vietnam'.

The Americal Division inspired little pride in its men:

First there was ... My Lai ... followed by the case of a former brigade commander charged with mowing down civilians from his helicopter and ... revelation of the use of chemical defoliant capable of inducing cancer.

Then . . . the commanding general was relieved in the aftermath of an attack on a firebase in which thirty-three GIs were killed.

'I'm afraid to tell anyone back in the world I'm with the Americal,' says one of the lieutenants, laughing sardonically. 'No one has much pride in the division. That's one reason morale is so bad.'[8]

Winding down led to more refusals to obey combat orders and the 'fragging' (murder attempts, often using hand grenades) of officers judged too enthusiastic about exposing men to danger:

. . . a gung-ho officer full of plans for daring patrols and ambushes, pleading with his commanding officer to give him 'a few more days to work the area by the stream' while his men cursed him silently – and not so silently: 'God dammit, if no one was looking, I'd frag the sonuvabitch.'

Counting the time before going home became a morbid and extreme preoccupation, men feeling that as there was no victory to be won, they were wasting time. The pointlessness of the war was accompanied by the serious erosion of the moral authority of those in charge, and many units discussed fragging without actually doing it.

Without a clear, achievable military aim and a morally justifiable reason for prosecuting a war, no amount of military leadership can hold an army together. In purely military terms, it has been successfully argued that the Vietnam War was actually won by US forces (but lost by Congress refusing to continue funding the South Vietnamese Army). In many ways therefore, it is remarkable that US ground forces held together as well as they did for a decade in Vietnam.

Infantry platoons – and their equivalent tank, artillery or engineer troops – are the basic building blocks by which wars are fought and won. Their efficiency, morale and determination depend upon the way the platoon sergeant and his platoon officer work together. This relationship varies greatly according to individuals, but without the experience and maturity of the sergeant combining with the youthful leadership of the officer, the section commanders who actually fight the battle will not be effective and the platoon will fail to function. The British Army sets great stock in a traditionally paternal sergeant respectfully guiding and teaching a young officer to the point at which he actually takes the reins himself. The Israeli Defence Force is very different, selecting its officers from the best NCOs. Platoon officers in the IDF are older and by definition better than their sergeants – the British paternal sergeant and youthful leader rolled into one.

In battle the paternal sergeant/officer relationship is put to the test.

The officer must come up with the goods, and his sergeant has to ensure that his officer does not fail – for everybody's sake. Parachute Regiment officers, having survived P Company selection, enjoy a high degree of respect from their men – but nevertheless they are very young, and combat is a very exacting environment. WO2 McCullum, a platoon sergeant in A Company, 3 Para:

We had some young officers who shone beyond all expectations, and others who did not. It was about fifty-fifty.

Going off to the Falklands was all 'gung ho'. Everyone wanted to go. The Falklands was our terrain (as it was the Marines'), our sort of thing, a perfect time and place for us. But once the bullets start flying and the artillery shells and mortar rounds start coming down, people think, 'What have we got ourselves into here?'

A lot of officers had never seen a man dead, with half his head shot away. There was a shock factor when this happened to one of his men. The officers were straight out of Sandhurst, aged eighteen, freshly into the battalion and now off to war. The shock of it was a big factor for them.

There were incidents of officers becoming paralysed at critical moments, having to be slapped about the face – even given the full fist – by their platoon sergeants, to force them to get a grip and do their job. This was entirely understandable. The platoon sergeants were aged around 29, each with six or seven Northern Ireland tours under their belts. They'd seen the dead and the dying.

There are moments in combat in which the officer must come up with the goods. Regardless of his inexperience, it is his responsibility alone to take critical decisions and lead the platoon. Like an actor, he is 'On' and must do his stuff:

In training, as the platoon sergeant you can let him get on with it, drop a bollock and make a mess of it. In battle, however, with the platoon in danger, you could never sit back and say, 'It's your baby, you get on with it'.

We were stuck on a ridge at Mount Longdon, just before the final part of the attack, and were told to fix bayonets, strip down our webbing and prepare to go over the top with grenades to clear the final position. I briefed the section commanders, and the platoon started preparing for this highly dangerous assault with anticipation and fear. We were the third platoon to go over, and while we waited, my platoon commander sat down beside me and said, 'Sar'nt, what do I do?'

I replied, 'You're fucking joking! What do I do? You're about to go over the top with the men and you're asking me what do I do, now!' I said, 'Listen, you don't need radios, you don't need nothing. Forget that. You're going to be so close to your section commanders that communication will be by word of mouth. You've got two point sections, work with them.

They'll tell you "Positions Clear", "Positions Clear", you've just got to follow them up through. I'll be here at the back, any problems you've got, always push me forward.'

But what a time to ask me! [good-natured laugh] There was no way I was going to say 'You wanker', you couldn't because he was giving it this . . . [gesture indicating fear]. He'd suffered a hard time a few days before, which I appreciated. He was obviously frightened. There was no way I was going to say, 'Fuck off, I'll take over.' But it was a shock to me, having him ask me that – at that time.

In fact, I knew that he understood exactly what to do. He was a good officer, but the fright factor had got to him. He just lost control, couldn't remember what to do. It was the most basic thing he had to do anyway – shouting at the people nearest to you . . . very simple.

wo2 McCulloch, then a platoon sergeant, B Company, 2 Para:

The platoon commander and I worked as a team, so that what one lacked in experience, the other could provide. He was on his own however in the battle, up at the front, commanding and co-ordinating the sections. During the battle, the men reacted to his voice. Afterwards they might think well of him for being in there with them – or adversely had he not been there. At the time they just get on with the job. When leaders didn't do what they should have been doing, somebody, like the platoon sergeant, would have a sharp word and put them right. In any case, in our regiment, the section commanders would just carry on. It's very much a question of face, like being in the balloon – you jump because there are three others behind you watching.

Discipline was never necessary because everyone knew what to do and got on with it. Sergeants major don't go round shouting. In battle everyone is in a team, depending on everyone else, so nobody needs to go round telling people what to do. On a few occasions, with people not reacting as quickly as they should, or feeling a little sorry for themselves, I gave short, sharp reminders that it wasn't just their lives on the line, but everyone else's too.

The platoon sergeant's job is to keep the men and their equipment ready to fight, and in actual combat to get casualties evacuated from the front line and ammunition resupply forward to the sections. McCullum:

I spent a lot of time looking after men with exposure and bad feet. During the battle, I was very busy; looking after our casualties, prisoners, ammunition. I never had time to get worried or frightened. It's not like being a Tom, in charge of nobody, with nothing to think about except what might happen to him. I had too much to plan for and think about to be frightened.

It was the younger lads that we lost, who went forward in twos to attack the positions man-to-man. Platoon sergeants are older and wiser. The boys do the job for you. The young lads report positions clear, and you just say, 'Let's get on!'

Platoon sergeants must pass on the benefits of their experience in such a way that the men believe what they say and continue to trust them. They must also get the men to do things that are dangerous – somehow without jeopardizing that trust; like coping with being shelled:

I explained my thoughts on artillery fire to the rest of the platoon, which seemed to make sense to them: If you are in a trench or bunker, to hit you a shell has got to land right on top of you, hitting an area eight feet by eight feet or less, with pin-point accuracy – which it is very unlikely to do. With the unit spread out over a huge mountain, you'd be particularly unlucky if this happened to you.

We were quite heavily shelled on Mount Longdon, but only one of my men snapped under it. This particular man was a section commander who'd been out on a limb from the rest of us, his section acting as sentry on the forward slope. After a day of shelling, he asked to be pulled back to our reverse slope positions. I said: 'Pulled back to where? We're all being shelled the same as you. You'd only come back to another bunker being shelled just the same.' 'No, no,' he insisted. 'They seem to know where we are, they're trying to hit us.' I told him: 'The shells are all over the place. He's not pin-pointing you, he doesn't know where you are – it just seems like that.'

A bit of fear was creeping in, helped by the shells. And especially at night, we couldn't sleep at all – but nobody broke under it, or became in any way desperate to get out of it.

McCullum's platoon had suffered the loss of a section in the blue-on-blue incident with C Company early in the campaign.

Having lost a whole section, I was given a collection of drivers and odds and sods as replacements, which I put into my rear section, along with this machine gun team.

On the way to Mount Longdon, we were coming under fire from artillery and small arms, with the odd lucky hit from a sniper or shrapnel. There was plenty of undulating ground as cover and peat trenches to get into. On crossing the Murrell River, one of the drivers had fallen in and became soaking wet. He started to gibber and shake, with exposure.

The surviving gun team and also the platoon commander had been seriously affected by the blue-on-blue. As well as having to take great care with the machine gun team, Sergeant McCullum had to keep his officer going. The platoon commander was the first to attend to the soaked driver:

I heard some squealing and found the platoon commander beating this man up. They were on the ground with the platoon commander on top shouting, 'Wake up, wake up.'

I put my rifle down and dragged the officer off. Whether this bloke was bluffing or not I don't know, but I got him some dry kit, and rubbed his hands and feet [to get some circulation going]. Mortar rounds were landing all over the place – but just sporadic fire. To warm this bloke up, I got him to raise his feet in the air, but one of the two men from the machine gun team rushed over and insisted that the driver's white feet were drawing enemy mortar fire!

On Mount Longdon, 3 Para were overlooked by Mount Tumble-down. As day broke, their sections on the forward slopes of Longdon came under fire from Tumbledown. Sergeant McCullum pulled his platoon back on to the reverse slope of Longdon, back into dead ground away from the fire. He heard panicky shouting from one of the sections, and discovered that two machine gun teams, including the pair who had survived the blue-on-blue, were still on the forward slope in view of Tumbledown, stuck twenty yards down in a bunker.

They were under heavy fire, which was breaking down the rocks in front of them. The section commander blamed them for having been too slow in getting out, so there they were, stuck . . . I was reluctant to give covering fire [to get them out], for fear of drawing enemy artillery. I shouted down, asking how much cover they had, and would it last until nightfall? There was artillery fire coming down all around, and the section commander was panicking. There was a forward observation team [artillery] close by, so I asked him to smoke them off [so they could withdraw behind the smoke]. Unfortunately the smoke [canisters] buried itself into the peat, so they had to wait. The FOO then tried to fire HE, but had to stop to let a Harrier come through. I was shouting instructions down to them all this time, to keep them from panicking.

By the time it got dark, they'd been under fire for over three hours. The Harriers took about 45 minutes to do their attack, then finally the HE came down and the platoon opened fire against the enemy positions. I've never seen people move so quickly.

I was very glad to see them, but unfortunately they hadn't brought any-thing with them. They'd left their weapons, the machine gun, ammunition and everything. I sent them off to make a cup of coffee. Later, as that section went forward in the darkness [as a night sentry] to cover in front, I stopped them: 'Where was their machine gun – *my* machine gun?' 'It's still down in the bunker on the forward slope', they said.

I then did the wrong thing, shouting: 'Get your arses down there and get it' . . . because they replied, 'No, you must be joking!' I told them they had to go down for it, but again they refused.

This was a serious moment – a mutiny in the face of the enemy which is a capital offence even now. The Parachute Regiment approach to such things, however, is to sort them out yourself, rather than fall back on military discipline – which is exactly what Sergeant McCullum did.

In the end I said, 'Fuck it, I'll go.' I got the platoon lined up again, under strict orders that if even an enemy .22 [the lightest calibre small arm] opened up, they were to give it all they'd got.

One of the two sat on the ridge line shouting out instructions where to go, and I crawled down, got the gun, webbing and ammunition and came back up. The section then deployed, and I went to sit with the platoon commander. I was soaking wet anyway, but there was also a terrible smell, which I realized came from my having crawled through an Argentine shit-pit. I was not in a good mood . . .

I wouldn't send any of those men [from the blue-on-blue] out on an ambush, or give them too much harassment. They'd been through a lot, and didn't need any more testing. They came through all right, and are still serving and enjoying it.

I always used to say, 'War's a bastard'. You've got to keep a wry sense of humour going, because if the platoon sergeant goes down, everybody else follows. You keep discipline going, never letting men slacken up, but you don't go round cracking jokes – it was too serious. The men were either happily working, frightened, couldn't give a fuck or indifferent . . . the characters pulled each other along, and they didn't need a big happy sergeant!

McCullum's platoon commander was never the same after the blue-on-blue: 'He lost a lot there. He'd been really badly frightened. While we were being shelled, I could see that he wasn't right. He'd not been the same since his first experience.' The Sergeant was nevertheless bluntly positive about this:

In fact it made my war a lot easier because I had to keep a constant eye on him, looking after him rather than getting worried myself.

He didn't like the war, he said it wasn't for him. At the end, when we were sitting on Mount Longdon, while Wireless Ridge was still getting pounded [with shells], he couldn't see the sense of it: 'Why didn't they leave?' He couldn't see the reality of having to keep hitting them until it was all over.

As they watched, three prisoners came up to them, half-naked, with unbuttoned jackets, their trousers dropped, laces undone [to make resistance impossible] hands in the air, trying to surrender:

It was my job [as platoon sergeant] to look after them. The platoon commander asked me what was I going to do with them? I said, 'What do you think I'm going to do with them? I'm going to shoot them, then dump them off the top of the hill. They're no good to me!'

It was the first time that I'd seen him – as a young lad – flare up at me: 'No you fucking won't!' 'Well I wasn't going to anyway. Only joking . . . only a joke.'

He really hated the war, the killing, yet when we first started off, he'd been keen, geeing the men up, we were going to do a good job . . . At the end of the play, he'd had enough; and at this silly joke, two days after the surrender, he'd snapped.

Sergeant French:

We spent ages in this dip in the ground. I'd love to go back now and see it again. The OC [Company Commander] was making serious decisions, finally deciding to try one last effort to go round the left-hand side to link up with B Company. If that failed, he was going to order us to remove our webbing and swarm over the top in one human wave, to take out the last bunkers.

I remember thinking, 'Fucking hell, this isn't the First World War. We don't do things like this!' We were however all prepared to get on with it, and do it. It all ended up being very unorthodox, fighting teams with grenades, going under machine gun fire to the bunkers and sorting them out at really close range.

In the confusion of combat, formal leadership and group organizations tend to break down. Corporal Kelly:

Platoons get mixed together in battle, and the guy with the strongest personality ends up taking over – regardless of rank. The guys then follow. People have smoke breaks – and lots actually start smoking! – and work out what they should be doing for themselves.

In the more extreme moments, decisions have to be made, and often it doesn't matter much what is actually decided as long as everybody gets on and does the same thing. By the same logic, the individual who makes the decision does not need to be the person officially in charge. Cooper:

The individual on the battlefield has the authority that he takes. I did things that were way beyond my authority [as a chaplain], for example sending the Welsh Guards back to Ajax Bay after the Galahad disaster because nobody else could take a decision. Not one of the Welsh Guards officers was capable of making a decision, they were so shocked, so I had to decide.

5 Infantry Brigade HQ was nearby doing absolutely nothing, completely inert, so I got two helipads running to evacuate casualties, then flew out the survivors. Despite the survivors having no kit and so being ineffective, their company commander refused to accept this, insisting that on the ship he had enough to re-equip the unit.

Cooper almost forcibly reminded this major that the ship was burning, then ordered him to go to his soldiers and compile a list of survivors and missing:

Only the brigade commander could have made the decision to send this battalion back. You get the authority you demand on the battlefield, rank tends to take a back seat . . .

With well-trained troops in combat, leadership seems to become a little like that of an ant colony; everybody knows what needs to be done and gets on with it. French:

We tried everything, Milan missiles, 66mm anti-tank rockets, people teaming up with the snipers and the artillery, all the different units joining up as one big bubbling unit dealing with the problems. If one thing didn't work, someone would try something else. The cohesion between all these different little units was marvellous.

In the end, leadership in battle comes from within the unit, from every person involved – rather than from individuals with rank, or over the radio.

Later, a similar cohesion developed between 2 and 3 Para on Wireless Ridge. I never thought two parachute battalions could get on so well, as they still do to this day.

It brings tears to my eyes to think about it.

10

COPING WITH CARNAGE

War and death go together. Although fighting and winning a battle can be elevated into either an intellectual chess game for commanders, or a professional job of work for tradesmen-like soldiers, the real purpose is killing. You kill the enemy and win the war.

During an attack, the fighting men are too busy to do much about casualties. Their comrades fall, either wounded or dead, and the attack moves on, leaving the bodies behind. Nobody knows who lived and who died until after the battle. Even then, it is impossible to know how comrades are faring in hospitals hundreds of miles away from the battlefield. It can be months later before friends are reunited – or discover that friends are dead. Platoon Sergeant 'Mac' French:

You don't know what happened to the casualties. The last time you see them is as they are fighting for life and the medics take them away – or when you have to move on and leave them. I don't remember thinking or worrying about my casualties until we got home. During the battle we were too busy, and at the end, so very tired . . . so very tired.

From the purely military point of view, once a man is dead or wounded, he is of no further use. Worse, if wounded, he becomes a serious burden to the logistical system. Care of the wounded, especially in a chemical or biological warfare environment, does not contribute to the killing of the enemy or help win the battle. Looking after enemy wounded is even more futile.

In most of the battles of the past, there has been no alternative to this cruel military logic – largely because medical science could not provide any but the most basic battlefield medical services. Without anaesthetics most would die of shock, and without antiseptics or antibiotics the rest would die of infection. There was little point in treating mass casualties. The Royal Navy led the way to an extent by carrying ships' surgeons – not from humanitarian considerations, but because without healthy crew, ships of the line could not fight. The British Army's medical effort started to grow during the Crimean War, its nursing staff being civilian volunteers like Florence Nightingale. Only in the last hundred years have armies provided themselves with formal medical infrastructure to deal with large-scale battle casualties. In the Boer War, and other colonial expeditions, many more soldiers died from disease than from any action of the enemy. Cleanliness, hygiene and disease prevention were identified as war-winning factors, so medical officers held sick parades, and health and personal hygiene became enforced soldierly virtues.

In battle, the same medical officers were then supposed to deal with mass casualties – waves of large numbers of very seriously injured people. Their effort has always seemed somewhat of a token gesture, Canute-like figures struggling against a sea of violence. Today they are backed by battlefield ambulances, field surgery units and field hospitals, although in the British Army at least, financial investment in the medical services has rarely been given the same sort of priority as that given to killing the enemy. Modern soldiers will not throw themselves into a battle unless they know that the medical back-up is the best that can be arranged. Why should they risk their lives if the army does not value their sacrifice enough to provide good medical services? If soldiers *believe* that they will be well looked after when wounded (no matter what actually happens), then they will fight. Thus, in purely military terms, medical services are a very important part of maintaining the morale and fighting spirit of the troops. In peacetime, however, the military importance of medical services cannot be demonstrated, so only lip service tends to be paid to them – a very unwise attitude. Setting aside any humanitarian considerations, as was discovered in the Gulf War, if you are serious about fighting and winning battles, your soldiers must be certain that they are supported by the best medical system.

When they are actually in combat, troops do not think in any detail about what will happen to them if they are wounded. They are frightened of being maimed and of the pain of wounding, but provided they believe they will be properly looked after, they get on with the job. The determination of troops to continue fighting is completely separate from any sort of calculation by individuals of the number of wounded or dead their unit might have suffered. In any case, no individual can see more than a few metres, so such a calculation is impossible. There is no simple correlation between the total number of casualties and whether an attack succeeds or fails.

It is unlikely that as the battle is being fought, anyone will be able to give first aid. It is therefore up to each individual to keep himself alive during these critical first moments after being wounded, which as the battle continues, can turn into hours. Personal first aid skills are vital for every soldier, as the means of self-preservation. Platoon Sergeant McCullum:

If you put one man to each of your wounded, you soon lose the whole platoon. This 'buddy-buddy system' will stop the momentum of your attack, and the momentum is what takes you through. The official line was that the wounded have got to be able to keep themselves alive, which the men accepted.

It's callous to order a man to move on when his best mate has just been hit. You have to bring up the medic, and then tell the man to carry on, which he does knowing his mate is being looked after. It depends upon the situation whether you order the men to leave casualties or not – you can't impose inhumane rules. However, although you can tell the men not to stop for their mate, in reality unless he's dead they'll stop for him, patching him up before carrying on. B Company were certainly doing that.

Battlefield first aid differs from the usual trauma first aid, in which airways are cleared and cardio-pulmonary resuscitation keeps people alive. These techniques are rarely possible or practicable in combat. Serious battle injuries are accompanied by severe loss of blood; soldiers cannot carry matched whole blood or plasma to replace the blood losses of others and have no time to carry out the delicate operation of inserting an intravenous drip into their mates. Patients whose hearts stop beating are unlikely to survive the long journey to the main dressing station or field hospital. Every member of 2 Para in the Falklands carried a half-litre bag of saline solution. Inserting a needle into a vein, particularly in a seriously injured man whose vascular flow may have become restricted by shock, is however, very difficult. Instead, Captain Steve Hughes (their medical officer) taught the insertion of tubes into the rectum of patients – a procedure that could take place on the battlefield before the men even arrived at the Regimental Aid Post. (The technique was practised on the sea voyage down, to much ribald comment.)

A summary of the basics of battlefield first aid – theory and practice – should perhaps introduce the thoughts and memories of those who had to actually do it. Stopping loss of blood from wounds is important, by applying pressure to points where the main blood vessels pass over bones (pressure points), tight bandaging and even tourniquets. The latter are dangerous as once the patient loses consciousness, in the confusion of battle a tourniquet may be forgotten.

The affected limb loses its blood supply and becomes necrotic, creating a surge of infection that can kill the patient or makes amputation unavoidable. Large holes, in the abdomen or thigh for example, can be stuffed full of some sort of wadding – a rolled-up jacket or pullover, or vacuum-packed shell dressings that have not been unwrapped – then bound up tightly with crepe bandage. Anything to stop the bleeding.

Being shot through the chest is in many ways preferable to a bullet through the abdomen, pelvis, shoulder or thigh. High velocity rounds have tremendous force, which is transferred to the tissue surrounding the wound. The chest is largely an air-filled space, and provided the bullet does not hit any major blood vessel and misses the spine, it will go straight through, taking most of its lethal energy with it. However, with both the lungs and chest wall punctured, air is sucked into the chest cavity with every breath the casualty takes, reducing the extent to which the lungs can inflate – and he slowly suffocates. The bullet's entry and exit holes must be sealed up, and the British Army's 'first field dressing' has an impervious outer wrapping that can be ripped in two for this purpose. Individuals with chest wounds can help themselves by sitting up and holding their hands over their wounds, but the feeling of panic as the slow suffocation begins is terrifying. A 'sucking' chest wound is easily stabilized at the Regimental Aid Post by inserting one-way valves into the entry and exit wounds, which let air out of the chest cavity on inhalation, sealing it for exhalation.

In war movies, the wounded are always given cigarettes – whether they smoke or not. Morphine (and cigarettes) are part of reassuring frightened patients, which, once breathing and bleeding have been attended to, is a most important treatment. However, morphine should only be given for certain types of wound; sedating the patient can lower his blood pressure and cause his death.

McCullum:

Although we were all medically trained, it was better to leave it to the proper medic. During the training, we'd been told about morphine speeding up the blood circulation and increasing blood loss. One of my blokes had been hit in the leg with shrapnel, and we wanted to make him comfortable and get on, leaving him for the medic. Unfortunately he'd got this thing about morphine fixed in his mind and absolutely refused to let us inject him.

Another lad had a bullet wound to the shin, which was bleeding. In trying to stop the loss of blood, I was making him scream – until I realized that he'd probably got a badly broken leg as well. We caused a lot of unnecessary pain to casualties through trying to treat them but getting it wrong. You can't play around with seriously injured people unless you are properly trained and well practised.

Battle casualties first see a doctor at the Regimental Aid Post. Although the doctor will carry out any emergency life-saving procedures that might be necessary, he has only the most limited resources, and so must use his expertise to make a very swift and critical assessment of each patient. This categorization is called 'Triage', in which the casualties are divided into three priority groups – a tough and practical decision as to who is to be treated, who can wait, and who is left to die.

The most desperate cases become 'Priority One', those in need of urgent resuscitation and surgery. A gunshot or shrapnel wound of the thigh is the most common wound of war – and is the most usual Priority One wound. With such a wound, the casualty will die quickly through loss of blood from a damaged femoral artery. Penetrating gunshot wounds to the chest are also Priority One, provided the patient is still alive. Lt Colonel Leitch, Royal Army Medical Corps: 'If the heart, the main arteries, or the spine have been hit, then the casualty is probably already dead [or will soon be so], and is therefore not Priority One.' Other chest wounds are Priority One: 'If nothing vital has been hit, the bullet will have gone straight through, deflating one of the lungs, which although immensely dangerous is easily repaired.'

McCullum:

The worst wounds we had were sucking wounds to the chest, which after Northern Ireland and first aid lectures you'd think would be quite straight-forward. The bloke gets hit in the chest, red froth on his lips and air entering his rib cavity – so you cover the entry and exit wounds and lay him on his side.

However, when the bullet goes in and twists, it breaks five or six ribs, the ends of which then dig into the wound and are very painful. With a lung wound, turning the man on to his side is so painful that the man will not let you do it, and will get back up again. We had one bloke died choking simply because he wouldn't lie down on the smashed-up side.

A hit in the abdomen is also urgent. The entry hole may be a simple hole with little fluid loss, but if the abdomen is distended 'like a drum', a major blood vessel has been punctured, and is filling the cavities between organs with blood.

Priority Two wounds are serious but not an immediate threat to life. Lt Colonel Leitch:

The amputation of a limb by shrapnel or from treading on an anti-personnel mine, although very painful is not immediately dangerous. In the shock of the injury, the blood vessels in the stump contract, reducing blood loss, and the wound is easily tied off.

Priority Three can be anything from a minor burn to a broken ankle, but also includes very serious injuries like an open head wound:

If you survive a head wound, the chances are that it won't get any worse, so you become a Priority Three patient. Lieutenant Robert Lawrence of the Scots Guards is a good example. A missile had ripped a piece of skull away, taking with it a piece of his brain. Blood vessels had been damaged, but because the wound was open there could be no build-up of pressure inside the skull. Once those blood vessels had been clipped off, he could wait.

Non-medical personnel do not understand the harsh realities of triage, particularly when doctors appear to be ignoring a serious head injury case. Other wounds are more urgent. Fitting one-way valves into chest wounds so that men do not suffocate, or cutting into drum-tight abdomens to find and tie off bleeding arteries, must be done instantly to save life – and with terrifying speed. An open head wound on the other hand requires time and infinite patience, which may be in short supply in the heat of a major battle. Head wounds need to be cleaned up (called debridement), the bits of bone, dead brain tissue and dirt carefully and painstakingly removed, then covered. Until a head wound patient can be removed to good surgical facilities, careful observation is all that can be done, checking for any changes to his condition.

Head injuries do become classified as Priority One if there is evidence of bleeding inside the skull. As intracranial pressure increases, the base of the brain (the brain stem) that controls the brain's automatic functions – particularly breathing and heart action – is affected. Unless the pressure is relieved rapidly, the casualty will die.

Battlefield triage is completely different from anything that happens in peacetime and so can only really be learned in combat. In the early days of a campaign mistakes will be made; in the darkness, screaming patients with lower limbs shredded from the blast of mines will be competing for helicopter floor space with ghastly head wounds and ashen-faced men clutching their abdomens in sickly silence. Those with head wounds and smashed lower limbs tend to be loaded on first. Once the helicopter has gone, it is too late for the real Priority One patient, the abdominal wound who is actually dying.

When high-velocity bullets strike flesh they create a shock wave that moves in front of the bullet, slamming through muscle tissue and organs. For a few thousands of a second a very large cavity is created inside the body. The bullet drags with it fragments of sweaty, filthy clothing, and, because the impact cavity is a partial vacuum, as it collapses even more potentially infecting matter is sucked into the wound. Often the surface of the skin immediately around the wound will be tattooed with dirt and debris. The infection that is sucked in by the bullet is considerable and due not only to dirt, but more specifically to the bacterium *Escherichia coli* that in combat covers soldiers' skin. In the long periods without any sort of sanitation on the battlefield, these organisms multiply outwards from faecal material around the anus. Almost immediately after the impact and penetration of the bullet, the muscle fibres in the area surrounding the wound start dying, the necrosing flesh increasing the risk of infection and gangrene.

Battlefield surgery is a two-stage process. The immediate and most life-threatening damage caused by the projectile is attended to first. Ruptured blood vessels are stitched up and vital organs roughly repaired. With the patient stabilized, the wounds are deliberately left open to allow oxygen to enter. In this first stage of battle surgery, which usually takes place under less than ideal working conditions, any structure, crushed nerve or shattered bone that still lives is preserved, to be dealt with later when more sophisticated procedures can take place in better conditions. Complicated reconstruction surgery can only be done in a proper hospital.

In the second stage, surgeons re-open the wounds and, once bleeding has been stopped, start debridement. Peroxide and a scrubbing brush might be used to remove dirt and muck in certain sorts of injury, but where the head, chest or abdomen have been penetrated, there is no alternative to the laborious cutting away of any obviously dead tissue and the removal of grit, dirt and bone splinters using forceps, scissors, scalpel and probe. Quite large cavities will be created by this severe cutting. Once the wound is clean and red raw, after being packed with gauze dressing and bound up with crepe bandage it is left open for three days to allow aerobic bacteria to clean out any infection that remains. In the Falklands, patients were moved from Ajax Bay to the hospital ship SS *Uganda*, where any remaining necrotic tissue was removed and more complicated repairs made.

After the battle for Goose Green, and at the end of hostilities in the Falklands War when British surgeons came upon Argentine wounded who had been treated by Argentine surgeons, they found wounds that had been cleaned up, then, as in normal civilian practice, sealed with clips. Because these wounds had not been left open, anaerobic infections like gas gangrene and tetanus were thriving. The Argentine doctors had attempted to overcome this with antibiotic tablets, despite the fact that drugs are unable to penetrate dead muscle tissue. British surgeons noted that their Argentine patients all had some kind of wound infection.

Explosions cause quite different injuries from small arms fire, and artillery fire causes both shrapnel and blast injuries, often at the same time. Shrapnel from exploding shell cases is razor sharp, scything and spinning through the air. Although it loses momentum quickly, quite small chunks can tear off whole limbs and cause terrible slashing and deep gouging injuries. Blast alone can kill through tearing off limbs, but also by causing massive internal injuries that may not be apparent from the outside. The rupture or contusion of viscera leads to internal bleeding and air embolus (fatal bubbles of air entering the blood stream). Local 'implosions' of very high pressures in certain areas like the eardrums, lungs and intestinal tract also cause serious damage. Respiratory failure ('blast lung') occurs 12 to 36 hours later.

For infantrymen, mines are particularly frightening. Whereas anti-tank mines explode only under the weight of a heavy vehicle, anti-personnel mines are intended for people, and to maim rather than kill. A crippled soldier, screaming out in agony for help is far more of a burden than a dead one, both emotionally to his comrades and logistically to the medical system. The flash and blast of the explosion can also temporarily blind those nearby and perforate eardrums. The blast 'de-gloves' the boots, trousers and flesh from feet and legs, sometimes leaving the bones intact. The extent of the subsequent amputation depends upon exactly how you tread on the mine. Royal Engineers Lieutenant Jon Mullin: 'If you stood on one with only your toe you lost your foot and ankle. If you trod on one with your heel, you lost your whole leg – either just below or above the knee.'

Unless in a completely open space, the blast of an explosion is usually accompanied by heat, particularly when vehicles are being hit by missiles and direct fire projectiles. Temperatures above 43° C cause burns, which affect the lips, mouth and pharynx, and unprotected parts of the body like the hands. Much higher temperatures are needed to cause pulmonary changes, but in the confines of any vehicle, the smouldering or burning of toxic materials (electric cable, hydraulic fluid, fuel . . .) causes immediate smoke inhalation damage, which develops into serious respiratory problems.

In the Arab–Israeli war of October 1973, which was fought largely using armoured vehicles, around 10 per cent of all wounded suffered burns, of which 30 per cent were serious (with third degree burns through the full thickness of their skin). Some 8 per cent had pulmonary problems, over half of whom were damaged to the extent of needing tracheostomy in order to be able to breathe. Comparisons with casualty statistics from armoured battles of the Second World War reveal the improved power of modern weaponry: many more tank penetrations with correspondingly more killed, wounded and burned. Although tanks are better protected today, increased weapon efficiency with over five times more explosive in shaped-charge warheads (an inverted 'V' that blows a hole through armour) has dramatically increased spall fragment injury to crews and the damaging effects of pressure and temperature.[1]

When a tank is hit by an armour-piercing or explosive projectile, even if the crew compartment has not been penetrated, the crew are nevertheless likely to suffer wounding from ricocheting spall fragments (metal scabbed off from the inside of the compartment), and a combination of burns, blast and smoke inhalation injury. Burns also lead to respiratory problems and infection, as large areas of the body are damaged and the body's immunological response is reduced. Land mines threaten a tank's crew only if their compartment is penetrated or if the vehicle is lifted off the ground by the blast, throwing the occupants around inside. The inside of a tank is a very confined space with dangerous steel projections.

Burns casualties are particularly difficult to treat on the battlefield. Charred and fused clothing must be cut away and the whole body examined to assess what percentage is actually burned skin. Loss of fluid is critical, so intravenous infusion is started immediately. Rather than ordinary dressings, white Flamazine spray, like shaving foam containing painkilling, antiseptic sulpha compounds, is then applied to seal, cool and sterilize the wounds. Burned hands are tied up in sterile plastic bags where the wounds can be kept under close observation. In the healing process, scar tissue forms that severely restricts movement, leaving fingers and hands contracted like deformed claws. Some burns are bad enough to require escharotomy, the slitting of both sides of each swollen member to keep the blood flow circulating. Without this painful procedure, reduced blood circulation to individual fingers causes tissue to die, with the risk of gangrene and loss of the limb.[2]

Surviving battlefield surgery depends very much on physical fitness, and the length of time that has elapsed since wounding. After lying for hours in cold, wet moorland waiting for helicopters to struggle through mist and driving rain, Falklands casualties arrived at Ajax Bay in bad condition – particularly Argentinians left by their comrades for dead. Some British casualties, perhaps because they were fit and highly motivated, benefited from the cold. McCullum: 'The cold slowed the bleeding down a lot, saving many who would otherwise have bled to death. They slipped in and out of consciousness . . .' The patients were cold (32°C as opposed to the normal 37°) which, apart from the hazard of cold exposure, altered the way the anaesthetics worked. Cold patients often stayed under for long periods after their surgery had finished. Their careful warming and reviving is time-consuming, particularly as front line operating theatres are usually without resuscitation or ventilation equipment. Patients have to be ventilated by hand, and warmed up by being given fresh blood and the application of hot water bottles.

The success rate of combat surgeons has increased greatly since the Second World War, although not in line with the dramatic increases in the power of modern weapons. The surgeon J. A. Ross reported that out of 1045 patients operated on by four surgeons at the Anzio beach-head in 1944, 65 had abdominal wounds (46 hollow viscera damage, 8 lesions to hollow viscera and 11 with no visceral lesion) all from blast injury. Only 33 of these were reported to be in a satisfactory condition later, and although no short cuts were taken in the surgery, two intestinal perforations were missed in one casualty. All thoracio-abdominal wounds were likely to die, and recovery was rare when compound fracture or traumatic amputation occurred with other injuries.[3] Comparison of these figures with battle surgery carried out 32 years later in Pakistan (during the Indo–Pakistan War of 1976), shows that burns and respiratory injuries were better understood and treated, improved vascular surgery saved more limbs from amputation and more men were sedated (using Valium). The use of the helicopter for casualty evacuation, however, was probably the most significant saver of lives.

Military surgery is very radical, and very general – which goes against the current medical trend towards surgical specialization. Most civilian surgeons do not know how to repair the massive and multiple wounds that occur on the modern battlefield. In combat, different levels of surgeon are needed; butchers initially, then general surgeons, then lastly in the field hospital, the specialists to make final repairs.

*

The experience of being wounded in action is not readily talked about by combat veterans. It involves a transformation from fighting soldier to victim – from being somebody who is active and potent, into a useless, supine burden. Being wounded but alive is the only acceptable and honourable ticket out of the combat zone, so this loss of status is also accompanied by a guilty and almost shamefaced relief.

Wounded soldiers rarely feel instant pain, just a shock of some kind. Their legs give way under them, for example, or they remember feelings akin to a sudden blow or a jolt of electricity. The pain follows, and a realization of what has happened – then sudden and overwhelming fear. The natural human reaction when wounded is to get away from noise. Although the noise of battle (which is considerable) is not harmful, it is very stressful and encourages fear. Most animals when hurt crawl away to some quiet place to control their pain and try to recover. Humans are no different. Private Nick Taylor, Support Company, 2 Para:

They say you never hear the one that gets you – it's true. The artillery shell that hit me landed just behind our Milan [missile] and took three of us out – which was the end of my war. I was unconscious for a short time, then awoke with a searing pain in my back. My section commander came over and stuck his hand straight down my crutch and said, 'Don't worry, it's all still there' and that I'd been hit by a 'shock wave'. Having been firing I was on my stomach. I didn't look round to see my legs as they hurt too much. I asked what had happened to them and he said, 'Oh, it's the shock wave. Your muscles have contracted, like cramp. Don't worry about it, you'll be up and about again in a few days.' Little did I know that he was lying through his back teeth.

They picked me up by the wrists and dragged me back fifty yards to wait for the medic. He gave me seven shots of morphine in an hour to calm me down. It hurt like hell, and as I couldn't feel my hands I was very worried. I kept getting my mate Blackie to squeeze them and because I couldn't feel him, kept asking if he was doing it. I kept blacking out and he slapped my face telling me not to fall asleep and that the helicopter would be there soon.

All my kit went as I was waiting there. People came along and asked for – or took – everything: my helmet, webbing, magazines – even my camera, although it might have been blown up.

The battle hotted up a bit and someone dug us a shell-scrape. There were about eight of us injured there, and we waited 26 hours to be flown out. One of the helicopters was shot down [killing Lieutenant Nunn; see Chapter 8], then by the time four of us were left, it grew too dark to fly us out. I felt very helpless, vulnerable and scared. I'd not looked at my legs, and couldn't move them. I had pain in the back, legs and arms, but I was still convinced I'd only got cramp. When they put bandages on, they gave me some bull story about easing the cramp. The morphine put me out of it pretty much anyway, but the time did drag very slowly. I thought I'd never be out of it. The bloke opposite me had his jaw all shot away and another lad was shot in the ankle. I kept looking at the bloke opposite and thinking, he's worse off than me. There were several dead Argies across the way too, and I kept looking at them as well.

I was put into a box on the side of the Scout, and could see the pilot's right arm through the little perspex window. Every time the helicopter banked I was convinced I was going to fall out. I'd never do it again. It really got to me. At Ajax Bay, they got us out of the coffin and into a holding area. The pain was getting worse and the morphine was wearing off. Hank had decided seven morphines were enough – he was worried he might have killed me!

The next thing I remember was being on the operating theatre table. They helped me get my trousers and pants down to the knees, and I looked down and thought, 'Fucking hell, where's it gone?' It was so cold and me being in shock, my dick had shrivelled up to nothing.

The cold, loss of blood and excess of morphine generated hallucinations:

There were these two women nurses in there too – at least they looked like women to me [there were no female service personnel on the Islands]. What must they think of me, I thought. I was sitting up on the table and they took my white thermal vest off – it was covered in blood. I knew I had a pain in my back, but still wondered where all the blood was from. That was the first time I saw my legs, all cut up everywhere. The left arm of my vest was also covered in blood. I was still convinced of this cramp story, but when I asked the surgeon he said, 'Oh yeah, and you've been hit in the back as well.'

Neither the medic nor I knew that my back had been hit too. I must have lost quite a bit of blood through that wound being unbandaged. Then I got worried that they were cutting my wind-proof trousers off me – they're like gold dust! They cut 'em straight up the middle with these huge scissors, and my boots up through the laces. I was gutted at that – and from knowing I'd been hit in the back. Then they gave me a jab and I was out.

Corporal Kelly, section commander 4 Platoon, B Company, 3 Para, was wounded in the final hours of the attack on Mount Longdon. His platoon were assaulting a strongly held Argentine bunker position:

I was coming across last, with nobody to either side. There was lots of noise with our machine guns firing and fire coming from all directions. After twenty or thirty metres a man went down in front, so I went over to grab him, to keep him in line with the rest. It was dark, so I didn't realize he'd been shot. As I got to him, I felt as if I'd been kicked in the back and side. I tried to stand up but my legs just gave way.

I rolled down, thought 'fucking hell' and then it started burning . . . inside us. I laid there for a bit, and everyone else realized we were being hit and had gone to ground. The platoon commander was trying to find out what was happening and where the fire was coming from. Once he'd done that, they went off to take the [enemy] trenches out.

With their second replacement platoon commander (the others having been shot), Kelly was acting platoon sergeant. Even though wounded and under fire, Kelly was still concerned with the progress of the battle:

The heavy machine gun was the main problem. It was dug into a really well-made sangar about 100 metres away and we just didn't have the fire power to take it out. We were in a little dip, and provided you kept really low, the fire went over your head. But if you sat up or kneeled, you'd be hit. After ten minutes, my wound felt stiff and I somehow knew I was going to be okay. I checked myself over, and couldn't find anything. I got the radio operator to have a look too, and eventually he found the wound. Because I was lying on a slight hillside, the small trickle of blood had run up my body and not down, so it turned out to be much lower than I'd first thought. We could find no exit wound, so we assumed the bullet was still inside.

I could move my upper body, but the whole of my hip had seized up from the bullet hitting it, a complete numbness. One of the younger guys was suffering badly from a sucking chest wound. He wanted to sit up all the time, but kept sucking more air into his chest cavity, slowly suffocating. Any time anybody moved at all, it drew more fire, so we knew he was in trouble.

The first attempt to get us out was by a big man called Scrivens who tried to carry [the chest wound] out, and a lad who held me up. A section put down covering fire as we all stood up, but another burst of enemy fire killed Scrivens and the lad who was holding me up, creating more casualties. Not being able to help or do anything was frightening. They had a re-think, then put down more covering fire and eventually got us all off, then moved us further down the mountain to the RAP.

After that first disastrous attempt to rescue us, I didn't want to be carried, preferring to try to walk, supported by others, rather than be carried on a poncho. I felt helpless and useless, and didn't want to be a burden to the others. I also realized that I'd have less chance of being hit again if I could walk on my own. I ended up on two guys' shoulders, and it was a pretty rough ride.

As we waited to be casevac'd I could hear the troops being briefed for the next stage of the attack. My guys didn't have time to come over and speak with me, but blokes from other platoons did. We waited there over eight hours, and I knew before I eventually left that my platoon had been disbanded – the survivors split between the other platoons in the company.

I didn't lose much blood because it was so cold. I didn't have any bandage at all on the exit wound in my chest for about ten hours. I didn't feel very cold until several hours after being shot, while we were waiting for the stretcher bearers. While we waited, the sucking chest wound died. Maybe it was a lack of compassion, but the noise of his terrible breathing was annoying, continually there, distressing to us. It was rasping, gasping for breath, him trying to sit up all the time. The medic was trying to do things, but he was dying . . . We wished that he would shut up, then suddenly the noise did stop. We called the medic, and he was taken away. We felt relieved that the noise had stopped – as it was seriously getting to us all.

It never affected us in the way of people breaking down or whatever. Somehow it didn't seem real, even though it was there. It didn't seem to affect anybody . . .

Kelly knew he had been very lucky with his wound:

The bullet had entered the edge of my ribs, and took a few bits of rib off then clipped the edge of the hip. Somebody laid a quilted jacket on to me to keep warm. I was put into the back of a BV [snow vehicle] which had a light inside. I fumbled around for my fags, and found I couldn't undo my trouser zip where the bullet had hit it. I then found a big hole – the exit wound. Another wounded chap (who'd been hit in the back) gave me a spare first field dressing which I used to patch myself up. I couldn't shout to anybody driving the BV until it stopped. I'd had one morphine syrette on the mountain and another before they moved us. I don't know if I needed it or not.

We flew to Teal by Scout, where they couldn't do anything for us, then on to Ajax Bay. I knew I was going to be okay, and was quite happy going down through the [casevac] system. [At Ajax Bay] they opened me up to clean out the wound. The round had gone through my water bottle, taking bits in with it. They had to open me right up to get the bits out, leaving the wound open for several days. It wasn't so much painful as the stink of the blood. They pushed a tube and gauze all the way through, then left the ends open to bleed. The exit wound was about two inches deep and the size of your hand.

Because of the severe cold on Mount Longdon, Kelly had lost very little blood. Looking back to being hit, he recalled that the shock was not as bad as he had expected it might be – which he guesses could be due to his subconsciously having expected to be wounded. 'I was lucky there was no infection, so all that remained was to have skin grafts for the entry and exit wounds.'

The memories of wounded men of the painful days and weeks of recovery, and of the long journey home, are often clouded by the drugs they are given to ease the pain, but also by the strong sense of having left their mates – and also of guilt at not doing their share of the fighting. By the time Private Taylor reached Ajax Bay he was in very poor condition: 'I woke up in the recovery room on a stretcher. I was gagging for a drink, but wasn't allowed to have one for 24 hours.'

Once he had stabilized after initial surgery he was taken to the hospital ship ss *Uganda*, where the more complicated repair surgery was done. She floated in a Red Cross 'safe box' 50 miles to the north, a haven of medical tranquillity guaranteed by international law. New patients found her a striking contrast to the main dressing station at Ajax Bay. The decks were carpeted, medical staff wore white, the stewards were Goanese – and there were female nurses. The amazement of patients was initially equalled by the shock of nursing staff at the condition of the filthy, exhausted men coming to them from Ajax Bay, 'their wounds unsutured' (it seems that in the normality of *Uganda* some medical staff were taken aback on first seeing battle wounds left open by surgeons to prevent anaerobic infection):

I can't remember going to the *Uganda* so I must have been pretty ill. They took me down these steep steps and I was worried at falling out of the stretcher. The sheets were all white and starched, lovely and clean. There were quite a few of our people there. I had three operations on my legs, and the doctor gave me some of the shrapnel he'd found.

We told stories of what we'd all done. We hadn't a clue what was going on in the war, unless casualties came on board to tell us. I still wanted to get back ashore and be with all my mates again, to get my own back on the Argies.

We were then transferred to *Hecla*, crammed into bunks four high and four wide. We met navy guys as well, until we were dropped off at Montevideo for the flight home by vc10. The war was still on, and not even my parents were told I was back in England. I had to phone them from hospital. It was all rather secret, being smuggled out of Brize by the back entrance so the press wouldn't find us. I didn't want to talk to anyone who wasn't in the army, and just wanted to get sorted out.

They kept me in hospital after all the others went home, but I did get a trip on Concorde and met the Queen when she came to visit. I was out at the end of June, four weeks after being hit. It took a year to stretch the muscles properly so I could run, and the holes took a long time to heal. I'd been hit thirteen times by shrapnel, on the left side, arm, back and legs. The other three guys in my section [who had been hit at the same time] were actually okay, but still got back-loaded to uk – even though one in particular, who had only been hit in the wrist, could easily have continued with the war. Being back-loaded annoyed them.

Uganda and the other hospital ships were Red Cross territory from which no combatant was permitted by international law to return to the battlefield.

Six casualties on *Uganda* with trench foot were particularly gutted because they'd thought that after treatment they'd be able to return to the battle. That made me feel good because I knew I'd got a good reason for getting out of it. We gave them a bit of a hard time, and they felt very bad – that they'd skived out and in the end wished they hadn't.

Corporal Kelly:

Talking to other guys on *Uganda*, for many with bones smashed, at first the pain was unbearable. After a while one of the guys told me he'd resigned himself to it. I was lucky as my life hasn't been affected by it [my wound]. Some of them were crippled for life.

Coming home was an anticlimax. We flew into Brize Norton – like returning through the back door. We were the last lot off the *Uganda*; they wouldn't let me off until the skin grafts had healed. I ended up with three weeks' sick leave, then the battalion had a month's leave, and I went back to work when they did. It seemed amazing to be back so fast. I'd been out of the system for a while, and being due promotion to sergeant, I needed to get on with it as soon as possible . . .

Nothing really got to me during the campaign. One thing got to me afterwards though: I clearly remember lying in intensive care on *Uganda* and a nurse asked me if I knew Corporal Steven Hope, and that he was a mate of mine. For some reason, at first the name didn't ring a bell, but she said he was 3 Para – Steve Hope. I finally recognized the name, and she told me to come with her as they were going to turn off the machine. He'd been shot in the head on Longdon. She asked what religion he was. I said C of E, so they got one of the two padres on the ship along, gave him last rites then turned off the machine. They then took him back ashore and buried him.

All the doctors have told me subsequently that this never happened, that Hope died ashore. However, I knew him very well indeed and he was three beds away from me on the ship. We'd joined and done P Company together twenty years ago. Why should I make up a story like this? I was very upset. It was so clinical, just turning off the machine like that. He'd been the OC's signaller and got shot by a sniper. They were lying down all together behind a bank and when everyone got up to move on, he stayed down and they realized he'd been shot. He'd never moved so they'd not known he had been hit. He never recovered consciousness.

Corporal Kelly did not make up this strange story, but perhaps it shows how a combination of sedation and grief can create what may have been a totally realistic dream, in which he acted out some of his emotions. With dreams, the emotions are the significant element, in this case Kelly's delayed reaction to the death of signaller Steve Hope – and possibly of other friends who had died that night on Mount Longdon.

The combat experience of medical officers and their assistants is totally different from the painful inertia of being a battle casualty. Within the medical profession, deciding to become an army doctor goes against the grain. Steve Hughes:

I joined the army to avoid becoming cloistered in the medical profession and get experience of orthopaedics and trauma. I had been attracted by the cohesiveness and bonding of the Parachute Regiment, particularly that of 2 Para, compared with the selfishness of civilian life. I never had any doubt over the rightness of what I was doing. As a doctor I was not going to be part of the fighting, but picking up the pieces afterwards – friend or foe.

Despite two years in Northern Ireland, 2 Para's medical system was poor. The sea voyage to the Falklands was invaluable. Hughes ran intensive courses for combat medics, and more general training across the battalion for everyone else:

On the way down in the *Norland* I said we needed a plastic infusion arm to practise putting up drips – and [2ic Major Chris Keeble] gave me the money so an infusion trainer could be purchased in UK for us. Those who could do it on the arm were allowed to try on a mate. This was a much more aggressive way of training than the RAMC policy of buddy-buddy care, company medic and RAP – which was far from being dynamic.

We taught self-aid; that if you are hit, you put your own finger in the hole, then drag yourself behind a rock and start your own treatment. Your mate secures the ground to make it safe for evacuation. There's no point in stopping to bandage a casualty if you can't move him anywhere. And you're more likely to lose the ground if you lose somebody else for every man injured.

The increasing likelihood of combat made his audiences even more attentive:

I did one particular lecture about combat care in which I asked the men to bring their concerns out into the open, throwing questions at me. They were more frightened about what they didn't know about, than what they did. Once you gave them the harsh realities, then at least they knew what to expect. Fear of the unknown was more important to them. They heaved sighs of relief discovering they were all concerned about the same things.

For example, they were very worried about the various misapprehensions that exist about wounds; for example, the John Wayne idea that any sort of abdominal wound means slow but unavoidable death. In fact 70 per cent of all wounds are to the limbs, not head shots or gut shots – which came as a great relief to them. If they were shot in the guts and were still alive, then they were going to stay alive because they'd be treated properly. I emphasized that they shouldn't assume they were going to die.

I was able to tell them about how most colostomies can eventually be joined back up again; how limb wounds would be treated; how their main problems were likely to be stopping one of their own bleeding vessels by putting a finger over it like you would a hole in the garden hose; that it was in their best interests to treat themselves and let their mates secure the ground.

For treating others, I stressed that as long as the airways were open and the bleeding under control, forget fractures, splints and everything else. If the guy is screaming and shouting then he'll be happier being alive at the end than if you'd filled him full of morphine and he quietly succumbed during a lengthy evacuation. They all understood this; it made sense. We were honest about the problems too; that there wouldn't be enough stretchers, and casevac would be difficult. HQ Company's defence platoon were organized as stretcher bearers, taking ammunition forward and bringing casualties back. We could break off a fire team from HQ to go forward for casualties, organized by the RSM – but it was far from ideal.

The attitude of 2 Para had always been realistic. They duly faced up to the hard medical facts:

The company commanders realized that it was up to them to get their casualties from where they were hit back to company HQs in any way that they could. We admitted that we didn't have all the answers – and we asked for ideas. They were nevertheless relieved to know what the score actually was, and had confidence in the back-up such as it was – the section medics, company medics and the regimental aid post. Each man knew what would happen if he was wounded. They'd met the Parachute Clearing Troop on the way down on *Norland*, so they also knew who would be doing their surgery. The fact that these guys wore the same coloured berets helped.

We'd had blood donor sessions before we left *Norland*, so they knew blood was standing by for when they needed it. They knew that a whole logistic set-up was ready to look after them, and they knew exactly what it was, which I think gave them confidence. They'd seen the system evolving on the way down and had trust in the guys running it. They were worried initially about pain, wanting to have morphine on them at all times. We were however able to educate them about this – that it was better to resuscitate the casualty than fill him full of morphine.

In combat, adrenalin levels are high anyway, and being wounded further floods the system. The effect of this is two-fold; adrenalin enables people to carry on and ignore pain, but can also increase fear drastically – and so increase pain. Fear and pain are inextricably linked. Drugs like morphine are not able to remove the pain; by making wounded men feel good they remove the fear, and the pain becomes controllable and so bearable.

Morphine is more of a treatment for the guy who is with the casualty and doesn't like the screaming. The screaming is keeping the man's airway open, and the adrenalin running round his system keeps him alive. Rather than trying to quieten him down, you're better off trying to get him evacuated. In fact the majority of guys who have been shot don't get a great amount of pain. Although we issued morphine to every man, not a lot of it was used, and surprisingly few had much pain because of the numbing effect of the impact of high velocity bullets – and also because of the psychological relief of having been wounded.

After the initial numbing effect of a wound, when pain does come, it is often experienced as a series of waves. When combined with fear and cold, pharmacological pain relief is very difficult to achieve effectively. Morphine may not actually give any relief at all.

Being shot is an acceptable way of getting out of the battle. The endorphins created by the relief of this realization remove much of the need for pain relief. Fear causes pain. Once a man had a wound, he knew exactly what to expect and to an extent his fear of the unknown was removed. Having come to terms with it [being wounded], they found it much easier to bear.

One particular man, Warrell, had been shot in the abdomen and was sitting in the RAP [at Goose Green] holding folds of his small bowel in his lap. I asked him if he remembered what I'd told him on the *Norland*. He was horrified by what he could see had happened to him – a very frightened young man – but was nevertheless reassured. I'd told them a story about when I'd been working in a hospital in Ely, of an old man of 70 who'd had a laparotomy [major abdominal surgery]. In a number of cases the wound breaks down after about ten days. He'd coughed, the wound had fallen apart and he'd found his guts had dropped out into his lap. There'd been no great drama; we'd wrapped his gut in sterile towels, taken him to theatre, shoved it all back in again and sewn him up. The guy was sitting up eating breakfast the next morning. On *Norland* I told them that provided it's all cleaned up and put back in again, having your guts come out was no great drama.

I said it's like the old boy I was telling you about. You've got your guts sitting in your lap like he had, plus a few holes as well that will have to be patched up. The severity of your injuries means that you have to be got to surgery pretty soon, and you'll be on the first helicopter out.

Warrell was reassured, and although he did not actually relax, became noticeably less tense – and a week later was back home.

On the battlefield the training paid off. As casualties came through the RAP, they trusted Hughes and his staff: 'They were being treated by the faces who'd told them what would happen to them – in exactly the way they'd been told they'd be treated.' Hughes's war had started slowly. After the landings at San Carlos, 2 Para's Regimental Aid Post was kept ticking over by a stream of problems associated with the men having got soaking wet during the landings – immersion foot and so on. They then sat on Sussex Mountains for a week 'not knowing what was going on, watching the navy getting hammered'.

Then suddenly we were off [to Goose Green]. There was one false start [when Brigadier Thompson cancelled the operation], then on the night of 26 May we set off at a horrendous pace – me totally knackered having been up all night with a guy suffering from renal colic.

We fell over lots of times, I buggered my ankle up and slipped into a knackered, automatic sort of mode. Eventually the pace slowed as the Forward Air Controller RAF Flight Lieutenant Jock Penman, a 56-year-old who wasn't really up to it, fell by the wayside. Then a man in A Company fell over and supposedly knocked himself out – although I was convinced he was feigning it and had jacked. I had to leave a medic with him.

It was bloody awful terrain, and eventually we collapsed exhausted in one of the outhouses of Camilla Creek House and waited for first light. The battalion sorted itself out, and dispersed from the house as it got light. Then the BBC World Service announced where we were – so we expected at any minute to receive an artillery barrage, which would put us out of action.

The Argentinians investigated, providing Hughes's RAP with its first customers: 'As it happened, all the Argentinians did was send out a fighting patrol, which got bumped by us. So we had our first casualties to treat – who thankfully were Argentinian.' Neither the medics nor Hughes had ever seen gunshot wounds before:

It was lucky that our first casualties were people we didn't know. It was easy to go and treat them – like a casualty department in the deserted house. The medics saw me start treatment then followed suit – I literally blooded them with Argentine casualties. They'd never seen real wounds – and afterwards I was quite impressed with their performance.

I was interested in the wounds, and took photos of some of them. The next day however, as our guys started coming in, the impact of their wounds was much greater. We'd never seen gunshot wounds on people we knew. I was so bonded with the blokes that it was hard to be the objective doctor, to the extent that I was never able to bring myself to take photos of our own wounded – it would have seemed callous. When I did take photos, it was of Argentine casualties. In fact, I told one of the blokes to take a picture of the RAP at work, and everyone else gave him a serious hard time for doing what they thought was taking advantage of our wounded.

The RAP worked in the open, in a gully surrounded by burning gorse – set alight earlier by phosphorus grenades in the attacks. Each man was carrying 60–80 lb bergans loaded with purely medical supplies and equipment:

We had drips, haemacell [a plasma substitute], Hartmann's solution, Kramer-Weiss splintage, lots of field dressings, crepe bandages to secure dressings more fully; I had a bag of drugs, and each of the guys had a breakdown of either a minor treatments pack – everything you need to treat D & V for example – or a supply of crystapen [injectable penicillin]. I had a list of what each had got so that I knew who had the back-up supply of penicillin and so on.

The main weight was the intravenous fluids – 4 to 8 litres each. We also had a small amount of food and some ammunition.

Hughes and his medics were each carrying around twice the weight carried by men in the fighting companies.

Despite being merely a group of men standing out in the rain, the RAP was organized like a field hospital: one man was the Reception, sorting out casualties into Serious or Minor Wounded, then allocating them to Major or Minor Treatment.

When the full two teams were together, A would treat and B would do the minor treatments and evacuation. Blokes would be just lying on the wet ground. I'd put a drip up and give antibiotics, then go round the others and tell the medics what I wanted doing and who were the priorities for evacuation.

Conditions at Goose Green were appalling.

It was raining most of the time, smoke constantly on the position. We foraged for corrugated iron sheeting and Argentine blankets to put over the casualties, and cuddled them together for warmth. We'd removed their equipment [to cut down the weight for the helicopters], and replaced clothing cut away to investigate wounds. We also took anoraks and parkas from Argentine prisoners to keep the casualties warm. There would be around ten casualties in the RAP at any one time.

I had my scissors tied with cord to the pocket of my smock so that they dropped to arm's length ready for cutting away bandages and clothes to inspect wounds. My drip cannulas were in the pencil pocket on the arm of my smock, and everything else was in my pockets.

We were all covered with blood – on our hands, covering our clothes, boots and equipment, and on the ground. We hadn't enough water to drink, let alone to wash anything, so were completely filthy. Blood-stained dressings lay everywhere, with the packing, polystyrene beads and empty boxes from medical resupplies ... As soon as we received casualties, I'd asked for our résupply to be brought up in the casevac helicopters so we were ready to go again.

There wasn't much screaming and shouting, everyone was pretty calm, although there was plenty of noise around. We were under artillery fire constantly, but luckily, through being in a peat gully, the rounds were landing either at the top and pinging bits of peat down on to us, or sailing over the top to explode 70 yards behind. There was a lot of small arms firing about 100 metres further ahead where the battle was being fought – triple A and missiles. One noise, a peculiar whistling, was only identified when we entered Goose Green. A multi-barrelled rocket launcher was lashed to the kiddies' slide, pointed in our direction.

The burning gorse and billowing, rolling cordite fumes created a fog through which at times we couldn't see each other or what we were doing.

When Colonel Jones was killed, Hughes decided to move forward from Coronation Point to deal with A Company's casualties – leaving his B team with D Company. They knew A Company were short of ammunition, so took as much as they could, plus a GPMG. The new location was known as the Bower:

We set about dealing with our own wounded, then sorted out the Argentinians – and tried to get everyone evacuated. We spent around eighteen hours there in the smouldering gorse. It was a series of runs of casualties, treating, then getting the helicopters in – before another batch was carried in. We had to keep our heads down after helicopters had left as the Argentinians could see us and would call down their artillery.

When we first arrived in the Bower, our casualties were ready for treatment. It was only once we'd casevac'd them that I realized there were Argentinian wounded still out there. We started treating them. From then on we worked on the basis of the most serious first, regardless of the nationality.

The Geneva Conventions are very clear that all wounded are to be treated equally, regardless of whether friend or enemy.

Then I ran into problems with the Army Air Corps, who refused to fly out Argentinians. They'd had a helicopter shot down [by Pucara], and clearly felt strongly about carrying enemy wounded. Two of the pilots in particular would wave away the Argentine casualties as we tried to load them – waving their arms and shouting, 'No Argies, no Argies'. These pilots didn't notice that some of the stretcher cases were not British, so I did get some Argentinian wounded out. I had one, however, only sixteen years old, shot in the arm and although he was walking, he'd lost a lot of blood. He looked very obviously Argentinian and the pilots simply refused to let him on. I'd put this youth back with the rest and try to get him on the next helicopter – but the next pilot refused too. We'd then have another surge of casualties, and because he was walking wounded, he'd end up being put back behind others more badly injured.

The next I heard he'd died in the night. I felt I'd failed him. To me it was important that we were treating human beings, not Argentinians or British. We were trying to treat everyone just the same – and I had thought that we would be better than them in this. I felt helpless that although it was my decision who was flown out and who stayed, I couldn't actually do anything about it.

For a long time I found that incident difficult to cope with – dwelling on it. I suppose I could have pulled my pistol and ordered the pilots to carry him, or wrapped him up in blankets on a stretcher so they couldn't recognize him as Argentinian? The trouble is you don't always think of the obvious in the heat of the moment.

The helicopter casevac operation was a desperate struggle against time that deeply affected Jeff Niblett (commanding B Flight of 3 Commando Brigade Air Squadron):

Only the most urgent cases were flown out, so you knew you had to get them back quickly. The back of the cab was filled with some very gory sights. Despite being able to see – and smell – the worst aspects of combat injury, you had to be detached and calm – and fly them home.

With stretcher cases the aviators tried to use the Scout, but always at the discretion of the medical officer in charge of the unit RAP. Speed was of the essence. They shoved them in as fast as possible on the principle that the rough handling was more than justified by the speed at which they would arrive at the MDS. The flight time was short – a 30-minute round trip to Ajax Bay including a refuel. The men were young and fit and by the time they were put into the aircraft they were patched up and reasonably well stabilized. Three could fit into the back of a Gazelle, and pilot Nick Pounds remembers two paras and one Argentinian in together, holding up each other's drips and hanging on to each other's legs. For wounded men, differentiating between friend and enemy seems to become irrelevant; their war is over and they are all suffering in the same way. For everyone else, the war grinds on. Even soldiers trained as medics find it hard to shake off the concept of 'enemy', even in seriously injured men. Steve Hughes:

My blokes found it difficult to cope with treating Argies, but they took their lead from me, and so treated them the same as us. I was proud of them for being professional enough to treat everybody the same, showing humanity for the vanquished foe. After a while there was compassion from everyone for the Argentinians – even from the guys guarding the prisoners. They even handed over sweets – despite our not having had food ourselves for 36 hours. One of the Argentinians who could speak English asked me: 'Why are you treating us?'

The distinction between medical activities, which the enemy are supposed not to jeopardize, and everything else in battle can in practice become very blurred. An enemy observation point on Mount Osborne could see 2 Para's RAP at Coronation Point, just beside an ammunition dump. The evacuation helicopters arrived full of mortar and small arms ammunition which stretcher bearers loaded on to their stretchers after dumping off casualties. The enemy OP was therefore fully justified in firing on the RAP – which they did whenever helicopters appeared. Hughes was in sole charge of treatment and casualty evacuation:

When the helicopters came in we'd grab anyone who was around to pick the stretchers up and carry them to the aircraft. Luckily we were able to keep it all moving.

Most of the time the medics did the technical stuff and I went round allocating priorities and giving instructions. If they couldn't do something, then I'd do it. We were close enough for me to be able to see what the others were doing and shout instructions across. Steven Russell, for example, was brought in with multiple cannon fragments down the right side of his body, deep fragments in the neck and punctures in the trachea through which air was leaking. There were holes in the side of his chest and nicks in his abdomen. The neck wounds were obvious, bleeding all over his uniform, which was shredded by the other fragments. We had to cut away the clothing to work out where the rest were, dress the wounds to stop bleeding, getting a drip up to replace the blood he'd lost, filling him full of antibiotics, titrating a small dose of pethadine intravenously for his pain – rather than injecting morphine muscularly – plus getting in a chest drain and evacuating him.

Russell was cold and had lost a lot of blood. Getting the drip up was difficult:

He was Priority One, and after putting up the drip I filled in a casualty card – one of the few that I actually did. I've got a photo of it; very shaky writing, my hands were covered in blood which is smeared over the card.

We'd started off with a number of bodies already there; Shorrock had a gunshot wound in his back and was lying half on his side. Bill Wenton and Irvin Gibson started treating him as they were his friends. I then got involved with Warrell, who'd been shot in the abdomen, and had his bowels hanging out. After we'd got his treatment under way I spotted Tuffin, whose body was half-hidden under a sheet of corrugated metal that had been put over the top of him. I asked, 'Who is that?' Somebody shouted back, 'That's Tuffin – he's been shot in the head.'

I went over to take a look. He had a big wound in the back of his head where the whole of the back of his occiput had been smashed out. Bits of brain were hanging out – but he was still conscious. He'd been there about five hours, so I knew as he'd survived this long he wasn't in any immediate danger. There was no point in evacuating him urgently even though everyone thought he was the most seriously injured patient. I also knew there wasn't a neurosurgeon at Ajax Bay.

Although he needed his brain cleaning out, it wasn't life-threatening. He would either survive, or die. The surgeons at Ajax Bay couldn't benefit him as much as they could someone with a gunshot wound in the abdomen, or who was actively losing blood – so he was a low priority patient. I put Tuffin down in the casevac order, behind other more immediate injuries. The medics obviously thought I'd put him to one side to die and were about to fill him up with morphine to kill him off. Someone suggested they check with me first – and I was able to stop them. I ordered someone to stay with him to keep him conscious and talking. Eventually he was put into a helicopter.

(Tuffin survived and is now living in Herne Bay, married with a baby. Hughes attended the wedding two years ago.)

We were just getting one lot of casualties ready for evacuation, when a fresh batch came in. C Company Headquarters had been hit. Roger Jenner had caught a few bits of shrapnel and Holman Smith was virtually dismembered – he was the signaller of the HQ. Then a guy wandered in completely bombed out, almost dragging his rifle behind him. He said, 'You've got to do something about Choppsie, my mate, he's been blown up, but is still alive. He's lying out there.' Part of me wanted to go straight away and try to bring this guy back, but the other part of me said No, you are part of the resources of this battalion, the doctor, an asset that cannot be squandered. They need you here.

I had to ask Bill Bentley to go – which went very much against the grain. The objective, rational doctor in me knew I couldn't afford to go, whereas the human side of me wanted to put my life on the line the same way as everyone else was doing. It was a conflict between the rational and the human sides of my personality.

Lance Corporal Bentley went forward with a stretcher team, and New Zealand Captain Mike Ford. Choppsie Gray was lying in full view of the enemy, well down the forward slope. As soon as Bentley and Ford reached him, accurate enemy fire opened up from all directions, which continued as they worked on him. His leg had been half blown off by a mortar round, and was lying in a small crater that had partly filled with blood. Bentley had to cut the rest of the leg off in order to get a tourniquet on. Morphine would not have worked. They had no time to give him anything else for the pain – and in any case, sedation would have been more dangerous than helpful. Gray was conscious throughout the amputation, mercifully blacking out several times. Bentley used his penknife, then put on the tourniquet.

After loading Gray on to the stretcher, for some reason Bentley put the severed leg on as well.

The two-man stretcher team ran back up the hill while Bentley was repacking his medical kit. He watched as a lethal shadow of enemy machine gun fire followed them through the grass, never actually catching up with them. He then realized that he was going to have to do the same, so after collecting what weapons and ammunition he could, he started moving slowly towards the ridge line. The enemy picked up his movement and started firing, so he legged it as fast as he could.

Bentley was a seasoned soldier who had seen service with the Armoured Para Recce Squadron, in Aden and so on. He was afraid, but he knew the true chances, analysing the situation as a soldier without being overwhelmed by it. He was shaken when he got back to the RAP, but shrugged his shoulders and carried on. It was the culmination of his military career – exhilarating in a way, achieving his ambition (just before leaving the army) of being an effective paratrooper. He was awarded the Military Medal, the citation reading:

L Cpl Martin William Leicester Bentley PARA Regt . . . courage and presence of mind in carrying out his duties . . . acted as an inspiration not only to the other medical orderlies, but to all who came in contact with him. With an immense pack of medical supplies on his back, L Cpl Bentley was to be found wherever the casualties were thickest, regardless of enemy shell and mortar fire, he not only dealt with his casualties in a calm, reassuring manner but boosted their morale with a continuous light-hearted banter.

When Choppsie Gray arrived at the RAP, having lost so much blood he was the colour of a corpse, and was unconscious. Hughes:

His veins had completely collapsed, so I had to do a cut-down – slicing through to find one. When I thought I'd found a vein I bunged a drip in. Although I wasn't sure if I'd got one, as a helicopter came in we just shoved him on. I didn't really hold too much hope for his survival.

After the battle, Hughes was told that when Gray was transfused at Ajax Bay, as the blood ran into him the colour returned and he woke up. After the trimming up of Bentley's amputation, he made a remarkable recovery.

A lot of the specific cases I've blanked out of my memory because I was overwhelmed by what happened that day. I can't confront individual circumstances. An extra screen seemed to come down in front of my emotions, shielding me. I couldn't afford to take anything more on board. As the day went on, I detached myself from what was happening. I felt as if somebody else was doing the job, and I was watching from a distance. This is a common psychiatric defence mechanism. I was outwardly functioning in the same way, but my emotions were disassociated from my functioning ability (in order to cope) and I became an automaton.

Black humour also played an important role:

At Goose Green, one of our wounded said he had a present for me, then pulled a hand grenade from his pocket and gave it to me. The others vanished behind rocks leaving me standing there on my own with this grenade.

When we first arrived at the barn in Bluff Cove, apprehensive about whether the Argentine 155s [their large 5.5 inch howitzers] could reach us, there were hundreds of flies crawling all over these naked light bulbs. I felt we needed some sort of joke, to break the ice, so I said, 'Somebody had better crap in the corner so all these flies will have somewhere to go when we turn the lights off.' Everybody creased up with laughter, and some were still chuckling away twenty minutes later.

When Bill went forward to Choppsie Gray, Choppsie said, 'I've lost my leg.' Bill said, 'No you haven't mate, it's over here.' At Fitzroy, a Scots Guards casualty from the Bluff Cove fire asked me if I minded if he smoked. I said, 'Well it doesn't really matter as you've only just stopped.' His clothing was still smouldering.

It was pure escapism.

Soldiers at the front line cease to think or worry about the wounded once the medic has taken over. They even think how lucky the casualties are to be getting out of the fighting and into a warm hospital bed. They only start to think about their injured friends when the battle is over – and they have the time. Steve Hughes was constantly asked how long-since-evacuated wounded men were doing:

Everybody seemed to think that I had some psychic link back to the doctors in UK, and could tell them how our wounded were doing. We did however know that they were all alive, which did wonders for morale. Warrell, the man with the abdominal wound, had a brother in the battalion, who kept asking after his health. He'd say 'The bastard! I knew he'd get home before me somehow. I bet he's shagging my missus.'

Unlike the soldiers, RMOs see the full carnage of the battle, all its horror funnelling through the Regimental Aid Post in a way that doctors and their assistants cannot possibly avoid:

The others may see a few mates wounded, or a bit of the horror of it, and they can work off their frustration and aggression by blatting off at the enemy. The medics can't get away from it, either through action or through switching off, because every time one lot of wounded has been evacuated, another load are brought in.

Even after the battle, it didn't stop. Once we got settled and packed after Goose Green we received a stream of wounded who had not thought themselves serious enough to stop fighting, plus all the sick who had simply been soldiering on during the battle. There were civilian injured too.

At the end, after the battle for Stanley, a stream of ingrowing toenails, piles, boils, diarrhoea, wound infections and other things that had been brewing during the fighting started to present:

Medically, before Goose Green the men were psyched up after a week of inaction, but were cold and wet, suffering from the weather. Early foot problems were not helped by the absence of fresh bread and vegetables in our diet. After a week or more, army compo rations need supplementary fresh rations. In the cold and wet, we were burning up more calories than we were eating.

Malnutrition has always caused problems during military campaigns. Despite the balanced diet of 'compo' rations, the Falklands was no exception:

By Goose Green we were beginning to slim down a bit, but after the battle we were able to buy things from the shop. We all had money on us, and paid for everything we wanted – bottles of whisky and boxes of Mars Bars. Locals gave us beer and food, and cooked for us as well, so we got some decent food.

Before Wireless Ridge, although psychologically there was a strong commitment to getting the job over, physically we were getting near the limits. On the approach march from Mount Kent to Wireless Ridge, we were so short of men that the cooks and bottle washers became stretcher bearers – the fat, idle knackers. Although we [the medics] were knackered and carrying heavy bergans, these lightly equipped men were so unfit they were slipping and sliding everywhere. About the only way we kept going was through the dubious pleasure of constantly kicking these characters to keep them going! It was a very harsh way to behave – especially as the doctor – but beating these fat bastards (who hadn't even done any cooking throughout the campaign) cheered us up quite a bit.

By the time we arrived behind Mount Longdon we were pretty knackered. When a supposed '3 Para company' were discovered to be wearing Argentine uniforms, our attack was postponed for twenty-four hours. We had only two days' rations for three days (a regular situation) so this delay gave us the chance to get more food brought up, and to try and rest.

During the attack it was very cold and snowing. I found myself listening to the combat net and hallucinating through exhaustion. I wasn't sure if I was hearing messages or not. We all virtually staggered to Wireless Ridge itself, and it was only the surge of extra energy created by the surrender announcement that enabled everyone to make the march into Port Stanley.

By Stanley most people had endured several bouts of D & V and had some kind of chronic wound or injury. Malnourishment and being out in the open for so long had also taken its toll on everyone. Going back by ship didn't help, either, as there were no fresh vegetables and the water supply was undrinkable. The ship's rubber water containers hadn't been correctly cleaned before being filled, and the water was tainted – tasting dreadful. Some of it couldn't be used in any way. There was however a limitless amount of beer! We ate rice with most meals on the ship, tinned vegetables and eggs. The problem of malnutrition was therefore never resolved until people actually got home.

Ajax Bay's meat packing factory was the only building in the area, the only suitable place for the Main Dressing Station, to which casualties were first brought. In its sepulchral interior, a casualty flow system was set up: stretchers came in through the main door to triage (to sort out priorities and documentation), moved on to resuscitation, to get the seriously injured fit for operation, and then to the two theatres themselves. The casualties then emerged into the post-operative area and high- and low-dependency wards – which were as far from the starched cleanliness of a hospital ward as could be imagined. They were flown out to the hospital ship SS Uganda as soon as possible.

Paratrooper Corporal Tom Howard worked as a medical assistant at Ajax Bay. A touch of rivalry between the Royal Marines and the newly arrived Red Berets of 5 Infantry Brigade's Field Surgical Team had been quickly resolved:

Everybody was making a concerted effort to do their absolute best. Nobody was going to shirk and the commandos and paras were on very good terms. The one overriding emotion is the absolute and utter exhaustion that we felt, of being totally drained. We didn't realize how tired we were until the end. We had eight hours on duty and eight hours off. During the off period, if we had lots of casualties we'd come in and help. During the eight hours off, we had to eat, wash, and sleep – getting around five to six hours' kip.

After a few days Rick Jolly [a Surgeon Lt Commander] requisitioned some rum and whisky, and gave each man a quadruple measure before going off duty, which was like liquid gold – a spirit lifter. I'd stopped smoking, but after being bombed I started chain-smoking, and gained tremendous relief from cigarettes . . .

During the wet nights, when we knew the helicopters wouldn't be flying, we'd pray that there would be no casualties.

The field surgical teams were completely isolated from the ground fighting, although they were the prime target for Argentine air raids. They saw however every wounded person that the war produced – a concentration of all its horror. There was little differentiation between Argentinian and Brit:

I wanted to save every casualty that came through; the Argentinians were wounded people the same as anyone else. One Argentine sergeant had a gunshot wound through the left shoulder and another through the right thigh, so we cut his clothes off him, to discover another entry wound by his clavicle on the right-hand side. The exit wound was way down in his groin, between scrotum and upper inside thigh. As I moved his scrotum to one side, I discovered a 7.62mm SLR bullet held in place by his testicles. He was babbling in Spanish, which one of the guys translated. He had a little three-year-old son back at home and didn't want to die without seeing him again.

Howard's own daughter was about two years old at the time:

I decided to do everything in my power to get him to see his son again – because I wanted to get back to see my little girl. We prepped him for theatre; put a Hartmann's in, banged in drips, broad spectrum antibiotics, cleaned and dressed the wounds, monitored blood pressure, pulse and breathing, gave him an ampoule of hydrocortisone, magnapen, an anti-tetanus jab and he went into theatre. He came out and went on to a stretcher in the recovery ward. He had terrible breathing difficulties, so I ventilated him on oxygen, but he was turning blue and becoming very cold. He sounded like he was suffocating.

I went to get one of the doctors, Major ——, and told him that the patient had got post-traumatic pulmonary oedema. He came and had a look, then told me to go and get the padre to give him last rites. I was so absolutely fucking gutted, really angry with him, because I knew this guy could be saved – and here was a doctor telling me to get the padre! Well I got the padre, but also asked the anaesthetist Colonel Knight to come too. He examined him, told me to give him a broncho-dilator and a diuretic – to remove the blood leaking into his lungs – and I catheterized him. He was cold, and as the hot water bottles were all being used on other patients, I filled my canteen with hot water, wrapped it in a towel, placed it on his stomach and covered him with a sleeping bag.

I'd been on duty for over sixteen hours. The nursing officer Captain Terry McCabe came over and said, 'You've become very attached to this patient. You'd better hand him over and go off shift, but I'm telling you now, don't expect him to be there when you get up in the morning.' I asked him what he meant. He said, 'It looks like he'll be dead then.'

I was gutted, feeling that I'd failed. I fell asleep, then next morning, I came through looking for him – and he was gone, away . . . the stretcher had been moved. I was devastated. Then, as I went through the low-dependency ward to get a cup of tea, I saw this Argentinian propped up on his elbow smoking a cigarette, talking to his mate in Spanish. I couldn't believe it. I went over to him and clapped him on the shoulder saying something like, 'God, you fucking gave me some problems yesterday', and laughed and smiled. He stopped talking and just stared at me, going 'Que?'

But I knew he was going back to his little three-year-old son . . . It didn't make any difference, as I never saw the guy again.

Blood was in constant short supply at Ajax Bay. Stocks had been created on the ships before the landings simply by lining soldiers up:

We took lots of blood from people on the ship, then kept it cool ashore by piling it outside the FST [field surgical team] covered with wet hessian. When we heard that casualties were coming, we'd put our smocks on with a belt round the middle, then fill the front with bags of blood to warm them up. We'd then wander round wobbling, making jokes about vampires. If one of the bags had burst it would have looked like a very serious wound.

On 1 June, after the ammunition explosion at Goose Green which injured several Argentine prisoners, the Ajax Bay MDS ran out of fresh blood. The injured had arrived with very low pulses and blood pressures, needing large amounts of blood before any treatment could be attempted. One had already died in triage. Surgeon Commander Rick Jolly called for donor volunteers from the PoW compound outside. Argentine Army Colonel Pioggi refused to allow his men to co-operate, so Jolly invited him inside the MDS:

. . . the colonel swaggers into theatre behaving as if he is the landlord rather than a guest. At the critical moment I step to one side and give him the full, Technicolor visual impact of Patient 275's dreadful wounds [one of the injured Argentinians]. The message to him via our interpreter is clear, and translates perfectly into Spanish: 'Sir. Some bastard booby-trapped the ammunition dump in Goose Green. This is one of your men, and there are others. We need more fresh blood.'

The bald-headed senior officer sways on his feet, unable to look any longer at the gore and blackened meat. He turns away, muttering: 'Cuanto – cual tipo?'[4]

Colonel Pioggi lined up 60 donors immediately. One week later, during the aftermath of the Bluff Cove disaster, medical squadron again ran out of blood and Chief Petty Officer McKinley (who was in charge of the blood bank) dragged everyone he could lay hands on into the MDS, testing their blood and taking suitable pints for immediate use. He matched the blood (a complicated and tricky process) on a six-foot table; there were no mismatches – an impressive record even under ideal conditions.

When helicopters arrived at the MDS everyone lent a hand. Royal Marine Lieutenant Paddy George: 'It was like MASH. At the first sound of the helicopters, everyone drifted up to the MDS to help. Everyone helped and these terribly burnt people were brought into the building.'

Tom Howard:

A young commando soldier really affected me badly. He was brought in on a stretcher. I turned around just as he arrived, and stopped gob-smacked because I just couldn't believe what I was seeing. He had both his legs blown off from above the knee joint, the tib and fib of both legs had been completely stripped of flesh – and the bones were splayed outwards.

I was speechless for probably thirty seconds, then I went over to this young lad – he had very light brown hair, a handsome, fit young man – and I held his hand. The only thing I could think of to say to him was, 'Don't worry, we're going to get you into theatre. We're going to repair the damage and don't worry. You're going to be going home.' Major Jowett the anaesthetist and theatre tech Rick Sanders came out of theatre and took his blood, so I continued holding his hand, talking to him. He was gripping it like mad, and looking up at me. As we were wheeling him into theatre he said, 'I want my mother, get my mother', then started to shout, 'Mum, Mum'.

I turned away and walked back into the ward, over to the window to have a quiet look outside. After a few minutes, I saw the stretcher come out of theatre, with Rick Sanders pulling a blanket over the face. I asked what happened: 'He arrested twice on the table. We started his heart again. The third time he arrested we couldn't get it going . . .' They'd discovered that a large fragment of metal had gone up inside his groin and ripped through all his intestines, liver, and ruptured his right kidney . . . he was literally blown apart inside. How he had survived that far was a miracle.

That particular case seems to have been representative of everything that Howard saw, and which was to affect him so seriously afterwards:

The death of that lad created a very powerful image inside me, which with the rest of the Falklands experience was a sort of catalyst. I couldn't believe that people could be so brutal as to have sat down and designed the mine that had done this thing to this boy. They could have been solving the food problems of the world, using technology to feed the starving millions . . .

This was a tremendous change for me, from having been a fully committed soldier. I started to turn to religion when I came back from the Falklands, particularly after I left the army . . .

I felt very sorry for the young Argentinian lads who came in – hypothermic, starving, wounded. Once we'd cleaned them up they were so grateful. We had piles of girlie mags sent down by the publishers, which were amazingly popular with them. They'd smile and laugh, giving us thumbs-up signs. There was never any animosity between the Brit and Argie wounded.

An Argentine Special Forces captain came in with a slight head wound. He spoke perfect English and turned out to be called Brown – born in Argentina, of Yorkshire parents.

This brought home to Howard the ultimate futility of war, an emotion that overrode all his logical and previously deeply held beliefs about the need for nations to be prepared to defend themselves from the Galtieris and Saddam Husseins of this world – as well as the Tojos, Hitlers and Mussolinis of the past.

I felt that the war was a dreadful, god-awful waste, a total change from my previous attitudes. My change of outlook started with the first mass-casualties that came in. In the end, I became very anti-war, and will never serve again – not even in the reserve.

After Goose Green, Howard was faced with having to deal with the bodies of friends: 'When the 2 Para bodies were brought into Ajax Bay for burial, I carried one of the young lads, Steve Dixon, to the grave. During the service I had a terrible sadness at the waste and mess of it all.' Later, after his surgical team moved south to Fitzroy, he cared for wounded from the Scots Guards' attack on Tumbledown:

When Lieutenant Lawrence came in, his brain was coming out of the top of his head. We'd had an earlier patient from 3 Para with a similar wound who had been conscious, but after evacuation to *Uganda* he'd died. Bob Lawrence had a massive triangular hole, which looked much more severe than the first one I'd seen.

He was lying on the stretcher and his brain was literally coming out on to the canvas. I remember holding a shell dressing to his head, and Terry McCabe [the nursing officer] coming up behind me and saying quietly 'Don't push too hard, just support it . . .' Lawrence complained about feeling cold and pins and needles down his left-hand side. I was amazed to be having a conversation with him, and was resigned to the reality of talking with someone who would be dead tomorrow. I'm astonished now at the recovery he's made. I found myself unable to understand how people could do this sort of thing . . . nobody deserves to be shot through the head with a high-velocity weapon.

The surrender was announced as I was holding his brain. I remember thinking how unfair it was that the war was over and this man was still going to have to die.

While the battle was still going on, from the Fitzroy FST you could see up to the hills where the Scot Guards were fighting on Tumbledown, a carpet of tracer rounds coming each way. The only sound was the odd distant explosion as a 66 went off. I was watching a real battle, and I remember wondering how people could survive . . . then I realized that what I was seeing was actually an advance warning of more casualties coming in.

The US Army in Vietnam, with fully equipped, well-trained medics on the front line and the 'Dustoff' helicopter casualty evacuation able to lift wounded men directly into air-conditioned surgical hospitals, provided GIs with a gold-plated medical system. Yet even in the low-intensity combat of the Vietnam campaign, battle conditions often prevented Dustoff from arriving within the vital first hour after wounding – 'the golden hour'. The British Army, conditioned by Northern Ireland, expects the war to stop to allow first aid and helicopters to fly in when someone gets hurt. Casualties find themselves on the operating table in the military wing of Musgrave Park Hospital in South Belfast well within the 'golden hour'.

If casualties can be treated within that first hour of injury, their chances of recovery are dramatically increased. In the case of large injuries, unless fluid lines are put up and blood loss stopped, and with the large amounts of what could simply be described as dead material flooding the body from the wound, toxic shock occurs, with kidney failure and death. McCullum:

One lad with a simple flesh wound to the upper thigh had to wait seven hours or so for the helicopter, and gangrene set in. In the end, he lost the leg right up high. One of our NCOs on his own in the darkness was badly wounded, but nobody could get to him. Throughout the night he kept coming on to the [radio] net pleading for somebody to pick him up, but we had to ignore it and get on with the job. His voice got weaker and weaker, until finally the calls stopped. In the morning we found his body, the radio still going, a morphine needle stuck in his leg. It's bad enough seeing people dying, but hearing a man on his own pleading for assistance then dying alone is terribly sad, and wound us all up. He was very popular in the battalion; we all knew his voice yet nobody could get to him.

In combat, with the battle still raging, casualties are not likely to receive medical help within the golden hour. The most seriously injured men will die, leaving the casualty evacuation system to handle only those who are strong and fit enough to survive lengthy evacuation. The Falklands boast that every soldier who reached the field surgical hospital at Ajax Bay alive survived, should be tempered with the thought that the marginal cases had already died in the extreme cold and wet, while waiting hours (and sometimes days) for evacuation.

Once a casualty arrives at the company aid post, he receives medical treatment to stabilize him for the journey back to the regimental aid post, which in a large-scale armoured battle can be from 800 metres to 5 kilometres away. British Army ambulances are too small to allow treatment to be carried out inside them, and are very uncomfortable for patients. Military ambulances operate a version of 'scoop and run', a practice that civilian ambulances gave up some fifteen years ago. The British Army has no paramedics able to go forward to treat patients, and their ambulances have none of the sophisticated, miniaturized roadside resuscitation equipment that civilian ambulance men use routinely, together with entonox gas-and-air pain relief and scoop stretchers (that avoid the need for patients to be lifted at all). The vehicles are designed so that intravenous infusion, resuscitation, splinting and bleeding control can be carried out as the ambulance drives to hospital.

The British Army made a number of unfortunate deductions from Vietnam and from their own experience in the Falklands. In Vietnam, the US Army achieved excellent levels of survival through having thoroughly trained medics forward with the fighting troops, and getting the Dustoff helicopters in quickly, evacuating men directly to surgical hospitals. The British military establishment decided that it could not afford to deploy enough high-grade medics forward with the fighting troops. Because of the vulnerability of helicopters to ground fire, flying up to the front line to collect casualties was quite sensibly judged too dangerous. In the Falklands it seemed that, despite the appalling conditions, the men's own first aid skills had been enough. It was decided that the high levels of medical aid provided for US troops would not be given to British troops. Not surprisingly, this decision has been the cause of much soul-searching among the RAMC and means that British troops in future wars can expect no better medical service than their forerunners experienced in the Second World War – and in many ways a very much worse service because the increased range and accuracy of depth-fire artillery means that medical evacuation chains are certain to be interrupted by artillery fire. The young soldiers of today's army expect the same levels of medical help that they see in American films about Vietnam like *Platoon* and *Hamburger Hill*, or at least the same as they would get after a civilian car accident. Their expectations are justifiably high, and in the preliminaries to any conflict, unless the medical services are able to match these expectations, morale and the will to fight may be adversely affected.

One interesting development in the Gulf War preparations occurred as the troop build-up in Saudi Arabia was getting under way. The British Army had sent the 7th Armoured Brigade accompanied by its integral Rhine Army medical facilities – which were woefully inadequate. The US Marine Corps, on the other hand, had a Rolls Royce medical set-up. Somebody realized that once British soldiers saw the disparity between what they could expect if hit, and what would happen to GI Joe, morale would be seriously affected.

So the British forces medical system was expanded far beyond that intended to serve the entire British Army of the Rhine in an all-out war against the Warsaw Pact forces. In the end vast numbers of medical personnel were drafted into the army from the reserve, civilians long released from military service, but whose dusty record cards bore some kind of medical qualification. It was an unprecedented effort to create an adequate and workable medical infrastructure that thankfully was not put to the test.

In the Falklands War, there was no equivalent medical expansion. A senior medical officer, asked to compare Gulf medical facilities with those of the Falklands, declared that this disparity had been acceptable because commandos and paratroopers were tougher and more self-reliant than the 'ordinary' troops that fought in the Gulf. In the Falklands the wounded expected to have to fend for themselves, and were trained to keep themselves alive. Most remained on the battlefield in the rain and snow without treatment for a day and more. Although the reply ducked the question, it was reasonable. We do not however know how many men died in the Falklands who, with a better evacuation system, might have lived.

Getting the man off the battlefield to medical aid is a big problem. One solution, practised by the Americans in Vietnam, is to have the medics on the front line already. In a large-scale, intensive war, however, the front line is too dangerous for medics to work, men simply cannot be spared from fighting the battle, and helicopter ambulances stand little chance of survival. Armoured fighting vehicles are not designed to carry casualties. Tanks can take stretchers perched vulnerably on their engine decks, but not inside. Armoured personnel carriers can only take four stretchers – and that leaves the crew out in the open. The Israeli Defence Force are unique in having designed their Merkava tank with a rear casualty compartment. The average British infantry battalion possesses only eighteen stretchers, which are supposed to be carried by the battalion's bandsmen. The Falklands showed that casualty evacuation often used all the spare manpower from every platoon.

Helicopters are the best vehicles for moving casualties, able to lift them directly back to the field hospital, but in addition to being very vulnerable to ground fire, casualties cannot easily be treated while being flown. With vibration, noise and sudden movement, delicate procedures like getting needles into veins is almost impossible. The arrival of helicopters at the front line before medics have finished intubating casualties or got drips going properly has caused casualties to be loaded before being stabilized. As many patients have died through helicopters arriving too soon as from their arriving too late. The front line of a conventional battlefield is in any case likely to be too dangerous for helicopter casualty evacuation.

The US Infantry published 'Combat Notes from Vietnam' throughout the war, to keep military men at home up to date with the latest tactical practice in the war zone. Extracts from Major W. K. Hoen's article from the first edition (published in 1968) shows how large-scale helicopter casualty evacuation worked in a low-intensity war – where helicopters could fly with reasonable safety:

When requesting DUSTOFF, it is imperative that a true picture is given of the pick-up site. If an insecure area is known in advance, gunship escort will be requested . . . Too many times in the past few months the ground commander has declared an area secure when it was not. As a result, several of our aircraft have received extensive combat damage and some crew members were wounded. Obviously when our aircraft sustain major damage, we have prolonged maintenance down-time and we cannot as effectively meet our commitments.

Just because an area is declared insecure, does not mean that the pick-up will not be attempted. The advance warning gives the pilot notice so that he can be better prepared to make the pick-up with the least amount of delay.

In making radio requests for Dustoff, grid references were always required in clear (not in code), to ensure that mistakes and delays did not occur.

The use of suppressive fires in hot LZs is encouraged. DUSTOFF likes to take advantage of everything available to keep Charlie's head down, but it is extremely helpful if the ground commander can give some prior warning to commencing fire. In the helicopter, it is difficult to tell whether the fire is incoming, or outgoing – and it is a real comfort to know these things.

There were serious problems when it came to risking helicopters to fly out dead men:

KIA [killed in action] is an ugly term and becomes even more unpleasant when there are misunderstandings and confusion tied up with it. Probably no area is in more need of clarification than the DUSTOFF procedure for KIAS.

Well, here it is in a nutshell – DUSTOFF will not, repeat will not go to any pick-up solely for the purpose of disposing of KIAS. Resupply ships or other support aircraft must be used for a mission of this type. DUSTOFF aircraft will take KIAS out of an area where the patients are being extracted if there is space available in the aircraft.

This is not intended as a cruel or impersonal policy against the soldier who has given his life for his country; this policy is simply a compliance

An immaculate and well-starred General Westmoreland in Vietnam. As in the First World War, reality for the 'grunts' actually fighting the war was very different to that perceived by commanders and staff officers giving the orders from clean, safe rear areas

A Tornado re-fuelling during the 1991 Gulf War, a delicate man-oeuvre the aircraft had to perform before entering Iraq and also on their return (often in darkness) from bombing raids, in order to have enough fuel to land safely

As HMS *Ardent* burns (sunk during the Falk-lands War), her crew, wearing orange immer-sion suits, line up along the rail to climb one at a time down a rope onto HMS *Yarmouth*. *Yarmouth*'s damage control teams spray *Ardent*'s deck and side with water to prevent them from becoming too hot

BELOW: A German soldier, 26 August 1918. On the battlefield, even today, treating serious head wounds requires time, clean surroundings, good light and the facilities of a properly equipped hospital. Those with head wounds are therefore a low prority for evacuation, and are put to one side – often to die. Those who live face the arduous journey back to a field hospital. Medical officers will only give space on transport to those capable of surviving this journey

ABOVE: A Royal Navy medical orderly helps a badly burned Falklands combatant ashore from a British hospital ship

LEFT: An innocent, peacetime GI, trained but blissfully unprepared for the realities of war

BELOW: A First World War underground dressing station, with less seriously wounded men receiving treatment. They appear blank and expressionless, except for the man squatting bottom left, who seems unnaturally and almost hysterically affected, and unaware of his surroundings

LEFT: British troops during the Gulf War taking photographs: a common reaction among modern (camera-carrying) troops to enemy dead. They would not take similar snaps of their own dead.

BELOW: Iraqi soldiers waving pieces of white cloth crawl from a bunker to surrender to British troops during the Gulf War. The British soldier on the right is gesturing to them to stay where they are

RIGHT: In an agony of fear, a Viet Cong prisoner awaits interrogation in January 1967 at the US Special Forces Camp at Thuong Duc, near Da Nang

with the primary mission of DUSTOFF aircraft – Save Lives and Evacuate the Wounded.[5]

The only solution to the very limited mobility of the battlefield is for more advanced resuscitation facilities to be positioned closer to the front line. Many lives could be saved by giving seriously wounded men surgery much earlier – opening abdomens to stop serious bleeds, doing tracheostomies, completing amputations and sealing up chests – on or near the front line. This sort of surgery is different from that practised in hospitals or by civilian emergency services and requires highly trained medics. Many doctors would be unable to do this sort of work. However, in battle medical corps men would not need all the training of a doctor to decide whether a patient's symptoms were caused by disease or injury. Battlefield diagnoses are usually quite straightforward: a grey-faced man with a puncture wound to a drum-tight belly has been hit by a bullet that has sliced a major blood vessel. He will die unless his belly is opened up and the bleeding stopped. Nobody is going to sue for medical negligence. Neither he nor the medic has anything to lose – provided the corps man has the equipment and basic manual skills to do the job.

On the battlefields of the future, with high-tech surveillance and long-range strike systems, all movement is likely to be very dangerous – whether by night or day. There will be no safe rear areas beyond the maximum ranges of artillery shells. Even the rear administration areas will be subject to heliborne and parachute assault and rocket attack. Medical treatment in a chemical or biologically contaminated environment is an even greater nightmare – to which a rather despairing lip-service is paid in training. Once chemical or biological agents have been used, field surgical units must be completely sealed to the outside world. The 'production line' must be divided into contaminated and clean zones, with decontamination units in between. Casualties are certain to be suffering from both wounds and contamination poisoning, protective suits having been punctured. Decontamination takes time, and must be very thorough to avoid killing unmasked staff and patients in the clean zone. I was shown one of these facilities working on simulated casualties during an exercise, and was forced to wonder whether the nightmare it represents would in reality be tolerable to medical staff, let alone their patients.

Nevertheless soldiers have got to be made to feel confident that, even in nuclear, biological and chemical warfare, they will be looked after if they are wounded. Most seem doomed to die from wounds and poisoning before their decontamination is complete, and the prospect for everyone in the air-tight tents seems bleak if they have to move or come under attack. However, provided the medical facilities are actually there, and that somebody with expertise and some kind of system is dedicated to taking care of the wounded in an NBC environment, soldiers will feel confident enough to carry on with their duties. They will not trouble themselves with the detail of whether or not the system actually works.

We are back to the role of medical services in maintaining the morale of the fighting troops, and to the suspicion that it does not in fact matter what the medical services are actually capable of doing – provided everybody believes in their capabilities. In the danger and immobility of an evenly-matched modern battle (both sides having high-tech weapons), will the US Army's splendid medical machine actually work – or will the troops have to look after seriously injured men themselves on the front line? Will its failure lead to a serious collapse of morale? By contrast, is the British Army's decision to limit its medical effort in fact a more responsible and realistic attitude, which British troops will understand from the onset of a conflict?

The fact remains that medical expertise on the front line saves lives, and that perhaps the only certainty for the future of battlefield medicine lies in having superbly equipped, high-grade and highly motivated paramedics on the very front line in sufficient numbers and with enough equipment to perform the sort of surgery that has been described. To achieve this in the British Army would require the Royal Army Medical Corps to demonstrate a much more aggressive attitude to the selection and training of high-grade personnel and demand equally rigorous support from the RAMC's hierarchy.

The Falklands War proved that fit, highly motivated soldiers can survive the severest multiple wounds provided they are resuscitated on the front line and treated within the golden hour. In the Falklands, the Ajax Bay Field Surgical Teams were organized specially for this sort of work, and as the conflict proceeded they found themselves having to perform much more complicated procedures through sheer necessity. Past war experience led to the so-called 'six-hour rule:', that casualties without immediately life-threatening injuries should ideally receive surgery within six hours of wounding, after which their chances of survival diminished rapidly. Resuscitation, antibiotics and intravenous fluids have today increased this time limit, but after surgery the so-called 'seven- to ten-day restriction' on moving the patient, cannot be ignored. Flying men out of theatre in a Hercules or VC10 aircraft a few days after laparotomy or other surgery could prove fatal.

Hospital ships that sail sedately back home as their patients recover on board are ideal, but realistically, as was planned in the Gulf, casualties are more likely to be flown directly out of theatre and back to the USA or UK. British Falkland casualties, when they were considered ready for return to the UK, were transferred to one of three converted survey ships (*Hecla*, *Hydra* or *Hecate*) for passage to Montevideo and onward aeromedical evacuation to the UK by RAF VC10. For the medical evacuation of Gulf War casualties, the plan was to fly wounded out of Saudi Arabia as quickly as possible, either to Cyprus or, more often straight to the UK. On arrival in the UK, mass casualties were to have been shared out between civilian hospitals once military hospitals were full. In Vietnam the seven- to ten-day restriction was adhered to; casualties were not moved after surgery until they were well stabilized – often waiting several weeks.

The International Red Cross is closely involved in the repatriation of both prisoners and wounded. Once wounded are evacuated to Red Cross hospital ships, they are on safe, neutral territory and cannot return to the combat zone. On occasion the Argentine hospital ship *Bahia Paraiso* came out to *Uganda*'s Red Cross box to receive the numerous Argentine casualties who had come through the British medical chain. From the *Bahia Paraiso*, they were taken by sea back to Argentina.

The safety of hospitals is a Red Cross concern. In land operations, field hospitals consist of 100 and more beds, located 20 to 100 kilometres behind the front line. They are virtually immobile, sitting targets for artillery and other indirect fire weapons. Pilots and artillerymen, able with modern munitions to destroy whole grid squares, could easily hit large medical facilities by accident. In future conflicts, ensuring that both sides know the locations of hospitals will be a particularly important task for the International Committee of the Red Cross.

In the British Army, few soldiers volunteer to become medics. The best become NCOs, and those who fail as riflemen become storemen, drivers – or medics. It is a peacetime paradox that those unable to make it as combat soldiers are entrusted with the lives of casualties in war, required to be able to resuscitate, maintain airways, put up intravenous infusions, staunch bleeding, administer pain relief and splint limbs. In addition, regimental medics are expected to run training courses in first aid for the other soldiers in their units. Unfortunately, but not surprisingly, the low quality of medics is equalled by the low quality of the instruction they give.

Effective battlefield first aid requires actual experience, of the sort that can only be gained in the casualty and emergency departments of hospitals. In the British Army, only special forces units like the SAS and SBS send their medics to work in civilian hospitals: indeed, probably only SAS or SBS trainee medics are of any use to the hospitals. The best work experience that most unit medics can expect is in the regimental sickbay, handing out bottles of aspirin and date-stamping 'excused boots' chits. The low regard in which unit medics are held by their peers does not bode well for future combat. Lt Colonel Bob Leitch, RAMC: 'The good are very good but inexperienced, and the bad are very bad and inexperienced – a lethal combination. How can you trust a man with your life if you can't trust him in other ways?'

Quality and realism in peacetime medical training is very much a reflection of the combat experience of an army. Units with recent combat experience know how vital efficient casualty evacuation and treatment is in maintaining morale and motivation in combat. The British Army, however, under pressure over the years to make manpower cuts and despite sporadic interest, has allowed its medical training to lapse. Attention has always been focused on fighting the battle – on tanks, guns and equipment. Medical support is too difficult, a logistical matter scorned by 'G snobs' (the Operations staff), ignored by everybody except the RAMC, who have comparatively little influence or leverage within the peacetime military system.

The British Army solution to the problem is convenient and traditional; bandsmen are to be stretcher bearers in war, leaving the 'real' soldiers free for the fighting. By continuing this tradition of centuries, musicians are given a justifiable war role, conveniently allowing regiments to retain their military bands. The importance that the peacetime British military hierarchy ascribes to military bands is well known, raising the question of whether bands or trained medics are the real priority. Bandsmen might be a convenient source of manpower for stretcher bearing, but they are far from ideal. Staff bandsmen are recruited either into boy service as musicians or as adults from civilian orchestras, lured into the army by higher wages. They may do very little military training and are kept busy playing band and orchestral music at a wide range of military and civilian events. Although the Royal Marines Band emerged from the Falklands War having done well in their medical role, they were working on board ship and, in general, were not required in battle, to carry stretchers for miles over soaking tussock grass.

The Israeli Defence Force, who must husband their limited human resources carefully, take first aid and casualty evacuation very seriously. The offensive spirit of their soldiers is carefully nurtured through training, to produce stable units whose members know each other well, and teams that have been together for years. An important part of their combat motivation is therefore 'achavatt lochameem' (translated literally as 'combatants' brotherhood'). This sense of brotherhood inspires heroism in combat; suicidal attempts to rescue wounded comrades under fire are commonplace, and wounded are evacuated to hospital as quickly as possible. The IDF also go to enormous efforts to recover their dead from battlefields, partly because the Jewish religion requires the proper burial of all the individual's body parts, and also as an extension of 'achavatt lochameem'.

With no dedicated military hospitals, in war every Israeli civilian hospital goes on to a war footing. Staff have already received military training, and many surgeons are experienced in dealing with battle casualties. Hospitals local to the battlefield act as immediate first aid and resuscitation centres. Stabilized casualties are moved deeper into the centre of the country, to hospitals further away from the fighting for less immediate surgery and recuperation.

Unlike their medical assistants (the US Army 'corpsmen'), military doctors, like chaplains, are not soldiers (sailors or airmen). In the British armed forces, doctors (and chaplains) find themselves in a strangely ambivalent position. Their professional duty is to their patients (and congregations) as individuals, yet they are employed by the forces as part of the 'servicing' of unit morale, to keep whole bodies of fighting troops ready to fight, and working to the orders of their commanding officer. In both theory and practice their ultimate responsibility is no longer to individuals but to the army, navy or air force, whichever pays their salary. (In civilian terms, this would perhaps be like general practitioners working for the benefit of their Local Health Authorities.)

Like everybody else in military life generally, doctors must conform and not 'rock the boat'. For example, a military doctor who embarrassed his CO by reporting alcoholism in the unit's sergeants' mess might not keep his job for very long. Medical problems are seen (usually wrongly) as an indication of low standards of administration, and therefore poor leadership in that unit. MOs are expected to keep 'dirty washing' within the family and to be loyal to their CO.

In the extreme, such 'loyalty' can extend to MOs being pressured to gloss over cases of bullying, marital violence, or mental illness – and, more usually, to condone training that they might consider injurious to the health of their patients, for example by officiating at regimental boxing competitions.

Doctors receive just enough elementary military training to allow them to play their part in the peacetime military community, but are not regarded as properly trained soldiers. Unit medical officers are usually young and newly qualified, often ill-equipped to stand up to a strong-willed, ambitious commanding officer. In combat doctors have to pick up the pieces, working under appalling conditions. A unit medical officer at war with his battalion could be compared with a general practitioner whose village is suddenly visited by some terrible disaster. He knows everybody intimately, having treated them and their families over the years for all the usual illnesses and domestic injuries. The community suddenly goes to war, sprained ankles and sore throats giving way to terrible wounds that he has neither the equipment nor the time to treat.

The unit medical officer finds himself part of the military mincing machine – working in the midst of an abattoir. After seven and more years training to save lives, he is part of the elaborate process through which men he knows well are killed and maimed. The men fighting the battle are aware when people nearby are killed or wounded, but in moving on, leave the blood and gore behind them. The Regimental Aid Post is a concentration of all the horror of battle, and the medical officer sees it all. There is no magical medical training that protects the sanity of doctors and their staff from the horrors they must deal with. On the battlefield medics are deeply affected by what they see. Lt Colonel Bob Leitch, RAMC:

Becoming familiar with the sight of carnage helps you to treat patients without freaking out. After seeing it over and over again, the horror disappears and you become able to make a quick clinical assessment of each patient. Blood doesn't concern you any more – it's just something to be cleared out of the way. If someone is screaming you know he's not too bad – but the guy who is pale and very quiet is the one you treat first.

It does however make you very aware of the vulnerability of humans, in a horribly obvious way.

Captain Steve Hughes, the RMO of 2 Para throughout the Falklands War:

Medical training doesn't prepare you for a battle. The combat environment is very different to an accident and emergency department in a hospital.

The worst you get [as a civilian] is working at the roadside as member of an accident team. If you break down and have to walk away, someone else can take over. In hospital there are police to protect you from drunks, back-up teams and consultants to call in. The lighting and technology are good and everything is nice and clean. Also you don't know the patients from Adam – they are complete strangers.

On a battlefield, there is the constant, great danger to yourself and multiple casualties arriving in great surges. There is no back-up, nobody to call on, and everyone is looking to you all the time. You can't just pop into the next room for a breather, because there is nobody else. You have to maintain the professional façade.

Doctors must learn to become objective about patients, but not to the extent that they lose their compassion. The human patient is not a machine and needs sympathetic communication and reassurance. Making rational, logical decisions without becoming either too emotionally involved, or too professionally detached is a difficult balance – and takes years to learn:

All doctors go through swings either way; young students being very supportive of patients, holding their hands ... and the other extreme of the impersonal consultant who has never learned to cope, lecturing and never listening to the patient.

Like the army, the medical profession has its own version of the stiff upper lip:

Only in the last few years have people started talking about this sort of thing. Facing a battle wound in a young man – especially if you are young yourself – you associate the wound with what could have happened to you or to patients the same age as your son or daughter. It's very difficult to cope with. Some doctors have to blot out such patients emotionally, treating them less humanely because it's too close to something that hurts ...

Patients vary, too. Some will drain you of everything you are prepared to give, leaving you exhausted. With them you have to set a limit. Others don't want anything at all because they have their own ways of dealing with their problems. You offer them an olive branch, then withdraw and deal with them mechanistically. You must respect their desire for privacy.

Stiff upper lip prevents many civilian doctors from recognizing the problem and talking about it, locking it all away, increasing their alcohol intake instead. Junior doctors are often hard-drinking, as they come to terms with the tragedy they see every day. Alcoholism is almost an occupational hazard of the medical profession, along with broken marriages, drug addiction and suicide.

Doctors haven't learned to address the stress of their job, but cover it up with drugs and alcohol. On the battlefield your only hope of survival as a doctor is to maintain a professional façade, drawing on the defence mechanisms built up through medical training in order to remain objective. In combat, you know all the patients coming through intimately – and their families. Your medics feed you info, too: 'This is Paul Smith, he's my best mate; his wife has just had a baby . . .'

You can't let this get through, because if your own emotions get overwhelmed you won't be able to treat them effectively. Somebody close to you can wipe your brain clean and make you ineffective.

In the Falklands, Hughes was very conscious of the heavy personal responsibility of his position, and the consequences if he failed to withstand the pressure:

If I was to show emotion and fold, I knew that my team would fold too – as they knew the guys even better than I did. When David Wood (a close friend) was killed and I went to see his body, I knew that the emotion was there – a tremendous room full of it that I just had to lock the door on. It wasn't the time or the place to deal with the grief. To see him with a 7.62mm entry wound in the middle of his forehead had a tremendous impact on me, but I couldn't allow that to register on my emotions at that time. I had to pretend the professional, detached persona and say: 'He's dead, there's nothing we can do for him. Go back to the guys you can do something for.'

We were so busy coping with casualties that we had no time to think. I was always worried. About the casualties we were holding, getting them evacuated, and then, once we were clear, about the wounded still out on the battlefield needing to be brought back to us. When all that was done, we'd start thinking about the artillery that was falling around us – and when the next lot would be coming down. You worried about yourself last of all, in a maelstrom of emotions that could only be controlled by intellectually latching on to something else, keeping the doors closed.

Hughes was aware at the time that in suppressing his emotions he was storing up trouble for the future. Working on the principle of 'physician heal thyself', he was banking on being able to unburden himself to his friend and mentor John Randall, a retired naval psychiatrist:

Throughout the battle I had John fixed in my mind as the man to sort me out – but three days after Goose Green I had a letter telling me he had died of a heart attack.

In the sorrow of that moment, an enormous explosion went off in an Argentine ammunition dump, throwing me back once again into the violence and bits and pieces of flesh everywhere. In that moment I came to terms with the fact that anybody close to me could die in the next minute.

I began to put everybody at a distance . . . the little boy inside me putting up barriers, because in his experience anybody who came close to him died.

After 2 Para's battle for Goose Green, in addition to recovering from the experience, they had to clean up the battlefield, which was a dangerous business. The disorder behind the Argentine artillery gun positions in particular was surprising: artillery and small arms ammunition mixed up loosely with boxes of mines and gun propellant charge bags. Suspecting booby traps, an ammunition technical officer had been asked to inspect; he declared the dump clear. The Argentine PoWs were in nearby sheds, and a few days later, their CO asked if the ammunition could be moved – in case it was hit in an air raid. As 2 Para simply did not have enough men to do this, the Argentine CO was happy for his men to do the job. The Geneva Conventions allowed them to volunteer (and be paid by the British for their work). Chaplain David Cooper:

Throughout the day there were explosions; mines exploding as sheep trod on them or just it seemed because they got bored with sitting in the ground – and Sappers doing demolitions. Then there was a tremendous bang. I set off on foot . . .

There was a figure on the ground in the field beside a huge fire of blazing charge bags, with ammunition exploding and artillery shells roasting in the flames. The RSM was trying to get a fire extinguisher going and lads were running up with stretchers. An RAMC sergeant was on the ground with one Argentine soldier on a stretcher, and I could see two others, one beside the fire, the second still in the flames screaming. We dragged the one on the edge out. He had lost one leg at the knee, and one at the thigh. An arm was missing and he had a huge wound in the chest – and was still alive. He obviously wasn't saying very much.

Because of the fire, we couldn't get near the other one, who was screaming in the flames. The only thing we could do we did – we shot him.

This fellow we'd got out, the flesh on his leg was gone and the wound had been cauterized by the blast, so the femur of his right leg was completely exposed down to the jagged ends of the bone, and his left leg was intact up to the knee. But the flesh simply ended at the knee joint, then just the splintered ends of the tibia and fibula. He was waving the stumps about, and as we were trying to put the drip up, we were being hit in the face by the splintered ends of these bones.

Hughes arrived with a Land Rover and medical equipment:

I got there to find an Argentinian with both legs blown off. In a parody of anatomy, his tibia was held on to the femur by only the ligaments of his knee, as you would see on a dissected cadaver – except it was also charred. Only the top half of the body was alive, the severed legs writhing around in agony. It did not look human, this half-cadaver, half-person – and it was dying. Nevertheless we (with Rory Wagon) tried to get a drip up, then got some morphine in. The thrashing about pulled the drip out and we couldn't get another line in. He died in the helicopter back to Ajax Bay.

At the same time we knew that [RAMC sergeant] Chris Fowler had shot another Argentine prisoner burning inside the pile of ammunition. The fire was so fierce that you couldn't get near it – charge bags and small arms ammunition going off. In the centre of this fierce heat, a human being had been screaming and writhing around. Chris Fowler had already pulled one man out of the fire, but couldn't reach the other. People were standing around horrified. Chris grabbed an SLR from one of the prisoner guards and fired several shots at the figure in the fire. When the fire died down, the body was just a charred mess – which David Cooper buried.

Afterwards we wondered whether as medics we would have had the courage to do that – a medic shooting somebody to put him out of his misery. Under the circumstances it was the only humane thing to have done – and tremendously brave.

David Cooper was deeply affected by the suddenness of this incident, at a time when the battalion and their prisoners had thought it was all over:

It seemed so unfair. The Argentinians had been through this battle and were trying to make the area safer for themselves and suddenly they were blown up. I'm convinced it was a booby trap, despite ATO having told us he'd checked and that it wasn't. It was the unexpectedness of it that catches you under the belt . . . like the *Galahad* bombing, too.

Shortly after the ammunition fire at Goose Green, the RFA merchant ships *Sir Tristram* and *Sir Galahad* were bombed. Yet again violence descended from nowhere, which Hughes and his team dealt with. Hughes:

I particularly remember the guys in the sickbay of *Galahad* – which was hit by a rocket that passed completely through the ship. Having already been injured, the war was far from over for them. The madness was so extreme there that one member of 9 Squadron, realizing that he was going to burn to death, got out his marine-issue clasp knife and cut his own throat. He in fact performed a perfect tracheostomy on himself, and survived.

David Cooper was dismayed by the unfairness and ignorance of the Red Cross:

The International Red Cross were almost unbelievable at their inquiry afterwards, in Stanley. Apart from anything else they said, they criticized Steve Hughes for not having personally certified all the Argentine dead – as being clinically dead – on the battlefield. They were so incredibly unaware of the circumstances to expect a battalion doctor to patch up his own men and enemy wounded, but also to go round certifying every single Argentine body as well. At the time I couldn't believe it.

Hughes was upset and concerned at what subsequently happened to Sergeant Fowler:

As the Red Cross Protecting Power, Brazil had lodged a complaint about this incident (on behalf of Argentina) and [after we got back to UK] the shit had hit the fan. There had been Questions in the House of Commons – I was dragged back from leave to answer questions from the Royal Military Police. I then heard that Heseltine [Secretary of State for Defence] repeated my words in the House that same afternoon.

People without the faintest idea of the circumstances under which Chris Fowler had acted, judged him and found him guilty. He had been written up for a medal for his other efforts, but because of this incident [shooting the burning prisoner] the citation was torn up. He was then formally accused of murder, a charge that was proved to be nonsense by the testimony of all who witnessed the incident.

Despite his complete exoneration, the shooting incident irreversibly branded Fowler:

While most of his peers in the Parachute Clearing Troop were commissioned, Fowler remained a staff sergeant. His army career was blighted.*

Steve Hughes's own horrific experiences as a combat doctor in the Falklands War were to stay with him and emerge years later in the frightening symptoms of Post Traumatic Stress Disorder. After leaving the army and becoming an orthopaedic surgeon, several years later, the madness he was slipping into forced him to the desperate lengths of admitting himself to an NHS mental ward – from which he had serious trouble escaping.

* Chris Fowler was eventually commissioned into the RAMC in June 1990.

11

AFTERMATH

Of all military operations, a night attack is the most severe test – of both units and individuals. Darkness offers many opportunities to avoid danger, and with few people within sight there is often little or no sense of unit cohesion to keep men going. Small groups of men fight the battle – sometimes on their own. Dead and the wounded are left behind, friends and enemies alike screaming into the night. In the aftermath of a night attack, as dawn breaks, men realize that in surviving they have come to the end of a long and testing journey. Some emerge from the test with a clear conscience, whereas others know that in the darkness they played safe or let down their friends. Their failure might be common knowledge throughout the unit, or an individual, guilty secret.

Before and during an attack every man's attention is focused on the attainment of the military objective – for example, the enemy's fortified trench positions. Despite the need for men to risk their lives in taking the objective, self-preservation is an important part of their determination; each man knows that the nightmare will end only when the objective has been taken. Often only a handful of men out of the hundred or more that might start a company-sized attack actually reach the objective – their comrades left behind dead, wounded, or still engaged in the many micro-battles that make up the battle proper.

The moment of success is the most dangerous time – when the defenders mount a surprise counterattack. In the moment of survival, achievement, relief and fulfilment, the attacker must become a defender – a very different sort of animal. At the height of his aggression, determination and ruthlessness, he must dig a trench and wait for the enemy to attack him. He comes down from the adrenalin 'high', tiredness hits like a sledgehammer. He hears about others, which of his friends have been killed, which wounded and which maimed and crippled. The reality of battle returns to swamp his euphoria, falling like the curtain at the end of a play.

Dennis Marshall-Hasdell joined 42 Commando on their Mount Harriet objective just as it was being secured against counterattack. Despite elation at the success of their assault, 42 Commando were also very frustrated. They expected to push on to take Mount William, but had been ordered to stop. Some felt this went against the basic military principle of maintaining the momentum of an attack. In fact, no further advance could be made until Tumbledown had been taken, which was 45 Commando's objective. The Argentines were shelling positions their infantry had just lost so, stuck on Harriet, men knew that every hour of delay would cost the lives of more of their mates.

Over the past days, the men of 42 Commando had gone from being cold, wet and pissed-off, through the tension and expectation of preparing for the attack on Mount Harriet, to the trauma of the operation itself. Having put their souls into a heart-stopping night attack, which demanded every ounce of their team spirit, determination and expertise, being ordered to stop was in Commando Brigade parlance 'the green rub' – 'a kick in the crutch'. Some claimed, unfairly, that the halt was being ordered 'because of all the 5 Brigade cock-ups, so the wooden tops [guardsmen] could get to do something.' Although elated at their success, 42 Commando were back as they had started before the attack – cold, wet and pissed-off.

The Argentine artillery started firing on the Mount Harriet positions as soon as 42 Commando's rifle companies arrived. At dawn their firing intensified, settling into a lethal sequence: 105mm batteries followed by the heavier 5.5 inch howitzers firing on to previously adjusted targets. Enemy shellfire claimed victims from among the survivors of the attack – its impersonal lethality unfair, frustrating and offensive.

After an attack, prisoners are always removed from the scene as quickly as possible, lest the attackers' anger be vented on them. The shelling made steel helmets essential. Few (if any) commandos carried them, whereas every Argentinian soldier was wearing one. Nobody cared where they took them from: Argentinian corpses provided some, prisoners others – in clear contravention of the Geneva Conventions. In the ruthless pragmatism of frontline logic, PoWs being evacuated to the rear areas had less need of helmets than men staying on shell-swept hillsides. The men's feet had been soaking wet for weeks, and were now wrinkled and sore – in various stages of painful trench foot thanks to the cheaply made and poorly designed British issue 'Combat High' boot. The Argentine issue boot was well-made, of thick, good-quality leather, water resistant with a heavy-duty sole. Argentine dead were duly stripped of their boots, helmets, jackets and equipment. A new phrase was coined – or maybe it was remembered from an earlier campaign; anything 'liberated' from the enemy was known as a 'Gizzet', the shortened version of 'Hey you, give us that'.

A very strong feeling of absolute ownership extends, for a time, even to the lives of the surrendered enemy who remain on a captured position. In the crucial moment as one group of enemy surrenders and others continue to fight, terrible mistakes occur. A surrendering enemy might seem suddenly to open fire, and so the outraged attackers kill unarmed, unresisting men. And yet once the fighting has stopped, the combatants of both sides find that they hold each other in a strange sort of mutual respect. Close combat gives a human face to an enemy, and makes men realize that he suffers too. When prisoners have been ill-treated, it has generally been at the hands of non-combatant troops in the rear areas – men whose lives have never been on the line. Sergeant McCullum:

Prisoners were a new element – I'd never taken any before. We'd captured thirty bunkers and they were all full. Once daylight came up, I realized I had lots of them. They were the dregs, no interest in fighting, stinking, poorly dressed and starving. There was no sense in searching them – these were terrified, hardly likely to have bayonets hidden up their arses.

Argentine soldiers also popped up out of nowhere, and on the spur of the moment some were blown away. Things like this happen in war. You get individuals who are maniacs in their own little paradise, blowing prisoners away and enjoying it. I made sure it never happened in my platoon, but I'm not saying it didn't happen elsewhere.

Why kill a man who's fighting a war that he doesn't want to be involved in? I was thinking that if it was my son, would I like to hear that an Argentinian paratrooper had blown him away when he surrendered? I'd have hated to hear of that happening. We were all human beings. They were people who didn't want to be in this war and they'd surrendered, so off they went to the rear. No matter what they'd done, mates they'd killed, who could tell which one of them did it anyway? If someone gets blown away by a shell, you can't go looking for the bloke who fired it . . .

B Company had a different attitude – because during their attack they were having to push on so fast. There was no time to look after their own wounded, let alone prisoners. What can you do, leave prisoners in the bunkers to shoot the guys following on? If when you are pushing forward, these people come running out of trenches with their hands up, what can you do? There isn't anybody to take them back – the blokes are in the middle of a fucking war. And you can't just leave them either. Do your blokes kill them, or call the platoon sergeant who's going to say 'Waste them'? If you stop the momentum of an attack for anything, prisoners, wounded or whatever, you've lost the battle. You just haven't got time. Had I been in B Company, having lost so many men, so many friends . . . I'd have taken prisoners in a different way – and I'm not saying how . . .

On Mount Harriet, with the prisoners gone, Marshall-Hasdell found himself in a very strange environment. He felt frustration mixed with elation, but also contentment and even satisfaction:

We ransacked the enemy positions; there were heaps of food and kit – duvet jackets and the like. It was a very comfortable, nice place. There was also a general feeling among all of us that nothing more could possibly happen, that this experience was as bad as it could ever get – now, or in our future lives – and that actually it was quite easy . . . very satisfying.

A Mercedes Land Rover was modified to re-charge the commandos' radio batteries and Argentine rations were judged excellent, especially the tinned beef.

The shelling was constant, but we soon worked out when they were coming and which ones we should take seriously. We became experts at taking cover. It was a bit of a game, using our technical experience to decide what the shells were going to do – although very wearing.

I watched a Scots Guards company commander being escorted by the RSM to a position where he could observe Tumbledown – which they were going to attack. Every time a shell came over, he hit the dirt while RSM Chisholm stood over him, encouraging him to continue, telling him the shells weren't going for them. He looked foolish, and very scared. Perhaps we were all scared but because of our experience we weren't showing it. The guardsman certainly did show it – to the whole unit. I didn't feel scared – even when shrapnel landed in the Argie stew I was cooking. Sometimes the shells were very close, but there was never the feeling of real fear. Everyone was very wound up – the feeling of fear driven out. I'm sure that if I was put in that position now, I'd be scared fartless.

There was lots of burying people, Padre Albert Hempinstall saying quiet prayers and covering corpses with stones. The equipment hunters were a pain – to the extent of taking laces from the otherwise worn-out boots of corpses. After burying the same man for a third time, Padre Hempinstall complained to the RSM. It seemed rather funny at the time.

There was a blasé attitude towards Argentine dead; no real attempts to cover them and no sense of disgust or horror. It seemed perfectly natural, and over a couple of days they were buried – but with no rush about it. 'Some bad things were happening, but no one was really bothered.' As men settle into occupation of a captured position, the lawlessness with which they have fought the battle continues in behaviour that would be completely unacceptable in normal life. Rings, watches and jewellery were taken from bodies – swollen fingers hacked off in the process. A reliable witness told me that a few men pulled gold teeth from corpses' mouths with pliers. In World War Two, American Marines carried pliers to pull out Japanese gold teeth, and after Waterloo, similarly 'liberated' teeth are said to have been re-used as false teeth by dentists. Marshall-Hasdell also saw evidence of this sort of behaviour and concluded that: 'Humans in war are really no better than animals.'

I stole chocolate and money from one dead man's wallet – as souvenirs. I can't tell you why I did it now, but at the time it seemed like the thing to do. You can't tell your nearest and dearest about any of it; it's impossible to explain what it was like. I was associated with it – it went on around me – and I found it quite amusing at the time.

These three days on Mount Harriet were the start of Marshall-Hasdell's later problems. In an alien environment, light years away from what he had been trained for, he felt he had lost control over his life. The shells were haphazard, random and impersonal, as uncontrolled as every other aspect of the madness. He felt he had seen the true, horrible nature of humanity revealed without any of the softening or camouflage of civilization. It was like the contorted reflection in a fairground mirror, and at the time he did not find it horrifying, a lack of reaction in himself that today concerns him greatly. Having seen humanity laid bare, he wants nothing to do with the way people really are – and never wants to see anything like it again.

I was kept going on Harriet by the thought of a certain rock at home in Aberporth, where I'd always sat and watched the sea.

McCulloch:

We went firm for about three hours [on Wireless Ridge], then as we started moving forward again, we were told to stop – 'Endex', all finished. This was actually a bit of an anticlimax as we were expecting to have to take Sapper Hill.

The battalion were nevertheless relieved:

On the aerial photos, we'd seen all the minefields so we knew it wasn't exactly the sort of place you'd want to go dancing through, not to mention FIBUA[1] through Port Stanley. However, after about five minutes of disbelief, people realized that the news was genuine and not a rumour. Relief swept in, and the whole thing turned into normal daily work.

McCullum:

When they surrendered, there was great relief and elation in the platoon. One lad, a real hard man who'd been a professional heavyweight boxer in Civvy Street, broke down in tears. There was pure joy at finishing, after a 70-mile tab. We'd done a hell of a good job.

The ending of the Falklands War was as strange for the commanders as it was for the combatants. General Moore and Colonel Pennicott flew into Port Stanley over the top of Government House, weaving in the darkness through a forest of radio antennae to land in the midst of a helicopter park. The landing site was in fact the football pitch beside Government House, and was surrounded by thousands of Argentinians, all armed to the teeth. Colonel Pennicott: 'The flight had been pretty hairy and seeing all these heavily armed men made the hair at the back of my neck stand on end.' A British reception committee took them straight to the Secretariat Building.

Menendez was waiting there with four of his cronies. They were immaculate – hands soft and clean, cleanly shaven. We had tried to smarten ourselves up a bit before we came, scraping our faces with razors in a sheep-shearer's hut, putting some polish on our boots, but it hadn't made much impression. We looked scruffy and haggard. Only their marine colonel had been in the field with his soldiers. The others clearly had never left the comfort of Stanley.

The surrender was actually signed on 15 June: the Argentinians were using Argentine time, and the Task Force used Greenwich Mean Time for operations as well as local time. It was agreed, to prevent further confusion, to date the signing as at 2359 hours GMT on the 14th. Coffee was then brought in. General Moore said to Menendez conversationally: 'Did you know that you nearly killed me yesterday?' – referring to the bombing of the Brigade HQ. Menendez replied, 'It was nothing personal.'

After celebrations with the Islanders, Moore and Pennicott stayed that night in Government House, which was heavily booby-trapped and had bodies in piles round the back. Pennicott encouraged his understandably very strung-up commander to unwind a little, leading him in a therapeutic whisky-drinking session. They then both moved carefully through the cleared part of the house to where they were to sleep.

Sergeant French:

We left Wireless Ridge and went straight into Stanley, where we raided an Argentine clothing store and took some of their rations. We were wearing the same clothes we'd landed with and were in bits, so we needed to get ready for further operations. We'd been living off our belt orders for several days, so we actually had nothing to eat.

McCullum:

Once we got to Moody Brook, 2 Para had secured Stanley and we were marching in three ranks. We knew we could relax, and people started slipping away to forage, for bottles of wine and the like.

Cooper:

I felt strongly that having fought the battle, we were not the people to police the place. The Islanders needed controlling, and had access to all sorts of arms. And when we got to Stanley, we didn't have the resources. A large number of military police should be hot on the heels of an attack to reorganize the system, reimposing law and order on both civilians and servicemen, and helping get fragmented units back together again. The fighting men, after their experiences, are not in the right frame of mind.

In Stanley, the civilians were doing quite a lot of looting, and the soldiers had no food, so they were taking Argentine rations. Once you've been in a situation where you destroy anything that is a threat to you, you lose all concept of private property. You destroy a building that might contain enemy, and if you need something, and the owner happens not to be there, because you've risked your life to take this town, you help yourself.

Civilization is one of the first things to go in a war, in the mind of the individual. To be effective as a soldier, you have to break free of the normal civilized constraints. Afterwards, you have to be brought back, a transition that has to be imposed from without. Having lived from one minute to the next, doing whatever you need to do, blasting away any difficulties, getting back to the frustrations of normal life can be difficult.

French:

There was looting afterwards in Stanley. For example, a Royal Marine officer parked a Land Rover outside the HQ at the Racecourse, foolishly leaving the engine running. As we jumped in and drove off, he shouted 'What are you doing in that Land Rover?' and all he got from us was, 'You fucking knob!' as we fell about laughing.

They brought these little discs out, saying which unit each Argentine vehicle 'belonged' to. We all made up our own discs, and nicked vehicles – including the 2ic of our company!

The Argies in the west of the town were being controlled by the RMPs and provosts, but at 6 a.m. on the second morning we were ordered into the centre to find they'd rioted and burned down some houses, chucking their own kit all over the place, apparently looking for food. Looking at the state of them, I could understand it. However, all these shiny-boot people [the RMPs] who had turned up after the fighting, didn't want anything to do with it. They couldn't control the Argies when they turned nasty.

Each of our platoons was given an area, and we formed 80-man working parties out of the Argies, with an English speaker in charge. They were told that if they ran they'd be shot, if they worked hard they'd be fed. They were simple conscripts. They worked hard and we gave them food.

That's the annoying thing about the bullshit of the British Army. An immaculate RMP came up to us while we were clearing up the streets with all these Argies and started giving the lads hassle. When they told him to go away, he got funny so I had to tell him that he wasn't needed, and because we were doing his job for him, it would be better if he pushed off.

The sheer numbers of hungry, neglected Argentinians were a great problem. They had killed several of their officers that night, which was also hardly surprising. Their officers seemed to have been permitted to shoot soldiers – and did, and so needed to keep their pistols as self-defence, which did not impress us. The whole situation was annoying because had we been allowed to handle the whole thing, we'd have got all the prisoners disarmed and organized, then fed them – as part of our standard battle procedures. The riot was completely unnecessary. But because the shiny people became involved, the proper procedures just didn't happen.

Both we and the Argentines needed to get out of Stanley because the sanitation couldn't cope. We were cleared up and gone after about five days – exercise over and back to normal life.

Sergeant McCullum:

Discipline did go for a while, even in my platoon which was fairly tightly run. One lad came back with a TV set! What the hell could he do with that – put it into his bergan? Others came back from somewhere with all these little sweetie miniature bottles of whisky. We got money together to buy some beer and have a party. We had our weapons and ammunition and were still ready for action.

The sergeant major did go round shouting at us, wanting to know where all the blokes were, saying the war was still going on. But it didn't feel like it any more. I certainly wasn't going to line the platoon up for daily inspections. We'd taken over a house, and each day we cleaned the floors and the cooker, in a disciplined daily routine. We weren't going to steal all the food from the owner's freezer, or break his pictures. If the lads got roaring drunk, they did it in the house, under my wing.

I did get the section commanders together at one stage away from everyone else for a severe debriefing, about how we'd won a war but hadn't been given any excuses to break up this guy's house. Nobody got out of hand; we were very tired, and spent the time mostly dossing in the house. I didn't have people running wild. My platoon toed the line. We were too spread out for the RSM to have much influence, and the CSM had to leave it to us, the platoon sergeants in each platoon house.

Formal military discipline had never been a feature of 2 Para's war

– in keeping with their informal but practical attitude towards everything they did:

In the battle, the only discipline came if we'd started to bunch up or get too close to other platoons – and was imposed by the CSM acting as lineman. He always gave me the hard time, not the platoon commander.

We had negligent discharges during the campaign; in one, a weapon was dropped and someone was hit in the leg. We couldn't charge people at the time, and back in UK, after coming all the way through the campaign we just couldn't do it. The guy felt bad about it, but he's still in the regiment!

At the end of hostilities, Dennis Marshall-Hasdell spent a week compiling information for the post-battle intelligence report. Initially flying in a Gazelle, then later driving a commandeered Mercedes jeep, he logged all the air force related hardware left behind by the Argentinians, before it could be tampered with or removed. Professionally this was fascinating; discovering large amounts of brand new US and Soviet equipment, in particular a radar-laid air defence co-ordination system and data link-part assembled, its American manuals still lying open. Also, the fabled land-launched Exocet that the experts had refused to believe could exist, was there for all to see.

There were amazing amounts of hardware, ammunition, rockets and artillery shells, with large numbers of live Argentinians with the shock of capture on their faces – wide-eyed, vacant and very depressed. We had GPMGs mounted on the back of our jeep as many of them were still armed.

Dennis flew back up to Wall Mountain, the scene of his rapid withdrawal and the abandoning of the laser target marker (see Chapter 9):

My best green beret had been in the bottom of my bergan, for the march into Stanley. However, when we got there it was all gone. Some bloody Argie had nicked it – probably as a souvenir. I knew that they had laser target markers of their own, but I've often wondered what their intelligence officers made of an LTM and my green beret with an RAF badge sewn on to the front.

I enjoyed analysing the Argentine air defence – and looking back on it, I also enjoyed Mount Harriet. I feel so very bad about it now – about how I felt and acted . . . so cold and callous.

A fellow RAF man, Tony White, came ashore and they occupied a house at Number Three Race Course. The outgoing inhabitants were their exact counterparts, the Argentine Air Force Intelligence team. Surprisingly, the house had been formally leased to the Argentine air force since 1972 by the Falklands administration. Their lease com-

plete with Royal Warrant 'to the Argentine Air Force' was framed
and mounted on one of the walls.

We'd wandered through minefields in the rush to get to Port Stanley. Dead
people were everywhere, with the shit and garbage of war. As on Harriet,
there was crap everywhere – in the houses, streets . . . maybe they did it
deliberately.

The job of cleaning up the battlefield was to take many months,
and had to be started immediately the fighting finished. The Royal
Engineers in particular, with the dangerous responsibility for marking and making safe the minefields, bore the brunt of this work,
transforming themselves instantly from combat duties to their peacetime role as civil engineers.

Before anything else could happen, the airfield and buildings in the
town had to be cleared of booby traps and the piles of assorted
munitions made safe. At the same time, the runway had to be repaired
to allow RAF Hercules transport aircraft to land. However, the
materials with which to do all this were simply not there. For
example, different grades of gravel and stone were needed so the
airfield quarry was reopened. Having just fought the war, the parachute engineer squadron had only high explosive from which to form
blasting charges – which at first produced useless boulders. As the
charges were increased experimentally, a newly sprouted and luxuri-
ous RAF tented camp half a kilometre away was showered with
debris, leaving no stone at all on the site.

A constant and uncontaminated water supply was vital. British
naval gunfire had destroyed the roof of Port Stanley's water pumping
station, causing the valves, filters and pipes to freeze up and split.
The winter was well advanced, and the weather had defeated the
civilian engineers, so a Royal Engineer section (led by Corporal Iles
of 9 Squadron) spent twenty-four hours rebuilding the walls and roof
in a blizzard, then fixed the equipment. The engineers also took on
the problem of the Argentine minefields, which were unmarked and
largely undocumented, making movement around the town impossible. Captured Argentine mine documentation was reasonable for
some of the fields but non-existent for others. In the latter days of
the war anti-personnel mines had literally been thrown about by
hand – the areas unmarked. Engineer Lieutenant Jon Mullin studied
Argentine mine-laying pamphlets and interrogated prisoners to
understand the theory behind their placing of mines, before risking
his men's lives clearing them.

Argentine sapper prisoners waiting for repatriation were persuaded for humanitarian reasons to help with this dangerous work. One engineer commanding officer had withheld mine location maps from British interrogators, but responded to appeals from 'brother sappers who would have to risk life and limb'. The Geneva Conventions are very strict about the work prisoners of war are permitted to do. The danger of clearing mines was obviously great, and the work was monitored closely by the Swiss Red Cross. Among the sappers, prisoners and captors got on well together. While minefields were marked, Argentine dead were also buried as both nationalities listened to radio reports of World Cup football matches. The prisoners were paid for their work, and escorted to local shops to buy tobacco and sweets.

Before the airfield was finally repaired to peacetime standard the RAF delivered mail by parachute. Letters from home are of very great importance to morale and are another Royal Engineer responsibility, so when one particularly inaccurate drop fell into a minefield on Sapper Hill, a 9 Squadron mine clearance team reverted to its combat role to breach the minefield and recover the bags.

With the war over, the mine marking and clearing operation was ordered to be done with an absolute minimum of risk. Nevertheless, an Argentine corporal was badly injured in an accident. An Argentinian officer accidentally entered a minefield while positioning a boundary fence, and the corporal following him stepped on to an anti-personnel mine. Medic Major Bob Leitch witnessed the incident:

There was a whacking great bang as an Argentine sapper trod on a mine, blowing off his foot – about ten metres away from where we were standing. My life froze, and we instantly went up on to our toes like ballet dancers, standing on one square centimetre of earth each. We looked at each other, eyes sticking out, the effect of adrenalin making your arse twitch and spasm . . .

Not a word was said, but as I was the medical corps officer, it was up to me to go across to the injured man. I counted to ten and thought of the war being over, of my four kids and what the hell my wife would say if I came home minus a leg and my balls. This was the moment of truth. As I hadn't got the moral courage to refuse, I decided to go to him.

Just as I was about to mince my way across, the Argentinian sapper troop commander looked at me, making it clear that this was his business, and that he realized I wasn't quite up to it. He walked across the mines, then carried his soldier over to me for a running repair, before being flown to [surgeon] Jim Ryan for surgery.

The corporal lost his leg above the knee.

The co-operation between Argentine and British sappers was rounded off when they were sent home by an enormous farewell party during which both national anthems were sung. Bob Leitch witnessed the Argentine sappers' departure:

It was dark and they arrived dressed in British combat kit, with rucksacks and loads of British rations. Having worked together clearing mines, an incredible empathy had grown up between them. As far as [British] 9 Squadron were concerned, these guys had proved themselves every bit as brave and competent as Brits. 9 Squadron were genuinely worried that when they arrived home in Argentina they'd be done in.

Most of 9 Squadron were at the jetty to see them off. The farewells included shouts of 'Tell them to fuck off when you get there', 'Do a runner', and 'Don't let the bastards grind you down'.

Bob Leitch had arrived in the Islands as the war came to an end, to be the staff officer responsible for clearing up the human aspects of the mess – the prisoners, the bodies and even the honours and awards. As a non-combatant, he saw clearly how the war had affected people:

Outside the confines of Jeremy Moore's HQ, there was an enormous amount of unpleasantness. The units that had done well in the war just wanted to get home. This was summed up in San Carlos, where the paras had painted a huge wings badge above the entrance to a sheep barn, with the motto 'Ubique' underneath and '2 Para, first to fight and first to Port Stanley'. Someone else had added in green paint '. . . and first to die you wankers'. There was a huge amount of petty rivalry, and accusations of looting and ill-discipline – all of which were totally unfounded. No one liked each other any more; they were classically knackered and cold, and just wanted to go home.

Leitch had come fresh from the UK, to reimpose a stable peacetime structure on the chaos that is always the aftermath of war:

I quickly realized that guys who have done the fighting cannot be used to sort out the vast amount of crap that is left after a war. People weren't thinking straight, problems reduced them to tears, to becoming irrationally upset over trivia. Surgeon Jim Ryan was a good example. He had to stay behind after the war to provide medical cover, at a time when [of the combatants] only 9 Squadron, the Welsh Guards and some artillery were left.

Both Ryan and anaesthetist Jim Anderson had worked tirelessly throughout the war, including witnessing the bombings at Bluff Cove then treating casualties from the fires. 'Jim Ryan had watched this

horror show from the shore, then carried out the triage and initial
first aid on all the victims before their evacuation to Ajax Bay.'
Anderson had actually been on the *Galahad* when it was bombed,
and had been deeply affected by not having been able to save his
friend Roger Nutbeem from the fire.

Now, after the fighting was over and most of the combatants were
on their way home, a horrifying accident occurred on the airfield:

A Harrier had been revving up to take off, but for some reason fired two
Sidewinder missiles. One of these bounced off the runway and exploded,
but the other hit a group of soldiers sweeping snow off the runway. They
were all in a row and the missile had gone straight through them, ripping
eight legs off six men. It was the most spectacular sight – a bizarre game of
skittles in the snow. Jim Ryan was the surgeon, with anaesthetist Jim Anderson in the piss-poor Port Stanley hospital.

The Sidewinder accident threw Ryan and Anderson with appalling
suddenness back into a medical emergency as bad as any during the
war:

These two men had to transform themselves from being exhausted and
completely fed up, suddenly to coping with a disaster equal to any that the
Ajax Bay surgical teams had faced during the war – but now they had no
expert backup. They were on their own.

Jim Ryan was incredibly cool. These six severely injured young men
desperately wanted to get back home – but were dying. He had to decide
which lives to save; which to operate on first, and also in that instant make
crucial surgical decisions about the quality of life they would enjoy in the
years to come . . . Should he amputate above the knee to be sure of saving
a life but creating a cripple? Or below the knee, so that the man could have
a good artificial limb and the chance of a normal life, but risk a surge of
infection (necrosis) killing him?

On his own, Ryan had no choice but to do both the triage and the
surgery.

A Board of Inquiry investigated the incident. The young pilot of
the Harrier was in the dock:

The Board of Inquiry for this incident was dreadful, like the First World
War. Everyone decided to get on with it, showing no emotion, writing it
all down in order to make a decision. The poor chap was really mortified
by what he'd done. I don't think he had actually flown in the war, which
made him feel even worse about it. He had to sit for hours in the corridor
outside.

At the end of the day it was found to have been some freak mechanical
thing, related to the ad hoc firing system used [during the war] for Side-
winders.

This was only one incident in the long, hard process of bringing order back to the Islands. The combatants' resilience had gone. They were not able to re-adjust from war to peace.

They were so tired and had lost all perspective, just wanting to get home. This feeling was contagious. We also still had 500 special category PoWs – senior Argentine officers kept back for interrogation – and needed to get them back home as well to Argentina.

For those on the Falkland Islands doing the actual work, the UK-based headquarters and support agencies seemed to be creating problems rather than solving them. The robust personality of the new garrison commander Major General David Thorne enabled the plethora of problems to be solved:

Everyone was interfering, especially the navy, but we pushed on regardless. Nobody could be pissed off with David Thorne around.

There were rumours of looting, stealing gold coins, and smuggling weapons back home. Weapons were everywhere. The leaders were taking things like helicopters, so the boys were packing .38 pistols and Mauser rifles. The UK hierarchy were getting very fed up with this, and put pressure on the command in the Falklands to discipline people. Combatants who were having to stay were particularly fed up. For example, T Battery Royal Artillery were based by the seashore, beside where the ship housing the Argentine prisoners was moored. Every night they could see the Argies enjoying good food, warmth and soft beds, while they were still stuck out in increasingly worsening weather, just off Navy Point. The ship was lit up at night, warm and comfortable and really looking nice.

One night, a sudden burst of tracer was fired at the ship from the top of the hill, the rounds dropping into the sea. The captain was particularly pissed off. We couldn't get down there that night [to investigate] and T Battery weren't answering the radio. There was severe consternation in Stanley and a general stand-to. Argie banditos were thought to be all over the place, deserters trying to shoot us up; stay-behind parties were attacking, the war had re-started!

The next morning we went down to T Battery. It was bound to be somebody farting about – a negligent discharge plus! They denied it. The weapons were all clean, the ammunition accounted for and nobody knew a thing.

This went on for about three nights. It was perfectly obvious what was happening. The boys in T Battery had just been through a war and nobody was relieving them. Everyone had gone home yet they were still stuck out on this hill, manning the Rapier missiles. Their entertainment was blasting away at the nice cosy ship – which drove the Provost Marshal up the bloody wall.

As combatant units mixed with the incoming garrison and 'clean-up' troops, the navy and RAF became more involved with the operation and tensions grew: 'There was an immense amount of infighting between the three services and the different units, particularly with 5 Brigade. [Task Force HQ] Northwood in particular were continually interfering in the detail of things – "micro-management". For example, Northwood asked Leitch to investigate alleged breaches of the Geneva Conventions; that the Argentine hospital ship *Bahia Paraiso* was supposed to have illuminated and shot up some SAS during the war, and that it had been delivering guns and war supplies to the Argies.'

These stories were nonsense, as Northwood should have known. I spoke with the *Bahia Paraiso*. On the night of the SAS raid [on Wireless Ridge] they'd heard a tremendous amount of noise and had turned on their lights to see what it was. As I was investigating all this, the International Red Cross were there too. Their head man would only say philosophically, 'A mote and a beam . . .'

During the war, the Red Cross had investigated British contravention of the Geneva Conventions, including the situation at the Ajax Bay logistic complex, where ammunition, the field hospital and a prisoner of war cage were grouped together (illegally). The complex provided a high value target for the Argentine air force, which was protected (it could be argued) by a 'human shield' of Argentine hostages. 'We had broken the rules of war ourselves quite seriously. What would have happened if Argentinian prisoners had been killed at Ajax Bay?'

The International Red Cross representatives were criticized during the war by British commanders for their lack of understanding of the conditions under which the war was being fought. Part of this criticism, however, was founded on a degree of self-righteous indignation at civilians interfering with military matters, and also through British commanders being surprised at the positive role of the Red Cross. In peacetime training exercises they are not even considered, let alone represented.

The Red Cross were bureaucrats, civil servants arriving with suitcases looking for hotels. They were used to Beirut where they could watch the war in comfort, and didn't know what they letting themselves in for in the Falklands. For all that they were impartial, honest and straight. They saw all the alleged horrors on both sides, and were very complimentary of the way we treated prisoners, considering the conditions we were under and that most of our tents and supplies had gone down in *Atlantic Conveyor*.

Their presence was vital, removing a little of the remoteness of the fighting; showing us that somebody in the real world was watching the war closely. They were real people in suits and Gucci shoes, at the outer limits of the real world trying to be urbane and civilized in this gloomy place.

Dennis Marshall-Hasdell had decided not to return to UK in the *Canberra*. He felt that on board the luxury liner, the voyage was certain to be a mass celebration of victory, which he thought inappropriate. He opted instead to go back in HMS *Fearless*, the ship in which he'd helped plan the war. The return voyage was busy; detailed staff debriefings on the build-up to the war, the war itself and the post-war intelligence operation. He re-wrote the Forward Air Controller's SOPs (standard operating procedures) in the light of what he had learned in the war.

I was very screwed up – to the extent of not telling anyone when I was coming home. My girlfriend – the daughter of really good friends in Aberporth – had been writing wonderful letters to me, and I returned thinking that I'd get married to her. As it turned out, she didn't really understand, and the things she wrote in the letters hadn't really been meant.

At home, the Falklands venture had created a carnival atmosphere, striking a peculiar, sometimes nostalgic chord that the media particularly were revelling in. All manner of stereotypes were adopted by those concerned in the crisis, learned from war movies perhaps, or generated by the sudden precipitation of events. The boring prosperity of the 1970s had been interrupted by high adventure, the whole nation suddenly conscious of the turning pages of history books. Knowing someone in the Task Force meant being exposed to a peculiarly intrusive concern – which often degenerated into crass curiosity.

HMS *Fearless* sailed into Plymouth Sound, the Duke of Edinburgh came aboard, and on landing, after a quick phone call, Dennis drove straight to Aberporth. The banners were out and an enormous piss-up ensued. His girlfriend, meanwhile, was in Southampton waiting for *Canberra*, which she'd assumed him to be on. He gave presents, his close friend Tony receiving a six-pound lump of shrapnel. He phoned his mother, then returned to Plymouth to sort out his military equipment.

Because we'd lost so much gear, it was more a question of writing things off than handing them in – which was quite amusing. I then returned to Aberporth for six weeks' leave – an unwinding process . . . my gut strings wound really tight . . . and they don't break.

Amid all the euphoria of surviving the battle and going home, as the Scots Guards were making their jubilant way back to the UK, a phone call from one of the outlying farms reported finding a soldier – Guardsman Phillip Williams.

Williams's name was on the list of missing. As far as his battalion was concerned, he was already a hero and on its roll of honour. His appearance six weeks after the end of the Tumbledown battle was a serious embarrassment to the Scots Guards, who after silencing their critics by a creditable performance were suddenly faced with one of their number who appeared to have deserted in the face of the enemy – the most serious military offence. Bob Leitch flew immediately to Fitzroy to collect him:

Williams was clean and tidy, well washed and his hair was combed. He was pale and slim, but certainly didn't look like he'd been living rough. He was supposed to have amnesia, with no idea of who he was or where he'd been. There was nothing much to be said, so we put him into the Wessex and got him back to the hospital.

Back at Port Stanley, the media had heard that something was afoot and were waiting. They were each as pro-army as you could possibly get; Christopher Wain, Nicholas Witchell, Brent Sadler, a man from the *Telegraph* and one from the *Sun*; all well stitched into the military organization and completely on our side. The army Public Relations Officer however was a plonker, completely wet and ridiculous. Faced with a red-hot story and the big guns demanding to interview Williams, he went to pieces, ordering them about, strutting up and down muttering about the case being sub judice, saying they were all subject to military law, and that they would not interview Williams.

Williams was kept in hospital with armed guards – to stop the press getting at him! We talked with him for a while, drinking a few beers, and the story came out. He was a runty little guy who'd joined the Scots Guards when they were at public duties. During the training in Wales, they decided that he wasn't up to being a rifleman, so they'd made him a stretcher bearer – which says a lot for the Guards' perception of the realities of war. Had they had any sort of combat experience they would have known that stretcher bearers have the hardest job of anyone in the battalion, both physically and mentally.

During the battle for Tumbledown, the commander of Williams's stretcher, one of the cooks, gave him the easier job of carrying everyone else's weapons. They were right out in the open, unarmed with shells falling all around, enough to scare the shit out of you. Williams was festooned with bandoliers of ammunition, two sets of webbing, several weapons etc., and found that he couldn't cope. The others said helpful things like 'Fuck off then'. In the end he just sat down and smoked a fag, intending to catch up with the others later.

According to an article by Mick Brown in the *Telegraph* magazine, Williams said that he was knocked unconscious by an explosion: 'There were explosions all around, and then a really close one that made me feel just a terrific amount of pain. I wasn't aware of anything, not even my own pain. It was like nothing.' When he got going again, the snow had started and he was completely lost. He speaks of wandering as if in a dream 'like being sedated'. At one stage he was close enough to an Agentinian observation post to hear them speaking. Eventually he reached the coast and a solitary hut, Port Harriet House, which a few days earlier the Scot Guards recce troop had abandoned in a hurry, leaving all their kit and food. Leitch: 'It must have been like the three bears! He rifled the kit and carried it up into the attic, where he stayed. I'm not sure exactly whether he stayed up there all the time, or whether he left and returned.' After the ceasefire the recce troop returned to find their food and gear missing, and assumed the Argentinians had been there.

I went up into the attic. It was a typical guardsman's effort, everything laid out neatly: two sleeping bags one inside the other, food in neat lines, and compo tins full of piss and crap around the outside. It was clean and immaculately organized and after six weeks he gave up only when the food ran out.

In these initial interviews, Williams seems to have been convinced that the army would treat him as a deserter, a conviction that (illogically) caused him to stay in hiding for so long, rather than immediately making himself known to Islanders and rejoining his battalion. 'As he said, he . . . was convinced they'd shoot him, so he daren't go back. He then had to concoct a story about amnesia.'

Unfortunately, by staying in hiding for so long, Williams himself created the suspicion that he was a deserter – a suspicion that was to drive him from the army and plague him for years after. 'The truth of the matter was that he wasn't a deserter at all – he'd just got lost, then wandered off. He just wasn't up to the difficult job he'd been given.' Guardsman Williams was a classic and unfortunate example of a unit not training a man properly, then demanding things beyond his capabilities:

I don't think he was battle-shocked at all. He was a kid of eighteen, and had no imagination. He was selfish and immature, but he did have all the natural skills to be a soldier and survive – but had not been trained to do it. When he sat down pissed-off, tired and fed-up, all his natural survival instincts came to the fore. His age, inexperience and lack of training were the cause [of his getting separated from the others]. Similar things could have happened in any other unit – except that the other units were properly trained. It was amazing that the Scots Guards were able to perform at all after only a brief exercise in Wales and a few weeks on the ships.

Although Guardsman Williams is an extreme case, he is not unique. Many combatants were affected psychologically by their experiences in the war. In the immediate aftermath, there was anger, confusion and the desire to escape from the emotions that war memories stirred up. Corporal Tom Howard:

By the end of the war, I couldn't have managed more than a few more weeks without having mental problems. It began to hurt me that people could do these things to each other – for a fucking piece of dirt in the middle of the ocean. Now, eight years later, I'm proud of the effort we all put in down there, of all the lads.

I'd started drinking heavily and smoking drugs by September 1982 – while I was still in the army. The combination provided an escape for me, and in Aldershot drugs were easy to get – from people in the army. We smoked hash – and even opium, sometimes – in the unit club. I don't know how we got away with it. I mixed with friends in 2 Para who had the same problems. We all used drugs and drink for the same purpose.

Steve Hughes was watching his soldiers in 2 Para closely, as they came to terms with having survived the war:

Both battalions were affected psychologically, and drank a lot, some on their own – not talking about it. People were bottling it up amongst themselves, thinking that nightmares and so on were peculiar to them. They felt lonely, thinking about the guys who'd died or been wounded and the horrific sights they'd seen.

These feelings, and more serious psychological problems that often develop from them, are well researched, particularly from Vietnam and the successive Arab–Israeli wars. In 1982 Post Traumatic Stress Disorder was well understood by army psychiatrists all over the world. Unfortunately, despite the very large body of psychiatric research into the longer-term psychological effects of combat, nobody from the army's Psychiatric Department came forward with any sort of guidance for Hughes as 2 Para's doctor, or for his battalion as likely sufferers of psychological problems:

The shame was that we didn't know enough about PTSD, and so although afterwards [on the voyage home and subsequently] we had the ideal opportunity to get everyone talking about their feelings, we were not able to do it. We just hadn't been told about it.

12

THE QUICK AND THE DEAD

In the aftermath of battle, combatants emerge from the tension and adrenalin surprised to find themselves alive. Before going into battle some otherwise agnostic individuals turn to religion for comfort, but afterwards, when psychological props are not as necessary, survivors often find a more genuinely religious dimension to their thoughts and emotions. Graham Carter:

I had a bullet bounce off my helmet, then when our own artillery shells came in on us [on Wireless Ridge], one landed fifteen feet away – but thankfully was a dud. It could have killed at least three of us.

Carter does not believe that his two lucky escapes were coincidental. Despite sharing the harsh (and realistic) fatalism of all paratroopers, he is quite certain that he was meant to live – and that 'somebody' was looking after his interests:

I first realized that I was being looked after on the night following Goose Green. It gave me confidence, but I wasn't absolutely certain that I was going to survive, and so I didn't feel I could take undue risks. I felt that during the campaign somebody was looking after me – and I'm a bit more religious now.

'Mac' French:

I don't remember being frightened on the battlefield. I was too excited – remembering what I'd been taught, staying alive, sneaking up on some bugger so that it would be him rather than me . . . But I was fucking frightened in the silent hours when nothing was happening, wondering what it would be like to be shot, in the final moments before you die . . . does it hurt? – no one can tell you.

For once I was glad I'd read the Bible and had something to believe in, and someone to turn to in those moments I really needed someone. I'd say a quiet prayer every now and then.

Sergeant French was less certain about surviving:

I never felt that someone was looking after me, who would ensure that I survived. I didn't know what was going to happen to me, and I had no premonitions. I just felt that it was nice to always have someone to talk to in my own mind – in prayers. I didn't feel like this all the time, and I'm not some religious maniac, but I did pray a lot – and I believe everyone did, in the quiet corners, just before you went to sleep . . . as you closed your eyes. People won't speak openly about this sort of thing . . .

Premonitions, either of surviving or of dying are common:

Some people think they are going to be all right. They reckon —— knew he was going to go. He shat himself a couple of hours before he was shot, and he stank to high heaven. It was a laugh and a joke with him, but they do reckon he had some sort of premonition.

David Cooper:

One warrant officer, as I was going round the day before the Wireless Ridge battle talking to everybody, told me that although he was not superstitious, tomorrow was the first anniversary of his wife's death. He was worried that this seemed to be too much of a coincidence for his death not to follow. There's nothing spiritual you can really say to someone like that. You can tell him not to worry about those kinds of coincidence – then perhaps ask how *he* feels about it.

Superstitious worries were common, even in the most rational of people. Medical Officer Steve Hughes:

After the battle for Goose Green, the ammunition explosion and then the fire on *Sir Galahad*, I wondered what on earth was going to happen next. I was expecting the unexpected, some fresh horror to eclipse that which had gone before – like a black cloud of expectation.

My 25th birthday was on the 12th of June. I had this sense of impending doom and became convinced that I was going to die on my birthday. It seemed logical that I should die on that date, a logic made unshakeable by the knowledge that the longer people were shooting at me, the more chance I had of being killed. It was a feeling of dread, a premonition of the certainty that I was going to live for 25 years, then die. The 'logic' of this was finally 'proven' by the date for our final assault on Stanley being named as 12 June. As it happened, the attack was postponed, and once my birthday was over – and I'd survived – the feeling of dread left me. When we did assault [13 June], I was never anything like as frightened as I had been all day on the 12th – when nothing much happened.

Soldiers are more frightened about being wounded than dying. I was worried about dying, but also about leaving the battalion without a doctor – of letting the side down. Fear is never rational, particularly when it is over-whelming and the irrational side of human nature emerges – and you become superstitious. People become very primeval on the battlefield . . . man's lowest level, at which all the veneers of civilization are stripped away. Standards of peacetime behaviour disappear and you function on pure instinct.

For combat veterans, soldiering and death go together. Although Church of England Christianity is the official creed of the British Army (Roman Catholics are referred to as 'left-footers', although certain Scottish regiments have Nonconformist padres), the actual religious beliefs of the barrack block vary from superstition through to Bible-punching, evangelical Christianity. In peacetime men may not be interested in thinking about death and religion, but in war such apathy disappears.

Regimental traditions interweave very naturally into the actual spiritual perception of many individual soldiers, sometimes connecting with concepts very much older than Christianity. There could even be a quasi-religious dimension that links soldiers throughout the ages. French:

Modern-day paratroopers imagine dying and being picked up by Pegasus and carried off to Valhalla. You can become fascinated with death, wanting to know what it's like – which is similar to wanting to know what it's like being in battle, or killing somebody.

Many peacetime soldiers feel that as part of their training (its climax) they should experience being in battle. As a development of that aspiration, some come to feel that they should perhaps have shot their rifle or had shots fired at them 'in anger', or even killed somebody. At one stage in the Falklands War I borrowed a weapon from a staff officer in the Special Boat Squadron. When I returned it to him, he asked if it had killed anybody.

The ancient profession of soldiering, festooned with regimental traditions and founded on the history of generations of military exploits, has an almost religious aspect to it. Regimental spirit is encouraged at every step, by parades and ritual, martial music, and a wide variety of non-military sports and out of working hours activities. Conventional religion is harnessed to work alongside and complement all this. (Even the Gurkhas' brand of non-pacifist Hinduism is an integral part of their regimental spirit – and hence their preparation for battle.)

However, none of the major religions of the world openly condones violence, so apart from the quasi-religious amalgam of regimental 'beliefs', real religion must have a more personal and individual role to play in military units. Chaplain David Cooper:

In what I represented, I was reminding the soldiers that there is a way of living other than by violence. War can dehumanize people, when they begin to regard the enemy as merely something to be killed. It was my job to prevent that from happening, reminding them they were human beings and that the enemy were as well. Of course, I had to do it in such a way that it did not blunt their fighting edge.

Doctors and chaplains share the same terrible dilemma: their duty to patients and parishioners as individuals conflicts with the job the military employ them to do. Doctors and chaplains are employed by ministries of defence to maintain the military efficiency and the morale of units – through looking after the bodily and spiritual health of individual service personnel.

Chaplains are concerned with the individual, but also with the aim of the unit, and helping people to achieve that aim. You have to recognize the men as individuals in very inhuman circumstances, helping spiritual and possibly psychological casualties – although I wasn't a barefoot psychiatrist. Ultimately the aims of the unit are more important than the welfare of individual soldiers might be.

Padres do not usually carry weapons, but Cooper is quite clear that this has nothing to do with the morality of killing in combat:

My pastoral work for the battalion was just as significant in keeping them fighting as would be somebody else's work in the unit. By supporting a fighting unit, I was as culpable for the deaths the battalion caused as the individuals pulling the triggers. The commandment says 'Thou shalt do no murder', not 'Thou shalt not kill'.

Cooper contributed fully to the military side of battalion life:

I'd always felt that the army doesn't know how to handle snipers, and the CO and 2ic supported my ideas. As I was keen on shooting, I was put in charge of training the battalion shooting team.

In Vietnam, the duty of chaplains (and psychiatrists) to keep the soldiers fighting placed them in terribly difficult situations. They were poorly regarded by Vietnam vets: 'They blessed the troops, their mission, the guns, their killing ... whatever we were doing ... murder ... atrocities ... God was always on our side.' One Catholic went to confession regularly: 'I'd say, "Sure I'm smoking dope again. I guess I blew my state of grace again." But I didn't say anything about killing.'[1]

Vietnam chaplains kept the men going – using Absolution to keep their guilt at bay. They are also reported to have given pep talks at funerals, urging the men to 'kill more of them'. Psychiatrists had a similar 'servicing' role, keeping men in combat and getting psychological casualties back into line units as soon as possible. At the heart of their dilemma is an essential conflict of interest, between the needs of the military for men to keep on fighting, and the needs of the individual. In more intensive warfare, the man who cannot continue in combat through some form of battle shock is a liability and it makes military sense to evacuate him as quickly as possible. However, Vietnam's 'low-intensity' hostilities (which could be very violent) made clear-cut distinctions between those who did not want to continue and those who were unable to continue very difficult to make. Individuals could be exposed to heavy combat – or to no combat at all. The growing climate of in-theatre opposition to the war put additional pressure on men to avoid combat, and on military authorities to keep the men's noses to the grindstone.

In most armies, in order to be able to do their jobs without interference, military chaplains and psychiatrists hold officer's rank. Some chaplains and doctors make soldiers feel aware of their rank during interviews, whereas others (notably Royal Naval chaplains) adopt the rank of the person to whom they are speaking. Both approaches have advantages and disadvantages; an authoritative father figure can give comfort and reassurance, or equally can upset patients by reacting 'just like a field grade officer'. The other approach, behaving like a friend of equal rank, is just as problematic; when chaplains or psychiatrists do not have the authority to remove men from battle, their sympathy is meaningless.

Vietnam soldiers who had witnessed or taken part in atrocities and sought help from chaplains and psychiatrists, found themselves caught in a trap. If they confessed to the events that were troubling them they risked court martial. Many who did take that risk found themselves being told that the incident was unimportant and that they should just soldier on. This complete lack of support – an opting out by counsellors – made them very angry. Other soldiers solved the dilemma by confessing to their feelings without mention of the atrocity:

During the interview with the psychiatrist, I was tearful and very emotional. I talked of being upset at the way the war was being run [rather than of guilt at the rape-murder he and others had committed].

The psychiatrist said: 'You're a specialist in the United States Army and you're sitting there with a red face and your eyes look like scrambled eggs. Man, you ain't no GI.'

That made me more upset and I answered: 'Oh, maybe if I was to prove myself by going and raping and killing some more girls for you. Is that what you want me to do, Major?'

Being in an impossible position the psychiatrist opted out, suggesting his patient see the chaplain – who was told rather more of the story.

In 'a fatherly way' the chaplain took the patient to the chapel, suggesting that he 'find the answer himself'. The soldier deserted.[2]

Despite David Cooper's very clear understanding of his military role in 2 Para, he realized that his responsibilities to the soldiers as individuals could jeopardize their morale and fighting spirit. He felt it was his duty to prepare them for the prospect of becoming a casualty or for the possibility of being killed – a stiff dose of reality that was certain to dampen the men's enthusiasm for the fight. More specifically, in the girding up of loins before battle, he believed it was vital that they understood that if they were wounded nobody would be able to stop to patch them up:

I felt I had to do this to prevent those who were wounded from feeling isolated and abandoned on the battlefield – and thus losing the will to live. I was also concerned that men whose friends were hit, who had been forced to go on without giving any help to them, would afterwards feel responsible for their deaths. It took a lot of thought as to how to present all this without frightening the soldiers to death, or scaring them to the extent that they wouldn't take any risks. I tried to make them talk about it, to bring the problems out into the open . . .

I couldn't do much to prepare them actually for dying; not many men want to be prepared for death by a priest. They were very superstitious; for example feeling that making a will was somehow inviting death. I told them that my belief was in a God who cared for them as an individual, who I thought had the authority to ensure that death wasn't the end of them as a person. I couldn't say any more than that without getting into things that I don't feel strongly enough to tell others . . .

There's not a lot I can say to anybody about what happens after death, and all I could say to soldiers is that God's authority transcends death. He cares for them sufficiently to ensure that they as a person do not face extinction at death.

Cooper's final church service before landing at San Carlos had been packed out – the entire battalion coming voluntarily together as a last act of comradeship:

As a clergyman I'm concerned with individuals. Once you get each person right, everything else [in the military sense] follows. I told the battalion of my beliefs, and also that I didn't believe in a God of Causes, that he was as much on the Argentine side as ours, that he was concerned with us as individuals of his creation – even though we were not in a situation he would want.

The soldiers may have taken some comfort from this – but I don't really know. Several years afterwards, a colour sergeant told me that although he had no time at all for religion, he will never forget the service we had in Stanley at the end of the war.

Immediately a battle ends, nobody knows how many have been killed or wounded – or their names. Even days after the battle for Goose Green, the soldiers knew only of their own companies and platoon, and were desperate for news of friends in the other companies:

At the church service, I read out the complete list of killed, wounded and who had been evacuated. Many learned for the first time of the deaths of friends and even family. This was followed by a normal church service, during which our emotions caught up with us.

Many men cried then – and not earlier on their company positions because they felt church was an acceptable place for such release. For the first time in their lives, many found that war had created circumstances in their lives that only religious language could address. Their normal lives did not bring such things to them. The service provided the language in which the soldiers could express their feelings, so although they might not have been religious, the words did allow them to make some sense of their emotions.

The units that fought in the Falklands War were very close-knit, with strong personal bonds between their members. The closeness turned casualties and deaths into deeply personal events, but while the war continued, soldiers had no time to stop and grieve for their friends: 'People's experiences were too shocking to cope with, so individuals kept shutting them away into some mental cupboard – which is fine until the cupboard becomes too full.'

A regular army of long-term professionals is different from a conscript force in that all the soldiers know each other and their families very well. Combat is therefore emotionally harder to endure:

For the professional, the dead and wounded are not just numbers but people you know well. The battlefield doesn't allow time for grieving, and so in losing friends, professional soldiers carry a much greater burden than ever before of the hard side of being a human being.

It's a double-edged weapon. Men fight better when with their friends but are more affected by the deaths. And they don't do it for the regiment, the Queen or even the cause.

With only a fifty-year history, some members of the Parachute Regiment feel they have an additional reason for fighting well:

Our men were very conscious of the examples set in the past – North Africa, Arnhem . . . We knew that when we returned to UK, we'd meet the people from 2 Para who actually fought in those battles. It's perhaps not the same as with the Guards – our traditions are not from the dead past. Paras are part of their own history.[3]

The feeling that the expectations of regimental tradition have been fulfilled is an important part of recovering from the emotional trauma of combat – and can help individuals come to terms with the deaths of friends. Through their history and traditions they know that others in past wars have endured the same grief, that the struggle was worthy and that they are not alone.

David Cooper emerged from the trauma of the war with the basics of his faith greatly fortified:

After the Falklands I abandoned a lot about religion, but I came away better equipped to be a chaplain, with the conviction that I'd got something that when the chips were down soldiers needed. I don't mean pushing the Bible or religion down their throats, but being somebody with the time to care for them as a person, and expressing a very simple belief that there is more to life than death.

The whole thing gave me a great boost as a chaplain, which as a job can be very wearing and demoralizing. You are usually on your own, fighting uphill with little support and not much confidence in what you are selling.

In his purely religious duties, during the war Cooper had made no attempt to evangelize, merely telling people what he believes:

In that sense I have often felt a poor clergyman – and this approach does lead to empty churches, which is depressing. However, I never felt it was my job to convince people of things they didn't want to hear, and I never said that if they didn't see things my way they'd be damned to eternity, as I know some military chaplains actually do.

As a chaplain, it's important to be seen to share [the danger, discomfort etc.], so that at least they see somebody who is prepared to take the same chances as them without even (as they see it) the freedom to reply in kind [by firing back].

Cooper did not believe the Argentinians were an evil enemy:

There were times when we felt closer to the Argentine soldiers than we did to the people back in UK – because they knew what it was like. The Argentinians were very nice blokes. Each side felt that they were responding to violence rather than trying to kill individuals. I'm not sure, however, whether I'd have reacted the same against the Japanese or even Muslims – who have such different attitudes towards life.

The paratroopers themselves shared their padre's humane approach to what had to be done. Private Graham Carter: 'It's hard to think that human beings could hate each other so much as to do these things to each other – but the irony is that there was very little hatred in this war. You just did the job.'

When hostilities ended, Cooper began to prepare his flock for returning to civilization – even though like them he was emotionally overwhelmed by the experience they had been through together:

At the end, I was alert enough to realize that our thoughts and the way we felt during the war were somehow important for the future. I told the soldiers during our service in Stanley that life would become easy again back home, but before that happened they should make an effort to remember how they felt now.

On the battlefield, being surrounded by mutilation and death causes a gradual desensitization and numbing of the emotions, which is described by ex-GI Jeff Needle writing in an anti-Vietnam War pamphlet:

A very sad thing happened while we were there – to everyone. It happened slowly and gradually so no one noticed when it happened. We began slowly with each death and every casualty until there were so many deaths and so many wounded, we started to treat death and loss of limbs with callousness, and it happens because the human mind can't hold that much suffering and survive.[4]

Seeing people die, whether or not you killed them yourself, has a terrible effect on individuals, creating very strong, long-lasting feelings of guilt. Psychological research into Vietnam veterans has revealed that men enjoyed the feeling of being the one to survive mutilation and death, that they enjoyed being surrounded by death, 'feeling alive' and even gaining a feeling of strength. In the process many felt they had gained an insight into the true nature of Man, but judging that the feeling of strength amid death must be perverted, came to regard this feeling (and to an extent themselves) as an embodiment of actual evil.

The curiosity of those who remain at home about what happens in combat, and about what individuals actually do, can be very hurtful. On returning home, war veterans seem invariably to be asked questions about what it is like to kill, and whether they have killed anybody themselves. Vietnam veterans were very touchy about such questions, particularly when asked how many times they had killed, or how they felt about doing it – especially when asked by children. The vets felt that their questioners were enjoying and being entertained by hearing about killing – and felt used.

A civilized society cannot ignore humans who have killed other humans. Killers are cast out, imprisoned or even killed themselves; they are considered by psychologists to have entered (in Lifton's words) a 'forbidden realm of control over life and death, which separates them psychologically from the rest of us'. War, however, turns killers into heroes, in the process celebrating one of the great human taboos. This is not in itself unnatural; the honouring of warriors who have killed for the tribe is probably the oldest of all tribal rituals. Vietnam veterans were in the strange position of having been given the sanction to kill, yet neither they nor their society accepted that the killings were legitimate. As a result, after Vietnam and the strong surge of anti-war feeling it generated, ordinary people in many countries have come to regard killing by soldiers in the same way that they regard killing by anybody else. Although this change of perception brings an element of blame to rest unfairly on those who are doing their duty on behalf of the rest of society, it is nevertheless a more honest and realistic attitude to warfare.

Memories of killing in battle haunt most soldiers – but they rarely talk about it. Being regarded as a killer (as Vietnam veterans certainly were) has the effect on the individual of adding a public shame to his personal guilt. Being asked about killing by non-military people is deeply upsetting, particularly as veterans know that if they admit that they have killed their questioners are likely to draw unfair conclusions about them as people – even to the extent of rejecting them. The prurient and basically indifferent questioning of freshly-returned combat veterans by friends, family and acquaintances can make them very angry. Mark Northfield (on returning from the Falklands):

Afterwards I couldn't see why any of us should have been treated as heroes. We'd signed on the dotted line, and just did our jobs. People would ask, 'Was it cold, and did you shoot anybody?' I'd ask them if they knew what it was like to kill someone, then tell them not to fucking ask me until they did.

Psychologists talk of 'survivor guilt' and 'death guilt' when discussing the reactions of people to incidents in which others have been killed and which can cause depression and other psychiatric and behavioural problems for long periods after the traumatic event. Survivors feel they should be grateful for being alive, and that they should be happy, which makes their actual unhappiness even harder to bear. The psychologist Robert Lifton found that Vietnam vets who survived ambushes that killed most of their comrades and friends felt joy at remaining alive, but a terrible guilt that their survival had been purchased at the expense of those who died. Men thought of themselves as ghosts devoid of luck, who had somehow betrayed their dead comrades by staying alive. They felt that they had been responsible for the deaths, and wished for death themselves. Many even saw themselves as already dead.

Lifton also says that Vietnam vets often identify closely with the veterans of the First World War rather than with those of the Second World War. The deadlock of the trenches seemed pointless and never-ending like Vietnam. A year after the poet Wilfred Owen's 'neurasthenia' (shell shock) was diagnosed, he was able to demonstrate in verse what survivor guilt felt like, a condition often described as 'death in life':

Mental Cases

– These are men whose minds the dead have ravaged.
Memory fingers in their hair of murders,
Multitudinous murders they once witnessed . . .
– Thus their heads wear this hilarious, hideous
Awful falseness of set-smiling corpses.
– Thus their hands are plucking at each other;
Picking at the rope-knots of their scourging;
Snatching after us who smote their brother.
Pawing after us who dealt them war and madness.[5]

Owen's problems started four months after a shell exploded, blowing him into the air and killing his brother officer Second Lieutenant Gaukroger. At first doctors diagnosed concussion, then shell shock. Owen thought out a diagnosis for himself:

You know it was not the Boche that worked me up, nor the explosives, but it was living so long by poor old Cock Robin (as we used to call 2Lt Gaukroger, who lay not only nearby, but in various places around and about, if you understand. I hope you don't!)[6]

Death guilt is at its strangest and most intense when men have come face to face with an enemy whom they have gone on to kill. Despite knowing that in such situations one must either kill or be killed, men still feel guilt at not being the one to have died. After describing killing a Vietcong with a knife, one man added, speaking softly: 'I felt sorry. I don't know why I felt sorry. John Wayne never felt sorry.'[7]

The sight of dead bodies, whether in a combat environment or at the scene of some civilian disaster, is deeply disturbing. The survivors of incidents in which others have been killed, and also those who come later to clean up the mess (police, firemen, ambulance crews), see damaged, mutilated bodies – sights that they are unable to forget. These unwanted memories can be so strong and frighteningly vivid that they haunt the survivors to a degree that can spoil and corrupt their lives. To them, after witnessing such carnage, the bodies of living people can seem horribly similar to the bodies of the dead. At one level, this makes the living constantly aware of the ease with which normal, healthy people can be transformed into corpses. Individuals move on from this realization to develop a sense of impending doom in their own lives.

At a deeper level, individuals may superimpose unwanted memories of mutilation and injury on to the people around them. Sex causes particular problems in this respect; living, naked bodies turn involuntarily into reminders of corpses. After fighting in the Wehrmacht in the Second World War, Guy Sajer wrote: 'As soon as I saw naked flesh [at the start of a sexual encounter] I braced myself for a torrent of entrails, remembering countless wartime scenes, with smoking, stinking corpses pouring out their vitals.'[8]

In combat men's attitudes towards death and dying vary. Vietnam soldiers had a fear of the filth and excrement of Vietnam – so different from the homogenized sanitation of America – fearing a dirty and sordid death. 'I wanted to die clean. It didn't matter if I died – but I just didn't want to die with mud on my boots, all filthy. Death wasn't so bad if you were clean.' Another had a recurrent dream throughout his time in Vietnam: 'I would end up shot, lying along the side of the road, dying in the mud.' Their expectations of death, fuelled by the glamour of films in which the stars died bravely, were severely dashed by the hard reality.

The US Army understood the political and military importance of protecting the public (and their soldiers) from the realities of death in Vietnam. When bodies were brought home they were often accompanied, particularly when the corpse was badly mutilated. The lead-lined coffin would be sealed and marked with a notice forbidding anybody to open it. A soldier (who perhaps had known the dead man) was often sent along to accompany the body, to ensure that this notice was complied with. The army regulations for this harrowing duty read as follows:

. . . each body in its casket is to have, at all times, a body escort . . . an effort has been made to find an escort whose personal involvement with the deceased or presence with the family of the deceased will be of comfort or aid.

Your mission as body escort is as follows: To make sure the body is afforded at all times the respect due to a fallen soldier in the United States Army. Specifically it is as follows:

1)   To check the tags on the caskets at every point of departure.
2)   To insist, if the tags indicate the remains as non-viewable, that the relatives do not view the body. Remember that non-viewable means exactly that – non-viewable . . .[9]

In peacetime training exercises, soldiers are only rarely required to practise dealing with the dead. Military trainers believe that too much reality in training frightens men rather than preparing them for combat, a concern that in the run-up to live operations becomes even more relevant. The result is that men have to learn what needs to be done for themselves – a process that occurred naturally in the Falklands. Sergeant French:

B Company were bringing their dead back into this little dip. Half a dozen bodies were there already covered with ponchos. When we went forward into the dip, I remembered thinking how blokes automatically laid out their own dead perfectly neatly, limbs out straight, hands on the chest – perfect. You couldn't have asked for any better on a drill square. This wasn't what they had been taught to do, or anything like that. They just wouldn't leave them all twisted, but in perfect straight lines.

The Argentine bodies, however, were being left where they'd fallen – as the battle was still going on.

Towards the end of 2 Para's Goose Green battle, chaplain David Cooper's main task was to find out exactly who had died and who was injured:

That evening I got hold of the RSM, Malcolm Simpson, the Ops Officer and Chris Keeble and said it was time for us to try to start accounting for our casualties.

At Warrenpoint [see Chapter 4] we'd made a bog-up of this. The circumstances hadn't been easy, and we'd told some wives their husbands were dead and others that they were alive, when in fact it was untrue in both cases. We agreed now not to release any names until we were certain.

To be absolutely certain, I collected and personally identified the bodies at our end, and Malcolm went back to Ajax Bay to do the same with any bodies moved back by the units that were following us up. That night I got lists of names from the companies of who were missing and where they had last been seen. Against that list, the RAP clerk told me who had been through the medical system, and companies were able to tell me some that were definitely dead – so I ended up with a comprehensive list of all the missing.

One of the names was an officer who I knew quite well, and I was extraordinarily upset about it. However the next day he turned up, having got stuck behind the Argentine lines while out on patrol. When he appeared I was very relieved and wanted to touch him, to shake his hand. I don't know why I felt like that; perhaps I saw in him some sort of particularization of a general feeling.

As the [Argentine] surrender was clearly going to happen, I got on with collecting the dead. With a lad from HQ Company I hijacked a Sno-Cat and we drove over to where D and B Company had been, to collect Jim Barry and the soldiers who had been with him. Because we didn't know where the minefields were, I didn't want to risk the living in order to collect dead bodies. We kept stopping to check wires across the track (which I was sure were from the Milan missiles[10] – but we had to check each one in case). The soldiers we had helping us initially kept their feelings at bay using humour: 'We're off to collect floppies – no, they'll be stiffies by now . . .' However, when it came to picking them up and pushing them into the Sno-Cat, they became very quiet. We'd then climb, the three of us, into the back with them.

Jim had been shot through the abdomen and had been biting his bottom lip and had a look of anxiety on his face. I sat in the back of the wagon looking at him, wondering what thoughts had been going through his mind in the moments before he was shot. The lad next to me saw my face and completely misunderstood my sombre look, saying, 'Don't worry, there'll be no mines here.'

We couldn't initially get helicopters to fly them back to Ajax Bay so we put them into the garden of the house being used by Tac HQ. There were dogs about that hadn't been fed for a while – which I didn't want to get at them. I went to the sentry and told him the bodies were by the hedge covered with groundsheets. The sentry was concerned and unhappy about this, and very glad when his stag [period of duty] was over.

The paras were emotionally very sensitive about their dead, and about the way 'friendly' troops had died:

I was collecting bodies from the earlier part of the battle in which a marine engineer had been killed. I had half a dozen bodies covered in groundsheets by the side of the track and was waiting for the vehicle to come and pick them up. One soldier came over and said, 'I hear there is a marine over there.' I said he was a sapper, and the soldier replied, 'The poor bugger, being killed so far from his friends.' He felt very strongly for the sapper, that he was among strangers, which was not the right way to die.

I brought [one of our men] back in a vehicle, leaving him to one side until we could move him back to Ajax Bay for burial. He'd been killed by a shell fragment, and one of the soldiers came to me and said, 'Have you seen him? Did you see that he's got tears in his eyes? He was crying when he died.' I asked the MO, Steve Hughes, if this was likely. [The man] had taken a huge lump of steel in his chest and Steve said he'd probably been killed outright. The soldiers however believed that he'd been crying when he died because he'd not been getting letters from his wife, and believed she'd stopped writing.

She had in fact been writing, which became clear after the battle:

The soldiers in his company were very upset by the tears story. They strongly felt that you shouldn't have to die with a question mark in your mind over your wife – a tragedy that had the added poignancy of his [supposed] anxiety being unfounded.

There was a very strong feeling that there is a proper way to die . . . that you shouldn't scream and writhe around shouting . . . We had one officer who was injured and we couldn't evacuate him for a while, and unfortunately he thoroughly choked everyone off (the soldiers thought it a poor show) by continually insisting that he should be evacuated. When we told him there wasn't anything to take him out in, he didn't believe us and kept saying, 'Look, if you ask the CO he'll tell you I've got to be casevaced now. You get on to the CO and ask him and he'll tell you.' We said, 'The CO's dead!' but that didn't make any difference. He was adamant.

There was also a strong feeling that there must be a proper funeral – even if it's only a foot you can find. You've got to do the right thing; and it was more than just respect for the dead. It was doing something for someone who'd given what you all expect you might have to give, only he's the one who has given it.

Most of the soldiers felt that once you were dead that was it, and I gave last rites on the point of death rather than afterwards. None of them asked my denomination. There's no place for that when the chips are down on the battlefield. The churches ought to appreciate that more.

I wasn't in fact with many of our men as they died. Most were either killed outright or died on their own before they were found; and every one who made it to our RAP lived. With Argentine soldiers, all I could do was make the right sort of noises as they died. Speaking no English, they nevertheless recognized the sign of the cross and so on.

The burials afterwards were really for the benefit of the living, although everyone has the right to a decent disposal of their remains.

In one particular instance, Cooper had to intervene in order that this be done:

A warrant officer from the [——] came to me and told me that the body of one of their officers who had been killed on the *Galahad* was still being carried around on the orders of their CO – who was intent on carrying the body with them back to UK.

Steve Hughes:

The body was in a body bag, being smuggled around from place to place, hidden tucked under CP tents or behind buildings. Most people in the brigade knew about it, and eventually [the warrant officer], a good friend of [the deceased], went to David Cooper and asked him to do something about it.

Cooper:

The warrant officer was very concerned about this – feeling that it just wasn't right. I assured him that it was very definitely not right, and bubbled [informed on] the CO (who seemed to have become unbalanced) to the brigade DQ, and the officer was buried. This sort of thing is understandable, but it's upsetting when the worst side of people comes out at a time like that.

After the Goose Green battle David Cooper's patience was tested to the very limit by the lack of support he had already experienced from the Royal Navy senior chaplain. The burial of 2 Para's battle dead was to make Cooper very angry. Earlier, he had run out of wafers and communion wine, and his telexed requests for resupply went unanswered:

I had to con some off the Roman Catholic chaplain who was coming round visiting on a very regular basis – and there was only one of him. I became annoyed that a senior chaplain couldn't be bothered to come and see another chaplain, albeit from the army, who'd come into his circuit. I'd have gone to find a naval chaplain if he'd joined our setup.

Then our Ops Officer Roger Miller came to me in Goose Green saying, 'There's a memorial service for "H" [Jones] and the others back at Ajax Bay. They're sending a helicopter so only 15 men can go – would you like to go?'

Cooper assumed that another chaplain at Ajax Bay would have buried the men once their bodies had been prepared and certified at the field hospital.

As it happened, I really did want to go. Although this is probably a very arrogant thing to say, as far as death was concerned I'd been carrying the battalion. I felt I'd been giving continually to others and needed someone to give something to me. I'd suffered personal bereavements in close friends who'd been killed, and there was nobody really that I could talk to about it. I thought that if I could go to the service without worrying about doing anything, just to take part would give me the help I needed.

But when I got off the helicopter some chaplain I didn't know (who turned out to be the senior chaplain) came up to me with a piece of paper. He said, 'There are the names. You'll need those.' I said, 'What for?' and he said, 'We've been waiting for you. You're taking the service. You're doing the burial. They're your soldiers!'

I said, 'Burial? I've come for a Memorial Service.' He said, 'No, they haven't been buried. This is the funeral!' So I said, 'This isn't the place to have an argument' and pulled myself together and went to the head of the trench, through crowds of people. Two Marine chaplains were there already, and as basically they [the bodies] were all 2 Para, the service was mine.

I said, 'Let's start' but nobody knew how. 'Where is the senior chaplain?' Nobody could find him, so I got hold of our RSM and said, 'Mal, to get this rolling, we're going to have to put the body bags into the grave, so start putting them in.'

We must have waited twenty minutes for the start of that service. At the end, everyone evaporated, no sign of anybody, so I stamped off to the helicopter and went back to Goose Green very annoyed.

Like commanders, chaplains need somebody to look after their welfare, and to maintain their morale.

I really felt let down. If the chaplain's trying to give to people, there's got to be somebody who takes the steam out of it for him, who he can have confidence in. I let off steam to Chris Keeble, then lodged a formal complaint against the senior chaplain with Brigade Headquarters. Anyway the DQ came down and made pacifying noises until I calmed down.

For most contemporary soldiers there can be little nobility attached to death in combat; the sight of the remains of their dead friends simply brings home the bitter waste of warfare. According to Steve Hughes: 'The most horrifying moment of the campaign for me was seeing the bodies of David Wood and "H".'

Under rain-soaked tarpaulins, while the battle for Goose Green was still going on, the bodies seemed like empty shells, the husks of their former occupants.

I knew that David Wood and 'H's bodies had arrived [at 2 Para's Regimental Aid Post] and were under a tarpaulin, but because I was busy with casualties, didn't go over to see them for some time. Bill [Bentley] had pointed them out among a pile of bodies behind some gorse bushes.

I went over there and lifted one of the tarpaulins, to find 'H' wearing a big green parka. When he was alive, because of his personality, he had seemed a physically huge man, but now, lying in the gorse, he was in fact small. David Wood was the same, a big personality, who really was a small, wiry Scot. In death they were both surprisingly small . . . and insignificant.

It was a serious shock to see people I'd seen a few hours before so full of life, joking, obviously in their element . . . and suddenly they were dead. It was horrific, but then there just wasn't the time to absorb it. During a battle with seriously injured casualties coming in all the time was neither the time nor the place for grieving, and part of me feels guilty for not allowing myself to grieve for them.

Part of the persistent horror [that Hughes still experiences] is guilt at not giving my friends the dues of grief in their departing. It was too painful so I locked it all away, and I feel now as if I have betrayed them by not acknowledging their worth by grieving . . . Perhaps PTSD is delayed guilt and grief?

The Operations Officer of the Scots Guards, Tim Spicer:

The worst job was tagging the bodies before they were flown out for burial. It was awful.

Spicer admits to being drawn to look at the bodies – a natural reaction:

I was technically interested in the wounds, in what modern weapons did to people. Some were unmarked, with a surprising absence of blood, although one in particular had lots of blood. I was curious, but was also very disturbed by the horror of it – particularly as I knew them all.

I had to do it as quickly as possible, then we put them on to the helicopters.

The bodies are my most vivid image of the whole war. I can see them as if it were all happening now. They were laid out in a row – like a dormitory where they were kipping. I didn't want to do it, but I just kept walking. It was a mix of curiosity and revulsion . . .

I was the architect of the battle, but not the perpetrator – fighting it with a radio and not a bayonet. I had more curiosity [about the dead] than the combatants might have had; they would have got over their fascination during the battle. I had more time to analyse it all, and here was the evidence – seven bodies, plus one so badly blown up that I don't remember seeing a whole body. I thought, why aren't they more messy? They weren't the first bodies I'd seen – I'd been to Northern Ireland. They were like a TV image of a dead body – clean. For the first few seconds I was amazed at the lack of visible damage, then we went through their pockets, bagging the contents to send home.

I didn't know what you were supposed to do – I'd never read the proper instruction on dealing with bodies. I knew you had to tag them, so we tied one to each man's jacket, and kept the other. You are supposed to leave one of the dog tags around their necks, and take the other. We left their dog tags. The burial teams would know what to do.

I had to ask the Sergeant Major to help me identify a couple, then we loaded them on to a helicopter and they were gone.

The bodies were flown to one of the field surgical hospitals for certification, documentation and bagging. Surgeon Commander Rick Jolly was responsible for the administration of the dead at Ajax Bay field surgical hospital:

Eleven more bodies arrived . . . piled on top of each other inside a Wessex. The bodies were stripped for burial, the cold, wet clothing cut away. Each pocket is emptied, and personal possessions logged and placed in plastic bags. All paras seemed to carry spare red berets to wear when the war was won. Several of these were too soaked with blood to be returned to relatives.[11]

Once each corpse was naked, Jolly examined it for cause of death. Each death had to be formally certified, and a Field Death Certificate completed.

After examination and documentation, each body is lifted into an opaque plastic liner, which is placed inside a thick grey PVC body bag with heavy zip and carrying loops. Each name is written in large indelible letters on the outside. The bags are built to withstand burial and any future exhumation. The RSM and a wounded company commander watched. Battle Casualty Occurrence Report forms are then completed.

Rumours quickly attach themselves to the dead, which can affect morale or the way the battle is fought unless quickly contradicted. Rick Jolly:

June 15th; after the ceasefire, the Scots Guards dead have been frozen into their rigor mortis positions by the cold. Their unusual postures have led to rumours that two were captured and executed by retreating enemy. The bodies were said to have been found with their hands tied and blindfolded.

Jolly carried out the post mortem:

One has been killed by a long range sniper shot to the head, the other by a fragmenting mortar round. In other words, they both died on the field of battle. I describe the findings to Lt Col Mike Scott their CO. No more is heard of this unfounded allegation.[12]

Major Bob Leitch was responsible for gathering together and burying the dead in the months following the end of hostilities, and for organizing the official War Graves Commission Cemetery on the Falkland Islands. This harrowing task proved to be distasteful for widely differing reasons:

The war was over but the press were still there, hanging around looking out for copy, digging out human interest stories. Nobody was being killed any more, so they started wanting to see the dead bodies . . .
I remember the helicopters flying press up on to the ridge so they could photograph bodies. The Argie corpses were left out in rows, and the helicopters would hover beside each one – press cameras clicking. Some of the pilots did this run so often that they developed names for each body: a fat one and skinny one, called 'Laurel and Hardy' for example.

Leitch was used to dead bodies, having experienced his first death (as an army nursing officer) when he was nineteen years of age. He nevertheless found his job very distasteful: 'I objected to the dead because they smelt bad . . . awful, lacked dignity – and they hadn't necessarily been just shot.'

Before being flown out to the Falklands, Leitch's unenviable job had been to notify wives, parents and family of the deaths of their husbands, sons and brothers:

. . . wearing my smart service dress, at eight o'clock in the morning. I had one particularly upsetting visit to make, to the parents of a Welsh Guardsman who had been killed on the *Galahad*. I drove round in my service dress and banged on the door, first thing in the morning. A little girl showed me in, to her mother who was sitting in the kitchen wearing a dressing-gown and pulling up her tights. She knew instantly what I was there for, and screamed at me to go away, then to demand why I wasn't down there, killed instead of her son.

The boy's father was a train driver during the train drivers' strike. I had first to find him, then tell the man's fiancée – who had apparently just discovered she was pregnant. On a crowded railway platform it took some time to find the father, and I was so obvious, dressed in all my uniform, surrounded by the other drivers. The man had a younger brother too, who I also had to tell. At the end of the day, my emotions had been rubbed completely raw.

Two days later, I was whipped off to the Falklands. While I was away, my wife went along to the guardsman's memorial service and we became quite good friends with his family. I sent them a piece of rock from Fitzroy and some photographs of where the *Galahad* had gone down. Then later I laid a wreath for the lad. So although we don't keep contact now, we welded together quite closely.

Leitch's new responsibilities on the Islands carried on exactly where his previous job had finished, which made it doubly hard for him:

You know quite a lot about some of these guys, their names, parents and family. You have a vision in your mind of what they were about . . . Then three or four months later you go out and dig up each body from its temporary grave, so you can put the man in a casket and send him home.

But when you dig him up you find he isn't at all like you imagined him. You find that he hasn't been shot, but blown to pieces by a recoilless rifle. Private A isn't lying with dignity in a body bag, or even a skeleton or partly decomposing corpse in a body bag, he's a series of lumps – *he's been blown to bits*.

Leitch found that there was no escaping from the reality of what was inside each body bag:

That's the real horror of it. If he's shot, the round goes in one end and out the other and that's him finished; he died. You can accept that. He's a dead body laid in front of you. It's when his entire face has been blown away, or his entrails are out, or he's got nothing from the navel down – only the top end of his corpse. You realize that at the end of the day, we're nothing more than hedgehogs or rabbits that you run over in the middle of the road.

Weapons impart huge amounts of energy that rip bits of our bodies off, so we just come apart – into bits. Some things are more grotesque than others. Head wounds destroy your face and your dignity. Your relatives can't recognize you, so what's left of you . . . ? What is there to say goodbye to?

And quite rapidly after you die you start to smell really bad. Your body fluids all pour out. We picked up one guy, I think he was a pilot, and I suddenly realized that you shouldn't ever bury anyone in an impervious groundsheet. As we picked him up to lift him into the Wessex, all this filth, this foul-smelling diarrhoea poured all over me and I had to go round for the rest of the day smelling like something unbelievable. I couldn't get it to go away.

I remember the smell as we dug them up . . . being given a polythene bag containing a ring and personal effects of one of the officers. His wife wanted him buried out there, but had asked for the ring. When I opened the bag, the stench was incredible, and now I cannot eat any sort of game meat – pheasant, hare, deer – because that is what it smells like, magnified a million times.

I thought this job was going to be quite straightforward; dig 'em up, put them in the boxes, then out to the ship where those gruesome guys would hose them down with formalin or whatever and get the bits together, seal them in a box and off home. It wasn't like that at all.

First we had to identify each one, from his dog tags – God knows why when I think about it. As they'd been dead a few months, it wasn't nice. It's worse if you have to nose around looking for things, particularly the dog tags around their necks. Some of them I knew and recognized. Several were people I'd trained with. It was really cold and gruesome, so long after the event.

Leitch had to find a site for the War Graves cemetery, in which the majority of the British dead would be permanently interred:

There were some beautiful moments too. I'd found this beautiful place . . . idyllic, a lovely little beach with grass, looking across the water, just beside Blue Beach – it would make you cry to see it. We sat on the beach; there were geese, and a horse that came down from San Carlos. I was feeling pretty maudlin, thinking of a friend who'd joined the army with me, who'd drowned in the SAS helicopter. I dug up some daffodils and made a little shrine for him behind some gorse bushes. I decided that this was a good place to be buried, and made my decision.

I then became quite carried away with the idea, thinking that no one should be shipped back to UK. It seemed ridiculous, to be dug up and reburied in Aldershot military cemetery where you'd be forgotten in ten years' time. Better to stay here where nobody would ever forget you, with your mates in this beautiful spot, with the War Graves Commission taking care of everything.

Despite being a paratrooper himself, Bob Leitch's emotional conclusion ran counter to the usual Airborne dictum of taking your dead with you. Steve Hughes, speaking of his Commanding Officer 'H' Jones:

'H' had always said that we would repatriate our dead – even though the official line was that they would be buried in the Falklands. He wasn't going to leave the bodies of his men buried on foreign soil where they could be desecrated. After exercises he would say that for real, he would turn the battalion back to pick up the dead and bring them home with us. He ended up being buried down there himself because, being a good CO's wife, Sarah Jones supported the official line.

Jones's expressed wishes as to what was to happen to his own body are not known.

Bob Leitch:

I received a letter from a girl enclosing a ten pound note to buy a wreath for her fiancé who had died at Goose Green – to lay on the 2 Para cross. Getting a wreath at that time of year in the Falklands was impossible; however, I spoke to some of the locals who refused the ten pounds and returned with a huge chicken wire and boxwood wreath with horrendous plastic flowers jammed in it – but it was beautiful.

The tenner went into the South Atlantic Fund, and we flew down to Ajax Bay and parked this thing with due ceremony by the cross. I photographed it, then sent the picture off with a letter to the girl. She wrote back, thanking me for what I'd done. She also said that eight weeks after being told of his death, she'd received a letter from him – which had been delayed in the post.

Having found the spot for the official War Graves cemetery, Leitch had to get it ready for the big opening ceremony:

I was working at Blue Beach with a troop of Pioneers on a sunny afternoon, digging the graves . . . They were good lads, but were fooling around being stupid, doing things like falling into the graves and coming out pretending to be Dracula. So I got them all together while they were having a fag-break and told them the story of the girl. I read her two letters – how the pictures made her feel close to her fiancé and so on. The boys didn't say a word, no more was said and we carried on working.

The cemetery was due to be opened with great ceremony. Secretary of State for Defence John Nott was coming, General Thorne [the Falklands garrison commander] was fussing around, and my boss was making life a misery. I'd got Harriers and Chinooks flying past, bands, ships sailing round, a bloke playing 'Flowers of the Forest' – this was to be a big do!

Everything was carefully rehearsed and organized; the little white crosses with names on so everyone knew who was where – so all we had to do was lower the bodies into the right holes. Then 2 Para's cross was brought in, complete with the girl's boxwood wreath and plastic flowers – the 'Bennie' [as troops described the islanders] wreath! I popped it to one side.

It was late in the afternoon before the big show and I was getting very tense. A Chinook load of the most beautiful red and green wreaths arrived, so I started to lay them out to see how they'd look. There was one from Maggie Thatcher, and from all the politicians and top brass, after reading some of the incredible inscriptions from the wives I was in tears. I had piles of these wreaths, and seeing that the Bennie wreath was now all brown and worn out, I lobbed it into the bushes.

The next morning I returned, to find this bloody wreath was back on top of all the others. I was in my Brigade of Guards mode, tidying up furiously. I chucked the damn thing away again and started laying out the flowers. I went away for a coffee and when I got back it was there again. I was about to get rid of it for a third time when a big, black Pioneer corporal came over and told me that the rest of the troop had so liked the girl's letters that they thought it should remain and be given pride of place above all the others.

If you look at all the official pictures, you'll see it there – in front of all the other enormous, beautiful wreaths! I think if I'd tried to get rid of it, I'd have been shot . . .

Collecting the Argentine dead was harrowing too:

Under this low overhang, a dead Argie in a grey greatcoat was jammed horizontally into a deep crack in the rocks. He'd been shot in the back, or maybe he'd been bayoneted and then shot to release the blade. Two of the Argentine prisoners got ropes and pulled him out by the head and ankles.

There then appeared another chap underneath, who'd been shot. It seems that the first man, after his mate had been shot, had shoved him into the rock cleft. Then as the Scots Guards came through their positions, he'd lain over the top to protect him – and somebody had killed him, leaving the first man to die later.

At the time I thought how could you do this, you bastards – kill a defenceless bloke while he's protecting his mate? Then you realize that it's not like that at all, that by the time you get into an enemy's defensive position it's all blind rage; just keeping going, stab, thump, kick, thump . . . and it's a wonder how anybody survives. Guys were shot with their hands in the air, surrendering. The bodies made this quite clear, and it wasn't just the strange positions of cold and rigor mortis. They were standing in their trenches and had been shot as the troops assaulted over the top of them, probably having been shooting themselves until the last minute.

Evidence of men being shot while surrendering is never preserved and only rarely witnessed by people other than the assaulting troops themselves who usually drag the bodies away soon after for field burial, in effect removing the evidence. Although technically a war crime, such shootings take place in the heat of battle, in moments of intense fear and great aggression:

Soldiers are not able to be so cold and calculating as to switch off their aggression – like some kind of psychopath. They are told to do things, then just keep going, doing what they've been told. It's all such chaos that taking surrenders is too dangerous until the fighting is completely over. The rules of the Geneva Conventions don't work in the heat of battle.

Sydney Jary in 1944:

. . . our padre John Williams drove over to see us . . . I suspect that our Adjutant had asked him to find out what shape I was in.

We had not gone far into the next field when we came across some grisly remains. One of our artillery shells must have exploded at the feet of a German soldier who had been digging a slit trench. His twisted and splintered spade lay by the side of the half dug trench beside which was a shallow shell hole. He had been disintegrated into small pieces of flesh and bone which lay scattered all over the field. Had I been on my own, I would no doubt have shuddered and quickly departed from this horror.

Draped over a wire fence nearby lay a parachute which our extraordinarily brave padre spread out as a shroud on the cold and damp grass. Then stooping he walked round the field, a lonely figure, reverently picking up every piece of that poor soldier.

To my shame, I stood and watched him. I lacked the courage to help. Somewhere beneath those damp fields just north of the Rhine that pathetic bundle must still lie.[13]

In contrast to this extraordinary act, a lack of respect for enemy corpses is common to most battlefields. The unwritten convention is that each side looks after its own dead. In the Falklands, because Argentine officers appeared completely unconcerned with whatever might happen to the remains of their men, it fell to the British to deal with them. It is hardly surprising to discover that Argentine bodies were not held in the same regard as British bodies by British soldiers. David Cooper (after the Goose Green battle) nevertheless tried to give them all a decent burial:

The Argentine dead were being stacked up by the airfield. The islanders refused to let us bury them, threatening to dig the bodies up and throw them into the sea if we did. I was getting very frustrated trying to clean up the battlefield, and we had also to look after the islanders, defuse the Argentine ammunition and account for our own dead. I asked the Argentine commander to help me identify his dead as some didn't have ID discs. He refused to help, saying he knew who they all were. By this stage I wasn't bothered about arguing any more, and I know they didn't account for their dead. They're still there now.

Northfield:

We'd been stiff-clearing with Argentine prisoners, collecting bodies and throwing them into a tractor, bringing them back. I didn't know you had to go and do that – John Wayne and Clint Eastwood don't have to do it. Their bodies just dematerialize.

Sergeant French:

We'd cleared the bodies off the position quite early, because we didn't want any left booby-trapped. Argentine bodies were taken back and put into this big hole.

The blokes started off dragging them down there by their arms, but the dragging made their trousers come off. The blokes stopped doing it because they were concerned that subsequent pictures [of Argentine dead] might lead people to think that they'd been buggering them. Instead they pulled them by the ankles. Nobody gave any sort of order for this. It was done at the Toms' level.

Everyone was curious about the enemy dead, looking closely at their weapons, equipment, kit and boots. I saw what I thought was a tailor's dummy; for some reason I was convinced that's what it was, thinking that the crafty Argentinians had been playing tricks. I went over and touched it. My fingers sunk into real flesh, completely pale and unreal looking, dead for about three days.

Carter:

Some lads had a sick sense of humour and were lying down between the bodies having their photos taken, with twenty or so bodies.

Northfield:

People were putting them into different shapes, putting fags into their mouths and taking photographs – for a laugh. This is the regimental humour, a sense of humour born out of shared hardship. Civvies would lock us up for some of the things . . . Humour is the way out, to lessen the burden of what you've just done, or what you are about to do.

Some of the blokes had never seen stiffs before, and found it was rather a novelty. If you've had death in your family, or have seen bodies before, you'd not do it. You have to realize that the Parachute Regiment has a very warped, sick sense of humour, and that a unit like the Royal Anglians wouldn't do this sort of thing.

In fact exactly the same occurred at the end of the Gulf War in front-line units. Horseplay with enemy dead is a fairly common way of proving something, that the enemy is dead whereas you are still alive. Men play macabre jokes, and pose for photographs with corpses, dead arms round their shoulders. These things sound dreadful, but are more a reflection of the harshness of the situation the men have just survived than a manifestation of their brutality. French:

In the aftermath of victory, it's something you do to assert your authority as the victor. It's an immature thing, but afterwards things start to sink in, and you couldn't do it. You certainly wouldn't ever do that sort of thing a second time.

There was strong disapproval from the men themselves of this sort
of behaviour – and even superstition. Steven Hughes:

Some guys collected Argentinian ears, but most regarded this as going over
the top. Having collected trophies in the night, one person had been slightly
injured at Goose Green. The boys regarded this injury as a warning to him,
and started to avoid him because he didn't change his behaviour. He was
subsequently killed.

There was always the superstition, almost a religion among the soldiers,
that offending against some moral or higher code would bring retribution.
They thought that people who behaved outside what they regarded as the
norm became somehow marked, and that something would happen to them.
They perceived a definite dividing line between good and bad on the battlefield. I heard afterwards that one particular man had been less than fair to
one of the wounded Argentinians – in effect torturing him. The wounded
prisoner then died. The man was subsequently wounded and maimed for
life.

In the uncertainty of the Vietnam War, men became hardened to
the sight of Vietnamese bodies, regarding them with a complete
absence of emotion, like 'sacks of potatoes'. (US bodies were different.) When living, the Vietnamese were perceived as a sub-species
rather like vermin, but as the war gained momentum their actual
bodies and the numbers of Vietnamese (synonymous with 'enemy')
dead came also to assume a particular military significance. Judging
the progress and success of the counter-insurgency campaign in Vietnam became impossible for US commanders. The numbers of enemy
dead therefore became their only method of gauging their success.
The grim statistic of the so-called 'body count' was used in many
ways, to evaluate the efficiency of units and also as a comparator
against the numbers of Americans killed in operations. The ratio of
ten Vietcong to one American was considered acceptable – not only
by commanders, but also by individual soldiers coming to terms with
the deaths of friends. Killing ten VC gave the death of one friend a
kind of justification. The VC also realized the importance of the body
count to the Americans, and went to great lengths to upset the ratios
by removing their dead after engagements.

The VC fought until dark, then escaped carrying away wounded, dead and
even empty cartridge cases. Often after long battles, not one cartridge case
could be found – or dead men would be found, with large tin cans filled
with cartridge cases ready for withdrawing.

The enemy also knew that we placed great emphasis on the body count.
Our men, being typically American, expected to see at least 10 enemy
bodies for every one of their buddies killed. The enemy felt he had won a

psychological battle if he could remove his casualties, leaving a sterile battle-field for our men to find, especially if he had inflicted some casualties on us.[14]

It has been said that there was little attempt by the Americans to link the numbers of VC weapons discovered with the body count because, from the disparity, it would be unacceptably obvious that many innocent civilians were being killed. There was also little incentive for officers to do anything about this statistical discrepancy. As Vietnam combat reports were so vital for officers' promotion, the body count was important to each one's career.

The 'truck count' was the air equivalent of the 'body count', and was related to the funds that the air force could expect to receive for future munitions purchase. 'Kills' were still considered important by pilots:

We plastered the place [a North Vietnamese military camp]; napalm, 500 pounders, the works. I know we had kills, you could see the people running all over the place, buildings burning. But do you know what happened? The grunts came in and reported 25 enemy killed by ground fire. All they did was shoot their M-16s into the corpses and then claim they'd killed them. The nerve. Can you imagine . . . the fuckin' grunts are stealing our kills.[15]

Body count played an important part in the My Lai massacre. Task Force commander Colonel Barker was described as 'an unusually aggressive and ambitious officer whose units were known for their high body counts and their capacity to gun down a lot of people'.[16] Both Barker and the Brigade Commander Henderson were said to be passing on down the line the hunger of their superiors for high body counts – bodies that the GI had, one way or another, to provide.

The process of determining body counts was far from being a straightforward counting of corpses, however. The figures were frequently fudged. For example, Charlie Company's tally for My Lai was given as 128. At Calley's court martial he estimated killing 'between thirty or forty . . . off the top of my head'. Company commander Medina thought fifty, and radioed in a figure of 310, which someone else pared down to 128. Only three weapons were found, so somebody else modified the figures to read '128 Vietcong and 24 civilians' – presumably so that readers could infer that civilians had carried off the 'missing' 125 weapons. The official report talked of 'contact with an enemy force' and quoted the commander as saying that 'the combat assault went like clockwork'. Charlie Company were duly credited with 14 kills, the remaining 114 from artillery fire.

In the actual counting of bodies, babies and very old people (who couldn't walk and who therefore couldn't be vc) were simply ignored. Those who could walk (before being killed) were included. The severed pieces of one corpse could be counted as several bodies, and a whole corpse might be claimed several times, by the man or unit that killed it, the patrol that found it, the HQ to whom it was reported and so on – according to the needs and ambitions of the various commanders. And once slain, a corpse was incapable of protesting its innocence: every corpse became vc. A member of Charlie Company, who took part in the My Lai massacre:

'If it's dead it's vc. Because it's dead. If it's dead it *had* to be vc.'
[The soldier boasting of a high body count] was sort of saying how much ... I hate the gooks – in terms that you can actually understand. I hate them a whole lot. I hate them even more than a whole lot ... so ... wow!, I killed 121 of them. That means I hate them more than anybody does ... And of course the only way you could determine who hated them the most was how many times you beat them or killed them or raped them or something like that.[17]

In the early seventies, as US participation in the Vietnam War wound down, the numerical decrease in American dead replaced the vc body count as the significant statistic. In the latter years, nobody was interested in knowing how many Vietnamese were killed.

Almost twenty years later during the Gulf War, body count was again a statistic of critical importance. In the build-up to hostilities, figures of 10,000 American dead were bandied about by both Iraqi propagandists and western opponents of the war. The actual numbers of Iraqi dead have never been released – because an accurate figure would be impossible to calculate, but also because in the magnitude of the Allied victory, any well-informed estimate is so large as to be obscene, especially if the ratio of enemy dead to friendly dead were to be estimated.

As Vietnam made clear, the numbers of dead bodies that a war produces is a very potent and politically loaded issue for western nations – a relatively new phenomenon. In the Gulf War, Allied military commanders were put under great pressure to fight without losing too many friendly lives (a politically determined number). This pressure dictated the tactics that were used and seriously limited the military options, but in the event the strategy proved unexpectedly successful in saving Allied lives. Instead, the Iraqi Army paid the price – in numbers that led to the ground offensive being halted prematurely, before Saddam's military power had been broken.

World media, keen to photograph war dead, undoubtedly shape international opinion during wars. (The photograph of one charred Iraqi soldier on the Basra road may in itself have prevented the destruction of the Republican Guard.) Broadcasting war into people's living-rooms every morning and evening turns real events into compulsive entertainment that can dominate people's lives at home.

Despite the unreality of odour-free TV screen corpses, the reaction of the folks at home can seriously affect the political resolve of nations to prosecute wars. The media are neither anti-war nor pro-military; they fluctuate between the two extremes. TV corpses provide the powerful antidote to the usually jingoistic coverage of what 'Our Boys' (the troops) are doing – but little of what appears on the screen bears much relationship to the reality of what is actually happening on the battlefield.

There was no official policy on whether war dead were to be repatriated or remain in the Falklands. Families were given the choice. Many of 2 Para's dead were brought home rather than being buried in the War Graves Commission cemetery at San Carlos. While the rest of the battalion went off on leave, as the senior chaplain in 5 Airborne Brigade, David Cooper was responsible for organizing the funerals:

[At the end of leave] I suddenly found myself with something like 30 bodies to be buried within a two-week period. I went on the road in a hired coach, with a firing party and bearer party. We drove round the country doing funerals, two and three each day. Some families lived in the Aldershot area, some elected for burial in the Airborne plot in the military cemetery at Aldershot, whereas others lived in different parts of the country.

So when the bodies arrived by ship, from Marchwood [in Hampshire] they were delivered around the country by undertakers. Those that came to Aldershot were brought to the gymnasium at 2 Para. The families agreed to have one large service at the garrison church, with separate private interments in the cemetery. The next-of-kin were guests of the battalion; we gave them a meal and looked after them, and they could spend as much time in the gym as they wanted.

After the big service, we moved down to the cemetery where the coffins were waiting, and buried them individually and consecutively. It was the only service I've ever been to with Roman Catholic, Jewish and Anglican clergymen all taking part together.

The other burials took us from Norwich to as far as Belfast and Glasgow,

covering enormous distances. We arranged the timings so we could actually
fit it all in. We went through the whole gamut of emotions from anxiety at
getting it right, to joking and sheer exhaustion. Then finally we were ground
down to the real sadness that the anxiety and joking had been masking.

Cooper felt strongly that the whole matter of these burials had
not been properly considered. From the start, when Prime Minister
Margaret Thatcher offered repatriation of bodies, neither the
churches, the MOD, the military units nor the soldiers had been consulted. Although many felt their comrades should be brought home,
others found comfort in knowing that their mates were at rest near
where they had fallen, amid the beauty of the Islands for which they
died. The usual British Army practice is for men killed abroad to be
buried abroad, their graves tended with much care by the Commonwealth War Graves Commission. A soldier might be forgotten in
some unkempt British municipal cemetery, never by the War Graves
Commission.

The funerals back in the UK were also a source of ecclesiastical
concern to David Cooper:

We had already buried these lads with a funeral service on the Falklands,
and yet I was asked to do another funeral service rather than a re-interment.
The re-interment would have been exactly the same for the parents, but
would not have been quite as wearing for the lads in the burial party – or
for me.

Sergeant McCulloch:

I was a member of the battalion firing party, going round all the funerals,
Belfast, Lowestoft . . . Because of having to get on to the next funeral, we
never had time to stop and talk to the families.

Some of the families were resentful, and one particular elder brother
started giving us aggro, blaming us for the death of his brother. He could
really have come seriously unstuck because the lads weren't in the mood
for an emotional civvy giving them all this crap. He just didn't know what
we'd all been through.

It was like a conveyor belt, and I wished we'd been able to spend more
time with the families, to say how sorry we were . . .

Private Northfield:

We had a lot of funerals, and I was in the bearer party for one. We dropped
the coffin twice in the rehearsals – he wasn't in it though. On the day, we
had to put lots of Brut aftershave on, because they really stank . . . One of
the relatives tried to get into the grave with him . . . we just wanted to get
out of it, go on the piss . . .

Graham Carter:

I went to Fred Slough's funeral at his home, which was very sad. I'd got to know him quite well. We'd had sorrowful times, and had exchanged a lot of views – he was the best I'd got to know anybody, really. I'd met another close friend in Stanley afterwards, from 3 Para, so we got pretty drunk and had what was really a grieving session together.

Once the last of the sad marathon of 2 Para funerals was well and truly done, David Cooper still had one last rite to organize:

. . . a memorial service at Aldershot with the Prince of Wales. I wrote the service, and knew that it would be emotionally absolutely correct, which the regimental colonel then tried to change. It was very obvious that he didn't have any idea of the effect his changes would have had . . .

The war had been over for several months, and yet Cooper had been unable to take leave. He was still carrying the burden of the dead for his battalion, a weight that nobody seemed willing (or able) to lift from his shoulders:

By this time I was exhausted and so asked not to go with the battalion on a six-month tour of Belize. The Chaplains' Department however didn't listen. Then when I was out in Belize [after various wrangles over whose chaplain he actually was] . . . I went into the jungle [on combat training], which I think was too much for me. I ended up being casevaced with pneumonia.

Realizing that the Royal Army Chaplains' Department were not interested in helping with his ministry, rather in using him for their own purposes, he decided to leave. He was offered a job as chaplain at Eton College, which with many regrets, he accepted, leaving the army in 1983.

After the Falklands, David Cooper was a distinct oddity in the British Army – a chaplain who had fought in two consecutive conventional battles, a paratrooper, and a small arms expert. By comparison, his fellow military chaplains were ordinary peacetime vicars, used to preaching to the wives and families of officers and ambitious NCOs in half-deserted garrison churches, and occasionally holding 'Padre's Hours' with restless, indifferent troops.

Cooper's ministry could hardly have been further from the insular cosiness of normal army life. But by the time he resigned, he was burned out, wearied by the lack of support from fellow padres, although still deeply committed to soldiers and soldiering, and to the army. 'I never in fact left the army, just the Chaplains' Department.'

13

ANOTHER KIND OF WAR

There is a terrible disparity between the idealized view of war (and heroism) expressed back home, and the reality of degradation and unspeakable suffering war veterans have witnessed, experienced and caused. Audie Murphy, the much decorated American Second World War hero, was quoted in his obituary as having said that no one gets over their war experiences. He kept a loaded German automatic pistol under his pillow until the day he died. Many war heroes have lived unsatisfied lives and suffered early deaths.

Major Bob Leitch observed Falklands combatants immediately the war ended, and then in subsequent years:

Everyone is affected to some extent by what happens to them in wars; and those who claim otherwise are either kidding themselves, or suffering from some unnatural and possibly psychopathic lack of human emotion.

War deeply affects individuals for decades afterwards. Julian Thompson:

When you talk to Second World War veterans from the Parachute Regiment, you can see that their whole war experience is with them all the time – that they can never forget it.

The nature of each person's war experience can affect their character afterwards. Thompson detects a distinct difference in attitude, for example, between members of the British 1st Airborne Division who fought at Arnhem, and 6th Airborne Division who were so effective in Operation Overlord and the crossing of the Rhine. Both divisions suffered heavy casualties, but 6th Airborne were successful, whereas the Arnhem operation went seriously wrong and turned into a heroic disaster.

Former members of 1st Airborne have an air of doom and gloom about them – a mixture of cynicism, anger, bitterness and pride. The feeling at the two Divisions' respective annual memorial services is also completely and identifiably different, even though each man would have different memories.

Specific incidents in combat can often be identified as the root cause of long-term psychological and personality problems in individuals. Bill Matthews, a Petty Officer in the Royal Navy during the Second World War, appeared to have been unaffected by what happened to him in action at sea – until a quiet period in dry dock towards the end of the war. He'd survived four years on the Murmansk convoys, including being sunk, then minesweeping on the St Nazaire and Dieppe raids, and the Normandy landings.

We were stuck in dry dock in Antwerp over the Christmas of 1944. The Germans were flying 'doodle bugs' at us. Whenever there was an air raid, the dockyard maties would rush off into the concrete bunkers – leaving us to our steel coffin in the dry dock.

There was absolutely no point to us being there – no work was being done on the ship. We were surrounded by petrol tanks, coke yards and coal depots. There were massive fires and explosions. It would rain black dust from the pulverized coke after an air raid, and we'd be absolutely filthy. One night 1100 marines were killed when a V2 hit the cinema. We rushed over to find everything gone – only smoking rubble. I even volunteered to join the army, at the time of the Battle of the Bulge! It seemed like a sadistic joke, that after missing death thousands of times I was going to die in Antwerp.

My nerves started to go wrong. I was sent on leave, praying that the bombing would be over by the time I got back. It was the first time I'd not wanted to return from leave. I'd gone beyond fear to resignation. I even took out life insurance on behalf of my mother, I was so sure that I wouldn't see her again.

Until we went into dry dock, we'd all been too caught up in the action, with no time to think. In Antwerp we had nothing to do – and so had time to think. It seemed very unfair to be left there – like lambs to the slaughter. We all felt like that.

At the end of the war I felt very unwell. My personality had changed from being a happy-go-lucky person to someone who was frightened by everything. I hoped that with time, I'd go back to normal. At the end of the war, the forces and the whole of the country were whacked out. Being unwell was quite common. A mate who stayed on the minesweeper, wrote and told me that when they had their medicals at the end of the war, 34 out of 80 in the ship's company had TB.

A career sailor, Matthews remained in the Royal Navy when hostilities ceased.

I joined carrier *Formidable*, and then spent several years in Gibraltar as a Petty Officer in charge of a group of stores – clothing, equipment etc. For the first six months of this job I was very worried and anxious until I got the stores into what I considered to be a state of perfection. My staff were a bunch of crooks – young fellows intent on stealing what they could. Clothing was a very attractive item and I was holding lots of cash. When I felt really panicky, I saw the Sick Bay CPO who fixed me up [with medication]. Having got through the bitter years of the war, I wanted to survive the easy years and get my naval pension. However at Pompey [Portsmouth], during my re-engagement medical, I was advised by the surgeon commander to get out [of the navy].

Matthews took this advice and left, in October 1949.

I wished I'd stayed in the navy; leaving it made me damn near heartbroken. I was too rocky at the time to see it, but the peacetime navy was so over-manned that they wanted to get rid of us. I married a landlord's daughter and was expected to help out in the pub after work. I ended up doing two jobs for very little money – and more stress. Having left the navy, the anxiety got worse, not better.

Matthew's medical problems have remained with him ever since:

The navy had taken out my appendix but really I'd got this irritable colon [a stress-induced condition]. I've got no control over it at all. It's really quite frightening. The worst thing you can ever do is lose control over your bowels in public. It's a vicious circle, triggered by stress and anxiety. One triggers off the other. I'm very doubtful about travelling because of it, although trains aren't too bad because they've got loos.

Anyone who serves in a war becomes vastly changed as a person. They'll never be the same as they were before. It makes or breaks people. After six years, it gradually builds up and seeps into your system so that you don't know any other sort of life.

Spending years in prisoner of war camps has an even more insidious and long-lasting effect on individuals. The recent release of Beirut hostages has focused general attention on the psychological effects of incarceration, in a way that simply never happened after the Second World War. In 1945, hundreds of thousands of released prisoners of war came home, without medals or combat experience to give them any sense of self-esteem. Apart from the physical toll, they had lost both liberty and dignity, as well as having been sub-jected to systematic degradation by their captors.

Harsh treatment was worse in Italian than German camps, and very much worse in the Japanese camps, whose racist sub-agenda was to lower for ever the status of the 'whiteman' in Asia. Some prisoners were made to wear arm bands inscribed: 'One who has been beaten in battle and who can be beheaded or castrated at the will of the Emperor'. Ten and twenty years later, the Koreans and Vietnamese were equally brutal for similar reasons. They did not recognize prisoner of war status, but regarded each captured United Nations or American soldier as a 'war criminal' to be degraded and tortured. The hatred and emotion created in the prisoner of war camps, particularly of former prisoners of the Japanese, lives on today. Men formed pacts to out-live the Emperor (he died in 1989); still spit immediately after coughing (a habit from the camps, so as not to swallow hook-worm coughed up from the lungs); and above all, cannot forgive.

It is impossible for anyone who did not experience the Japanese camps to comment on the survivors' attitudes to their former captors. For many, the mere sight of a Japanese car brings a flood of unwanted memories. To expect them to forgive is insultingly unreasonable, yet forgiving, as the only way of ending their self-destructive hatred, would relieve them of great personal stress. Forty years of hating takes its toll: ill-health, nightmares and all manner of psychological problems remain. Many Second World War veterans don't see why they should forgive and forget Japanese atrocities, particularly as they feel that the Japanese have never shown the slightest remorse. A former officer imprisoned by the Japanese in Burma:

We prayed every day for the prisoner's miracle – to survive. We were asking for the impossible, yet we succeeded – in the face of Japanese orders that we were to be massacred. The order was dated August 1944 and we'd already been made to dig the trenches. The atom bombs saved us because they left no time for the guards to carry out their orders. Millions of lives were saved by the atom bombs – so don't you ever call it luck that we survived. It was the miracle for which we'd prayed for years.

After the Japs had left our camp, the Australian padre gave a Service of Thanksgiving, wearing the dirty surplice he'd hidden for so long. He harangued everybody: 'Why did *you* survive when others died? Don't waste the new life that you've been given. Be humbled and get it right.'

Forgiving the Japanese would be disloyal to all our friends who died, so we said little and re-built our lives, refusing to be drawn on what it was like. We all acquired various survival techniques – tricks that we'd used to cheat the Japanese authorities, that we had to learn not to use on our return, like getting through the gate at a railway station without a ticket; you smile at the ticket collector on the right while showing the one on the left an empty hand . . .

Now today, some of us have decided to speak out, to influence the new generation who haven't suffered . . .

The Far East Prisoners of War (FEPOWs) have distinctive problems that are only now beginning to be recognized. The determination that led them to survive the camps, and the desire to make the most of a 'life after death' enabled many to build successful careers and raise families. The price of that 'will to survive' was high in terms of mental and physical health. Half a century on, most have retired, their families left home, and possibly wives have died. For the first time they find themselves alone, without work to distract them from their emotions. Many FEPOWs are only now coming to terms with their deeply rooted long-term psychological problems – admitting the unhappiness that has underlain all the effort and determination of their lives after the camps. Theirs is now a very different kind of war.

The majority of returned prisoners keep quiet about their experiences:

Most of us were loth to report any ill-treatment we had received, and we all made light of our medical ailments. We were riding on the crest of a wave and did not want to be delayed any longer than necessary. We wanted to be home.[1]

Returning PoWs were given double rations for only six weeks (two eggs rather than one), after which they took their chances along with everyone else in rationing that lasted nearly six years. The effect of incarceration remains with many: 'There were many bad dreams, and for a long time I was always looking over my shoulder for the guard.' The long-term medical effects were never accurately determined at the time. Returning PoWs vanished into the woodwork as quickly as they could. Apart from serious physical conditions caused by malnutrition and general ill-treatment (such as burning and tingling limbs from beri-beri, and various forms of arthritis from beatings and overwork), the psychiatric effects were marked.

A survey of American World War Two prisoners of war revealed that over forty years later 82% of the former FEPOWs were psychiatrically impaired, and that 60% had anxiety disorders, 18% depressive disorders and 28% PTSD. Of former Korean PoWs, 73% had psychiatric impairment, 60% anxiety disorders and 47% PTSD. Of the European theatre PoWs, 60% had significant psychiatric symptoms, 33% anxiety disorders (11% with PTSD), premature dementia and depression (17%). Of all American PoWs (totalling 142,227 from the two World Wars, Korea and Vietnam), 83,430 were still alive on 1 January 1986, of whom more than 90% were from World War Two.[2]

*

For professional soldiers coming home from war, returning to the peacetime military routine and a peacetime hierarchy that did not experience the fighting can be almost as difficult as enduring the war.

At the end of the Falklands War, 3 Commando Brigade commander Julian Thompson was surprised at the lack of interest in what he and the other in-theatre commanders had been doing:

I do feel that once the war was over, the hierarchy were not interested in what had happened – or in any lessons that might be learned from it all. Neither Mike Clapp [COMMAW] nor I received any sort of debriefing from Northwood or from Admiral Fieldhouse. This lack of honest debrief makes me feel they weren't interested.

The navy's apparent lack of interest extended to the actual combat performance of individuals. They decided that it was unfair to those who did not fight to allow Falklands war service to influence promotions. Julian Thompson could not understand this attitude:

Although we [who fought in the Falklands] were each the equivalent of those who didn't go, the big difference is that we've all been tested by war – and can actually cut the mustard when required.

A feeling of 'them and us' still remains strong today:

After the Falklands, we came back to a country that didn't have a clue, and we don't want to talk to them about it because they don't understand. The career people in the armed forces who didn't come south have a sort of jealousy of those who did.

Steve Hughes:

I had trouble with brigadiers and the like who had never been near a battlefield. They thought because I was junior I should agree with them – whereas what they were saying I knew to be wrong. It's like someone in England writing a travel brochure about Australia then refusing to listen when someone else returns from there and says, 'Rubbish, it's not like that.'

David Cooper:

For the six months after returning, Aldershot was the most peaceful it had ever been. There were few fights and little drunkenness, as the paratroopers felt they no longer had anything to prove. Some problems did occur however with new soldiers trying to prove they were as tough as the others.

Within the platoons, the soldiers knew who had been effective and who had not. Whilst there was nothing like recrimination, they were keenly aware of who had hung back – but nothing was ever said. Of course, through knowing what combat is like, everybody understood how these things happen, and nothing would be said.

Some soldiers felt very restless and left the army on returning to UK. Then after a year or so, finding civilian life boring, they returned. The usual turnover of Parachute Regiment personnel reduced the combat experience of 2 and 3 Para to something more normal after about a year.

We were very conscious in returning home and in the months that followed, of the team we had created dispersing, never to be together again. Soldiers recover better from a war if they can stay with the people they fought it with. New officers found it very daunting taking over battle-hardened platoons and companies, and one new commanding officer who had not been in the war caused serious upset in his battalion (3 Para) by telling them to 'forget the Falklands,' as if it had been an insignificant operation.

Major Godfrey McFall took over as second in command of Support Company, 3 Para in February 1983. Despite ten years' experience in the Parachute Regiment and four Northern Ireland tours, he was apprehensive about commanding battle-hardened troops.

I found the company very professional – and somehow awesome . . . They'd crossed a threshold that I hadn't. They had a composure about what they were doing, with an enthusiasm and respect for training. They were very keen to do things by the book and spoke of the war as having been just like courses at Brecon. They'd learned tricks of the trade like making base plate anchors for the mortars to stop them sinking into the mud on soft ground. The mortar fire controllers could hit targets four thousand metres away with just one round. They also knew how to break the rules with common sense and safety . . . The rifle companies were equally professional, and knew far more about the reality of warfare – for example that a section attack, supposed to take only fifteen minutes or so, can easily take all day. They had evolved all sorts of sensible drills too, which were kept going afterwards . . . They had also learned of the boredom of war – that it lasts a long time and nothing may happen for most of that time.

Their attitude towards officers had changed:

Before the Falklands, they hadn't realized what officers actually do in war – providing a level of intellect vital to the success of operations. Having seen it for themselves, they had a much greater respect for officers than when I'd served with them before.

They were also very clear that they expected their officers to be 'straight', having found that honest, uncomplicated leaders would continue to be 'straight' on the battlefield.

During this period, I learned respect for them – that they weren't just followers to be ordered about. I mellowed greatly in this family of men who had killed a lot of people and been mortared for three days themselves. I remember them all particularly well – there were very close relations between all of us, whether we'd been in the Falklands or not.

Some officers, and soldiers and NCOs, had failed the test of battle.

I noticed that as far as the soldiers were concerned, those who hadn't performed as it was felt they should have performed, were unobtrusively ostracized.

Getting back to normal peacetime soldiering was not easy:

All of them had problems readjusting to being back after the war. They'd each learned more about themselves as individuals. Their values and approach to life had changed. The families and their friends knew this, too, seeing a different person in each of them, having to make adjustments themselves in order to cope.

They were more introverted than before and had acquired an uncharacteristic humility. Some no longer wished to soldier (about 10 to 20 per cent), feeling they'd done their bit. Some feared that their own wells of courage had dried up, or felt fulfilled by having been in combat and fought in a war – preferring to move on to try something else. We saw a few PTSD-type episodes – with men getting drunk and so on, but I didn't have much to do with that. Most of those who didn't do well in the war had the honesty to realize it and leave. Several people I knew very well, did not change at all. They'd done well in the war and continued on as before. I also know a few who became bitter and twisted afterwards.

Carter:

Afterwards, we lost a lot of blokes to Civvy Street, and exercises were a real pain after the real thing. I went on to Patrol Company [who recce ahead of the battalion], something new. I'm not sure if I've been helped or hindered by what happened down there. On the ship on the way home, our platoon commander advised me to go elsewhere as he said I wasn't Parachute Regiment material [Carter was in fact awarded the Military Medal]. I enjoyed PT so now I'm in the PT Corps, but they don't seem to be able to give me the jobs I actually want to do – making me do the jobs they want. I'm pretty frustrated really.

Taylor:

It was very difficult, getting back to digging in on Salisbury Plain and firing blanks. Morale was on a high immediately after, then went to a complete low. Looking back, we were being kept busy so we didn't dwell on our thoughts.

Northfield:

Afterwards, Aldershot was our town, beer was half price, and everyone surprisingly well-behaved. A lot of guys got out because it wasn't the same. The discipline seemed petty and stupid, but I stuck it. Some people developed drink problems – but the regiment has always had a tradition of hard drinking anyway – but it tends to be social. Maybe the camaraderie of social drinking helped people unwind.

French:

Getting back to normal military life was a real problem. We'd lost most of our kit – or at least you could say to the storeman you'd lost it all on Mount Longdon.

Then when blokes went off on courses to Brecon, learning about what they'd just done for real, they had a hard time – either from others, or because they brought it on themselves.

There were loads of parties, which I wonder at now as it seemed to glamorize what we'd done. In some ways it would be better to be the loser of a war, as you'd at least understand the reality of what you'd done. If I ever have to remember it – to tell stories to civilians – I always tell them of our landing craft getting stuck on a sandbank, so instead of storming the beach we had to wait for over an hour then transfer to smaller craft. I tell them about nicking the Land Rover in Port Stanley, and watching the Wireless Ridge battle from our grandstand on Mount Longdon – the happy times . . .

McCulloch:

After leave, on dry exercises, we settled back into the mould very quickly. Not being an emotional regiment, we just got back to it again. The grieving was done in the Falklands; you thought about them for five minutes, then that was it. We live with death all the time. Think of all the people we've lost in Northern Ireland . . . we're used to it.

The Gulf War affected many Falklands (and Vietnam) veterans, particularly from the Parachute Regiment, who when I was interviewing them in January 1991 seemed unlikely to be going:

Some of these units in the Gulf are going to be crying their little eyes out, because all of a sudden they're going to be asked to stand up and be counted. They've heard all the war stories, and about all the heroes, then suddenly they're going to be asked to become these people. And they're in for a big shock. Instead of just saying as we did, 'Let's get it finished.' A lot of them will have that attitude, but equally a lot won't – which is a shame. Our training teaches you to take the knocks, then get up and carry on, which makes us the effective force we are at present.

The importance and significance of their memories of combat soon became apparent to each – even as early as the voyage home. Chaplain David Cooper's instinctive exhortation to 'remember how you feel now' was clearly important, lest the values and emotions of the battlefield be forgotten. 'Mac' French:

Everyone stole things in Stanley – as mementoes or souvenirs. Strangely, on the way back home, we were all throwing these mementoes into the sea because they didn't compare with our actual memories. It all lives on in our minds rather than in something we'd taken . . . things we'll never forget. I don't talk about it like this, even though I'm not ashamed of what I did . . .

Returning to normal life is partly a transition to an ordered existence, but also a coming to terms with what has happened. Combat was like the Wild West, completely lawless at every level. Within very broad limits, everybody had been licensed to kill, able to get away with virtually anything:

However, you do get a conscience afterwards, which you have to come to terms with. What you've done is not necessarily wrong if you've acted for the cause. The cause can carry the responsibility. But if you've acted for your own personal satisfaction, then you may have done something wrong. You'll pick up the tab mentally.

. . . This person always comes back to me, haunting me, so perhaps I'm on the verge of picking up the tab myself? I shot him twice in the head, and although I didn't stop to check he was dead, I knew he was. I ask myself now, did I have to do that? Could I not maybe have taken him, and handed him back [down the prisoner of war chain]? If I had ignored him, would he have shot the OC? We knew they'd waved the white flag at Goose Green then killed people. It was a stupid thing they did . . . we weren't going to take any chances. In some ways he was a victim of one of his own side's mistakes.

At the time I was quite happy with what I did. But it's funny how as the years go on, when I have a quiet moment, I always think of him . . . I've said a lot of prayers to his family – I mean that. I'm not proud of what happened, but I'd do it again if I had to, for a just cause. But if I had a chance to take him prisoner I would. We're not here to destroy each other, it's wrong.

But you can't explain this to people, they don't understand, and I wouldn't want anyone to take it lightheartedly. It's not a lighthearted subject. They laugh and ask what it's like to waste spics. You can't blame them though, because they've never experienced it.

The saddest moment for me was afterwards, crying, thinking of the boys who weren't going home – Ginge McCarthy, Stevie Hope . . . It started the day after the surrender, with thinking of Ginge as he had been the night before, looking down on Stanley from Mount Longdon . . . and thinking that tonight, he ain't with us any more, that he won't be seeing any more lights ever again.

Cooper:

People did feel guilt at surviving, while nobody talked openly about it. Soldiers covered up for it at work, and some behaved strangely at home. For example a wife told me of her husband who every evening would walk down to the end of the garden and stare up at the sky for an hour, then come back in. He would never tell her what he'd been thinking about.

Survivor guilt is probably more common in armoured units when a tank goes up and just a few men of the team survive. There was however a lot of it after the Falklands, and I was very aware of it in myself – that because I was alive, it meant I'd not done enough. There've been many deaths of veterans that could have been accidental or suicide. It wouldn't surprise me if it turned out that Falklands veterans had a higher rate of suicide than others.

(In the Vietnam War 53,386 US soldiers were killed. 110,000 Vietnam veterans to date are thought to have committed suicide.)

At times I have a feeling that the dead are the only ones who have really given everything. When you are in a world that doesn't recognize you, from which you find yourself alienated and frustrated, I can very easily see that feeling turning into the belief that it would be more comfortable to join your friends who are dead.

Taylor:

The funerals made you think a bit. I went to six. You'd hear that they'd been shot, but it didn't sink in until they were in the six-foot grave. It made me feel very lucky. They were hit once and died, and I was hit 13 times.

People have long memories and call me a 'half term merchant', but because I was wounded, I can joke about it. Anyway, I doubt if someone who skived off with trench foot would feel guilty. Getting trench foot is your own fault.

I knew two corporals who were killed. They'd been really good at their jobs, my heroes. They'd trained me ever since I joined the battalion. I was astonished, amazed to hear they'd been killed – as I watched TV to see them buried at Ajax Bay. I wonder now why they were killed and not two wasters who couldn't do their jobs . . . ?

Cooper:

The wives helped each other a lot at this time, and there was little counselling – probably the soldiers would have been angry thinking that they were being portrayed as mentally disturbed. Few men talked to their wives, although snippets of information were exchanged at Wives' Clubs and so on. The soldiers were supported in an unorganized sort of way, by the wives and by our families officer.

The wives particularly commented afterwards that there were levels of their husbands' personalities that had been exposed to their friends that even they were unaware of, that only emerged in the imminence of death. Marriages polarized, they either got better or worse. They wanted to know more than their husbands would tell them.

Keeping emotions bottled up is the start of most post-trauma problems. The cupboard analogy is frequently used by veterans:

You put your experiences into a sort of mental cupboard, and when the cupboard is full you can have problems. The cupboard can burst open at any stage, perhaps under some extra pressure. If people gloss over their experiences without coming to terms with them, they create problems in the future. And some people never recover.

The transition from a combat environment to normal life is a problem in itself:

Many peacetime soldiers find the complexity of civilian life difficult to cope with. War heightens all the common purposes and attitudes of military life into an exceptionally simple reality, in which individuals surrender themselves to the higher calling of the common cause – to something far more important than themselves.

There is something in men (perhaps not in women) that makes them need to give themselves in this way, perhaps part of some primitive pack instinct. The military life, especially in war, gives a satisfaction to men that civilian life cannot provide. Some ex-servicemen find they can't settle in jobs; they complain of civilians' lack of commitment, of there being nothing to serve and of being taken advantage of. They often end up going into business for themselves.

To bring in the religious side, the disciples immediately after the Resurrection appear to me to have suffered from something very like Post Traumatic Stress Disorder. They'd dedicated their lives to an ideal and a charismatic leader, who had come to a violent and bloody end. They were in the same state as soldiers who had come to the end of a battle, but had lost it. Men need some sort of group commitment to an ideal, which is perfectly satisfied by army life in war.

On returning to normal life you become frustrated with people who seem devious, and get short-tempered because nobody understands what life is really all about. It's like having seen the Holy Grail; you can't rest until you can get back to it. I can fully understand how men become mercenaries, when their own army isn't providing them with a war. There is satisfaction in the subordination and commitment to an ideal that occurs in war.

The self-sacrifice, commitment and drawing together of men in war brings out the best in people . . . the blossoms that grow on the dunghill of war. Being inspirational, this seems to be essentially good, but generated by a desperately evil environment, which creates a very strange paradox. It is a tragedy of human life that men will give so much for war and so little for peace.

The scars of war are the complex and (mostly) normal reactions of normal people to very abnormal events. The emotions raised by war and combat are so strong that only veterans understand them, hence the importance of keeping combat units together after wars. These emotions must be worked through by individuals in their own time, but when a veteran finds himself on his own, away from the people with whom he experienced combat, or when the unexpiated strength of his own emotions overwhelms him, a whole spectrum of physical and psychological problems emerges. However, before discussing these problems, a number of points must be made:

More than 20 per cent of the population in general require some kind of psychiatric help during their lives. Moreover, everyone suffers from perfectly normal stress at work and in the home. The effect of that stress on each individual depends on many factors: family history, personality, social problems – and the nature of the stress. Members of the armed forces have similar problems to civilians, plus a number of unique stress-inducing factors created by their environment. Military selection, training and comradeship to an extent improve their statistical chances of avoiding mental problems, but do not give any sort of immunity, especially when the stresses to which they are subjected in war are so great.

Servicemen are just as likely to develop psychiatric problems as the one person in five of the normal population. Their problems might be inherent (organic); a young soldier's family background may predispose him to mental illness. He might be a loner, finding it difficult to mix with others, feeling threatened by socializing, and live as the result in his own internal fantasy world. Military recruitment tries to weed out such individuals, although 'schizoid personalities' may live normal lives with no problems. But if this kind of person is thrust into a war environment, with all its extreme stress factors, he stands a good chance of developing full-blown schizophrenia. It may not happen immediately, as an acute psychotic reaction, but he will have a higher chance of developing a functional psychiatric illness than anybody else. A soldier with no predisposing factors, when exposed to the stress of battle might experience fear, sadness and bereavement with guilt and nightmares afterwards. Later, he might develop PTSD as a normal reaction to the trauma of combat – as opposed to an actual psychiatric illness.

'Battle shock' and 'shell shock' are non-medical terms used to describe what may happen to individuals actually on the battlefield. They are serious psychiatric conditions that almost certainly will affect casualties after the war – possibly for the rest of their lives. Attempts to predict who may succumb to battle shock have been shown to be futile, although its onset can be delayed by good leadership, comradeship and training, a strong sense of purpose and other positive factors. Studies of past wars show, however, that in time the psychological shock of battle will render every soldier incapable of fighting. Post Traumatic Stress Disorder, on the other hand, occurs after a traumatic event (and its symptoms must last at least one month). PTSD is a normal person's response to an abnormal, life-threatening event well beyond the normal range of human experience.

The process of going to war has already been discussed. Individuals take with them a burden of worries and fears that become critical to their ability to withstand the stress of battle. Life is in any case very unsettled for both servicemen and their families, so levels of stress can be very high anyway. Families are placed under even greater strain as men prepare to go on real operations. Quarrels may develop and, with other problems that may not be resolved before the man departs, increase the chances of individuals developing psychological problems before, during or after combat.

The range of war-induced psychological conditions includes most of the usual mental illnesses. Psychotic conditions lie at the more serious end of the spectrum: schizophrenia, manic depression or psychotic depression. Anxiety neurosis, depression and the minor psychological problems suffered by people in the course of everyday life are at the other end of this spectrum, with PTSD in the middle. Mental illness apart, war also induces serious yet very normal psychological reactions. Bereavement particularly is a complicated and also very important emotional process for humans, which soldiers rarely have the time to work through. In war friends are killed without warning, and in shocking and deeply upsetting ways. The danger and impetus of the battle makes the process of normal grieving impossible. Survivors may feel anger, but, in the tiredness, fear, danger and speed of combat, have no time to reflect on and come to terms with these deaths.

Combat veterans therefore rarely suffer only from PTSD. They question the purpose of all the suffering and destruction they have witnessed – becoming depressed. They may try to deal with their symptoms by drinking and taking drugs – becoming alcoholics and drug addicts. They may become violent, and fall foul of the law.

The term PTSD emerged from research done by the Americans after Vietnam, to differentiate symptoms caused by the acute trauma of war from similar symptoms that might have other causes. Before Vietnam the same condition had been called 'war neurosis', 'anxiety state', 'adjustment reaction' and 'mixed anxiety state'. Vietnam vets were noted to have specific patterns of symptoms, characterized by hyper-vigilance and involuntary memories of nightmare experiences.

These are now known to be a common reaction to a horrific experience of any sort of violence – not just war. The actual scale of the post-Vietnam problem helped with recognizing PTSD as a condition. More than 2.8 million individuals served in US armed forces in South-East Asia between 1964 and 1973, of whom a million were exposed to hostile, life-threatening events.[3] Over half these people (500,000) developed serious PTSD, which disrupted their whole lives, and *all* Vietnam veterans still have PTSD symptoms to some degree.[4]

PTSD has all the characteristics of both depression and anxiety states: the avoidance of others and an inability to show emotion, combined with sleeplessness, irritability and hyper-arousal. Most sufferers are depressed, which can make them feel physically tired and even ill, feeling helpless about their condition and very isolated. Frequently drugs and alcohol are abused as 'self-medication'. Sufferers may deliberately cut themselves off from close friends, family and spouses 'who do not understand'. Irrational outbursts of anger and irritation make family and work life difficult, while extreme rages make sufferers fear they will lose control and damage the people around them. (Their 'solution' is to seek isolation.)

Rage, generated in combat and directed at the enemy, on returning home becomes directed towards authority in a general sense, and specifically towards superiors at work, parents, military authorities, government, the 'Establishment' and the 'system'. Soldiers leave the army, and may then be unable to hold down jobs or work as part of an organization. They feel used and exploited, and have confrontations with superiors and fellow workers whom they mistrust.

The spouses of PTSD victims complain of coldness and lack of tenderness or care. The sufferers themselves are aware that they no longer share in the enjoyment of life as they remember it from before they went to war. Their lives feel drab and grey, without happiness or pleasure, even though their circumstances may remain the same. They feel *unable* to experience the joy any more, and often describe themselves as 'emotionally dead'. This 'psychic numbing' is uncontrollable, a natural defence mechanism that enabled them to cope with the fear and horror of combat. However once combat (the period of trauma) is over, the emotional shield remains in place. Feelings of love and compassion become very uncomfortable to PTSD sufferers, particularly if they believe that by allowing themselves to feel emotions again they will completely lose control – being (for example) unable to stop crying. Psychologist and Vietnam veteran Tom Williams:

Many of these [Vietnam] veterans go through life with an impaired capacity
to love and care for others. They have no feeling of direction or purpose in
life. They are not even sure why they exist.[5]

'Survivor guilt' can develop into a destructive self-castigation for
supposed incompetence at having caused deaths. This irrational feeling of guilt is common with many combat veterans, whether or not
they develop PTSD. My father (the historian John McManners) is
plagued with guilt at the death of two of his soldiers in the siege of
Tobruk fifty years ago: 'I am haunted by . . . an error of judgement
which cost the lives of two of my own men. I saw them die. I try not
to remember and mostly I succeed.' Survivor guilt has led Vietnam
PTSD victims to pick fights with the biggest opponents, crash their
cars (in single-auto accidents) and take heroin. More constructively,
others have become compulsive blood donors, finding relief in giving
blood so that others may live. Medics are particularly prone to survivor guilt, incapable of remembering the people they saved, blaming
themselves for the deaths of even hopeless cases.

In war, extreme vigilance and specific learned survival techniques
are vital, but, like psychic numbing, when combatants return home
these responses cannot simply be switched off. War veterans are
very attuned to anything out of the ordinary, disliking, for example,
people driving or walking too close behind them. They are startled
by loud noises and may take evasive action, throwing themselves to
the ground or taking cover behind buildings. Particularly in America,
many veterans sleep with weapons beside them, or sleep so lightly
that any slight disturbance brings them to full and often aggressive
wakefulness.

Anxiety that in battle can save your life, by making you more alert,
can make life back home unbearable – for family as well as sufferer.
The emotion that generates anxiety is fear. The normal 'flight or
fight' response is greatly increased in war veterans, an adaptation
to the combat environment that helped them survive. Turbo-charged
anxiety is however very destructive in normal life, the body over-
reacting to mundane difficulties as if they were life-threatening.

The actual reasons for PTSD sufferers' sense of terror can be difficult to determine. PTSD creates such strong but groundless fear in
sufferers because it always relates to the trauma they have already
suffered. In being exposed to terrible danger, and the sight of the
mutilation or death of others, people encounter a reality of life
hitherto unknown to them. Having experienced the unthinkable
once, victims of trauma react as if the unthinkable might happen to

them again, anticipating other situations when disaster might strike. In this totally real fear, trauma victims feel very alone – especially because they cannot communicate the reasons for their fear to anyone else. If PTSD sufferers can accept that their anxieties are a self-generated 'fear of fear', and not actually caused by the trivial problems that appear to stimulate them, they will begin to control their emotions, which requires courage and a lot of effort. It can seem to sufferers very unfair that 'normal' people should be free of fear and spared this effort. 'Normal' people, however, have led very sheltered lives, and remain blissfully unaware of the darker side of reality.

Once PTSD sufferers have harnessed their emotions, in coping with something that others cannot even imagine they become stronger and more realistic as people, entering a dimension of human experience that the safety and triviality of modern life denies to others. If they are not able to control the powerful negative emotions generated in PTSD, their health, happiness and social lives decline. 'Fear of fear' is an endless and destructive loop. Fear destroys self-confidence and the individual sinks in real and measurable socio-economic terms, a process known as 'social drift'. In its extremes, social drift is often accompanied by drug and/or alcohol problems, and can end in vagrancy.

Individuals suffering from PTSD do not enjoy their anxiety. On the contrary, it exhausts and defeats them, making them feel ill. Most wish they could return to being 'as they were before'; they fight hard to stay above water, exercising great strength to keep their lives together. Advice from spouse, family, friends and even family doctors to 'pull yourself together' is therefore both hurtful and unhelpful. If individuals were able to do so, they would already have done it.

Night brings reminders of trauma, forcing many to use drugs (particularly marijuana) and alcohol in order to sleep. Nightmares, of being shot at and having nowhere to run, re-living particularly horrifying events, or of some unspecific dread, are common. They wake for no apparent reason, or rise early still very tired. Wives report partners sleeping fitfully, calling out, even grabbing or attacking them. Memories of combat (or just unnamed dread) also intrude into veterans' minds during the day, uncomfortable thoughts that cannot be controlled. Some replay (and re-write) past events exhaustively in their heads, feeling guilty and angry at what they see as their failure to take the correct action at the time. Smells, noises and other stimuli are powerful reminders which cause memories to flood back, even creating short periods when the individual actually re-experiences past events. Flashbacks can last for a few seconds to several hours, and have led to serious confrontations between armed veterans and police. (Veterans' combat experience and expertise with weapons makes them a very dangerous adversary for even armed police.)

The disturbing changes of personality caused by PTSD, from cheerful extrovert to withdrawn, miserable introvert, also seriously affect families and friends. Spouses and children are most deeply hurt, particularly when sufferers walk out on them (because their combat experiences have made them feel dirty and unworthy of family life, or because of psychic numbing). Some counsellors estimate that more than thirty other people can be affected by each individual PTSD sufferer.

Every person suffering from PTSD will have a number of related symptoms, but may only seek help when he or she can no longer cope with them. For every identified case, therefore, there are many more struggling unhappily but coping. Many will be unaware of their problem, or will express it in different terms, as I discovered when sitting in on group psychotherapy sessions with Falklands veterans at the Royal Naval Hospital *Haslar*, in Portsmouth. A merchant seaman from the *Herald of Free Enterprise* ferry sinking, expressing his anger:

People in charge should be able to make mistakes that maybe cost time or money – but their mistakes should never cost people's lives. The *Herald* disaster was so big, so many people . . . responsibility shouldn't all be laid at the feet of a few men. I don't know how they must be feeling now [three years later] – they must feel dreadful. There were plenty of others who should be blamed – Department of Transport officials who hadn't done proper safety checks . . .

His intrusive thoughts and memories:

It's like a huge jelly inside you. You try to keep it there, stop it from getting out, but as you cover all the holes, it manages to get out somewhere else. You think about it all the time, you can't get away from it for a minute.

'Y', a recently retired Royal Marine Warrant Officer and Falklands veteran, found leaving the comradeship of the marines very difficult:

In the forces you've always got something to think about, something to look forward to. Everyone is geared up to getting the job done – together. Civilians are very different. They don't seem to care about the jobs they are supposed to do. They don't think about anything except four o'clock when they knock off. They are all brain-dead. It gets me very angry.

'Y' says that his anger is partly frustration at the change in his work, but accepts that it is too strong to be justified:

I was driving on this quiet road in our minibus and pulled out to overtake this Volvo that was crawling along. As I got alongside, he accelerated. I put my foot down and he accelerated again. I suddenly became angry like I've never been before. I banged on the steering wheel, I shouted at him . . . I was absolutely incensed. The minibus didn't have the acceleration to get past him, so when a car came in the other direction, I had to pull in behind him.

I then followed him home. I was going to grab him by the throat and kill him – throttle him. On the drive, I calmed down a bit. I got out of the van and asked him why he had done it. He was all [well-spoken and pompous] and gave me all this 'driving along at 35 mph like any good motorist' routine. I told him he was lucky his daughter was with him, and walked away.

Sailor 'X', from HMS *Coventry* (sunk by Argentine bombs), spoke of his inability to concentrate:

I've just started a new job and last week the boss explained what I would have to do. I found afterwards that I hadn't listened to a word he'd said. I'm wandering around at the moment trying to work out how to do the job – what needs to be done. He said to ask him if I wasn't sure – but I don't want to do that.

I like to spend a lot of time on my own. I go out fishing and don't come home until four in the morning. I'll have a few hours sleep in the chair then go off to work. I often get up at midnight or thereabouts and go off and read a book all night. I don't seem to get at all tired.

'X's anxiety and tension is so great that although he doesn't feel his tiredness, he is certainly affected by it:

I find that a simple two-minute job can take me all day to do. At the end of the day, I look around surprised at how the time has flown by. I can't work out what I was doing or how I managed to make the job last so long.

Others were concerned that their lapses in concentration were so complete that they lost whole chunks of time. When driving they would suddenly find themselves miles further on – sometimes on the wrong road. They worried about how they got there. 'Y' talked of going to visit his parents and being unable to concentrate on what they were talking about, thinking instead about his work and what he had to do the following week. 'X' commented that very often, at home, he 'just wasn't there' mentally and that his wife felt very lonely, even though he was with her.

Solitude is important to PTSD sufferers: 'Y' told us of joining the National Trust, taking afternoons off work to visit the houses and gardens, watching other people and enjoying being by himself. Another marine felt that in the Falklands, for the first time, he'd

really learned how to worry. His anxiety was quickly re-labelled
'fear' by the group – as the underlying emotion that is the cause of
feeling anxious.

Another sailor who had also served on HMS *Coventry* told of
returning to his ship after four weeks on the PTSD treatment course
at RNH *Haslar*:

When I left the ship, everyone was friendly, but when I came back no one
would talk to me. They all thought I'd been skiving off – having six weeks'
leave that they hadn't been given, making everyone else work harder doing
my job for me. They took the mickey – about me having come here, and I
found all the friends I thought I had weren't talking to me any more. I
lasted about a week before I had to come back to *Haslar*. Now I've been
drafted to [a shore-based job]; everyone is friendly and I'm happy.

A leading hand's wife was concerned that coming to *Haslar* on the
psychiatric course was going to upset her husband's promotion:

They're so careless with the information. Everyone in the ship ends up
knowing that he's coming here and that he's got psychiatric problems. He's
up for his promotion to petty officer now, and it all depends upon how
sympathetic his superiors on the ship are going to be, as to whether he gets
it. I don't know how easy it will be going back to the ship after all this.

Royal Navy psychiatrist Surgeon Commander Morgan O'Connell:

We are responsible for what we do and for our own emotions. We have to
learn to cope with them. For some people, life in the services becomes
unbearable and they have to leave.

It is important for both combatants (or accident victims, who equally
can suffer from PTSD) and their families to accept that PTSD represents a normal reaction to trauma. Without such acceptance, recovery is impossible. Unfortunately for combat veterans, there are
deep-rooted military prejudices against what many regard as a
'wimp's charter', a powerful conservatism that refuses to address the
problem of PTSD or other adverse reactions to having been in combat.
The attitudes conveyed by terms like 'stiff upper lip' or 'machismo'
are longstanding denial mechanisms, by which military men refuse
to admit that they or their soldiers could become psychological
casualties or suffer from PTSD. 'That sort of thing might happen to
other units, but not to us.'

Sergeant Dwight W. Johnson is a good example of how even military psychiatrists avoid blaming the stress of combat for psychological problems. Johnson won a Congressional Medal of Honor in
Vietnam for rescuing a close friend from a burning tank despite heavy

crossfire. However, when the tank exploded, burning to death the rest of the crew, he hunted and killed face-to-face a number of Vietnamese soldiers in retaliation (between five and twenty). Immediately after this he required psychiatric hospital treatment, which continued on his return to the USA. Johnson was diagnosed as having 'depression caused by post-Vietnam adjustment problem'. There was nothing in this diagnosis about the actual combat, his grief for the friends he saw burn to death in the blazing tank, or the anger that made him go berserk. He had persistent bad dreams, and guilt over surviving when his friends died – and for (as he said) 'winning a high honor for the one time in his life when he lost complete control of himself'. Most of all, he wondered what would happen if he lost control again – in Detroit? He believed he was failing to cope, that it was his fault that he hadn't readjusted to society after returning from Vietnam, that he was weak, maladjusted and inadequate.

Three years after his heroic action, at the age of twenty-four Dwight Johnson was killed by the manager of a store he allegedly attempted to hold up at gunpoint. His mother commented: 'Sometimes I wonder if Skip tired of this life and needed someone else to pull the trigger.'[6]

The admission that combat affects every normal person exposed to it challenges the whole ethos of military training and discipline. In this deeply sensitive area, military understanding of the problem is understandably very slow. Psychiatrists have not helped by using technical terms that are widely misunderstood by laymen. Patients who seek professional help complaining of feeling anxious or depressed are not impressed at being told after psychiatric examination that they are suffering from 'Anxiety' or 'Depression'. They knew that to start with. Everyone gets anxious or depressed, so military men could be forgiven for not taking psychiatric diagnoses seriously. There is however a great difference between the clinical diagnosis of anxiety or depression, and simply being in that particular mood. Freudian terminology might be more helpful; the word 'Melancholia' for example accurately describes serious depression.

The effects of psychological problems are far from simple, particularly in the armed forces. A significant amount of mental illness remains undiagnosed until it becomes a serious problem, by which time the sufferer has become convinced that he or she is defective as a person. Family, friends, workmates and superior officers are likely to have contributed greatly to this conviction, and will have suffered to some extent themselves in the process. The individual's military reports will not be as good as they should be, and he or she may have committed chargeable offences. Thus from the basic problem of the psychological condition, a whole host of other difficulties develop – known as the 'ripple effect'. Careers are ruined, marriages break down and lives are blighted.

Nobody suffering from appendicitis would be accused of weakness of character, but where any sort of psychological problem is concerned, quite unfairly, the sufferer seen as having the characteristics of the disease, which becomes a 'character weakness', linked with cowardice and ascribed to those more susceptible individuals who are assumed not to be as tough as everybody else. Steve Hughes:

I've come across many Second World War people who get very aggressive about PTSD or refuse to talk about it, describing it as 'just a lack of moral fibre'. If they had truly come to terms with it, they would be able to talk rationally about it, explaining that the war hadn't affected them in that way. So in fact they are putting up defensive barriers to protect their own inadequacies.

Some Falklands people were unaffected: John Crosland [a company commander in 2 Para] says, 'Well, there must be something about me that means it has no effect.' Bill Bentley says the same. It's gone over their heads. However, many people speak of their fathers never talking about the war, or getting funny talking about it – and even violent. Everyone says, 'It's the war'. If however you talk to the father himself, he'll insist he wasn't affected by it.

It has been calculated that from World War Two onwards, around 30% of all wounded have been psychiatric casualties. Of all casualty evacuations in the Second World War, 23% were for psychiatric reasons.[7] (At one stage more men were being discharged for psychiatric reasons than were being newly drafted.[8]) Unfortunately, in many of these cases men were discharged with diagnoses that ignored their combat experience, referring instead to other traumas – in childhood, relations with parents and so on. Such men still feel ashamed, guilty and wronged. In the Falklands, psychiatric casualties were officially estimated at between 5 and 10% of the number of physically wounded.[9] This is said to be lower than the usual figure because of the high quality of the troops and the relatively short duration of the war. Trench foot and cold exposure have a psychological aspect, perhaps concealing the true numbers of psychiatric wounded. A significant number of other cases however emerged after the war as PTSD, and in other guises such as hysterical deafness. It is suspected that many more cases than have been actually diagnosed exist hidden away under other problems ('occult PTSD').

Some people do not believe that PTSD exists. Many family doctors know very little about it, assuming sufferers to be time-wasters and inadequates. Sufferers are thus often kept quiet with Valium and other benzodiazapines, which are of no use in treating PTSD and may create serious dependency and other problems. Some doctors simply refuse to believe that anybody could be affected by something that happened decades ago. There is recent scientific data to support PTSD's existence, suggesting that a single experience of terror can actually change brain chemistry. These chemical changes have the effect of so increasing sufferers' sensitivity to adrenalin surges that normal events can cause repetitions of the sorts of reactions that the trauma itself caused. Only serious stress can induce these changes. Dr Dennis Charney, Director of Clinical Neuroscience at the US National Centre for PTSD:

Victims of a devastating trauma may never be the same biologically. It does not matter if it was the incessant terror of combat, torture or repeated abuse in childhood, or a one-time experience like being trapped in a hurricane or almost dying in an automobile accident. All uncontrollable stress can have the same biological impact.

The more intense the trauma and the longer its duration, the more likely it is to cause PTSD, which can last for decades or clear up spontaneously or through therapy. Increased chemical activity and changes have been observed in the brain stem, hypothalamus and pituitary gland, over-producing the hormones that mobilize the body for an emergency – even in situations that offer little or no threat. By contrast, observed hyperactivity of the opoid system (which lessens feelings of pain) may be the reason for emotional numbing and the inability to experience tender feelings that often accompanies PTSD.

When modern-day soldiers leave the army and are separated from the friends with whom they went to war, it can be difficult to determine whether their behaviour is due to any psychological problems they might have, or just normal 'squaddie' behaviour. Private Northfield:

Any one of the former paratroopers who were charged with civilian offences might have had PTSD-type problems ... or in fact were they just acting in the same way as they did in the army – going down-town, getting drunk, taking their clothes off, doing a Zulu Warrior ... ?[10] If one bloke on his own tries this sort of stuff in his home village in Gloucestershire, he gets locked up. Is this guy ill, or just unable to switch into civilian mode?

Isolation is probably the single most significant cause of post-combat (and post-trauma) problems. Cooper:

Many people after the Falklands found themselves getting inordinately angry and short-tempered, and equally easily depressed as well. They couldn't explain what they'd been through, and also they were coming back to live in a world whose values they'd seen were hollow and irrelevant. We came back to a rail strike. The soldiers were saying that these people [the rail workers] were getting paid the same as us, yet they don't get shot at – and here they are going on strike. What does that mean for us? It made the soldiers feel divorced from the rest of society.

The soldier can't describe what fighting is like; it is all-absorbing, of his emotions as well as his mind. The re-telling of it doesn't involve the emotions, so cannot ever be accurate. It's therefore much easier for soldiers not to talk to civilians about it.

Isolation can also be created by the hostile reactions of civilians to returned veterans – as happened to the servicemen from Vietnam.

Civilian populations don't always recognize their responsibility for the deaths that war brings. Soldiers are only the instrument of an electorate who have decided en masse that they want an army. The soldier might be the one doing the dirty work, but the responsibility for what he does must ultimately lie with the society that puts him there.

The conflict for the Vietnam veteran came from returning to a society that not only refused to accept responsibility for what he had done, but criticized him for it, despite the fact that he'd gone there on its behalf. Returning veterans found themselves regarded as criminals when all they had done was what Uncle Sam had ordered.

The sorts of post-combat reaction that began to be recognized after Vietnam are not confined to modern soldiers, but also occurred after the First and Second World Wars. For example, Frank Richards was the author of *Old Soldier Sahib* and *Old Soldiers Never Die*, about his experiences as a private in the First World War. For a time between the wars he found it impossible to settle into civilian life, living in South Wales ostensibly as a tramp, but in fact following his daily routine as a soldier, pitching camp at night and setting himself daily route marches. Men have always had problems in settling down after a military life, particularly when returning from war to the peacetime army.

Tom Howard, an RAMC Medical Assistant, started to experience nightmares soon after returning from the Falklands:

I heard a former GI from Vietnam talking of smoking dope in order to actually go into combat. I was contemptuous of this unprofessional, stupid behaviour. I used dope afterwards purely to gain relief from nightmares.

The nightmares were vivid and terrifying:

I was in a broken-down, ruined house with an SLR rifle. A line of soldiers were rushing towards me and shooting. I realized that before I could shoot them all, I would be overrun. Then I'd feel the bullets hitting me hard in the chest, shoulders, legs and arms. My girlfriend told me that I'd jerk as if I was being shot, before waking up terrified. I was drinking very heavily too, getting out of my head every night, then driving home.

In 1983 Howard was posted from Aldershot, away from his friends in 2 and 3 Para. He went to the military doctor, concerned at his condition:

I was shaking like a leaf and begged not to be sent away from my mates. She promised to sort it out, and gave me some sleeping pills. Ten days later nothing was done and I was sent to Germany. When I got to Germany, the drug supply dried up.

Howard was still a very capable medic, a positive legacy of his war experience:

A woman and three little girls were seriously injured in a road traffic accident. A Ford Taunus was upside down having crashed into a Coca Cola truck. I pulled the door open, then switched off the ignition. One of the little girls had slammed her head between the two seats, completely removing all the tissue from the top of her head. Her larynx was crushed and jaw broken. She'd stopped breathing, so I had to force her jaw open with a pair of scissors from the glove box, then give her artificial respiration. There was petrol everywhere, so I had to get them out quickly.

As luck would have it, our brigadier was in the traffic jam, and saw me at work. I ended up with a GOC's commendation. I seemed to know exactly what to do, and the idea of the danger of it – from fire – never occurred to me.

The drinking and nightmares were getting the better of him, however.

I realized that something terrible was wrong with me. I went to see the doctor, but could only cry. He got me a psychiatric appointment, where I was given an EEG test. Unfortunately the psychiatrist, who was aged about 70, told me that I had a very immature personality and that I needed to pull myself together. I could have fucking killed him.

I left the army because I didn't seem to be going anywhere, getting good reports but not being promoted. My wife had left me and returned to UK after a very bitter break-up. I felt I was coming apart. For the first time ever in my career, I failed a course – my sergeant's promotion – as I couldn't get my act together at all.

I got into the drink because it helped me sleep, and gradually the amount I needed increased until an evening's entertainment became a bottle of scotch in front of the telly. Alcohol dependence sets in fairly quickly, although the drugs were not a problem. If the Service Investigations Branch had caught me, I'd have spent 18 months in Colchester [the army's jail]. In 1984 the army did not want to know about PTSD – even though there was a lot of it about.

I never had any more medical treatment until 1988, when the nightmares were so bad that I just had to seek help. The GP was Jewish, and understood the problem – because of similar problems his own parents had suffered after surviving Auschwitz. He referred me to Woolwich [military hospital].

I turned to religion when I came back from the Falklands, particularly after I left the army. I spent several weeks in a monastery, and it frightened me. I realized that I'd found something ... such sanctity, and spiritual uplift. I could have fitted in so easily there, and never left. It sounds like a joke, but at the time I had a very beautiful girlfriend – and in the mental struggle of it she won, so I left the monastery. Now I don't smoke or drink – although I still have bad nightmares. I'm not a lost cause or a hopeless case – as I was when I left the army.

Dennis Marshall-Hasdell's problems started in June 1983 when he failed an aircrew medical. He was found to be deaf in one ear from repeated exposure to explosions – a common war injury. At a subsequent RAF medical, serious back trouble was also discovered, a common effect when a tall man carries enormous, over-loaded bergans. With his back getting worse, Marshall-Hasdell left his many friends in 3 Commando Brigade, returning to RAF Finningley. Outside the close-knit, almost family environment of the commandos, he started to go downhill. His back problem had been tentatively diagnosed as a misplaced disc. At Finningley he found himself increasingly troubled by it to the extent that he had to lie on the floor to relieve the pain.

I was beginning to realize that losing my flying category was inevitable, that I would never fly a fast jet again, or command a squadron. My RAF career was over. I was filled with a confusion of conflicting emotions and changing attitudes; I desperately didn't want to lose my flying category, but also I wanted to be back with the Commando Brigade.

He was posted to the Officer Training Squadron for a ground tour teaching young officers adventurous pursuits. His loss of medical category was kept secret.

My boss was a career creep. He used to send memos rather than bother to speak to me. He was a diabolical example to the young officers, a fat, unfit slob. He also seemed to hate me – resentful and jealous. The whole thing became very petty – which I couldn't be bothered with.

Marshall-Hasdell had also broken up with his girlfriend, and was aware of pressure building up inside him, although at this stage he was experiencing no specific problems. Then his corpulent boss wrote one memo too many. Marshall-Hasdell stalked into his office, dragged him from behind the desk and threatened him: 'If you send me another memo, I'll crack every one of your fingers.' He then returned to his own office and carried on working. A summons from the wing commander, who knew of the medical situation, followed shortly. In the wing commander's office, for the first time Marshall-Hasdell completely broke down. The station medical officer sent him away on three weeks' sick leave – for a rest.

Arriving at his empty house in Plymouth, he phoned Aberporth friends to explain what had happened. They suggested that after a good night's sleep he drive up to them, then contacted another RAF friend who came immediately to the house. By the time he arrived, Marshall-Hasdell was sitting in the hall holding his head in his hands and moaning. 'I just didn't know what was wrong, or what was happening to me. It was very scary.' The next day, feeling better, he drove to Aberporth, where the nightmares started:

They were horrific, major nightmares; complete jumbles that woke me up in a cold sweat. I would go to sleep, then have another one – maybe four or five in succession. They were never the same – never anything you could pin down. It was always to do with the Falklands, and something to do with the head, garrotting, decapitation – that kind of thing. And I would wake up choking.

Marshall-Hasdell returned at the end of sick leave to Finningley, where the air force's administrative system had taken over; 'Form 8A action' had been initiated – 'compulsory psychiatric treatment following a breach of discipline'. Six sessions with the RAF psychiatrist followed:

It was clear he didn't understand any of what I was saying. He kept telling me that I'd have to live with my memories, that remembering was good for me, that they would always be a part of my life. And then I told him of one particular thing, and to my amazement he started crying . . . I didn't cry.

This part of Marshall-Hasdell's story was for him particularly disturbing. When we talked, several years later, as with the RAF psychiatrist for several days he would not tell me what it was. Then the full story emerged:

On Harriet I'd seen it all; the dead people, heard the screaming . . . I sat on the Mount with a naval gunfire forward observer, the two of us on canvas fishing stools, maps laid on the ground, binoculars round our necks, looking for targets. We were completely in the open, oblivious to enemy shells or small arms fire. The forward observer was given an artillery battery for an hour at a time and we played, picking targets, dropping shells, enjoying it.

Having watched the enemy positions for several days, they knew who the enemy company commander was, had seen the RSM going round shouting, and had identified the bolshie soldiers who refused to leave their trenches.

Then two men moved from their trench to a small quarry that we thought they were using as a loo. The hour being up, we'd lost the guns so we had to request them back again. The forward observer was teaching me the artillery procedures, and between us we plonked fire down on these two men. We chased them from one piece of cover to the next for about fifteen minutes, until eventually we got them. The battery commander then took the guns away from us for a more important target. The men did not reappear, so we assumed they were dead.

At the time we actually enjoyed it. We were so detached and uncaring . . . and only afterwards did I realize how cold-heartedly professional, callous and unnecessary it was.

Eight years later, he felt deeply ashamed of this particular episode. The forward observer, on the other hand, when Marshall-Hasdell asked him about it, did not seem to accord the event any particular significance, and seemed unaffected by it – which puzzled as well as disturbed Marshall-Hasdell. This lack of reaction was not callous or indifferent. The war was far from over and the Argentine positions the two men were shelling would probably have to be attacked. The enemy on those positions might fight, and if allowed to organize themselves, could kill large numbers of friendly troops. He was carrying out the important artillery task of 'harassing fire'.

Just as each battlefield job has its own aims, objectives and dangers, each specialist has his own particular cross to bear. Artillerymen, from heavily camouflaged forward observation posts, must bring down savage fire on other less fortunate human beings who have no opportunity to fire back. There is no question of being unfair, inhuman or callous – it is simply one of the cruel realities of war. Had Marshall-Hasdell been doing his own job directing Harrier strikes on to suitable targets, he would have been secure in the knowledge that each target was important enough to justify risking the jets – even 'deserving' their attentions. He would have risked his own life standing where he could see both the target and the approach of the aircraft. He would have planned the safest exit route for the jets, away from enemy anti-aircraft fire, and very carefully evaluated the effect of the strike. Like the forward observer, the humanitarian aspect of doing his own job might not have struck him so forcefully – if at all. Unwittingly, in doing the observer's job, Marshall-Hasdell took on a burden of guilt that by rights was not his. Also, he was doing something he did not actually have to do – unlike the observer. In psychological terms, the military 'system' ('Mac' French's 'cause') was responsible for his actions and would absorb the guilt, whereas Marshall-Hasdell had inadvertently left himself morally stranded – he was on his own. He is not ashamed of anything else that he did in the campaign, and does not understand the logic of feeling guilty about those particular killings but not about others. How can one death be somehow justified, and another not?

His Wing Commander boss at RAF Finningley partly understood the cause of the breakdown, agreeing that he should be free of the trivial administration of the courses and stop working with his over-weight antagonist. However, soon the caving, climbing and hill-walking were getting harder and more painful. Rather than ease up, he took more and more painkillers – readily supplied by the station medical officer – so, although his back was getting worse, he was able to overcome it.

Looking back, I realize that the standards I expected of my staff and students on the Outward Bound-type courses I was running, were increasing. I was pushing them more and more. As the only green bereted RAF officer, with what for the RAF was unique Falklands war experience, the young officers expected a lot of me. They too worked very hard to come up to my require-ments, but really, I can see now that the standards were too high.

I was trying to produce some kind of combat-ready person rather than an all-round navigator. When I wrote their reports I'd ask myself, 'Would I want to go to war with this person?' No one ever mentioned it to me, but I was being too exacting for what the system required. I was also less accepting of weaknesses in others.

From the time I returned to the RAF I felt unusual, out of place, completely isolated and for most of the time, unhappy.

Throughout the troubled period before he left the RAF, Marshall-Hasdell was physically and mentally ill, at times to the extent of being irrational. He had to make crucial decisions under great strain, with no help or support from anyone. Three years later and relieved of the enormous strain he was under, he realized that he made several serious mistakes:

The RAF had me by the balls and they knew it. I could be easily manipulated. I wasn't given a chance – although everyone was very kind. I never felt that anything was done with my best interests at heart. I felt threatened by what was going on, as though they were playing everything down ... 'You're not as bad as all that, old chap ...'

Over the following eighteen months, Marshall-Hasdell battled simultaneously with depression, chronic back pain and an intractable RAF bureaucracy which seemed determined to minimize his entitlement to compensation. Even when agreement had finally been reached, it took the intervention of his MP, Geraint Howells, before payment of his pension began, and in the meantime he fell deep enough into debt to be compelled to sell his house – at a loss. Finances apart, Marshall-Hasdell was also very worried about his health and his future prospects:

I was convinced that because of my back I'd be in a wheelchair in ten years' time. But I took up the place I'd been awarded at Aberystwyth University and settled down to become a student. I enjoyed student life. I hardly ever socialized with other students and apart from the symptoms, was quite happy.

In his final year, with a girlfriend, he socialized more. He told her something of what he had been through:

I had to tell her a bit about it because of the night problems. When you spend the night with somebody, and wake up screaming or being violent, it's only fair to tell them a bit of what it's about.

I was quite happy and relatively under control. Trivial stress would cause lapses. The car breaking down, gas bills, arguments with people ... would lead to disrupted sleep, nightmares, flashbacks. Emotionally I was up and down a lot, and often cut myself off from everyone else at Aberporth for a week or so at a time. On reflection, I treated her very badly ...

After the breakdown at RAF Finningley, Dennis had taken to heart the RAF psychiatrist's professional advice that his Falklands experiences were a part of his life, that he should not try to reject them and that the feelings were actually good for him. His self-therapy was therefore to cut out all the trivia that made him so stressed, avoiding life for a while. He also drank, hitting the bottle until he felt better.

I felt that life was too short to worry about trivia. I'd survived three days being shelled on Mount Harriet. How could the car breaking down be as bad as that? I'd cut myself off from the trivia of life so as not to be so badly affected by it. The more I lived like that, the more I believed that I could never have any sort of career again – because of the effect stress had on me.

There was also the double guilt at having survived, then letting the trivia get the better of me – when others who had died would have been glad simply to be alive. Dick Nunn [see Chapter 8] would have been delighted to have a broken-down car . . .

I was just about coping, but not even beginning to solve the problem – which was very destructive.

Dealing with people was another problem. An able, active person, he threw himself into a wide range of activities; becoming a Community Councillor, leader of the local Air Training Corps, running the area Duke of Edinburgh's Award scheme . . . but being busy brought conflict with other people.

At university, I'd been able to drive home 30 miles down the road to avoid confrontation. There's no real pressure at university anyway. I try not to argue with people – to avoid the stress – but real life isn't like that. After clashes with others I thought for a time that I was the catalyst. It was only through Tony [a close friend] that I stopped thinking I was always to blame, and stopped moving myself into complete isolation . . . I'm giving up all my activities.

A lack of respect for authority is a common attitude in PTSD sufferers.

The Establishment – in the form of the Air Training Corps hierarchy for example – is anathema to me, so for my peace of mind, I gave up running the local branch. I find it hard to compromise my own principles, which are much more clearly defined now than ever they were when I was in the military. I can only adjust my position on something if it won't compromise my principles.

I do recognize that a lot of this is paranoia.

I have no space in my life now for the pettiness, trivia and awful, unnecessary anger of human life. People get upset at pathetic things, especially when you have seen what they are capable of doing to each other. I am frightened of ever getting angry again myself, that I might again become that cold, callous person who enjoyed killing. Any sort of aggro upsets me now, because I know of the potential I have for violence – having been so violent myself. It's changed my whole concept of values. So many things are done today with no thought of the future, from large-scale environmental pollution to throwing litter on the pavement. I was like that – doing all manner of things because I might be dead in an hour's time. I feel cold and horrible to think of it now.

I wonder if I actually learned from any of this? I wanted to do more of that kind of work, and I'm frightened now that without my medical downgrading I might have. I was getting quite good at that sort of thing . . . I then got involved with interrogation . . . What's the point of interrogating people? It's frightening for me to think that if I hadn't been medically downgraded, I would have continued.

I'm still worried about this inner drive to join with the Establishment and do this sort of business. It's wrong for humans to do that sort of thing to each other. If our leaders knew what actually happened in wars, then wars wouldn't happen. All I've ever done is satisfy the demands of the system – and been good at it.

War changed Marshall-Hasdell (temporarily) into an unthinking, callous person – which he never wants to be again. War also makes individuals more inclined to be themselves, and afterwards more uninhibited, which peacetime military people find hard to accept:

People don't let you live life unaffected. If you get too good at what you do, they reject you . . . they get jealous, and can't accept you for what you are. I'm no saint, but I just can't cope with the jealousy of others, when they react adversely to me doing things well. All I want to do is live in harmony with [my wife] – and I wish the same could happen to the rest of society. I get upset when this doesn't happen. Ambition is a problem . . .

He reasons that in order to be good at something, you have to be cold, pushy, callous and professional. On the battlefield ambitions were unchecked, and turned into a nightmare. So knowing what unbridled ambition can do, Marshall-Hasdell has deliberately divested himself of it.

I'd like to live in a caravan and get away from everyone else, so as not to have any hassles. Activity seems to create hassles, so I want to give up all activity . . . I've no ambitions any more, because I'm afraid of them being unworthy. I don't want to be 'cured' of whatever it is that's wrong with me – for fear of returning to what I was before . . .

Dennis Marshall-Hasdell has pushed on with his life, getting married and working hard towards finding an academic niche that will allow him to live peacefully beside the sea in Aberporth. After a year of concentrated study, he became a Russian linguist – an intensive course from which several other students dropped out, one with a nervous breakdown. Passing this test has restored his sense of self-esteem and created hope for the future.

In the Falklands Honours and Awards, Royal Marines Lieutenant Jeff Niblett was given the Distinguished Flying Cross – the first to be won by a Royal Marine.

The corps are very reticent about awards, reluctant to acknowledge gallantry because throughout their training, all marines believe they are capable of it. I cannot therefore validate my experience in terms of winning the DFC. I did my duty and feel humbled – it is a very great honour to me. Others did as much – yet they didn't receive any recognition.

Life in the services goes on without much of a pause, even after a war. After Christmas 1982 (having returned from the Falklands in July), Niblett was posted to a new job, the demanding training to become a QHI (qualified helicopter instructor), which he passed. However, for the next four years he describes himself as never feeling 100 per cent: very tired and lethargic, isolated, irresponsible, disliking authority and suffering new-found anxieties. In particular he felt heavily burdened by his family responsibilities, which he linked with the Falklands and the deaths of officers and men for whom he had been responsible during the war. He felt guilt at their deaths, emotion that spilled over into feelings for his family.

In October 1983 Niblett returned to his old combat unit, 3 Commando Brigade Air Squadron. Then in June 1985 he moved to a staff job in HQ Commando Forces, which he enjoyed greatly. Throughout this busy time, he was conscious of 'not being right within myself.'

I had to spend lots of time away from my family – week-ending, or on three-month deployments in Norway and exercises. As the Squadron QHI I was very busy. The job distracted me from getting to know my family. My personal life was empty. In any spare time I had, I would sit and do nothing – cutting myself off from people I knew, which was miserable for the family. My wife knew from the bad nights that something was wrong. It was nothing specific; pure disturbance, something subconscious keeping me awake. Your family react – they know you're not okay, then you seem to turn against them . . .

The deaths of members of his Falklands Scout flight, particularly Lieutenant Richard Nunn, weighed heavily:

When you lose someone close to you, someone you like very much, you feel anger at the safeness of the normal world, turning against people and the environment in which you once felt comfortable. You come to distrust and resent authority – the people you work for, your parents. You cut yourself off, isolating yourself.

People who haven't been through trauma don't understand. The corps [Royal Marines], with their macho image, expect you to be strong, when in fact you feel personally weak. It feels as though you are letting yourself and the organization down – so you create an artificial environment for yourself. It's very difficult to educate people about a problem they've never experienced. Few people have been through violent action. I have a particular respect for the grunts [infantrymen] – I was one myself before I took up flying. On that bare-arsed terrain, fighting at night – and being expected by everyone to WIN – is very frightening.

Others [in the military] cannot apply combat rules to what they do because they are peacetime soldiers. And you have to avoid banging on about the Falklands and its lessons. It was a unique experience that no one else can understand.

Few people could go through a war without hardship – even if they never saw any enemy. The pressure is relentless and affects everyone. In 1987 I met a steward from one of the merchant ships who was undergoing psychiatric treatment. He'd never seen even an Argentine jet, yet the pressure had got to him. Being stuck on the ship, he had no way in which to relieve it. At least on the ground, we could do something. I've no time for those who can't understand . . .

Jeff Niblett believes the 'uncertainty factor' is important:

When the Falklands crisis started I'd actually left the squadron – been given my prezzie, had my leaving run and handed over to Dick [Nunn]. It was the peacetime mentality; I was marking time before my next posting.

He had left behind several unresolved problems:

We were just back from three months in Norway, our first child was only seven months old, we'd exchanged contracts to sell the house – but hadn't yet found one to buy. And into all this, I suddenly went off to war.

Every day seemed like a week, carrying our homes on our backs, 33 days on compo with no apparent end in sight, and the uncertainty of how things were going. There were setbacks, weather problems, tragedies such as Bluff Cove, which made it seem a very fragile environment for living in.

In 1987 Niblett was selected as a student for the Royal Navy Staff College at Greenwich. Academically, the course started well, but after four weeks, reading a newspaper article about Falklands post-battle trauma by Royal Navy psychiatrist Surgeon Commander Morgan O'Connell, Niblett found himself confronting an unpalatable truth:

The article leapt out of the page at me. I identified with every symptom like someone was hitting me over the head with a hammer. I had nightmares, anxiety, emotional instability, irrational outbursts; I alternated from being close to my family, then very cold to them and isolated. All this was complicated by subconsciously knowing that something was wrong with me – but also feeling very guilty about it. The emotions completely take over, yet in all this you have the illusion that you are still in control and doing what you should do.

I'd been sent a PTSD questionnaire[11] which I had thrown into the bin – a common reaction with PTSD sufferers. I'd no stability in my life, although I was in an environment I was very used to.

From the time my son was eleven months old until he was six was a sad period, when he didn't receive proper support from me as his father. It was very, very sad . . .

Niblett has made a Falklands album, a private collection of pictures,
letters, newspaper cuttings and memorabilia. On the front cover, the
two volumes are dedicated to his son – 'for the time when he is old
enough to understand'.

I'm a very reserved person, guarding myself against intrusion. I wouldn't
talk about the Falklands. I couldn't. At the end, after the Remembrance
Service, it felt like the closing of a book. Far too matter-of-fact . . . which
led to my problems of 1987.

After reading the newspaper article, Niblett had psychiatric sessions
with Morgan O'Connell – very traumatic, horrific treatment.

The more he asked, the harder it was for me. It all came to a head during
a Staff College visit to naval bases in the West Country. While the others
were in Plymouth, I was due at Portsmouth for another psychiatric session.
I was emotionally knackered and cancelled the appointment.

We had a party that night, then on the Friday morning during the first
briefing, my DS informed me in an embarrassed way that I was ordered to
be escorted to the sick bay at HMS *Drake*. There I was grilled by a vicious,
retired RN four-ringer psychiatrist, who ordered me off the staff course. I
was 'in urgent need of treatment', and was ordered to report to RNH *Haslar*
on Monday. I had a dreadful weekend.

On Sunday, I drove to Greenwich to complete some outstanding work,
then attended lectures as normal on Monday morning. After a time, I was
summoned to my DS, then to the commodore – who had neither sympathy,
nor any understanding. It was very unsettling. I was ordered to clear my
belongings out of Greenwich and go to *Haslar*. On the way there, I nearly
crashed the car. After lunching in the wardroom at *Haslar*, I crossed the
car park to G Block – the psychiatric wing. The chief petty officer behind
the reception desk seemed to me to be insubordinate. He told me they were
expecting me, and that I could call him John, and he'd call me Jeff! I bit
his head off.

I was ushered into a group therapy session, where a simpering occupational therapist asked if I wanted to make a rug or a basket. We were in a
big room upstairs, overlooking the sea wall. One inmate was staring at the
waves nodding his head up and down, while another sat beside the TV
jabbing the remote channel changer every few seconds. The rest of them
were a motley crew of civvies. I left, refusing to participate.

Then Morgan O'Connell arrived, in a furious rush. A second doctor was
present at the ensuing interview – a buffoon who insisted on repeating
everything I'd said over the last four weeks. I was knackered, having slept
very little over the weekend. I cut the discussion short, demanding rest, and
so was sedated on a side ward until the next morning.

When I came to the next morning, the chief petty officer was reassuringly
patronizing and got me some breakfast. I decided to get dressed. I had

slip-on shoes with no laces, but when I came to put on my trousers, the belt was missing. They'd taken away anything that I might commit suicide with! I stormed to the desk, demanding that the Chief return my belt.

The more the CPO pleaded ignorance of the whereabouts of the belt, the more Niblett believed it had been removed for his own protection. As a full-scale search started, Niblett decided to check his car, where he had changed out of uniform into civilian clothes the previous afternoon. With horror, he saw the belt where he had left it. The embarrassment of being a Royal Marines officer admitted to the Royal Navy's Psychiatric Wing, and his underlying tension, were boosted to new levels:

I walked back into G Block, and whenever someone asked me about the belt it was as if I'd seized up. All I could say was, 'Disregard, disregard'.

I was formally admitted as a psychiatric patient, which meant I was forbidden to leave the block. I was not however prepared to accept the smothering sort of wet blanket of the psychiatric system. I knew I was ill – but I wasn't mad.

Psychiatric institutions have a way of making anybody feel that they have gone mad, turning their rational reactions to abnormal situations into crazy, illogical tantrums. Niblett's rejection of the system was the best thing he could have done:

I needed time to think. I decided to go into Gosport for lunch. As I strode through the entrance lobby, the Chief attempted to stop me, saying I wasn't allowed to leave. I told him to watch carefully as I walked out of the door.

Niblett bought fish and chips, read the paper, then returned to *Haslar*. Morgan O'Connell approved his having marched out of G Block as demonstrating a very positive attitude towards his problem, which could only be cured through self-therapy. Niblett was then formally discharged. Had he not stormed out, he would have remained a mental patient.

He returned home, returning frequently to *Haslar* over the next few months for therapy sessions.

Through June and July I went to see Morgan O'Connell. In these interviews, he asked penetrating questions designed to get at the root of the problems. He reduced me to tears in every session – which brought out all the repressed emotion.

After four weeks, O'Connell asked if Niblett would like to make a trip back to the Falklands, to re-live the incidents in situ. Applying for official flights was a tortuous and embarrassing process: 'I was a Falklands casualty in UK, wanting to be aero-medevac'd to the Falklands – which the RAF refused to understand.' Niblett was feeling very conspicuous and sensitive:

There is a stigma attached to having psychiatric treatment. People joked about it. And when you've got a DFC, you've earned a degree of notoriety – but covertly, people say that you are mentally sick, and have zero sympathy for you.

When he really needed sympathy and understanding, Niblett felt instead that he had become the butt of gossip, ignorant conjecture and jokes. War heroes are supposed by peacetime servicemen to maintain their stiff upper lip – not take psychiatric treatment.

Finally, in July 1987, after a great deal of opposition and bureaucratic difficulty from the RAF (over who should pay for the trip), Niblett flew back to the Falklands in a half-empty Tri-star.

I wanted to visit Dick's grave. He'd been moved from the mass slit trench to a proper War Graves Commission graveyard. I wanted to pay my last respects at his final resting place.

Travel from Port Stanley out into the 'Camp' (as the rest of the Islands is called) was difficult, but luckily in the Upland Goose Hotel he met a band of civilian helicopter pilots on contract, two of whom were former Royal Marines. They understood immediately why he was there, and working round their own schedules, flew him to wherever he wanted to go, picking him up at the end of each day.

We [Niblett and O'Connell] spent the first day at Goose Green walking the battlefield, finishing up in the settlement itself. I saw it for what it really is, beautiful, no violence, and with only some of the debris of war, clothing, blankets, some CBU [cluster bomb units] casings. Like a time capsule, I could visualize everything that had happened there.

We went to San Carlos on Thursday; to Ajax Bay, the settlement and to the cemetery. On Friday we went round Port Stanley – to the house where we'd stayed after the surrender. And as the plane took off for the flight back to UK, the intense relief I felt was like coming out of a tunnel.

After summer leave, Niblett had one more session with O'Connell, who then discharged him from treatment. Having been removed from the Naval Staff College under such inauspicious circumstances, Niblett is under no illusions but that his career has suffered, even though: 'Morgan O'Connell has personally kept the case notes, so my official records show only "treated at RNH *Haslar*".' He was then sent to the United States Marines staff college at Quantico, Virginia.

The Argentine marine who led their initial raid on Moody Brook was there, and we became friends. He'd only spent one day in the Falklands, flying home as soon as the airfield was captured. He wouldn't talk about it. My DS had suffered from PTSD after serving in Vietnam, and I was able to talk to him about that.

Niblett and his Argentine counterpart delivered the final presentation of the course – about the Falklands War:

I told my story of the war. Then after his summing-up the Divisional Colonel asked me to talk about PTSD – throwing me straight into the deep end. It was a taboo subject. No one had ever talked about it there . . . They had lectures on combat leadership, but never anything negative.

At the end of an unrehearsed and deeply personal talk, Niblett received a standing ovation, the only one afforded any speaker during the entire course.

His gradual emergence from the shadow of PTSD was saddened by news of a less fortunate victim, a friend from Niblett's former flight:

During the war —— had been tireless, a real pillar of strength . . . He'd come up to me after the Goose Green battle saying, 'We've got a serious problem, boss. I've just run out of pipe tobacco . . .'

During a bout of depression, he had sealed himself into his bedroom with the family lawnmower, then started it up, dying of carbon monoxide poisoning. He left a note saying that, since the Falklands, there had been nobody he could talk to.

Steven Hughes left the army to become an orthopaedic surgeon. While on call at his London teaching hospital, he suffered a profound, incapacitating panic attack.

For no obvious reason, I was suddenly overwhelmed by a crescendo of blind, unreasoning fear. I referred myself to the duty psychiatrist, was sedated, then admitted to the psychiatric ward of my own hospital. Nothing General Galtieri's men did compared with the terrors my own mind invented that night – or the terror of losing my self-control.

It was a vicious and unresolvable circle:

I couldn't let go in case I lost control, and the more I battled against the fear, the more my panic increased. I'd been physically and mentally exhausted when they sedated me, and the next morning, in the cold light of an ordinary Sunday with the consultant and my parents visiting I felt foolish – but far from sane. What had happened to me? What would stop it happening again?

To save embarrassment, the psychiatric staff attempted to find Hughes a bed in another London hospital. Eventually he was transferred – under escort. The duty registrar was apologetic; their only bed was in the forensic psychiatry ward:

So one hour later I was in a side room – a cell – in a ward for the criminally insane. I amused myself with the thought that two years with the Parachute Regiment must equate to a criminal record.

Hughes found that none of the staff were talking to him. Staff and patients were indistinguishable, drugs were dispensed from a hatch on the ringing of a bell. After 48 hours he began to get restless:

Getting agitated was counter-productive, so I lay down on the bed to calm down. Then a nurse told me to pack for yet another move. Hurriedly bundling my possessions I was escorted to a waiting ambulance. After an hour in London's rush hour, I arrived at one of the famous Surrey 'bins'.

The new ward was less forbidding, although the summons to medication and the absence of staff uniforms and name tags were the same as on the previous forensic ward. Hughes found himself under a 'close supervision order' – despite being a voluntary patient. A nurse would accompany him at all times.

The duty psychiatric registrar decided that I was neither dangerous nor suicidal and so dismissed my 'minder'. However after he had left the ward, one of the nurses appeared. If I wasn't to have a minder, they had decided to take my tie and belt. In jest I suggested they also take my plastic laundry bag in case I put my head in it. I was left with an untidy pile of soiled clothes. I was about to remark that one could always hang oneself with one's trousers, but checked myself.

Hughes had to wait three days to see the consultant – the only person who could discharge him. During that time he made friends with fellow-patients, and was visited by family and friends.

Thank God for the telephone. It was easy to imagine becoming lost to the outside world. Among the patients I found talent and compassion, besides sadness and torment – many remarkable people with surprising abilities, but temporarily lacking the capacity to cope with the world outside. It was us against the system.

He was duly released by the consultant for two weeks' convalescence at home, where after twelve days it happened all over again:

Panic consumed me, again out of the blue – this time at a Trauma Conference at the Royal Society of Medicine! I sought sanctuary in a casualty department nearby. This time I really felt I was losing my grip on sanity. I will never forget trying desperately to divert myself from the unhinging of my world – bizarre fixations on mundane things . . . an electric socket, a patient trolley . . . was this madness?

A young student nurse talked me out of the fog, calming me down until the psychiatry senior registrar arrived. Thankfully he decided against admitting me. Agitated but functioning I drove home – the only remaining sanctuary. There my parents persuaded me to contact a naval psychiatrist friend, Morgan O'Connell, who'd been with the Falklands Task Force. As I put down the phone from speaking with him, I had a flashback. I found myself back at Goose Green in the rain and smoke and horror. I felt the fear, the despair, the grief and the anger; an overwhelming maelstrom of emotions long since buried deep in my soul.

Doctors find it very difficult to diagnose and treat members of their own families, let alone themselves. Hughes knew all about his complaint – but until this moment had not related it to himself. He had even instigated and written a research paper on the incidence of PTSD in members of the Parachute Regiment. Hughes now realized that he had PTSD. His parents called the local GP, and Hughes was admitted to RAF Wroughton, in Wiltshire, for five weeks' in-patient treatment.

My subsequent treatment was not pleasant, but it was the way out of the abyss, and the route back to normality. I started to address what I had never acknowledged, let alone come to terms with, from those black days of 1982.

Like Jeff Niblett, he returned to the Falklands to exorcize his memories:

I felt very apprehensive about going back because I didn't know what was going to happen and whether I would be able to cope. It was a fear of the unknown, very similar to how I'd felt before going on the army parachute course.

Going back to the Falklands also meant a return after five years to service life. The first day boosted Hughes's self-confidence:

They tried to fly us by Chinook [helicopter] out to San Carlos in bad weather. During the flight the windscreen broke and the de-misters and wipers packed up, forcing them to fly with the loadmaster sticking his head out of the side door telling them where to go. Outside was a blizzard. The young soldier passengers were beginning to puke up with anxiety, but I was thinking, 'This is great – nowhere near as bad as operational flying. Nobody is going to shoot us down.' It was exciting but not dangerous. It was obvious from the way the others were behaving they had no idea of what it was like in war. After this incident, they were a bit wary of me, as someone who had done it for real.

This flight for me was the transition back ... I knew I could survive in this environment, in both peace and war.

Because the visit was not officially sponsored by the MOD, a number of people were obstructive, in particular a WRAC staff officer who refused to do anything to help.

The Islanders, however, went out of their way to be helpful – they knew I was coming, and either knew me, or knew all about me.

The first bit, in the cemetery, didn't get through to me as I had expected. It was too formal, and I needed more than that to start triggering things.

Accompanied by his psychotherapist and a young infantry platoon commander, Hughes walked the Goose Green battlefield exactly on its eighth anniversary, starting from Camilla Creek House at 0200 hours, stopping and keeping to the same timings:

The others could only see it as dark farmland. When the sunlight came up over Darwin Bay, to them it was a beautiful, serene place. For me it was eerie. I could feel the emotion of death, blackness, despair and hell on earth. The memories of my friends dying there were with me all the time. I hadn't reached such a level of emotion and pain until then. I felt desperately alone, that nobody could understand how I felt. I couldn't describe it to the others. Not having felt the desolation, pain and loneliness during the war, I was feeling it now, for the first time.

Coronation Point had been the last place I saw David Wood and 'H' before they died. Being there in the darkness exactly eight years later started off the re-living process for me.

During the battle, Hughes had moved his Regimental Aid Post from Coronation Point to the Bower, behind A Company's positions on Darwin Ridge. Eight years later, in darkness, they arrived there:

At the Bower, all I could see were bodies, helicopters and smouldering gorse bushes. We went on to the spot where 'H' had been killed, saw the cairn and planted a tree. I'd never been there before, and only finally understood what had happened when I saw it. I can't see it as a beautiful place; the blackness makes it a most unpleasant part of the world.

The next day in Goose Green, meeting people at the memorial service disrupted the re-living process for me. Although we went over to Fitzroy and Stanley, Goose Green had been the key. I didn't feel Wireless Ridge was important, so we didn't go back there.

Hughes's Falklands visit did not stimulate a miracle cure, but started a longer process of gradual catharsis. A few months later he suffered a further panic attack:

. . . all the pain and grief came back with a vengeance, and I felt desperately alone. Over the three or four months that followed I worked through the slough of an awful despair, alternating with anxiety.

I was using panic and anxiety as a means of avoiding the pain, keeping my brain ticking away thinking and worrying, but not feeling. I was swopping between pain and anxiety, and when I couldn't stand the pain of the emotion any more, I'd replace it with panic. For two weeks I couldn't work, and my boss had me to stay in his house.

His problems were not simply due to the events of 1982.

We all have disruptive elements in our lives that make us unhappy, some of which we come to terms with, others we just lock away. Something of the magnitude of the Falklands will trigger them all off together, and the cup of despair overflows.

Treatment is essentially self-administered, but requires a fundamental reappraisal of life: 'Instead of only dealing with the overflow, you might just as well get rid of the whole cup.' There is no going back to the way things were before, nor is there any 'cure'.

You need to develop defence mechanisms to be able to cope with future episodes – building yourself up in order to be able to cope in the future. The end result of it all leaves you a better person.

The Gulf War has produced its crop of PTSD cases, generated as much by the long and agonizing wait for the 'Mother of Battles' to begin, and the threat of chemical and possibly biological weapons, as by the actual combat. Allied ground troops were spared a fight, occupying positions that the air force and artillery had neutralized, but they were deeply affected by some terrible sights. The body collection teams in particular, having trained to handle large numbers of Allied dead, found themselves burying dead Iraqis as if they were household rubbish. The Iraqi Army were certainly seriously traumatized by the battering they took, and thousands of individual Iraqi soldiers are likely to have suffered considerable long-term psychological damage.

For the first time since the First World War, the British Army deployed field psychiatric units in the immediate rear of Gulf War front line regiments. In the event these battle shock recovery units ('BRUs') had few actual patients, but ran a 24-hour-a-day informal consultation service that kept them busy throughout the long build-up to the land war. Their presence was an indication of the seriousness with which the psychological dimension of modern combat is now taken.

Once the land battle was won, however, the effort to minimize psychological battle casualties does not seem to have been transferred to ensuring the long-term mental health of combatants. After Gulf War hostilities ended, the measures that are today well known to be so effective in reducing the incidence of PTSD in soldiers returning from war seem generally to have been forgotten. The field commanders at every level were deeply emotionally involved themselves so, to a very understandable extent, they discounted suggestions of PTSD in their troops. Their intense relief at the outcome of the operation and the strong pride they felt in their men's achievements overcame any thoughts about the psychological effect of the war. Stiff upper lip prevailed. Having won a war, real men don't need psychiatric counselling. Several officers in both the RAF and the army have made disparaging remarks to me about the BRUS – one in particular saying that the chaplains were more effective. In the tidal wave of desire to get away from every reminder of the battlefield, back to peacetime military life, it is no surprise that the RAMC's field psychiatrists were not listened to.

As in the Falklands, Gulf soldiers and airmen were desperate to return home as quickly as possible, and so were flown back to go straight on leave. Many of the units in which the war was fought were broken up, soldiers returning to completely different parent units which had not fought in the war – and which therefore did not understand what these men had been through. Furthermore, the ground forces had not actually fought a battle, which left many of them frustrated and angry, particularly as Saddam Hussein's power seemed undiminished. Several have described their feelings as 'Like a jet standing at the end of the runway waiting to take off, engines revving furiously.'

An RSM described the emotional effect of the war as being 'like training for months to jump over a 400-foot cliff, then when you reach the edge discovering it to be only four inches high'. The troops' sense of anticlimax and disappointment, together with relief at their own survival plus the horrors they saw inflicted on the enemy, formed a powerful emotional cocktail.

At the time of writing, a few months after the first anniversary of the Gulf War, the number of officially diagnosed cases of PTSD among serving British Army Gulf War soldiers is over 500. Army psychiatrists believe the actual number to be 'very much greater', and that it will 'increase dramatically, probably exponentially'. Judging from past wars, as individuals begin to experience PTSD symptoms, which in time get the better of them – forcing them to seek medical help, this rise will become apparent. All wars are a tragic waste of life and effort, and many Gulf soldiers feel that as Iraq's Republican Guard was not destroyed, their effort was pointless. (In a purely psychological sense, there are similarities with Vietnam.) History may yet prove Gulf War veterans to be peculiarly prone to PTSD.

One of the unsolvable riddles of human behaviour is the incredible good that can crawl unscathed from the gutter of war. It seems that humans have to struggle, suffer and endure in order to appreciate life, gaining our life force and humanity from a deeply rooted, possibly primeval need to push ourselves. So despite all the blackness and misery of combat and its after-effects, good can emerge in the individuals who are put to the test in this way. They have seen human life stripped of all its pretensions and niceties, and in the painful process of coming to terms with their radical new outlook, may become stronger people.

Senior officers in the armed forces, however, preoccupied with peacetime affairs, have been too busy to be concerned with the post-combat reactions of a relatively small number of servicemen; perhaps they subconsciously regard sufferers as sub-standard individuals of defective character. The manpower wastage caused by this attitude is enormous, particularly as only the most experienced, combat-proven individuals are affected. If post-combat PTSD sufferers remain in the forces (many find that for various reasons they have no choice but to leave), their suitability for responsible operational posts is very likely to have been questioned. A psychiatric question mark in the margins of a confidential report is usually the end of most military careers – or at least a severe limitation on promotion. Thus as a casualty of battle, a sufferer from PTSD does not concern the armed forces to the same degree as a person needing rehabilitation after a gunshot wound or sports injury. The PTSD victim is of doubtful military value, and will probably leave anyway.

There is however a groundswell of changing attitudes in the services today. In the build-up to the Gulf crisis, in the autumn of 1990, the Royal Navy put teams of psychiatrists into each of the ships that sailed for what was to become the war zone. These teams briefed officers, NCOs and men in the light of what had been learned nine years earlier in the Falklands War, teaching them what psychological symptoms to look for and how to deal with them. Royal Air Force psychiatrists treated the returning Beirut hostages, and their own aircrew taken prisoner after being shot down in the Gulf.

For the army, the Gulf War created several distinct groups of post-trauma suffers: the hostages (a group of soldiers working in Iraq before the crisis brewed up), fighting troops affected by the long build-up to war, troops captured and tortured during the war, and fighting troops affected by what they saw during and after the war – particularly personnel from the body collection units, who spent the build-up to the land war behind canvas screens and security fences training to process Allied bodies, and were quickly labelled 'ghouls' by other soldiers. Resentment built up between these volunteers and other troops, originating in a general and natural fear of death developing into a specific fear of being 'processed' by the body teams. In the event only Iraqi bodies were processed. Nevertheless, this resentment surfaced after the war when the survivors of incidents in which troops were killed by 'friendly fire' met the men who handled their friends' corpses. Today the Gulf War body handlers are a significant psychologically affected group.

The army, because it has so many more men who in war are directly exposed to violence, has the greatest potential problem, and has come under the pressure of steadily increasing numbers of soldiers with post-combat stress difficulties. The largest and as yet unquantified cause of army post-trauma cases is Northern Ireland. Many soldiers serve there without incident, but at any time violence may erupt, pitching men into scenes of carnage the equal of any battlefield. Emotions are further stretched by the normality of life in Northern Ireland and the effect of the violence on ordinary people – reminding soldiers of their own families. The bitter hatred gets them down too, particularly when soldiers have no choice but to accept abuse, enduring being sworn at and spat upon, as well as the better-publicized shootings, bombings and rioting.

An army psychiatrist estimates that an average of fifty soldiers during each battalion tour of duty in Northern Ireland suffer some kind of psychological problem, which informal counselling within the unit is able to sort out. However, around ten men from each unit experience problems that persist, which only formal psychiatric treatment can resolve – this works out at around 140 cases each year. These figures indicate that during the last two decades of the Troubles, several thousand soldiers have developed serious psychological problems as the result of their service in Northern Ireland alone. (The Ulster Defence Regiment, permanently serving in the Province, seems likely to have even more serious problems.) These figures do not however equate with the numbers of men actually treated by army psychiatrists; thus either the bulk of those affected leave the forces, or soldier on without their problems being diagnosed. As many units return regularly to Northern Ireland, men with existing psychological problems find themselves back out on patrol, caught between their personal pride and desire not to let their mates down, and their private fears – hapless victims of their own 'stiff upper lip', and the lack of understanding of their comrades (see

Appendix II for a case history of a Northern Ireland PTSD victim).

In the wake of the Gulf War, the steadily increasing pressure of post-trauma cases on the army has prompted Adjutant General Sir David Ramsbotham, with the Second Sea Lord and the Air Member for Personnel, to instigate the first formal MOD study into post-combat trauma in the armed forces. It is thought that a PTSD treatment centre will result. Although the will now exists at high level to confront the complex issues that this whole problem raises in the armed forces, PTSD prevention is achieved largely by educating people about the condition. Sadly, there remains a lobby within the hierarchy of all three services which believes that educating soldiers about the psychological effect of combat will somehow create a generation of weaklings who will use PTSD as an excuse not to continue doing their duty. This patronizing, peacetime attitude (held largely by those who have never heard shots fired in anger) is an insult to the courage, dedication and intelligence of everybody serving in Britain's armed forces.

The best treatment for PTSD would be to accept the fact that everyone involved in some kind of traumatic experience, whether it be a gunfight or bombing in Northern Ireland, a war, or any kind of violent disaster such as a serious car crash or fire, is liable to develop it. Prophylactic treatment could then start immediately after the event for everybody. Debriefings are usual after most military operations, conducted by intelligence officers. A psychological debrief could easily be built into this process, to identify the emotions and fears of the individuals concerned, reassuring them that their feelings are entirely normal and will go away. This reassurance (and what is known as 'normalization of emotions') would prevent PTSD in most people, and detect it in its earliest stages in others, allowing simple treatment to limit its effect.

Psychological (or emotional) debriefing could be carried out within the units themselves, by the chaplain or suitably trained platoon commanders or NCOs. Army psychiatrists are convinced that with counselling for every person involved in any incident, operation or traumatic event, most of the soldiers who would otherwise develop psychiatric problems could be cured before the problems even start.

The Vietnam War produced very large numbers of PTSD cases, which continue to increase twenty years on (affecting more than half of those who saw combat). Vietnam cannot be compared with the Falklands because most of the GIs were conscripts sent to war without choice, while British soldiers are volunteers with pride in what they are doing and the Falklands was fought by elite units. (Moreover they were in action for weeks rather than months.) We cannot compare Second World War figures either; whole nations were involved for years, fighting for their survival. Men were conscripted, and afterwards took up an equally desperate struggle to rebuild the economies of their ravaged countries – all very different from the circumstances in which Vietnam veterans returned home.

Although we have the official figures of psychological battle casualties from past wars, it is not easy to differentiate between physically wounded who were also psychologically affected, and those who were not physically wounded. As has already been mentioned, the actual numbers of psychologically wounded can remain hidden behind various physical diagnoses; some experts believe that in the Falklands War, trench foot and cold exposure casualties in particular may also have been psychologically affected, succumbing while others suffering similar physical problems soldiered on. Their injuries were no less real nor serious for not being purely physical.

The Falklands War could have been the golden opportunity for British Army psychiatrists. Fought by two closely integrated brigades and a relatively small number of people over a short period of time, it offered the ideal subject for the first comprehensive study of how professional troops react psychologically to modern war. The emergence of PTSD has never been fully plotted in military formations (although after the Gulf War the US Army may now have achieved this), so methods of treatment within the military environment cannot be properly evaluated.

Unfortunately, although many individual British Service psychiatrists do as much as they are permitted to do, there has hitherto been little positive MOD interest in studying PTSD. Despite the relative ease with which it could have been done, there have been no official surveys of Falklands veterans to determine how many have experienced PTSD symptoms. Dr Steven Hughes and Lt Colonel O'Brien carried out an unofficial survey of 2 Para (Hughes' own battalion) and 3 Para, compared with 1 Para (which remained in Edinburgh during the war). They discovered that five years after the end of the war, 50% of the Falklands veterans remaining in the army admitted to symptoms suggestive of PTSD, and 21.9% admitted to symptoms that suggested they were actually suffering from the full PTSD syndrome. (On the principle that the less affected stayed in the army, the ones that had left could be argued to have an even higher incidence of PTSD.)

If these alarming figures were to be duplicated in other Falklands units, a serious problem (and much suppressed unhappiness) would be revealed, with even more serious implications for future wars. However, without any sort of baseline survey of the condition, further studies to determine the effectiveness of treatments cannot even start.

An enormous can of worms is, however, being opened by the MOD, which may be one of the reasons for the delay in finding the can-opener. Once PTSD is officially recognized as an affliction caused by combat, the MOD will become liable to compensate victims, as they are for physically injured people. In many ways therefore, and for many reasons, it was easier for the MOD to ignore the problem.

The simple fact is that Parliament does not vote money to the MOD to treat or support servicemen or women who are no longer fit enough for the armed forces. Once injured beyond rehabilitation, service personnel are essentially on their own, shuffled sideways from the Defence vote on to the Welfare State. Thousands of participants in past conflicts are in this position.

Whether this situation is morally or administratively acceptable is not my concern in this book. One thing is however certain. In battle servicemen and women give their all, trusting that if anything goes wrong they will be looked after properly by the services. If for political, legal or financial reasons the government and responsible ministries do not wholeheartedly respect this trust (they seem at present to take it for granted), there is the danger that it may disappear. The effect of this would be far more damaging to the security of the nation than any defence cut.

EPILOGUE

Having finished writing this book, I was much saddened to hear of the death of one of the four members of my own Falklands War forward observation team. In my book *Falklands Commando* I wrote of Sergeant 'Des' Nixon:

Des Nixon is a Yorkshireman, older than the average gunner, having left the Army then come back in. He is a very experienced soldier who had been a gun 'Number One' (commanding his own gun and crew) in the Royal Artillery's elite parachute regiment. After several adventures as a civilian, he decided to come back into the Army, relinquishing his former rank of bombardier, starting again at the bottom. He is as hard as nails and absolutely uncrackable, with a direct and sometimes very gentle sense of humour. His shortness and fair hair give completely the wrong impression to anyone looking for trouble, and when pressed the Nixon reaction is swift and absolute. The rest of the team referred to him as the 'Old Man' or 'Des the Shovel' [after successfully defending himself from attackers one night]. More often than not the 'Old Man' showed the younger members the way home.

At the end of the book, reflecting on the psychological effect of the war, I wrote:

The most universal attitude of soldiers is the belief that whatever is going on they will not be the one to get hurt or killed. When others are killed the worry is short-circuited by saying 'if it's got your name written on it, then no matter what you do, it's going to get you'.

This optimistic fatalism is the only way to avoid becoming convinced of the inevitability of death, or worse – mutilation. It would be an impossibly brave man who carried on convinced that he was not going to survive. I suspect that such things as shell-shock occur when the resilience of the individual has been taken too far and the optimism is destroyed. Probably then you are unable to carry on and simply crack. Des Nixon used to mutter to himself, 'I'm a rubber duck and you won't crack me,' and he was right.

However, on returning from the war, his first marriage broke up. Then, after his second wife left him for the third time in November 1991, Des's cup full of troubles overflowed and he couldn't cope. He'd been depressed for many years after the Falklands, suffering but soldiering on (in our commando unit). Then when it seemed that his second marriage had irretrievably broken down, he reached the point when all his resilience was finally gone. He took his own life. I wish I'd had the chance to speak with him.

APPENDIX I

Ministry of Defence Statement on the Loss of RAF Tornado Aircraft in Combat During the Conduct of Air Operations Against Iraq

A total of six Tornado GR1 aircraft were lost in combat during the conduct of air operations against Iraq. In each case, the aircraft were flying in formation with others. Investigations have now been completed into the circumstances of each of the losses, making the best use of the evidence available. Conclusions on the cause of the loss could be reached in four of the cases, but not for the remaining two. The results of the investigation are set out below.

On the morning of 17 January 1991 Flt Lts J. G. Peters and A. J. Nichol took part in an attack on an Iraqi airfield with 1000lb bombs. On departure from the target the formation encountered Anti-Aircraft Artillery (AAA) fire and received multiple surface-to-air threat warnings. Flt Lts Peters and Nichol manoeuvred, apparently success-fully, against a missile threat warning, but soon afterwards their aircraft was hit by a missile from a previously unidentified military installation. The crew continued to fly the aircraft for over three minutes before being forced to eject with fuel leaking from the right wing, and flames on the side of the fuselage. The ejections were successful, although both crew members suffered minor injuries. The crew were both captured and held as prisoners of war (PWs) until the cessation of hostilities. The wreckage of the aircraft was found and inspected by the investigating team. Fragments of metal were extracted from the aircraft wreckage and analysed. The investigating team concluded that the aircraft was hit by a surface-to-air missile while leaving the target area. The crew were then faced with a series of problems culminating in loss of control of the aircraft at which point they ejected successfully.

On 19 January 1991 Flt Lts D. J. Waddington and R. J. Stewart took part in a night attack against an airfield in SW Iraq with 1000lb bombs. The formation flew into Iraq at low-level. Shortly before commencement of the loft delivery the formation came under fire from surface-to-air missiles. Flt Lt Waddington attempted to take evasive action, but a missile detonated to the front right hand side of the aircraft. The pilot became unconscious and the navigator initiated command ejection while the aircraft was at high speed. Both pilot and navigator received injuries during the ejection and parachute landing. They were captured and held as PWs until cessation of hostilities. The wreckage of their aircraft was found and briefly inspected by the investigating team; the Accident Data Recorder was recovered for analysis. The investigating team concluded that the aircraft was shot down by a surface-to-air missile during the run-in for a loft attack.

During the early hours of 24 January 1991 Fg Off S. J. Burgess and Sqn Ldr R. Ankerson flew on a mission to attack an airfield in SW Iraq with 1000lb bombs from level flight at medium altitude. Shortly after having released their weapon load as planned there was a large explosion behind the aircraft and the crew thought they had been hit by a surface-to-air missile. They turned towards the Saudi border with flames spreading along the aircraft wings. The aircraft became difficult to control and the crew prepared for ejection, which they did once control was finally lost. The crew suffered very minor injuries as a result of the ejection and descent. They were both captured and held in captivity until the cessation of hostilities. The wreckage of the aircraft was found and briefly inspected by the investigating team; the Accident Data Recorder was recovered for analysis. Shrapnel fragments recovered from the aircraft wreckage were analysed and indicate conclusively that premature detonation of one or more of the 1000lb bombs had occurred, damaging the aircraft to such an extent that the crew had no option but to eject.

On 14 February 1991 Flt Lts R. J. S. G. Clark and S. M. Hicks flew on a daylight medium-level mission as part of a formation of Tornados and laser designator Buccaneers to attack an airfield in central Iraq with Laser Guided Bombs (LGBs). Just prior to weapon delivery the crew received radar warnings but with only seconds to weapons release, continued with the attack. Only one of the two LGBs was released, with the other remaining hung-up. Shortly after, the Buccaneer crew reported a visual sighting of two SAMs fired from a site to the North of the target. Flt Lts Clark and Hicks attempted to take evasive action and to jettison external stores. Despite the crew's actions a missile exploded beside the aircraft, rupturing the canopy beside the pilot's head and smashing the majority of front cockpit instruments. Flt Lt Clark could not contact his navigator. Immediately after, there was another explosion from a second missile. Despite the extensive damage, including both wings being peppered with holes and no apparent control over the engines, the pilot still had limited control and flew the aircraft for a further two or so minutes before initiating command ejection when he found he could control the aircraft no longer. The pilot sustained a minor injury to his left leg as a result of ejection and descent. Flt Lt Hicks was found to be dead. Flt Lt Clark was subsequently captured and remained as a PW until cessation of hostilities. The crash site was located outside the area of Iraq later occupied by coalition forces and was inaccessible to the investigating team. But on the basis of Flt Lt Clark's report and interviews with other members of the formation, the investigating team were able to conclude that the aircraft was lost as a result of an enemy SAM attack which killed the navigator and severely damaged the aircraft, causing the pilot to eject.

On the evening of 17 January 1991 Wg Cdr T. N. C. Elsdon and Flt Lt R. M. Collier took part in a JP233 mission against an Iraqi airfield. The formation planned to attack the target on a westerly heading before turning to the North. After a further 10 miles the formation were to turn to the East and leave the area. As they approached the Iraqi border at low level, the formation encountered AAA fire which became progressively more intense towards the target. All four aircraft delivered their weapons and turned onto the northerly heading. As the aircraft turned onto the next, easterly, track a fireball was seen by one of the crews. The leader instigated a radio check in, but received no reply from Wg Cdr Elsdon or Flt Lt Collier. It was subsequently concluded that their aircraft had been seen to hit the ground while leaving the target area. Both aircrew were killed in the crash.

On 22 January 1991 Sqn Ldrs G. K. S. Lennox and K. P. Weeks led the first of two formations delivering 1000lb bombs in a night attack on an Air Defence site in western Iraq. The weather was good with excellent visibility, and they carried out a successful attack despite heavy AAA fire. Approximately five seconds later the leader of the following formation saw a fireball erupt in the distance. Closer investigation revealed a series of fires on a hillside to the right of the track where the fireball had been. As Sqn Ldrs Lennox and Weeks failed to check in after the attack, the leader realized that this fire trail was probably caused by their aircraft crashing. Both aircrew were killed in the crash.

The crash sites in these last two cases were located outside the area of Iraq later occupied by coalition forces and as such were inaccessible to the investigating team; the investigations were therefore confined to interviews with other members of the formation. The investigating team considered all possible factors in attempting to establish the reason for these two losses. There were several potential causes, including aircraft malfunction, hostile action, aircrew reaction and aircraft handling, but the lack of any firm evidence makes it impossible to reach a positive conclusion, and in each case the cause must remain undetermined.

The outcome of these investigations will be included in the continuing assessment of the campaign.

APPENDIX II

Interview with Northern Ireland PTSD Victim

Private X, an infantry soldier who returned home four weeks ago from an unexpected tour in Northern Ireland, is suffering from classic PTSD symptoms. He found it very hard to readjust to coming home after a previous tour in 1989, but this time it's worse. He wakes up in the early hours of the morning and cannot get back to sleep, suffering terrible nightmares that take him back to memories of his tours in Northern Ireland, memories that he tries desperately but unsuccessfully to forget. He is easily angered and very irritable, to the extent that his family life is suffering. His wife knows that something serious is wrong, but as he refuses to speak to her about it, there is nothing she can do to help.

On his first tour, Private X shot dead a terrorist – an experience that did not appear to affect him at the time, but which now haunts him:

He was a bloke the same age as me. You don't think of that until it happens. Once you've pulled the trigger, it's never, ever the same again. You live in fear for your own life, trying to keep the memories at bay.

The tour lasted two years. His company was based at Aldergrove but was sent on short tours (usually six months) elsewhere in the Province. His first incident was in the early hours, an 800-pound bomb in a South Armagh village meant for soldiers, which instead killed a mother and seriously injured her three-year-old daughter.

I didn't deal with the mother, but talked to the little girl. All you can say is that you'll be all right. They were innocent people in the wrong place. I felt very bitter towards the IRA. She was crying, scared, confused. I tried to calm her down, get her name and find where she lived. Getting information out of a three-year-old when she's frightened, scared and confused is very hard. You shouldn't have to do them sort of things straight away – even though it's necessary. You shouldn't have a soldier with a rifle who's going to scare her even more – it should have been a woman, someone who cared.

I feel guilty that it wasn't me that got killed by that bomb. It should have been one of us and not a three-year-old and her mum.

The bomb was intended for us, and people in the houses – a strong Catholic estate – treated us as if we'd put the bomb there. They spat in your face, called you a murderer. It was devastating for me, from that moment on. At the checkpoints they scream at you 'British murderer' and spit . . .

The next incident was in Londonderry, when I was doing top-cover in one of the green vehicles. My mate was facing front, me rear and he spotted a cheesewire, stretched across the road between lamp posts – intended to take our heads off. He shouted 'Wire!' and as I was about to move, it took off the top of my helmet. You heard the twing of the wire go off. Apparently they often attach a bomb to the wire, but hadn't in this instance. I was lucky my head didn't come off.

Soon after that the other company was shot to pieces in another shooting – nobody hurt, but all very shaken up. Then a bomb went off and threw several vehicles off the road, turning them over despite the heavy armour that weighs them down. Everybody was very slow reacting, stunned with disbelief that the IRA had managed to get a bomb into such a heavily patrolled area.

The second tour was unexpected, a sudden 'Spearhead' deployment, with the battalion split into different groups – Coalisland, Dungannon, Cookstown. After a tip-off in the first week, the army ambushed a group of IRA trying to attack the Coalisland police station. Private X was ordered to let the terrorists through his roadblock, and soon after heard the gunfire of both their attack on the evacuated police station, then the army ambush as they attempted to make their escape. Four terrorists were killed, the remainder wounded. X's section was ordered to the hospital to search the terrorists' relatives before allowing them to visit the wounded.

I could understand that they'd be upset, so I tried to be as polite as possible and still do my job at the same time. One bloke started swearing, calling me a murderer, fucking British bastard, wanker . . . He swung at me, so I moved back. Two more cars arrived and started to come out at me. About twelve people were around me, so I called the other soldier over to help me retreat back to the hospital doors. We were advised not to let anyone in until we'd got their names and addresses.

This was around midnight now, and the abuse continued. We had to keep the relatives there and watch them. A big ginger-haired man who stank of whiskey kept coming up and putting his face really close to mine and asking how I felt being a murderer. I tried to calm him down, saying, 'Look, it wasn't me who pulled the trigger – if it had been I wouldn't be standing here watching you. Your blokes were in the wrong. They were carrying ammunition. They knew the penalty, so let's calm down and you'll get to understand more later.'

Every time one of them left the room to go to a car, or for a cigarette, we had to search them again – in case they'd picked up a weapon. They got very narky, angry and vicious at us, trying to punch us and spitting in our faces. We had to take it – stand there and wipe it off our faces – because the RUC didn't want a riot in the hospital. And the kids kicked us in the ankles. The thing that stuck in my head was a three-year-old kid coming up and saying 'You murdered my Dad.' That hurt quite a bit inside . . .

Private X felt guilty for causing grief to these relatives – a throwback to the guilt of having shot a man himself.

We should only kill terrorists in the last resort. If we do shoot one, we've still got to give him first aid afterwards. Our aim is to save lives as much as prevent terrorists doing their work. I feel so much for the relatives – in so many ways. They've got families just like us.

Our role is to support the RUC, and it's right that we are over there. But we never know who the enemy is. You could be walking down the street, and although there are known PIRA, you don't know until something happens who they are. They dress the same as us, walk round the same as us.

I don't feel sorry for the blokes that got killed. They were caught doing something they shouldn't have been doing. I feel sorry for the kids that will have to be brought up without a father, for the families . . .

I accept that I'm a soldier, and that if my card is marked, then that's the way it goes. But this is peacetime, and our role in Ireland is to help people. Lots of soldiers however talk about going out there and having the chance to kill a terrorist. But when it happens they won't like it.

After the incident [on his first tour, shooting the terrorist], on the ground I was always more nervous, worrying that I might not be able to react like that again. I still can't say in my own mind whether the terrorist was going to shoot – although I've tried very hard to persuade myself. I just can't say whether or not he had his finger on the trigger and was about to shoot. It's probably the most scary thing that anyone can go through.

I'm all right during the day in my job, but when I go to sleep I dream about what happened and it wakes me up – like waking out of a nightmare. When I can control that dream, I can sleep.

Close family see it more than anyone else – because you can't hide it from them. They weren't too happy about me going back this last time – but it's my job.

After the first two and a half years in Northern Ireland, I came home jumping over fences at car backfires. My parents didn't understand. It took time to adjust to normal life in England.

The bad dreams came after the incident for a couple of months but I bottled it up … bottled it up. I was getting a lot of migraines, and was given pain killers (coproxomol) which got rid of it.

Since then, I've become more nervous, irritable and jumpy. Happiness doesn't seem to last as long as it used to, going towards other things than what it should do. I lost touch with my parents, and found I couldn't get my wife to understand what I was going through.

I went into my own little space …

Getting treatment is difficult:

It's very hard being in the army. That you can't go to any other doctor, to someone comfortable you can talk to outside. I don't however feel uncomfortable because the MO is an officer. There should be special times outside sick parade, when you can see the MO for personal reasons. He'll understand that, and maybe understand better why you are there.

However at sick parades, he's not to know that you feel uncomfortable, that it's personal. Maybe he could help a lot more, and the other medics would know not to ask you about it – like they do at sick parade. You tell the medics you've hurt your arm, then when you get in there [to the MO] you feel uncomfortable, so you tell the MO you've hurt your arm. Then you leave.

Now I'm unhappy; I hide it from my wife and family as I can't tell them just how unhappy I am. And even though we're back from Northern Ireland, the threat continues. We still have to keep looking under our cars for bombs. We lock our windows and doors, shutting the curtains so nobody can see you're at home. You watch derelict buildings or walk around them. Wires sticking out of doorbells, a dust bin put in the wrong place … you watch out for these things. It's in your head all the time. You can't get rid of it.

EAST FALKLAND

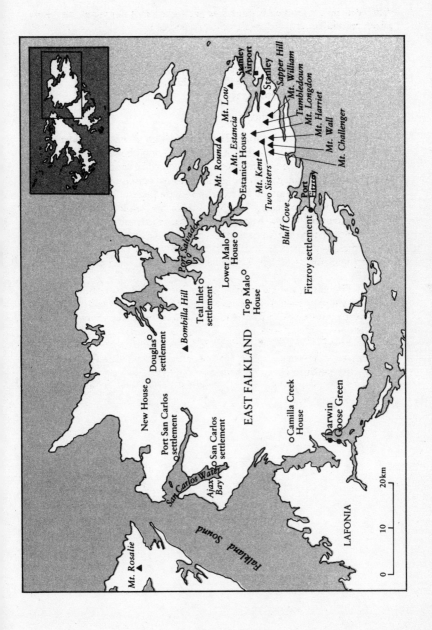

NOTES

1 FIGHTING THE PEACE

1 M. Rosenberg, *Occupation and Values*; see Norman F. Dixon, *On the Psychology of Military Incompetence* (London, 1979), p. 401.

2 Anthony Beevor, *Inside the British Army* (London, 1990), p. 55; the example is of a late-entry captain and his family.

3 Both were promoted from major to major general in peacetime. Progression in peacetime to higher ranks is very much more politic.

4 Sydney Jary, *18 Platoon* (Carshalton Beeches, 1987), p. 117.

5 R. G. L. von Zugbach, *Power and Prestige in the British Army* (Aldershot, 1988), p. 93.

6 Zugbach, pp. 68, 70.

7 Zugbach, p. 66.

8 Zugbach, p. 103, table.

9 Reuvan Gal, *A Portrait of the Israeli Soldier* (New York, 1986), p. 128.

10 Gal, p. 119.

2 IN THE SHADOW OF WAR

1 Transcription of the Parachute Selection Course Officer's opening talk, given to courses at Browning Barracks, Aldershot, in 1986.

2 From the verse-play *Hassan* (1922) by James Elroy Flecker; the Master of the Caravan has asked a group of travellers: 'But who are ye in rags and rotten shoes / You dirty-bearded, blocking up the way?'

3 From personal conversations with Iraqi officer cadets posted to the Royal Military Academy, Sandhurst, in 1973. They still had this test before them – and consequently were not looking forward to going home.

3 FORCING THEM TO FIGHT

1   Brigadier P. Abraham, 'Training for Battleshock', *Journal of the Royal Army Medical Corps* (1982), 128, pp. 18–27.

2   *Ibid.*

3   Lord Thomson, Secretary of State for Air, in a speech in the House of Lords on 14 April 1930, said that many of the conscripts were better educated than officers who took to the field at Waterloo.

4   General Montgomery, writing to the Secretary of State for War, told of the CO of an infantry regiment whose men had fled their trenches under mortar fire. The CO and his RSM had stood in the road behind the positions, armed respectively with pistol and sub-machine gun, to force the men back. Montgomery was not impressed with the CO, who complained (with justification) that his men had been kept in the line too long. 'Not a proper chap,' he commented.

5   The 12th Article of War read: 'Every person of the Fleet, who through cowardice, neglect or disaffection, shall in time of action withdraw or keep back, or not come into the fight or engagement; or shall not do his utmost to take or destroy every ship which it shall be his duty to engage, and to assist or relieve all and everyone of His Majesty's ships, or those of his allies, which it shall be his duty to assist and relieve too shall suffer death.'

6   William Moore, *The Thin Yellow Line* (London, 1974); Julian Putkowski and Julian Sykes, *Shot at Dawn* (Barnsley, 1989).

7   Sir Laming Worthington-Evans, Secretary of State for War, in a statement on 31 March 1925.

8   According to Brigadier General Brudenell White, Australian Chief of Staff.

9   *The Medical Department of the US Army in the World War*, vol. 10 (1929).

10 The widow of Lieutenant Herduin, of the 347th Infantry Regiment, received compensation from the French government after threatening to sue his divisional commander for murder. Lieutenant Herduin, who had already been decorated for bravery, was shot (with Ensign Millaud) after he withdrew the remains of his regiment – 42 men – at Verdun in June 1916, having endured attacks and bombardment that culminated in shelling by their own artillery. The general demanded their immediate execution, without any sort of trial and carried out by men from their own regiment.

11 Ill-discipline was not confined to 2 Para alone, who in fact were asked to patrol Port Stanley to prevent other units from misbehaving.

4 COMMITMENT TO FIGHT

1 Crossmaglen security force base is a heavily fortified concrete bunker in South Armagh, with very cramped, submarine-like accommodation for the soldiers.

2 R. J. Lifton, *Home from the War; Vietnam Veterans: neither victims nor executioners* (New York, 1974), p. 40.

5 FIRST BLOOD

1 Jeff Needle; see Lifton, p. 224.

2 Captain Jack K. Tarr, 'Preparation for Vietnam', *Combat Notes from Vietnam* (Fort Benning, Ga., 1968).

3 Airburst and PD (point detonation) are both types of fuse used on artillery shells. Airburst explodes above the ground in a lethal shotgun blast of shrapnel, whereas PD detonates the instant its point hits the ground.

4 No such ambivalent orders were ever issued by 3 Commando Brigade, the men's confusion being part of their transition from peace to war.

5 The detail of the Bluff Cove saga is described in Chapter 18 of *Reasons in Writing* by Ewen Southby-Tailyour (London, 1993).

6 'Idleness' is a Guards term for anything they disapprove of. Inanimate objects can be 'idle'; loose threads on a uniform are 'idle ends', to have them a chargeable offence.

7 DOING BUSINESS II — LAND FIGHTING

1 Sydney Jary, *18 Platoon* (Surrey, 1987), p. 93.

2 Jary, p. 80.

3 Cohen and Gatti, *In the Eye of the Storm* (London, 1991).

4 Jary, p. 17.

5 Beaten zone: the small area over which the rounds from a tripod-mounted machine gun spread ballistically when fired in long bursts aimed at the same precise point.

6 DF'd: invented military verb meaning 'to be shelled'; from 'defensive fire', a technical term meaning a pre-registered target (sometimes only co-ordinates on a map) on to which fire can be brought quickly.

7 The Belgian FN, a version of the 7.62mm SLR that could fire on automatic — a facility removed from the British version to prevent soldiers wasting ammunition.

8 Louch pole: a pivoted gun mounting allowing the weapon to swivel in all directions including up and down; generally used to fire at aircraft.

9 A 66mm anti-tank rocket, shoulder-launched, short-range, crude

but very effective, particularly at close range against people in trenches.

8 DOING BUSINESS III – AIR WAR

1   Unattributed quotations in this chapter are from conversations I had with a number of different individuals, all of whom prefer to remain unidentified.

2   The 'basket' is the zone around a laser guided bomb target into which the bomb must be placed for the guidance system to bring it on to the exact pinpoint of the target.

3   VVAW, *The Winter Soldier Investigation: an Inquiry into American War Crimes* (Boston, 1972), pp. 48–50; see Lifton, pp. 347–8.

4   Fred Branfman, 'Era of the Blue Machine: Laos, 1969–', *Washington Monthly*, July 1971, p. 19.

5   Major G. L. Tippin, 'Lessons Learned, Vietnam', *Combat Notes from Vietnam* (Fort Benning, Ga., 1968).

6   VT: variable time artillery fuses, that explode the shell automatically fifty feet above the ground, creating a lethal shotgun effect of shrapnel below.

9 COMMANDING THE CONFUSION

1   Captain Edmund C. Stone III, 'Small Arms Safety', *Combat Notes from Vietnam* (Fort Benning, Ga., 1968).

2   Jary, p. 19.

3   Martin Middlebrook, *Operation Corporate* (London, 1985), p. 264.

4   Lance Sergeant Tam McGuiness, 2nd Scots Guards; see Middlebrook, p. 361.

5   Seymour Hersh, 'Cover-Up', *New Yorker*, 22 January 1971, p. 54.

6   Lifton, p. 48.

7   Lifton, p. 52.

8   Lifton, p. 332.

10 COPING WITH CARNAGE

1   Lt Colonel M. S. Owen-Smith, 'Armoured Fighting Vehicles Casualties', *Journal of the Royal Army Medical Corps* (1977), 123, pp. 65–76.

2   See description in Rick Jolly, *Red and Green Life Machine* (London, 1983), pp.113–14.

3   J. A. Ross, in *Journal of the RAMC* (1979), 125, pp. 32–8.

4   Jolly, p. 93.
5   Major W. K. Hoen, 'Dustoff', *Combat Notes from Vietnam* (Fort Benning, Ga., 1968).

                        11 AFTERMATH

1   FIBUA (fighting in built-up areas): street fighting and house clearing using at least one hand grenade for each room; this kind of operation takes up large numbers of troops for long periods of time, and casualties are always high.

                    12 THE QUICK AND THE DEAD

1   Lifton, p. 163.
2   Lifton, p. 164.
3   This is unfair on the Guards, who in fact have more Second World War battle honours than the Parachute Regiment.
4   'Please Read This', pamphlet circulated by the New Mobilization for Peace Committee and the Vietnam Peace Parade Committee, 1970.
5   *The Collected Poems of Wilfred Owen* (London, 1963).
6   See Lifton, p. 130.
7   Lifton, p. 120.
8   Guy Sajer, *The Forgotten Soldier* (London, 1971), p. 355.
9   Glasser, *365 Days* (USA, Braziller, 1971), pp. 260–1.
10 Milan anti-tank missiles unroll a very fine wire as they fly, through which the firing point guides them on to the target; some anti-personnel mines are set off by trip wires strung across likely approaches.
11 Jolly.
12 Jolly, p. 129.
13 Jary, p. 114.
14 Tippin, 'Lessons Learned, Vietnam'.
15 Branfman; see Lifton, p. 355.
16 Lifton, p. 60.
17 Lifton, p. 189.

                    13 ANOTHER KIND OF WAR

1   Geoffrey D. Vaughan, *The Way it Really Was* (Budleigh Salterton, 1985), p. 70.
2   Steven Oboler, 'American Prisoners of War', *PTSD: a Handbook for Clinicians* (Cincinnati, 1987), p. 131.
3   *Mental Health Problems of Vietnam Era Veterans* (President's Commission on Mental Health, Washington DC, 1978).

4 Tom Williams, *PTSD: a Handbook for Clinicians* (Cincinnati, 1987), p. 8.

5 Williams, p. 11.

6 Obituary, *New York Times*, 26 May 1971.

7 A. J. Glass, 'Psychotherapy in the Combat Zone', *American Journal of Psychiatry* (1954), 110, pp. 725–31.

8 W. J. Tiffany and W. S. Allerton, 'Army Psychiatry in the mid-60s', *American Journal of Psychiatry* (1967), 123, pp. 810–21.

9 Brigadier P. Abraham, 'A Lesson from the Falklands', paper given at the Second International Conference on Wartime Medical Services, Stockholm, 1990; 777 British servicemen were wounded in the Falklands.

10 'Doing a Zulu Warrior' entails standing on a table and stripping to the chanting of onlookers.

11 The Royal Navy circulated all Falklands veterans, asking questions that would allow an almost instant diagnosis of PTSD to be made. To my knowledge the army did not attempt anything of the kind, and has not done so for the majority of the troops who returned from the Gulf War.

INDEX

The Pacific Campaign

The Second World War at Sea

Dan van der Vat

The Pacific Campaign is a judicious re-examination of the war at sea between the Allies and Japan from 1941 to 1945. For Japan, it was a self-inflicted classical tragedy. For the US, the war became the triumph that confirmed it as the greatest power on earth. And for both, it was an avoidable conflict made inevitable by mutual underestimation and misunderstanding. It is a story of error and heroism, terror and, just occasionally, humour.

Ranging from Cabinet meetings to foxholes on steaming tropical islands, from events under the sea to dogfights in the air and the huge set-piece battles on the surface, van der Vat's account, a sequel to his definitive *The Atlantic Campaign*, examines the crucial actions on both sides, including the highly damaging effect of inter-service rivalry and the increasing importance of intelligence-gathering systems.

The Pacific Campaign takes an entirely new, expansive and questioning look at the largest naval conflict in history.

'Fast-paced narrative . . . a fresh and very lively look at the war in the Pacific.'   *Publishers Weekly*

'Looks set to become the accepted reference work on that theatre of war.'   *Belfast Telegraph*

ISBN 0 586 20696 5

The Honourable Company

A History of the English East India Company

John Keay

'The first accessible narrative history of the English East India Company which has appeared for some time . . . Keay recounts his story with the sweep of a James Michener, but one anchored in the meticulous scholarship of historians . . . Commercial successes and failures, battles and politics from Table Bay to Tokyo Bay are treated with verve and clarity.'

Christopher Bayly, *The Observer*

Over two centuries, the East India Company grew from a loose association of Elizabethan tradesmen into 'the Grandest Society of Merchants in the Universe' – a huge commercial enterprise which controlled half the world's trade and also administered an embryonic empire. A tenth of the British exchequer's total revenue derived from customs receipts on the Company's UK imports; its armed forces exceeded those of most sovereign states. Without it there would have been no British India and no British Empire.

ISBN 0 00 638072 7

Shining Path

The World's Deadliest Revolutionary Force

Simon Strong

Shining Path – in Spanish, *Sendero Luminoso* – are already the stuff of legend. Like the Khmer Rouge, they possess ruthless, utter dedication and unnerving efficiency. Their full name is 'The Communist Party of Peru by the Shining Path of José Carlos Mariátegui and Marxism, Leninism, Maosim and the Thoughts of President Gonzalo', and they are bringing Peru to its knees.

Shining Path is the first study of this devastating revolutionary group which has brought a third of Peru under martial law and caused economic damage amounting to £9 billion, and one that demonstrates that the revolution is alive and well in a tragically divided country still haunted by events of five hundred years ago.

'A very good introduction to a dramatic subject that is at the heart of the dilemma in not only Latin America but all Third World countries'   Mario Vargas Llosa

'Simon Strong has written a compelling book which deserves to be very widely read indeed . . . Indispensable reading for anyone who wishes to understand the world in which we live'
                                       Anthony Daniels, *Sunday Telegraph*

Harold Wilson

Ben Pimlott

'One of the great political biographies of the century.'
A. N. Wilson, *Evening Standard*

'The rehabilitation of Wilson has begun – and Ben Pimlott, the best British political biographer now writing, has made a hugely impressive job of it . . . His narrative of the young Wilson, from sickly boy scout to academic pupil of the formidable William Beveridge, and then to chirpy junior minister is quite outstanding – clear, thoughtful and gripping. This early part of the book is central to its larger achievement, since Pimlott shocks the reader out of basic anti-Wilson prejudice by demanding a human sympathy for him. The little, blinking, stubborn boy, hiding his hurt with cocky self-confidence, lives on as a permanent presence within the powerful politician . . . Some biographies enter the political discourse at once, thanks to their innate qualities and lucky timing. There are so many echoes of the Wilson years in the politics of today that this happy fate must surely belong to Pimlott's book. Wilson's soured relationship with the press (and the terrible problems it caused for him) – the conflict within him between national leadership and good party management – even the growing debate about national decline – are all suggestive and worth lingering over. As, indeed, are almost all of these 734 well-researched and finely written pages.' Andrew Marr, *Independent*

'A masterly piece of political writing.'
Bernard Crick, *New Statesman*

'The narrative gallops along, sweeping the reader with it in a rush of excitement. A mass of complex detail is marshalled with the art that conceals art.' David Marquand, *Times Literary Supplement*

'Fascinating . . . Pimlott the X-ray has produced another work of formidable penetration.' Roy Jenkins, *Observer*

ISBN 0 00 637955 9

Talking Blues

The Police in Their Own Words

Roger Graef

'Roger Graef understands policemen . . . He misses nothing. On every page of this hefty book, raw police nerves are exposed . . . Graef has put his finger firmly on the pulse of the modern force and I believe he does it with accuracy, fairness and affection.'

John Stalker, *Sunday Times*

Talking Blues is an emotional mosaic, a collective portrait of the British police. Serving officers of every rank from all over the mainland and from Northern Ireland speak with painful but impressive frankness about the demands of their work, about the loneliness and questionable leadership that often comes with it, and about the dangers of policing an increasingly violent society.

Intimately and sometimes disturbingly portrayed in their own words, the men and women interviewed here are by turns fearful and brave, angry and amused, idealistic and cynical, and often very moving. It makes you glad that someone is doing their job, and very glad that it isn't you.

'It is an absorbing, comprehensive and valuable analysis of the careers of "a group of ordinary people asked to do extraordinary things".'   *Listener*

'A riveting book . . . tells you more about what it is like to be a police officer than all the drama series, documentaries and polemics you are likely to come across.'   *New Statesman*